Alfresco 4 Enterprise Content Management Implementation

Install, administer, and manage this powerful open source Java-based Enterprise CMS

Munwar Shariff

Snehal Shah

Rajesh R Avatani

Jayesh Prajapati

Vandana Pal

Vinita Choudhary

Amita Bhandari

Pallika Majmudar

[PACKT] open source
PUBLISHING
community experience distilled

BIRMINGHAM - MUMBAI

Alfresco 4 Enterprise Content Management Implementation

First published: January 2007

Second edition: June 2009

Third edition: July 2013

Production Reference: 1030713

Published by Packt Publishing Ltd.
Livery Place
35 Livery Street
Birmingham B3 2PB, UK.

ISBN 978-1-78216-002-1

www.packtpub.com

Cover Image by Maria Cristina Caggiani (mariacristinacaggiani@virgilio.it)

Credits

Authors

Munwar Shariff

Snehal Shah

Rajesh R Avatani

Jayesh Prajapati

Vandana Pal

Vinita Choudhary

Amita Bhandari

Pallika Majmudar

Reviewers

Piergiorgio Lucidi

Hetal Patel

Acquisition Editor

Kartikey Pandey

Lead Technical Editor

Ankita Shashi

Technical Editors

Madhuri Das

Veronica Fernandes

Pragati Singh

Dominic Pereira

Project Coordinator

Hardik Patel

Proofreaders

Mario Cecere

Amy Guest

Indexer

Rekha Nair

Graphics

Abhinash Sahu

Production Coordinator

Arvindkumar Gupta

Cover Work

Arvindkumar Gupta

About the Authors

Munwar Shariff, as a co-founder and Chief Technology Officer at CIGNEX Datamatics, brings over 20 years of industry experience and proven technical leadership. He oversees the enterprise architecture solution team and provides strategic planning to achieve business goals by identifying and prioritizing technology-based services and solutions. Defining initiatives and setting timetables for the evaluation, development, and deployment of pioneering technologies are his areas of expertise.

He is an entrepreneur, open source technologist, and author of the following four technical books:

- *Plone Live*
- *Implementing Alfresco*
- *Alfresco3 WCM*
- *Alfresco3 ECM*

He contributes to the open source community by journaling submissions on open source CMS, and has been a featured speaker at AIIM USA, JBoss World, DAM Conference, Plone Conference, Linux World, Gilbane, CTC, Yahoo OSCMS, Saudi Government, and CA World.

Munwar has also served on board at the Plone Foundation and is currently a board member at CIGNEX Datamatics.

I take this opportunity to thank Doug Dennerline (CEO of Alfresco) and Paul Anthony (CEO of CIGNEX Datamatics) for maintaining the partnership for the past 8 years. Our consulting team at CIGNEX Datamatics presented us with the various flavors of Alfresco implementations that we would not have possibly imagined. We used those throughout the book and we are thankful to them. Special thanks to our marketing team - Nirav Shah and Madhuram Yadav for the motivation and support.

Snehal Shah has extensive experience in implementing Enterprise Web Applications using J2EE technologies. At CIGNEX Datamatics, he has rolled out numerous Alfresco deployments worldwide in the areas of Document, Web Content Management, and Share. He has also worked on applications based on Liferay and Moodle products. Prior to CIGNEX, he has worked on various J2EE-based solutions using cutting-edge technologies.

He has worked with clients in the education, legal, and marketing domain across the world. He has worked on defining the architecture for various projects that involve multiple product integrations. In his previous organizations, he was involved in deciding technology paths of the organization and involved in various internal trainings in the technical part.

He holds a Bachelor in Computer Engineering from Deemed University, DDIT, India. He has also worked as a technical reviewer for the books titled *Alfresco 3 Cookbook* and *Alfresco Share*.

I would like to thank my parents for allowing me to realize my own potential. Many thanks to my lovely wife Payal, who always encouraged and supported me to achieve this goal. My main source of motivation came from my little niece Mahi, who taught me to keep on trying for the goal we have set for ourselves despite many failures, which encouraged me to take up this challenge and fulfill it.

Rajesh R Avatani leads the Alfresco Practice at CIGNEX Datamatics. He has earned his Masters in Computer Application from Basaveshwar Engineering College, Bagalkot, India

He is well versed with all the phases of the Software Development Lifecycle and has strong hands-on experience in leading and implementing Java, J2EE, Object Oriented Architecture based projects, and Alfresco-based ECM Solutions. He has around 5 years of experience in Alfresco. He has mainly worked on Alfresco integration projects as a Technical Architect and Project Manager, in other terms, as a Techno Manager.

He has worked on projects where Alfresco was integrated with Liferay, Drupal, and other web applications. He has also implemented the Contract Lifecycle Management System developed on Alfresco. He has successfully implemented Alfresco-based ECM solutions for various industries into healthcare, finance, insurance, banking, education, and so on.

I would like to thank Munwar Shariff for giving me the opportunity to write this book.

Jayesh Prajapati is a Senior Consultant at CIGNEX Datamatics. He has extensive experience in implementing Enterprise Web Applications using J2EE technologies. For the past six years, at CIGNEX Datamatics, he has rolled out numerous Alfresco deployments worldwide in the areas of Document and Web Content Management. He has worked on Performance-tuning projects where Alfresco was deployed in clustered and load balanced environments. He has also implemented Integrated Content Management Portal (ICMP) where Alfresco WCM is used as the central repository and Liferay as Portal. He has also implemented Alfresco WCM to serve Flex-based portals. He has worked with clients in the travel and hospitality, healthcare, academic, and high-tech domains. He has been involved in providing training on Alfresco Document Management.

Jayesh holds an MS in Computer Applications and Information technologies from the North Gujarat University, India

I would like to thank Mr. Munwar Shariff, Chief Technology Officer, and Mr. Manish Sheladia, Co-founder and Global Head – Strategic Accounts, at CIGNEX Datamatics for their encouragement and continuous support. I would also thank my consulting team, especially Faizan Shaikh and Yogesh Prajapati, at CIGNEX Datamatics who helped me implement the various examples found in this book.

I would also like to take this opportunity to thank my wife Hetal Prajapati, my families and friends. Without their support, this would not have been possible.

Vandana Pal is a Senior Consultant at CIGNEX Datamatics. She has more than 4 years of experience in the IT industry. She has an extensive experience in implementing Enterprise Content Management (ECM), Web Content Management, and System Integration. Vandana holds a Bachelor of Engineering degree in Information Technology from the Gujarat University.

She started her career with open source products such as Alfresco and Liferay. She has hands-on experience in implementing Alfresco-based solutions for various domains such as media, healthcare, and finance. She has extensively explored and implemented Complex workflow, UI customization, web scripts, and performance tuning in Alfresco. She has provided in-house training for Alfresco. She also has an experience of teaching Engineering students for a few months.

I would like to thank Munwar Shariff, Chief Technology Officer, and Manish Sheladia at CIGNEX Datamatics for their encouragement and continuous support. I am thankful to the consulting team at CIGNEX Datamatics who helped me with real-life examples implemented with Alfresco. I would also like to express my gratitude to my family and friends for all their support throughout.

Vinita Choudhary is a senior consultant at CIGNEX. She has extensive experience in working in a variety of environments with cross-functional, multi-cultural teams as a business analyst and has provided feedback on usability and functional gaps in process flows and proposed solutions.

She has re-organized existing repository of documentation, written guidelines for document creation, filing and change control, wrote reference and training material for software developers and published the same. She is involved in providing presales support to the sales team and has worked on process streamlining for the company and various documentation aspects. Vinita holds a Masters in Computer Applications degree from Gujarat University, India.

Amita Bhandari is a senior consultant at CIGNEX. As a senior developer, she has rolled out numerous Alfresco deployments world-wide. She has extensive experience in implementing Enterprise Web Applications using J2EE technologies such as JSP, Servlets, Spring, Hibernate, Web Services, Web Scripts and MVC Frameworks.

She has worked with clients in media and gaming, healthcare and e-governance. She trained many students in Java and advanced Java technologies. She holds a Masters in Computer Applications from Rajasthan University, India.

Pallika Majmudar is a consultant at CIGNEX Technologies. She is very experienced in Java/J2EE domain including the frameworks such as Struts, Spring, Hibernate, Web services, and Web scripts.

She has worked on various CMS applications for the customers in United States, Hong Kong and India. She has implemented Alfresco for clients across verticals like Media, Healthcare, Hi-tech and Communications. Pallika has earned her Masters in Computer Application degree from Gujarat University, India.

About the Reviewers

Piergiorgio Lucidi is an open source ECM Specialist and a Certified Alfresco Trainer at Sourcesense. Sourcesense is an European open source systems integrator, providing consultancy, support, and services around key open source technologies.

He works as a mentor, technical leader, and software engineer, and he has over 9 years of experience in the areas of Enterprise Content Management (ECM) and system integrations. He is an expert in integrating ECM solutions in web and portal applications. He regularly contributes to the Alfresco Community as an Alfresco Wiki Gardener, and during the Alfresco DevCon 2012 in Berlin he was named as an Alfresco Community Star.

He contributes in the Apache Software Foundation as a PMC Member and Committer of Apache ManifoldCF. He is also the project leader of the CMIS, Alfresco, and ElasticSearch connectors. He is a project leader and committer of the JBoss Community and contributes to some of the projects of the JBoss Portal platform.

He is a speaker at conferences dedicated to Java, Spring Framework, open source products and technologies related to the ECM and WCM world.

He is an author, technical reviewer, and affiliate partner at Packt Publishing, where he wrote the following technical books:

- *Alfresco 3 Web Services*
- *GateIn Cookbook*

As a technical reviewer, he also contributed on these books:

- *Alfresco 3 Cookbook*
- *Alfresco Share*

As an affiliate partner, he also writes and publishes book reviews on his website Open4Dev (http://www.open4dev.com/).

> I would like to thank Packt Publishing for giving me another great opportunity to contribute in a renovation project based on Alfresco.

Hetal Patel is a Senior Consultant at CIGNEX Datamatics, and has extensive experience in implementing Enterprise Web Applications using J2EE technologies.

He rolled out numerous Alfresco and Liferay deployments worldwide in the ECM and Portal domain.

He is also a certified Alfresco corporate trainer, certified Alfresco Engineer, and provides Alfresco Developer and Administrators training worldwide.

www.PacktPub.com

Support files, eBooks, discount offers and more

You might want to visit www.PacktPub.com for support files and downloads related to your book.

Did you know that Packt offers eBook versions of every book published, with PDF and ePub files available? You can upgrade to the eBook version at www.PacktPub.com and as a print book customer, you are entitled to a discount on the eBook copy. Get in touch with us at service@packtpub.com for more details.

At www.PacktPub.com, you can also read a collection of free technical articles, sign up for a range of free newsletters and receive exclusive discounts and offers on Packt books and eBooks.

http://PacktLib.PacktPub.com

Do you need instant solutions to your IT questions? PacktLib is Packt's online digital book library. Here, you can access, read and search across Packt's entire library of books.

Why Subscribe?

- Fully searchable across every book published by Packt
- Copy and paste, print and bookmark content
- On demand and accessible via web browser

Free Access for Packt account holders

If you have an account with Packt at www.PacktPub.com, you can use this to access PacktLib today and view nine entirely free books. Simply use your login credentials for immediate access.

Table of Contents

Preface

For the past 13 years at CIGNEX Datamatics, our focus has been on proving value to our customers using open source alternatives to the commercial CMS products. We talk to customers who have done multi-million dollar implementations of proprietary software, and faced all kinds of challenges, including vendor lock-in, rigid code base, and expensive upgrades.

Alfresco 4 offers a true Enterprise Content Management (ECM) system by providing an open source alternative to Microsoft SharePoint, Documentum, and FileNet. Everyday, over seven million business users in 75 countries rely on Alfresco to manage four billion documents, files, and processes — behind the firewall, in the cloud, and even on their mobile devices (as per the information listed on Alfresco's website, www.alfresco.com). It is the most popular Java-based CMS with over 25,000 active forum users and with more than 300 application extensions in forge. And most importantly, it is created using completely open standards. This excited us a lot, and we started implementing Alfresco since 2006. We have trained many users, administrators, and developers in Alfresco. This book distils the hands-on approach of our training courses into a concise, practical book.

This book focuses on business needs rather than technical syntaxes. We start by showing you how to do something — a step-by-step example. We explain how that process works. Then, we explain what other options are available, and how they fit into the overall picture. We hope this helps you "generalize" from such examples. We hope that you take advantage of this book by setting up a flexible enterprise content management system for your company and customers.

Your feedback is very valuable to us. You can contribute by reporting any errors you find in the book, making suggestions for any new content that you'd like to see in future updates, commenting, and blogging about it.

What this book covers

This book will take you through the complete cycle of implementing, customizing, and administering your Enterprise Content Management installation. The topics that this book covers are as follows:

Chapter 1, Introduction to Alfresco, includes an overview of the architecture and the key features of this software.

Chapter 2, Installing Alfresco, provides tips to choose the right installation for you, and also throws light on installing the software and explains how to start using it.

Chapter 3, Getting Started with Alfresco, gives basic information about the Alfresco Explorer and also provides you with various ways of configuring Alfresco as per your business needs.

Chapter 4, Implementing Membership and Security, describes working with users, and setting up security, including LDAP and Active Directory integration.

Chapter 5, Implementing Document Management, describes how to use Alfresco as a smart document repository, providing automatic version tracking and control, and accessing the repository from the Web, shared network folders, or FTP.

Chapter 6, Implementing Business Rules, teaches you how to automate document management tasks with business rules and various content transformations.

Chapter 7, Extending Alfresco Content Model, explains how to design custom content types.

Chapter 8, Implementing Workflow, teaches you how to automate your business process by using the advanced workflow concepts of Alfresco.

Chapter 9, Integrating External Applications with Alfresco, describes how you can integrate Alfresco with other external applications, such as Liferay Portal, iPhone, Facebook, iGoogle, Microsoft Outlook, Adobe Flex, and the Ffmpeg video transcoder.

Chapter 10, Alfresco Administration Operations Using Alfresco Share, explains how you can administer Alfresco using the Alfresco Share user interface.

Chapter 11, Customizing the User Interface, explains how to customize the user interface and create your own dashboard layouts, presenting content in custom ways that are relevant to your business.

Chapter 12, Search in Alfresco, explains how to make content easy to find using search, content categorization, and metadata. This chapter also includes a detailed description of Alfresco's Open Search features.

Chapter 13, Implementing Imaging and Forms Processing, describes how to collect paper documents and forms, transform them into accurate, retrievable information, and deliver the content into an organization's business application.

Chapter 14, Administering and Maintaining the System, explains effective administration and maintenance of the system for efficient performance and high availability.

What you need for this book

The default installation of Alfresco software requires installing the Windows enterprise version, `Alfresco-enterprise-<version>-installer-win-x64.exe`, which can be downloaded from the SourceForge project location (`http://wiki.alfresco.com/wiki/Download_and_Install_Alfresco`). Now, Alfresco is hosting its own community download area, hence you can also download it from `http://www.alfresco.com/products/ecm/enttrial/`. Select the download package, and you will be asked for the username and password of the Alfresco content community.

At the time of writing this book, the latest version was Alfresco Enterprise 4.1.2 and the `Alfresco-enterprise-4.1.2-installer-win-x64.exe` installer file is approximately 470 MB in size.

This installer will install the following:

- Java Development Kit (JDK) (if no JDK is installed on your machine)
- Apache Tomcat 6.0.32
- Portable Open Office 3.2
- The Alfresco Explorer web application, packaged as a Web Archive (WAR)
- The Alfresco Share web application, packaged as a Web Archive (WAR)
- SharePoint Protocol support

To install and run Alfresco, you need at least 500 MB of disk space and at least 512 MB RAM on the desktop or server.

Who this book is for

This book is designed for system administrators, experienced users, or developers who want to install and use Alfresco in their teams or businesses. Because Alfresco is free, many teams can install and experiment with its ECM features without any upfront cost, often without management approval. This book assumes a degree of technical confidence, but does not require specialist system administration or developer skills to get a basic system up and running.

Alfresco is particularly suitable for IT consultants who want or need to set up a flexible enterprise content management system for their clients, be that for demonstration, development, or as a mission-critical platform. This book gets you to that result quickly and effectively.

This book also helps business users to make decisions about migrating from the existing proprietary ECM to Alfresco 4.

This book is not a developer guide. However, various examples in this book will help developers to extend Alfresco's functionality and to integrate Alfresco with external systems.

Although no knowledge of Alfresco is presumed, exposure to HTML, XML, JavaScript and related web technologies will help you to get the most from this book.

Conventions

In this book, you will find a number of styles of text that distinguish between different kinds of information. Here are some examples of these styles, and an explanation of their meaning.

Code words in text, database table names, folder names, filenames, file extensions, pathnames, dummy URLs, user input, and Twitter handles are shown as follows: "Alfresco comes with a property called `policy.content.update.ignoreEmpty`, which controls the execution behavior of a rule."

A block of code is set as follows:

```
<config evaluator="string-compare" condition="Advanced Search">
  <advanced-search>
    <content-types>
      <type name="custom:pressrelease" />
    </content-types>
    <custom-properties>
      <meta-data type="custom:pressrelease"
                                property="custom:PRDate" />
```

```
    <meta-data aspect="custom:CustomerDetails"
                           property="custom:CustomerName" />
    <meta-data aspect="custom:CustomerDetails"
                           property="custom:NewCustomer" />
  </custom-properties>
 </advanced-search>
</config>
```

When we wish to draw your attention to a particular part of a code block, the relevant lines or items are set in bold:

```
<property name="custom:CustomerName">
    <title>Customer Name</title>
    <type>d:text</type>
    <protected>false</protected>
    <mandatory>false</mandatory>
    <multiple>false</multiple>
    <index enabled="true">
        <atomic>false</atomic>
        <stored>false</stored>
        <tokenised>true</tokenised>
    </index>
    <constraints>
        <constraint ref="custom:name_length"/>
    </constraints>
</property>
```

Any command-line input or output is written as follows:

```
export -user admin -pwd admin -s workspace://SpacesStore -path /
companyhome -verbose Intranet.acp
```

New terms and **important words** are shown in bold. Words that you see on the screen, in menus or dialog boxes for example, appear in the text like this: "Select the **More Actions | View Details** link to view the **Details** page of the space."

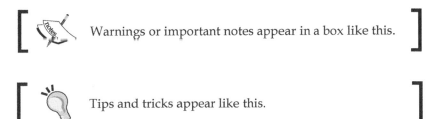

Warnings or important notes appear in a box like this.

Tips and tricks appear like this.

Reader feedback

Feedback from our readers is always welcome. Let us know what you think about this book—what you liked or may have disliked. Reader feedback is important for us to develop titles that you really get the most out of.

To send us general feedback, simply send an e-mail to feedback@packtpub.com, and mention the book title via the subject of your message.

If there is a topic that you have expertise in and you are interested in either writing or contributing to a book, see our author guide on www.packtpub.com/authors.

Customer support

Now that you are the proud owner of a Packt book, we have a number of things to help you to get the most from your purchase.

Downloading the example code

You can download the example code files for all Packt books you have purchased from your account at http://www.packtpub.com. If you purchased this book elsewhere, you can visit http://www.packtpub.com/support and register to have the files e-mailed directly to you.

Errata

Although we have taken every care to ensure the accuracy of our content, mistakes do happen. If you find a mistake in one of our books—maybe a mistake in the text or the code—we would be grateful if you would report this to us. By doing so, you can save other readers from frustration and help us improve subsequent versions of this book. If you find any errata, please report them by visiting http://www.packtpub.com/submit-errata, selecting your book, clicking on the **errata submission form** link, and entering the details of your errata. Once your errata are verified, your submission will be accepted and the errata will be uploaded on our website, or added to any list of existing errata, under the Errata section of that title. Any existing errata can be viewed by selecting your title from http://www.packtpub.com/support.

Piracy

Piracy of copyright material on the Internet is an ongoing problem across all media. At Packt, we take the protection of our copyright and licenses very seriously. If you come across any illegal copies of our works, in any form, on the Internet, please provide us with the location address or website name immediately so that we can pursue a remedy.

Please contact us at copyright@packtpub.com with a link to the suspected pirated material.

We appreciate your help in protecting our authors, and our ability to bring you valuable content.

Questions

You can contact us at questions@packtpub.com if you are having a problem with any aspect of the book, and we will do our best to address it.

1
Introduction to Alfresco

Enterprise content management (ECM) is the fastest growing category of enterprise software. Customers who are implementing or upgrading ECM systems are facing issues such as vendor lock-in, high maintenance costs, and lack of standardization. Open source technologies and open standards are becoming powerful alternatives to commercial closed-source ECM software. Alfresco being a stable player in this market has gained a lot of momentum by providing content management solutions to enterprises using open standards and open source based technologies. Alfresco is positioned as "Visionary" in Magic Quadrant for Enterprise Content Management (as per Gartner's ECM report 2012).

The latest release of Alfresco has an Enterprise Edition as well as a Community Edition. The Alfresco Community version is an unsupported product and is designed for use by developers and technical enthusiasts in non-critical environments. It serves as the research vehicle for new features and as the platform for the Alfresco Community. Constant innovation of the Alfresco Community renders a daily build, offering the latest functionality.

The Alfresco Enterprise Edition is production ready, stress tested and certified build that is supported by Alfresco Software Inc. It is fully a supported, Alfresco product that can provide support to corporations and governments that require commercial **Service Level Agreements (SLAs)**.

This chapter provides an introduction to Alfresco and outlines the benefits of using it for your enterprise's content management requirements. It also introduces the features of the latest release of Alfresco, Version 4.2, as of May 2013.

By the end of this chapter you will have learned about:

- The overview of Alfresco
- Key features of Alfresco software Version 4.2
- Alfresco products including Alfresco Mobile and Alfresco Workdesk
- Using Alfresco for your document management, business process automation, records management, team collaboration, web publishing, secure file sharing, and mobile content management requirements
- The future roadmap

Overview of Alfresco

Alfresco was founded in 2005 by *John Newton*, co-founder of Documentum, and *John Powell*, former COO of Business Objects. Its investors include the leading investment firms Accel Partners, Mayfield Fund, and SAP Ventures. The proven track record of its leaders, the features in the technology, the open source business model, and good venture capital backing of the team, as a combination makes Alfresco different.

Leveraging the benefits of open source

Enterprise customers can reduce costs, minimize business risks, and get competitive advantage by adopting the right open source based business software solutions. Based on publicly available pricing from a range of vendors, a white paper from Alfresco shows how it is possible to save, in the first year of implementation (based on a 1000 user configuration), up to 89 percent of the cost of SharePoint purchases and up to 96 percent of the cost of other ECM solutions by using Alfresco's open source ECM. You can reduce the cost of software solution acquisition, deployment, and maintenance by bringing the community into the development, support, and service process.

Alfresco is the leading open source alternative for enterprise content management. It couples the innovation of open source with the stability of a true enterprise-class platform. The open source model allows Alfresco to use the best-of-breed open source technologies and contributions from the open source community to get higher quality software produced more quickly and at a much lower cost.

State-of-the-art content repository

The following diagram explains the overview of Alfresco content repository and its integration with external systems such as virtual filesystems, web applications, knowledge portals, and web services.

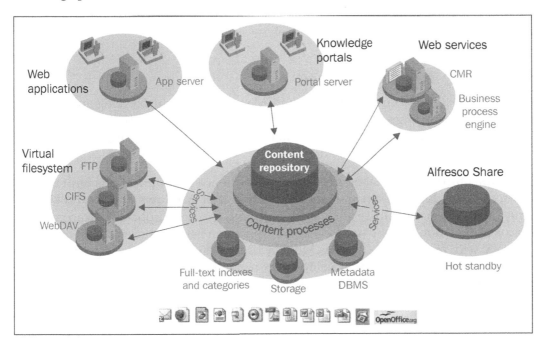

A content repository is a server or a set of services used to store, search, access, and control content. The content repository provides these services to specialist content applications such as document management, records management, image storage and retrieval systems, or other applications that require the storage and retrieval of large amounts of content. The repository provides content services such as content storage or import, content classification, security on content objects, control through content check-in and check-out, and content query services to these applications.

What distinguishes content management from other typical database applications is the level of control exercised over individual content objects and the ability to search content. Access to these services requires wrapping the calls in security to prevent unauthorized access or changes to content or its metadata. The finer granularity of this security and its complex relationship with other objects such as people and folders requires a more sophisticated mechanism than provided by a traditional database security.

The complex requirements of these services imply that much of the business logic of the content repository can be as large as or larger than the database itself. Almost all the content repository vendors provide proprietary service interfaces to encapsulate the breadth of functionality required. Despite having tried over the last 10 years to standardize these interfaces, it is only over the last two years that any progress has been made. In 2005, the Java community adopted the JSR-170 standard interface and Alfresco's content repository is based on these standards.

Scalable architecture

The single most important aspect of any ECM system is the underlying architecture. Alfresco supports pluggable, aspect-oriented architecture out of the box by leveraging the open source standards and components such as Spring, Hibernate, Lucene, CMIS, JSR-168, JSR-170, and JSE6.

The architecture is based on open standards and hence the applications built using Alfresco can be deployed on any environment such as Windows, Linux, and Mac, using any relational database such as MySQL, and Oracle. Applications can run on various application servers such as JBoss Application Server and Apache Tomcat, can work with any browser such as Mozilla Firefox, and Microsoft Internet Explorer. More over the applications built using Alfresco can be integrated with any portal such as JBoss Portal, and Liferay Portal.

In any enterprise, the amount of content you will manage will keep on increasing. In some organizations such as media, pharmaceutical, and healthcare, the content increases exponentially every year. Hence scalability is a critical issue when evaluating the ECM solution.

Due to modular and light-weight architecture, Alfresco is highly scalable. Alfresco provides horizontal scalability by having each tier in the architecture deployed on multiple servers. Similarly Alfresco can scale vertically by partitioning and load balancing in a multi-server environment.

Open standards-based underlying components

Open standards protect enterprise investment, promote innovation, and make it easier for IT departments to support the software. By adopting open standards for their ECM requirements, enterprises can lower the risk of incompatibilities with existing technologies. The enterprise application integration becomes easier with open standards.

Alfresco is completely built on the following open standards:

- Java 1.7
- WebDAV – IETF web-based distributed authoring and versioning
- 5015.02 – US Department of Defense (DoD) certified for records management
- JSR-170 – Java Content Repository (JCR) API
- JSR-283 – Next generation of JCR
- JSR-168 – Portal integration standard
- CMIS – specification supported by all major ECM vendors including IBM, and Microsoft
- Spring 2.0 Aspect-Oriented framework
- Apache iBatis (replacing Hibernate from Alfresco 3.4 version onwards)
- AIFS (Alfresco Intelligent File System) supporting Windows files sharing (SMB/CIFS), NFS, and FTP
- Open Office 3.3

Globalization support

If your enterprise has a global business model, it is very important for you to provide content in multiple languages. Most of the enterprises look beyond their geographic borders for new markets. The majority of the web users speak little or no English. Hence ECM systems should be designed with globalization in mind.

Alfresco out of the box supports major languages including Chinese, Dutch, English, French, German, Italian, Russian, and Spanish.

Security and access control

Protecting unauthorized access to the content is the key requirement for enterprises. This is true for corporate websites, intranets, extranets, front office, and back office applications.

A nice thing about Alfresco is that the permissions can be applied at a space (folder) level or can be set for each individual content item. Out of the box, Alfresco supports relational database-based membership systems and also supports external identity management systems such as LDAP, NTLM, Kerberos, and Active Directory.

Essential library services

Library services are required if you want to manage, leverage, modify, and control the content in an ECM system. Alfresco provides library services such as Check-In/ Check-Out, version control, auditing information, and content streaming.

Using Alfresco, you can define the library services to be executed automatically based on the business rules. For example, every edit to the content can version the content automatically. Or every check out can move the content to a specific location based on the business rules.

Alfresco provides additional intelligence to the content by adding metadata (data about data), business rules, security rules, and collaboration rules dynamically, using aspect-oriented programming. Alfresco also provides features such as content metadata extractors, content transformers, translations, and auto categorization to make the content intelligent.

Business process automation

Business process automation increases productivity, reduces costs, streamlines processes, and shortens operation cycles. Alfresco includes **Activiti** (http://www.activiti.org/) as a business process management and automation solution. This would help manage document life cycle with security and audit trails capabilities. Alfresco extends the support for JBoss JBPM workflow engine which was the default workflow engine for the earlier versions.

Enterprise integrations

Alfresco provides open-standards based protocols to integrate with external applications. Some of the application integration examples are mentioned in this book in *Chapter 9, Integrating External Applications with Alfresco*. Alfresco could be used as an embedded repository or as an external content repository. Because it is open source, you can reuse the integration components for your business applications saving time and money.

Alfresco now integrates with applications such as Facebook, ViewOne Pro, and iGoogle, and gadgets such as iPhone. Alfresco integration with Drupal (PHP-based web content management system) is a perfect example of how cooperation between open source projects can yield innovative solutions more rapidly than a proprietary model.

Alfresco integrates with Ephesoft, offers the customers access to a comprehensive production capture solution, including automatic document classification, data extraction, and validation for both Internet-based distributed capture or centralized environments.

Alfresco integrates with an open source J2EE-based leading portal framework called Liferay. Alfresco Liferay bundle is an out of the box solution, which provides an excellent portal-based ECM solution.

Alfresco integrates with external identity management systems such as LDAP and Active Directory and supports centralized security and single sign-on.

Alfresco Enterprise 4 – an overview

Alfresco Enterprise 4.0 is built on the Alfresco Surf platform. This platform enables you to build dynamic, REST-oriented web applications and collaborative websites. The Surf platform is designed to work in a number of different web environments. It includes content oriented components designed around the Yahoo!® User Interface (YUI) Library and Adobe® Flash® for dynamic uploads and previewing of content and other information. The new user interface components make it much simpler for users to develop new collaborative web applications. It is also enabled to work as a Web Part in Microsoft SharePoint Portal.

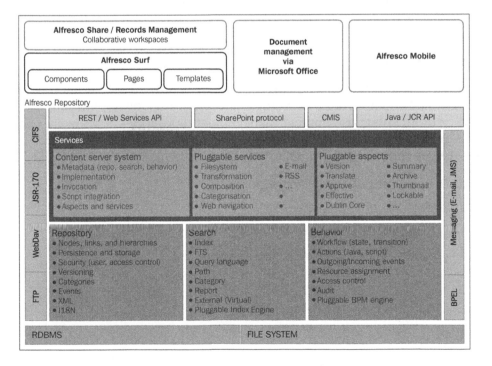

Alfresco Share

Alfresco Share delivers out of the box, collaborative content management. Alfresco Share simplifies capturing, sharing, and retrieval of information across virtual teams, boosts productivity, and reduces network bandwidth requirements and e-mail volumes between project team members.

Alfresco 4 releases include many enhancements to Share such as improved user experience and advanced management tools. Share now also supports plug-in extension modules to extend, replace, or remove components within Share without changing the OOTB code.

Alfresco Repository Public API

The Repository Public API provides content and collaboration services for customizing and developing Alfresco applications. Introduced with Labs 3b, it offers services such as site management, site activities, tagging, commenting, thumbnails, blogs, wikis, and forums to support social collaboration. These new REST APIs are based upon ATOM Publishing. The Repository Public API has two forms:

- A RESTful API for remotely connecting to the repository as used by Alfresco Share
- A JavaScript API for developing extensions to the repository (as used in web scripts, actions, and so on)

Alfresco CMIS implementation

The **Content Management Interoperability Services (CMIS)** specification defines a domain model and a set of API bindings that can be used by applications to work with one or more Enterprise Content Management repositories or systems. The CMIS technical draft specification has been developed jointly by EMC, IBM, Microsoft, Alfresco, Open Text, Oracle, and SAP. The CMIS implementation will benefit by:

- Write once, run anywhere application
- Integrate multiple repositories
- Business process across repositories
- Learn one UI for all repositories

Alfresco Version 4.0 includes enhanced CMIS features such as the following:

- Consolidated AtomPub and Web Services impl. behind OpenCMIS Server
- Access to OpenCMIS Client API within Repository (in-process)
- Single-Sign On support with CMIS
- .NET OpenCMIS Client API (via Apache Chemistry)

For more information on Alfresco and CMIS, please see `cmis.alfresco.com`.

Microsoft SharePoint Protocol support

Alfresco is now the first ECM to offer Microsoft Office SharePoint Protocol support. Available at a lower cost and with no additional client installation, it is remarkable. It also allows choice for hardware, database, operating system, application server, and portal products.

Social content publishing

Social content publishing is a new feature added in Alfresco 4.0 release to allow you to publish content from Alfresco to social platforms. The current out of the box support is for the following social platforms:

- Facebook
- Flickr
- LinkedIn
- SlideShare
- Twitter
- YouTube

Solr search

Many improvements were made to the search service in Alfresco from 4.0 release onwards. Alfresco provides Solr as an alternative to previous in-transaction, Lucene-based indexing and search. Solr can be deployed and scaled on a separate tier.

Activiti workflow for Business Process Management (BPM)

Prior to the 4.0 release, Alfresco used **JBoss JBPM** as the workflow engine. The 4.0 releases now include the full integration of the Activiti engine into the repository. A new installation of 4.0 will also include JBPM, but it will be disabled by default. This is to support backward compatibility.

iPad and Android usability improvements

Alfresco 4.2 releases include mobile usability improvements for the share interface. For example, the editor for content creation, wiki, blogs, and forums is more users friendly. Features such as HTML5 drag-n-drop (in supported HTML5 browsers), and multi-file selection in the standard file upload dialog are supported.

Alfresco products

Alfresco Enterprise version comes in various product forms. This is to allow you and your content to move from desktop to cloud to tablet to smartphone. Wherever you are, access your files and share them with those who need them. For more details about these products, visit www.alfresco.com.

Alfresco Enterprise On-Premise

Alfresco Enterprise On-Premise helps customers to have customized versions as per the organization needs. Customers can scale the installation as listed based on the demand.

- **Single server**: Alfresco can be installed on a single server including the database, application server, and Alfresco application. Suitable for proof-of-concept projects or for small, departmental deployments.

- **Horizontal scalability**: Alfresco can be installed in a cluster. Additional servers can be added or removed from the cluster to meet user demand. This high-availability style configuration offers a higher level of reliability and resilience, and can be scaled out as you grow.

- **Vertical scalability**: To increase performance, the Alfresco application can be separated into different tiers so the content server, share application, search server, and content transformation server can be run on separate servers, each optimized to the workload.

- **Alfresco index server**: Content indexing can be run on a separate system to remove the indexing load from the Alfresco servers. All of the nodes in the Alfresco cluster can use this central index server, which can be scaled independently.

Alfresco in the cloud

Alfresco in the cloud is a fully managed **SaaS (Software as a Service)** offering that helps your organization keep control of its content while providing your users with powerful ways to access their content securely on any device, anywhere.

Alfresco Mobile

Alfresco Mobile is a free mobile document management app for iOS and Android smartphones and tablets, which enables you to view all your content stored in your Alfresco On-Premise or Alfresco in the cloud account.

Alfresco Workdesk

Alfresco Workdesk is a business solution that includes the Alfresco enterprise content platform, offered on a per-user basis. Alfresco Workdesk allows users to focus on just the content that is relevant to them, at just the right time, on the device of their choice, based on their role in the business process.

How you can benefit from Alfresco

Alfresco offers **enterprise content management (ECM)** such as document management, collaboration, records management, enterprise search, and imaging. You can configure and customize Alfresco to address your business requirements. Some of them are listed here for your reference.

Using Alfresco for document management

Using Alfresco you can implement document management solutions such as enterprise document management, digital asset management, and contracts management.

Alfresco document management features provide organizations with all the services necessary for creating, converting, managing, and sharing electronic documents. Built on industry-standard open source platforms, Alfresco provides version management and search capabilities.

Built-in data management and transformation engine provides you with the ability to transform the data into required formats based on the business rules. Integrated workflow provides you with the full control over the document life cycle, management, and process flow.

Digital asset management provides a single access point for all your rich digital media and its underlying metadata information throughout the extended enterprise. Alfresco centralizes storage and provides easy, efficient, enterprise access to digital assets, and allows them to be quickly repurposed, which streamlines processes and saves money.

Whether it's an employment contract, purchase agreement, maintenance contract, or collaboration agreement with a business partner, completeness, validity, traceability, and unalterability must be guaranteed if a company is to protect its commercial interests. Alfresco's document lifecycle management features ensure that people in various company departments, divisions, and regions can work together to support all processes relating to a contract throughout its lifecycle—from creation through fulfillment and modification to termination.

Key features include:

- Flexible metadata management
- Full audit control
- Transformation of data
- Security and version control
- Indexing and full-text search
- Locking, check in/out
- Offline briefcase synchronization to access content offline
- Taxonomy and categorization of content
- Advanced search with combined metadata, location, and multi-category search
- Soft deletes and deleted documents recovery support
- Scheduled jobs and actions
- Management of web assets

Using Alfresco for records management

Using Alfresco, you can implement records management solutions such as enterprise records management, compliance, imaging, forms management, and business process management.

Alfresco records management features provide a secure, auditable environment for creating, declaring, classifying, retaining, and destroying records. Organizations can ensure compliance by defining and enforcing policies for records use, storage, and disposition, with a legally defensible audit trail.

Records management capabilities are modeled to support the US Department of Defense 5015.2 Records Management standards. Alfresco provides file plan templates for numbering, classification, disposition, and other metadata population of records. Disposition includes the transfer of records and/or the ultimate destruction of the record.

Predefined reports will provide you with information about recent records, records due for cutoff, records retention due for expiry, records due for transfer, and records due for destruction.

The lifecycle determines the disposition of the record including when the records will be cut off or grouped together, how long the records will be held, and what happens to the record after the hold period expires — whether they are transferred to a records holding area or whether they should be destroyed.

By integrating with Scanning and OCR technologies, Alfresco provides end-to-end solution by collecting paper documents and forms, transforming them into accurate, retrievable information, and delivering the content into an organization's business applications. The information then is full-text searchable and goes through various lifecycles based on the organization's defined business process management.

E-mails are considered as records in some organizations. Alfresco enables you to drag-and-drop e-mails from Microsoft Outlook into the file plan space. The system will extract the metadata from the e-mail files and populate information such as who the e-mail is from, who the recipients are, and the subject of the e-mail. E-mail content is stored in a secure and scalable repository and is full-text searchable.

Key features include:

- Record plans
- Automatic conversion from proprietary office formats to long-term vendor neutral formats such as **Open Document Format (ODF)** and **Portable Document Format (PDF)**
- Vital records information management

- Record cutoff information management
- Record holding and retention management
- Record transfer process
- Record destruction management
- Record lifecycle management
- Archival policies
- Disposition schedules
- Restriction of user functions
- Audit trails

Using Alfresco for collaboration management

Using Alfresco you can implement collaboration solutions such as corporate and departmental intranets, knowledge management, and client and project extranets.

Alfresco collaboration features provide the infrastructure, integration points, and tools required for accessing, sharing, and distributing content among users or systems. Built upon industry-standard, open source platforms, Alfresco helps you to quickly define and develop environments for teams (project teams, associations, research, and so on) that will streamline processes, reduce costs, and improve time to market. Users can manage and collaborate on documents, web information, and forms within a single system through a consistent user interface.

A comprehensive security model based on individuals, groups, projects, and team spaces provides you the highest level of control. The solution leverages the existing infrastructure such as LDAP or Active Directory for authentication and authorization.

A web-based rules engine enables business users to define the business and content rules appropriately without the help of programmers and IT. Alfresco supports a graphical tool to define the workflow and business process management for content flow in collaborative environments.

Users can discuss the content using the discussion forums and discussion threads tied to the content. Users can subscribe to content and receive e-mail notifications when content is added or updated. The solution supports both inbound and outbound RSS syndication to share content beyond inside and outside corporate firewalls.

Interfaces such as **Common Internet File System (CIFS)** and WebDAV allow each team member or departmental system to map the folder on the server as a local network drive. This enables bulk transfer of files between your local system and the central server repository. Users can use their favorite editors to edit the content that is mapped in the local network drive.

Knowledge Management (KM) refers to a range of practices used by organizations to identify, create, represent, and distribute knowledge for reuse, awareness, and learning across the organization.

Key features include:

- Team spaces
- Full audit control
- Discussion forums
- Message boards
- RSS syndication
- Ad-hoc security
- Version controlled content repository
- Full-text search of various content items
- User controlled routing
- Integration of enterprise systems
- High availability, fault tolerance, and scalability
- Business process-driven content management

Using Alfresco for enterprise content search

Most of the ECM systems do not consider search as an important part of enterprise content management. Search helps to locate information quickly, generate business reports, and helps to make business decisions. The following features of Alfresco will provide you an enterprise search solution:

- Provides single point access to enterprise content repository
- Provides full-text search of documents
- Helps to index the documents and provide metadata search
- Helps you to build and share reports using saved searches
- Helps search for users and collaborative groups
- Searches archived content

Applications of Alfresco

Since the architecture is flexible and extensible, you can build various applications using Alfresco such as:

- Enterprise document repository
- Intranet
- Enterprise knowledge management portal
- Scalable content repository
- Corporate websites
- Marketing communications
- On demand publishing
- Compliance and records management
- Financial applications which involve security, forms handling, and approval process
- Research portals for collaboration and sharing of information

Alfresco's website (`http://www.alfresco.com`) has a list of customer case studies. Going through these case studies will help you understand the type of applications you could develop using Alfresco.

How does the future look with Alfresco?

This book is based on Alfresco Enterprise 4.1.2. It is an update on the previous book which was on the Alfresco 3.0 release. The Alfresco system has evolved towards a state-of-the-art, one point solution to the ECM needs.

Alfresco is geared towards an enterprise content platform that you can use in the cloud or behind your firewall. Alfresco is built for the portability of the tablet and the power of the cloud.

There has been so much interest from international organizations, governments, and multi-national corporations that translation seems a natural extension of the Alfresco model.

Alfresco has weaved itself into a number of other products. Products such as Quark, Acrobat.com, CAStor, and Adobe LiveCycle are just a few to mention who have incorporated the ECM into their product in some way.

Better support options

Alfresco comes with multiple support options. Firstly, it is supported by the company Alfresco, which gives users direct access to Alfresco's engineering team and most recent bug fixes.

At any given point in time, the following three support alternatives exist for Alfresco open source software:

- **In-house development support**: As the source code is open source, you can train your developers in-house to support your application built using Alfresco.

- **Community support**: Alfresco already has a big community world wide. With a growing community, you can always get help through Alfresco community forums, though the quality of support can vary.

- **Alfresco enterprise network support**: Alfresco Inc. provides the highest quality option for production and development support. This support is provided to the company's customers using the Enterprise product. It includes direct access to the engineers who write the Alfresco code, the up-to-date bug fixes, configuration assistance, and a range of other services.

Free upgrades

For every new release, you will get free upgraded software. You might have to take care of your specific customization to upgrade to the later version of the software. It is important to follow best practices while implementing Alfresco, so that upgrades are easier and less expensive to handle.

Implementing the example solution using Alfresco

Subsequent chapters of the book contain examples to help you implement your requirements such as collaboration, customization, and document management using Alfresco. The examples are an attempt to solve similar content management problems which are encountered in a typical enterprise.

By providing examples in this book, the idea is to:

- Engage you, and keep the material feeling real-world.

- Help you apply the features of Alfresco to business decisions. You see in the fictional example that decisions are made for particular reasons, and can contrast those reasons (and thus the decisions) with your own situation.

- Give the book an overall theme—even a narrative engine to keep things moving and not feel like technical documentation.

Where do you get more information?

The best place to start looking for more information is Alfresco's corporate website (`http://www.alfresco.com`) itself. You can find the latest news and events, various training programs offered worldwide, presentations, demonstrations, and hosted trails.

Alfresco is 100 percent open source and all the downloads are available from the SourceForge website at `http://sourceforge.net/projects/alfresco/files/`.

Alfresco Wiki (`http://wiki.alfresco.com`) contains documentation such as tutorial, user guide, developer guide, administrator guide, and roadmap.

Alfresco discussion forums (`http://forums.alfresco.com`) are the best place to share your thoughts, and to get tips and tricks about Alfresco implementation. The discussion forums are available in multiple languages.

If you would like to file a bug or to know more details about the fixes in a specific release, then you must visit the bug tracking system at `http://issues.alfresco.com/`.

Summary

Alfresco is the leading open source alternative for enterprise content management. It couples the innovation of open source with the stability of a true enterprise-class platform. The open source model allows Alfresco to use the best-of-breed open source technologies and contributions from the open source community to get higher quality software produced more quickly at a much lower cost.

Alfresco provides key features for a scalable, robust, and secure content management system to deliver trusted and relevant content to your customers, suppliers, and employees.

Alfresco enterprise content platform can be used in the cloud or behind your firewall. Alfresco is built for the portability of the tablet and the power of the cloud.

2
Installing Alfresco

One of the remarkable features of Alfresco is the ease with which it can be installed and deployed. The simple out of the box installation is quite straightforward with preconfigured options that are aimed at having a complete, working content management system in no time. This chapter provides you with a basic understanding of Alfresco architecture, various installation options, and the key terminologies used. By the end of this chapter, you will be well equipped with the information to make a choice on the suitable operating system, database, application server, and other software required for your installation. This chapter is essential reading for anyone not already familiar with Alfresco.

By the end of this chapter you will have learned:

- The overall architecture of Alfresco
- How to determine what is the right installation option for you
- The full installation of Alfresco
- How to install Alfresco and all the required software
- How to install Alfresco components
- The AMP installation script

Installing Alfresco

Before directly delving into installation, it is important for you to understand the architecture behind Alfresco and various installation options available to you. This will help you to make good decisions in selecting the suitable software for your business application.

Out of the box installation architecture

The out of the box deployment of Alfresco is a typical web application architecture consisting of different layers as shown in the following diagram. This new architecture is basically N-tier and delivers more scalability without massive hardware and software investment. It also accommodates more users with the existing hardware resources. The layered architecture of Alfresco provides the benefits of easily manageable, flexible, and highly scalable content management solution.

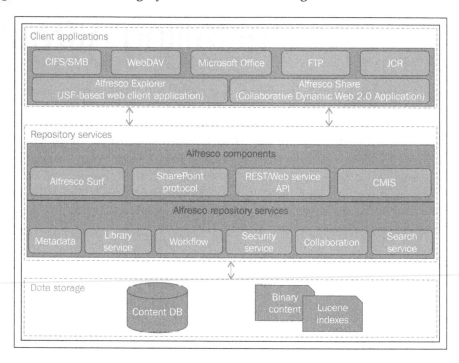

Client applications layer

The client applications layer contains the actual application as a web browser on the user's machine; basically the presentation layer. Out of the box Alfresco provides two client applications: Alfresco Explorer and Alfresco Share. Alfresco Explorer is pure document management web application whereas Alfresco Share is Web 2.0 application which provides dynamic collaborative support. In the next couple of chapters we will talk about these two applications in detail. Along with these two applications, Alfresco provides the support for CIFS, FTP, WebDAV, Microsoft Office, and so on. Refer to *Chapter 9, Integrating External Applications with Alfresco*, for more information on the different client applications integrated to leverage the services provided by Alfresco.

Repository services layer

The repository services layer consists of Alfresco components and services. This new architecture has clear separation between the presentation tier and the repository tier. The Alfresco RESTful API provides access to its services via HTTP which makes it accessible to other tools and applications. The SharePoint protocol support offers Microsoft users greater choice by providing them with the first open source fully-compatible SharePoint repository. Companies can leverage existing investments in Linux, Java as well as Microsoft .NET connection software to significantly reduce their SharePoint total cost of ownership and maximize their hardware and software investments. The Content Management Interoperability Services (CMIS) specification defines a domain model and a set of API bindings, that can be used by applications to work with one or more enterprise content management repositories or systems.

Data storage layer

The data storage layer stores the data in a relational database and filesystem.

There is a reason for using both database and filesystem as content storage. Any content within Alfresco consists of two elements, the content itself and information about the content (metadata).

The actual content can be anything from simple documents (HTML and XML) to images, audios, and videos. The actual content and its related versions are stored as binary files in the filesystem. Storing content on a filesystem has its own advantages. It allows for very large content, random-access streaming, and options for different storage devices. It is important to note that Alfresco is agnostic with respect to the filesystem it utilizes. It is possible to configure Alfresco to use a vast diversity of filesystems.

Alfresco uses Lucene and Solr, popular open source search engines, to provide metadata search and full-text search capabilities of the content. Apart from the actual binary content, indexed files are also stored on the file system.

The content metadata consists of information which includes elements such as:

- The format of the content
- Date created
- Language
- Security settings, which are stored in the relational database

Components of Alfresco applications

The application server hosts the user interface and domain logic. It provides an abstraction and enables communication between the client and storage layers. In the case of Alfresco, the application server houses Alfresco applications (such as the Alfresco Explorer and Alfresco Share) and the Alfresco repository.

The Alfresco repository provides a set of reusable cross-cutting content management services such as content storage, query, versioning, and transformation, which may be utilized by one or more applications.

An Alfresco application provides a complete solution tailored for a specific area of content management such as document management and records management. The user interfaces for all these applications are referred to as Alfresco Explorer and Alfresco Share. Alfresco Explorer is the JSF-based client, which is highly customizable and configurable according to the user specific requirements. The out of the box web client gives you a lot of packaged functionality. With the web client management console, you can manage users, security, content, business rules, and so on. Additionally, Alfresco Share introduces a new, simplified, easy-to-use, and adept knowledge worker UI; the current JSF client will still be available and unchanged.

How can you access the application

There is no installation or configuration required for the Alfresco user interface. Any number of web browsers can connect to the application without prior client installation costs.

The out of the box installation comes with Alfresco Share and Alfresco Share web client where you can connect to the Alfresco repository through web-based applications.

Apart from these applications, Alfresco out of the box installation supports various client applications to access Alfresco content with web services or protocols such as FTP, WebDAV, and CIFS:

- **File Transfer Protocol (FTP)**: It is useful to transfer files from your local filesystem to the remote server.

- **WWW Distributed Authoring and Versioning (WebDAV)**: It is primarily designed for editing and managing files on remote web servers in a structured way. For example, an application such as Adobe Photoshop can directly open and edit a file in the Alfresco content repository. This gives you the flexibility of using your own favorite editor to edit the content on the Alfresco server.

- **Common Internet File System (CIFS)**: It maps Alfresco content as your local filesystem folder.

- **Web services:** Most of the ECM products, in the market-store content, are in a proprietary format, which is like a "black box". Alfresco content is stored as per the JCR (Java Content Repository-JSR 170) open standards. Any JCR-compliant client application can read the content which is stored in the Alfresco repository. This is one of the key selling points of Alfresco. An API is provided out of the box so that you could connect to the Alfresco repository from your applications through web services or JCR integration.

- **CMIS:** Alfresco supports **Content Management Interoperability Services (CMIS)** for interoperability between ECM systems. It specifies a domain model and protocol bindings for web services (SOAP) and AtomPub. If you want to use CMIS in Java-based application, you can use the Apache Chemistry implementation of OpenCMIS. It provides bindings for both the AtomPub and SOAP protocols. You can see the example of using Alfresco repository in Liferay using CMIS in *Chapter 9, Integrating External Applications with Alfresco*.

Which installation option is suitable for you

Alfresco is 100 percent open source software, which is developed using open standards. Hence it runs on various operating systems, relational databases, application servers, web browsers, and portals and supports various languages. Let us examine all the choices and determine which option is right for you.

Enterprise and Community editions

Alfresco currently provides two types of product download options:

- Alfresco Community Edition
- Alfresco Enterprise Edition

Both the options have the same code base and features, and are 100 percent open source. For both the options, you can use Alfresco documentation (wiki), community support (forums), and community contributed add-on products. Alfresco Community Edition is free. Alfresco Enterprise Edition includes per-CPU license fee.

The Alfresco Community Edition is an unsupported product and is mainly designed for developers and technical enthusiasts in non-critical environments. Alfresco Community Edition releases early, often, and renders a daily build, offering the latest functionality. It doesn't provide scalability and high availability certifications. Community editions are not updated with the latest bug fixes; those are provided in the Enterprise editions. A feature such as JMX tools support is also not available with the Community Edition.

I would recommend this to use as the research vehicle for new features and as the platform for the Alfresco Community and consider it as a test drive before you install.

If you are implementing Alfresco for major corporations, financial, insurance, government, or healthcare organizations, I would recommend you to go for Alfresco Enterprise Edition support. The primary benefit is that with the support of Alfresco and its certified partners you would get a stable, reliable, certified, and supported application with warranty and indemnity. Your Alfresco version will be certified on all available stacks such as Linux, Windows, MySQL, and Oracle. You will benefit from Alfresco support which includes problem resolution, compatibility advice, and migration advice and upgrade support. You will receive 24 x 7 support from Alfresco experts for mission critical applications. You can know more about Alfresco support stack by going to `http://www.alfresco.com/services/subscription/supported-platforms`.

Operating systems – Windows, Linux, UNIX, and MacOS

Choosing an operating system to run Alfresco will be based on various factors. For some companies it depends on in-house expertise. For example, if you have administrators and IT staff who can easily manage business applications running on Microsoft Windows platform, then your choice could be to go with the Windows operating system. For some companies it is based on the integration requirements with the existing systems.

If you do not have any preferences, I would recommend you to go with the Linux operating system for production use. Linux source code is freely distributed. Tens and thousands of programmers have reviewed the source code to improve performance, eliminate bugs, and strengthen security. No other operating system has ever undergone this level of review. The key advantages of Linux are listed as follows:

- The best technical support available
- No vendor lock-in
- Runs on a wide range of hardware
- Exceptionally stable
- Supports many tools and applications you need
- Interoperates with many other types of computer systems
- Low total cost of ownership

Databases – MySQL, Oracle, MS SQL Server, and PostgreSQL

The data access layer of Alfresco is implemented using an open source software component and **ORM (Object Relational Mapping)** tool called **MyBatis.** If you have already chosen the Microsoft Windows operating system, then the natural choice for you could be MS SQL server. If you already have Oracle license, then Oracle database is the best choice for you. You will get PostgreSQL by default with the Alfresco installation.

If you do not have any preference, I recommend that you go with the MySQL database which costs nothing if you go with the open source version. The MySQL database has become the world's most popular open source database because it is consistent, and also because of its fast performance, high reliability, and ease of use. It's used in more than 10 million installations ranging from large corporations to specialized embedded applications. MySQL runs on more than 20 platforms including Linux, Windows, OS/X, HP-UX, AIX, and Netware, giving you the kind of flexibility that puts you in control.

Application servers – Tomcat and JBoss

Alfresco runs on any J2SE 5.0 complaint servlet container. Hence there are no application server specific dependencies. However it is important to make a choice of the application server before moving into production.

Alfresco uses the **Spring** framework and not the **Enterprise Java Beans (EJB)** framework. So there is no dependency on JBoss or any other application server which provides the EJB container. **Spring** is an open source application framework for Java/JEE. The Alfresco repository uses the Spring framework as the core foundation of its architecture. If you are developing a standalone application, then Tomcat might be a good option. Apache Tomcat powers numerous large-scale and mission-critical web applications across a diverse range of industries and organizations. It is the most widely accepted web servlet container in the market.

On the other hand, you must consider using JBoss application server, which has the highest market capture (> 35 percent) in J2EE-based application servers in the world. JBoss internally uses Tomcat and hence you get the benefits of Tomcat servlet engine as well.

Alfresco application is implemented in a way to utilize JBoss cache's ability to distribute and maintain data caches, making it possible to build large-scale systems that outperform traditional enterprise content management systems. Alfresco also utilizes the clustering, failover, and load balancing facilities of the JBoss application server to increase scalability. Alfresco uses JBOSS jBPM tool and Activiti for business process management features.

If you have already invested in JBoss, then Alfresco provides complementary industry-leading enterprise content management technology to the JBoss enterprise middleware system suite.

Portals (optional) – JBoss Portal and Liferay

It is optional for you to go with a portal of your choice; if you already have an enterprise portal you can integrate Alfresco with it. If you do not have a portal in place and you would like to leverage the portal framework, then you can consider using either JBoss portal or Liferay portal. Both of these are based on J2EE technology; both of them are open source and open-standards based and both of them have Alfresco built-in support.

The JBoss portal provides an open source platform for hosting and serving a portal's web interface, publishing and managing its content, and customizing its experience. While most packaged portal frameworks help enterprises launch portals more quickly, only JBoss portal delivers the benefits of a zero-cost, open source license combined with a flexible and scalable underlying platform. The JBoss community portal project no more exists. It's been managed by JBoss community and GateIn. The new portal introduced with their combined effort is known as the GateIn Portal framework. You can read more about this from http://www.jboss.org/gatein.

Liferay is the most downloaded and popular open source portal with 40,000 downloads per month. It runs on top of any J2EE servlet such as Tomcat, so a full installation of JBoss is not required, but it can run against most full application servers out of the box including JBoss, JRun, BEA WebLogic, and Orion. It has a full set of web service interfaces to the portal. Liferay supports more than 800 portlets (products) and has wider adoption in the market.

Choosing the suitable software for your installation

You need to make the best choice of software to install Alfresco. If you do not have any specific requirements, you might consider a complete open source stack for production usage and go with the Alfresco Enterprise Edition on the Linux operating system, with MySQL database running on the JBoss application server with the Liferay portal.

Installing Java SE Developer Kit

The very first step for installing Alfresco is to install Java SE Developer Kit. Alfresco requires Java 1.5 or higher. If you already have JDK, then skip this.

To Install Java SDK, follow the given steps:

1. Download the JDK 6u33 update from `http://www.oracle.com/technetwork/java/javasebusiness/downloads/java-archive-downloads-javase6-419409.html#jdk-6u33-oth-JPR`.

2. After downloading, double click on this file to automatically proceed the installation.

3. Accept the license agreement. Click on **Next**.

4. In the next window for custom setup, choose **defaults**. Click on **Next**.

5. In the next window, choose the desired browsers to install Java [optional]. Click on **Finish**.

6. Test your installation by typing the `C:\>` `java -version` command on the command prompt.

7. Create the `JAVA_HOME` environment variable to set the path of the Java SE Developer Kit.

Installing Alfresco bundled on Tomcat

For convenience, Alfresco provides the bundle of Alfresco to install on Tomcat. This bundle includes a configuration file for the Tomcat server, together with the Alfresco web application archive (`alfresco.war`) file, the Alfresco Share web application archive (`share.war`), batch files, sample extension folder, and so on.

Steps to install Apache Tomcat

In order to install Alfresco on Tomcat, you first need to install Tomcat. The latest version of Alfresco uses Tomcat 6. The following steps describe the process to install the Alfresco bundle on Tomcat.

1. Download Tomcat 6.0.26 (`http://archive.apache.org/dist/tomcat/tomcat-6/v6.0.26/bin/`).

2. Unpack the Tomcat bundle in `C:\Alfresco\tomcat`.

3. Create the following directories required for the Alfresco extension:
   - `<TOMCAT-HOME>/shared/classed`
   - `<TOMCAT-HOME>/shared/lib`

4. Edit the `<TOMCAT-HOME>/conf/catalina.properties` file to add entry for the directories created in step 3. In case you created different directory names, use them in the following statement:

```
configuration.shared.loader=${catalina.base}/shared/classes
  ,${catalina.base}/shared/lib/*.jar
```

5. Copy the JDBC drivers to the `<TOMCAT-HOME>/lib` folder. If you are using the MySQL database, copy the connector JAR file.

6. Make changes in the `<TOMCAT-HOME>/conf/server.xml` file to set the character encoding UTF-8 on the Tomcat connector. By default, Tomcat uses ISO-8859-1 character encoding when decoding URLs that are received from a browser. Reach to the connector section in `server.xml` and make the change as follows:

```
<Connector port="80" protocol="HTTP/1.1"
URIEncoding="UTF-8"
connectionTimeout="20000"
redirectPort="8443" />
```

Steps to deploy Alfresco on Apache Tomcat

To install Alfresco on Tomcat, you need to download the Alfresco enterprise package from `http://support.alfresco.com/`. This bundle contains the required files to deploy Alfresco in Tomcat. Download the Alfresco enterprise zip package as mentioned:

1. Browse to the Alfresco support portal.

2. Log in to the support portal with the credentials you have, browse to **Online resources | Downloads | Alfresco Enterprise <version> (from left navigation) | Click on "<version> Alfresco Enterprise zip package"**.

   You will get the `alfresco-enterprise-<version>.zip` file.

   Within this file, you will get the following files and folders:

   ○ `Bin`: This folder contains batch file / shell scripts and JAR files for the Alfresco module management. It also contains DLL files to support CIFS.

   ○ `Licenses`: This folder contains the structure to copy Alfresco and third-party license files.

   ○ `web-server`: Under this folder you will receive library files, web archive files for Alfresco and Share, and directory structure with files to extent Alfresco.

   ○ `readme.txt`: This file contains information regarding the bundle file.

Let's talk about how you will deploy the previous files to configure Alfresco on Tomcat.

1. Stop the Tomcat server if it is already running.

2. Copy the `alfresco.war` and `share.war` files from the `web-server/webapps` folder to the `<TOMCAT-HOME>/webapps/` folder.

3. Replace the `<TOMCAT-HOME>/shared` folder from the `web-server/shared` folder and rename `alfresco-global-properties.sample` to `alfresco-global-properties` file.

4. Start the Tomcat server to deploy.

Installation of other Alfresco components

Alfresco uses various open source components for different purposes. You can install and configure them based on your business requirements. In this section we will see how to install those components and configure it with Alfresco.

Installing SharePoint protocol support

If you have installed Alfresco using full setup then this support will already be there. Otherwise follow the given steps to add the SharePoint protocol support:

Download the `alfresco-enterprise-spp-<version>.zip` connector functionality for Microsoft SharePoint protocol support from `https://support.alfresco.com/ics/support/DLRedirect.asp?fileID=34833`.

To install SharePoint support, follow the given steps:

1. To install this module, copy `alfresco-enterprise-spp-<version>.zip` in `<alfresco_installation_folder>\amps`.

2. Run the `apply_amps.bat` file available at `<alfresco_installation_folder>\bin`.

3. Start your Alfresco server to deploy the newly created `alfresco.war` file by AMP.

4. Verify that your SharePoint AMP is applied properly to Alfresco by checking the `/webapps/alfresco/WEB-INF/classes/alfresco/module/org.alfresco.module.vti/context` path directory.

Installing the Alfresco license file

If you want to use the Alfresco Enterprise edition, you require a license file. Alfresco Enterprise edition comes with a 30 day evaluation license. If you don't provide any license file, then you can evaluate it for 30 days. After that it will expire and you will only have read-only access to the repository.

Steps to download the Alfresco license file

1. Browse to the support portal and click on **Request Support** on the menu bar to submit a ticket.

    Use the following information to the create ticket:

    ◦   Issue type: I need a license key from the list.

    ◦   Select the Alfresco Enterprise version: The version for which you want the license key from the drop-down list

    ◦   Select a priority: Question/how-to/enhancement (it's very important to provide appropriate severity to the ticket as the license retrieval process is automated and will be counterproductive if higher severities are set to the ticket)

    ◦   Fill up the **Subject** and **Problem Description** fields

2. Submit the ticket and note down the ticket number. You will receive the license via e-mail.

To install the license file

1. Shut down Alfresco if it's already running.

2. Browse to the `<alfresco_installation_folder>\tomcat\shared\ alfresco\extension\license` directory.

3. Drop the downloaded `.lic` extension file into this directory.

4. Restart the Alfresco server.

After the successful installation of this license, `.installed` will be appended to the file name and it begins to utilize the terms of your license immediately.

Installing and configuring the MySQL database

As mentioned earlier in this chapter, the content in Alfresco is stored in persistent back-end systems such as a database and filesystems. So for the persistence of metadata, we need some database. Alfresco by default uses PostgreSQL to persist the metadata. You can change the default database configuration to MySQL by following simple steps:

Steps to install MySQL

[If you already have installed MySQL on your machine, you can skip this section.]

1. Download the MySQL package from `http://dev.mysql.com/downloads/`. Alfresco requires MySQL 5.5 or higher.

2. After downloading, navigate to your download location and unzip the package.

3. Double-click on the `setup.exe` file to automatically start the installation.

4. You will see the welcome message screen. Click on **Next**.

5. Select the typical setup in the next screen and choose the default selected options for the next screens.

6. Once that wizard completes, you will have an option to configure MySQL server instance. Select **Configure the MySQL Server now** and click on **Finish**.

7. Now you will see the welcome screen for the MySQL server configuration wizard window. Click on **Next**.

8. Choose the default selected options for the next screens.

9. Select UTF8 Character set when asked.

10. Accept the Windows option: Install it as a Windows service as shown in the following screenshot. Click on **Next**.

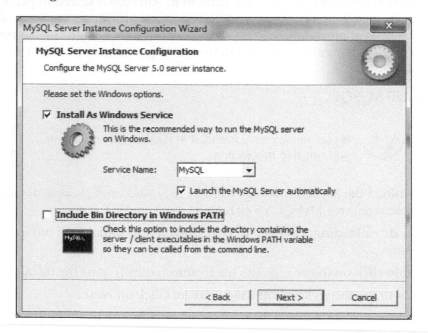

11. In the next step, provide the password for the root user. Click on **Next**.

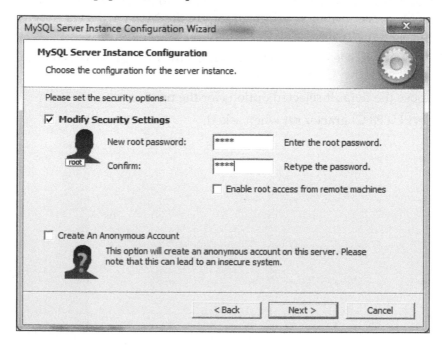

12. In the next screen, click on **execute** to start the configuration.

13. Open the MySQL command-line client from **All Programs | MySQL | MySQL Server 5.0 | MySQL Command Line Client** and provide the root password.

14. Now to test your installation, type the following command:

```
mysql -u root -p
```

Steps to set up the MySQL database for Alfresco

1. Login to MySQL. Create a database for the Alfresco instance with the database name as `alfresco`. Create a user called `alfresco` with password as `alfresco` and grant all permissions to it. See the following code snippet for creating a database:

```
create database alfresco default character set utf8;

grant all on alfresco.* to 'alfresco'@'localhost'
   identified by 'alfresco' with grant option;

grant all on alfresco.* to
   'alfresco'@'localhost.localdomain' identified by
   'alfresco' with grant option;
```

Once done with previous step, a MYSQL database will be created with the following credentials:

  ○ Database name: `alfresco`

  ○ Database username: `alfresco`

  ○ Database password: `alfresco`

2. To confirm the database is created, login to MySQL with the `mysql -u root -p` command.

3. At the MySQL prompt, execute the command, `show databases;` you will find the database created as Alfresco.

Steps to configure the MySQL database for Alfresco

To convert the default installation to MySQL, we simply need to modify one file in the `<alfresco_installation_folder>\tomcat\shared\classes` directory that is set to use default database. The file is `alfresco-global.properties`. To change the Alfresco installation to MySQL database, the following changes need to be made in `alfresco-global.properties`:

1. Comment out the PostgreSQL connection lines using #.

2. Add the following lines to set host, port, and name to the location of your MySQL JDBC driver. Change the host and port if you have installed MySQL on a different machine.

    ```
    db.username=alfresco
    db.password=alfresco
    db.name=alfrescodb.driver=org.gjt.mm.mysql.Driver
    db.url=jdbc:mysql://localhost:3306/${db.name}?
       useUnicode=yes&characterEncoding=UTF-8
    ```

3. Copy the Database Connector lib.

4. Download the MySQL database connector JAR (`mysql-connector-java-5.x.x-bin.jar`) file.

5. Copy the `mysql-connector-java-5.x.x-bin.jar` file in `<alfresco_installation_folder>/tomcat/lib`.

6. Restart the Alfresco server.

Installing OpenOffice

For the document transformations such as office to PDF, OpenOffice is used, which is basically a cross-platform office application suite. OpenOffice is an optional installation that provides access to a range of document transformations in Alfresco. The following installation steps could be helpful, if you have not selected the OpenOffice option during Alfresco installation:

Steps to install OpenOffice

1. Download the latest stable version of OpenOffice from `http://download.openoffice.org`.

2. Install the downloaded file, the wizard will start.

3. Click on **Next** on the welcome screen of the installation wizard.

4. Leave the installer location as is and click on **Unpack**.

5. Fill up the customer information and click on **Next**.

6. Choose the `OpenOffice.org.Writer` module, which is the only module used by Alfresco, the others are not required for Alfresco. Change the installation directory to `<alfresco_installation_folder>/OpenOffice` by clicking on the **Change** button. Click on **Next**.

7. Optionally, select the files for which you want OpenOffice to be the default application for, and click on **Next**.

Steps to configure OpenOffice as a headless service

1. Open `<alfresco_installation_folder>/tomcat/shared/classes/alfresco-global.properties`.

2. Uncomment the following two lines and change value of `ooo.enabled` to `false` and save the file:

   ```
   ooo.enabled=false
   jodconverter.enabled=true
   ```

3. Restart the Alfresco server to reflect above changes.

Installing Flash Player

Installing Flash Player is optional but if you are using Alfresco Share then it is advisable to install this as Alfresco Share uses the Flash Player for viewing Flash previews. It is also used when you want to make use of the multi-file upload facility.

Steps to install Flash Player

1. To install Flash Player, download the latest version of Flash Player from the Adobe's Flash Player download site (`http://www.adobe.com/products/flashplayer`).

2. Follow the wizard steps to install it.

Installing SWFTools

Installing SWFTools is optional. For previewing the PDF files, Alfresco Share uses the pdf2swf utility of the SWFTools. This generates one frame per page of fully formatted text inside a Flash movie.

Steps to install SWFTools

1. To install SWFTools, download the latest version from its website (`http://www.swftools.org`).

2. Follow the installation wizard steps to install it.

Installation folder structure

Let's take a peek into the installation directory `<alfresco_installation_folder>` to look at the folders:

- `alfresco`: All the shortcuts to installing, uninstalling, starting, and stopping Alfresco as Windows service, and restarting, stopping and starting of Alfresco as a normal console application, from the **Start** menu of Windows points to this folder.

- `alf_data`: All the Alfresco content and Lucene indexes are stored in this directory.

- `amps`: All the AMP extensions files are required to be put in this folder and then use the `apply_amps` script to perform the update to Alfresco explorer.

- `amps_share`: Similar to the `amps` folder, all the AMP extensions files for Alfresco share are required to be put here and then use the `apply_amps` script to perform the update to Alfresco explorer.

- `bin`: This directory contains scripts for applying AMP files and cleaning the Tomcat folder after applying the AMP file. It also contains the module management package JAR file, which is used for applying AMP files to Alfresco through scripts.

- `java`: As is evident by the name, it contains the Java Development Kit. All the Alfresco development is done using Java as the core programming language.

- `licenses`: This directory contains the licenses for Alfresco, MySQL, and Apache and licenses for the other third-party applications used inside Alfresco.

- `tomcat`: Again, as evident from the name, this directory holds the Tomcat installation where Alfresco application is deployed as a WAR file. You can see the `alfresco.war` and `share.war` files in the `webapps` subfolder of this directory.

- `openoffice`: This directory contains the entire portable office suite installation that is used for word processing, spread sheet processing, and so on.

- `imagemagick`: This folder contains installation files of the ImageMagic module.

- `README`: This file gives information about using CIFS and some troubleshooting tips.

You can uninstall the program by clicking on the `uninstall.exe` application.

Starting and stopping Alfresco as a console application

The options for starting and stopping Alfresco as console application can be viewed by navigating to **Start | All Programs | Alfresco Enterprise | Alfresco Enterprise Service** as shown in the following screenshot:

The options are as follows:

- **Stop Alfresco Enterprise Server**: This option is used to stop Alfresco. It stops the MySQL server and the Tomcat application server.

- **Start Alfresco Enterprise Server**: Use this option to start Alfresco as a console application. This will start the MySQL server and the Tomcat server.

- **Alfresco Explorer**: This option is used to open Alfresco web client in the browser.

- **Alfresco Share**: This option is to open Alfresco Share in the web browser.

- **Alfresco Website**: This option is to open the Alfresco's website in the web browser.

Alternatively, you can always start, stop, and restart the Tomcat application server, and the MySQL database server manually, by going to their respective directories. It gives more control to the user. However, the console option gives batch files to perform the start/stop procedures in a consolidated way, relieving the user of any unwanted errors.

Configuring Alfresco as a Windows service

You can also configure Alfresco as a Windows service in a standard Alfresco/Tomcat installation. With the default installation, Alfresco is bundled as a web application that launches within Tomcat. To configure Alfresco to run as a Windows service, you need to set up Tomcat to run as a Windows service.

Steps to configure Alfresco as a Windows service

1. Open a command prompt.

2. Go to the `<alfresco_installation_folder>/tomcat/bin` directory.

3. Use the following commands:

   ```
   service.bat install alfresco

   tomcat6 //IS//Tomcat6 --DisplayName="Alfresco Server" \

     --Install="<alfresco_installation_folder>/Tomcat/bin/tomcat6.exe
   " --    Jvm=auto \

     --StartMode=jvm --StopMode=jvm \

     --StartClass=org.apache.catalina.startup.Bootstrap
   --StartParams=start \

     --StopClass=org.apache.catalina.startup.Bootstrap
   --StopParams=stop
   ```

   ```
   service.bat install alfresco

   tomcat5.exe //US//alfresco --DisplayName "Alfresco Server"

   tomcat5.exe //US//alfresco --JvmMs=256 --JvmMx=512 --JvmSs=64

   tomcat5.exe //US//alfresco
   --JavaHome<alfresco_installation_folder>/java

   tomcat5.exe //US//alfresco --Environment
   ALF_HOME=<alfresco_installation_folder>/

   tomcat5.exe //US//alfresco --Environment
   PATH=<alfresco_installation_folder>/bin;%PATH%

   tomcat5.exe //US//alfresco --StartPath
   <alfresco_installation_folder>--Startup auto
   ```

4. To uninstall the service, go to the `<alfresco_installation_folder>/tomcat/bin` directory and enter the following command:

   ```
   service.bat uninstall alfresco
   ```

5. To edit your service settings, go to the `<alfresco_installation_folder>/`
    `tomcat/bin` directory and enter the following command:

    ```
    tomcat5w.exe //ES//alfresco
    ```

6. To start the service, locate the service named Alfresco Server in your
    Windows Service control panel, and start Alfresco from this control panel.

Installing TinyMCE language packs

Alfresco supports the German (de), English (en), Spanish (es), French (fr), Italian (it),
Japanese (ja), and Dutch (nl) language packs in translations. On complete Alfresco
installation, all the language packs get installed by default. If you want translation
support which is not supplied with Alfresco installation, then you need to install
the TinyMCE language pack. Use the following steps to install the language
pack manually:

1. Download the desired language pack from the TinyMCE website
    (`http://tinymce.moxiecode.com/download_i18n.php`).

2. Unpack the language file:
    *   For Share, unpack the ZIP file to `<alfresco_installation_`
        `folder>/tomcat/webapps/share/modules/editors/tiny_mce`
    *   For Explorer, unpack the ZIP file to `<alfresco_installation_`
        `folder>/tomcat/webapps/alfresco/scripts/tiny_mce`

3. Clean your browser cache before testing the newly installed language pack.

Installing on Linux

Alfresco provides a nice package that includes all of the programs you need for using
Alfresco on your Linux machine. Download it from the customer or partner's portal
by selecting the latest version of the `alfresco-enterprise-<version>-installer-`
`linux-x64.bin` file.

This installer file contains Tomcat, OpenOffice, and Alfresco. Make sure you have
permissions to execute the installer. Make sure that you have JDK 6 installed on your
machine before installing Alfresco.

Use the following command to change the permissions on the installer so that it can
be executed:

```
> chmod a+x ./alfresco-enterprise-<version>-installer-linux-x64.bin
```

Become root (super) user to install by executing the following command (for some platforms that have the super user account disabled by default might require su -s):

```
> su
```

Now execute the installer directly on the command prompt as follows.

```
./alfresco-enterprise-<version>-installer-linux-x64.bin
```

Follow the instructions presented by the installer:

1. You will be asked for the language in the **Language Selection** prompt. Select **English** by pressing *1* and press *Enter*.

2. In the next option, you will be prompted for **Setup Type**. Select **Easy** and press *Enter*.

3. You will be asked for a location to install the software in the option. If you want to keep the default location, press *Enter* or provide your desired path to install Alfresco. If you are root, the default of /opt/alfresco-<version> will be selected. If you want to change it, /usr/local/alfresco-<version> will often be another good choice.

4. In next options, the installer will ask for providing port number to insert for database, web server domain, Tomcat server, shutdown port, SSL port, AJP port for Tomcat, and Alfresco RMI port. If you want to keep the default port keep pressing the Enter key or provide your desire port information.

5. Now in the next prompt, the installer will ask the admin user for the password. Provide your desire password and press the *Enter* key.

6. As discussed earlier at the beginning of this chapter, Alfresco provides support for SharePoint protocol to access the Microsoft document and update it directly in the repository from office software. Provide the port number for SharePoint protocol support and press the *Enter* key. The default port for SharePoint is 7070.

7. Provide port number for OpenOffice. Alfresco uses OpenOffice to transform a word document to PDF. Provide a port number if you want to change the default port or press the *Enter* key.

8. Now the setup is ready to install. It will ask for a confirmation. Press the *Y* key and then the *Enter* key to continue with installation process.

9. Once the installation part is done, the installer prompts to view the Readme file. Do not forget to read the contents of the Readme file, as it contains information about using CIFS and some troubleshooting tips.

Installing extensions with the AMP installation script

Alfresco provides extensions as an AMP file, which we can install with the help of the Module Management Tool in Alfresco. The Module Management Tool supports the installation of AMP modules including upgrades to later versions, enabling and disabling of installed modules, deinstallation of installed modules, and listing of currently installed modules.

Using the Module Management Tool with a script

For installing any AMP module in Alfresco, please refer to the following steps:

1. Download the particular AMP file with the `<extension-module>.amp` extension.

2. Copy the `<extension-module>.amp` file to `<alfresco_installation_folder>\amps`.

3. Stop the Alfresco server if it is already running before applying the AMP file. Run the `apply_amps` command available at `<alfresco_installation_folder>\bin`, which will install the particular module.

4. Delete the `alfresco` folder in `webapps` if it exists and restart the server.

Using the Module Management Tool from the command prompt

You can apply the module file to `alfresco.war` using the command prompt. You can use the following command to apply the AMP file:

```
java -jar alfresco-mmt-2.1.jar [args]
```

In order to use this command you need to set some JAR files on the class path. Run the `<alfresco_installation_folder>/scripts/setenv.sh` file before running the previous command to set JAR files on the class path. You will also have to set the `ALF_HOME` and `CATALINA_HOME` environment variables.

Let's understand the commands you can get with the MMT tool.

- `install`: You can use this command to install files found in the AMP file to the `alfresco.war` file. See the following example that demonstrates the use of the `install` command:

```
java -jar alfresco-mmt-2.1.0.jar install /opt/alfresco-
recordsmanagement-2.1.0.amp /opt/alfresco/tomcat/
webapps/alfresco/alfresco.war
```

- list: You can use this command to list the details about all modules currently installed in the WAR file. Check the following command:

```
java -jar alfresco-mmt-2.1.0.jar list /opt/
alfresco/tomcat/webapps/alfresco/alfresco.war
```

You can use MMT with Maven as well. You can visit http://wiki.alfresco.com/wiki/Managing_Alfresco_Lifecyle_with_Maven for more information.

Some of the extension modules available with Alfresco are alfresco-enterprise-spp.amp for SharePoint protocol support, alfresco-fb-doclib.amp for Facebook integration and alfresco-recordsmanagement.amp for Records Management sample functionality.

Summary

You have so many options to choose from while installing Alfresco. Alfresco installers on Windows and Linux operating systems make the installation process so simple that you could install all the installation software such as JDK, MySQL, Alfresco, SharePoint protocol, OpenOffice, and Office Addins within minutes. On the Windows platform you can run Alfresco as a service or as a console application. You can refer to various documentation regarding installation and other things at http://www.alfresco.com/resources/documentation. In the next chapter you will learn about different terminologies and configurations of the Alfresco repository.

Getting Started with Alfresco

Now that you have installed Alfresco successfully, it is very important to understand the terminology and configurations of Alfresco repository before using it. This chapter provides you the basic information about Alfresco Explorer; a web-based client application used to access the repository and also provides you various ways of configuring the repository as per your business needs. By the end of this chapter you will have learned how to:

- Log in to the Alfresco Explorer application
- Use the Administration Console and perform system administration tasks
- Use Alfresco for basic document management
- Configure personal dashboard wizard
- Configure file server, audit, and email subsystem
- Define multilanguage support
- Perform advance configurations such as high availability and multi-tenancy
- Create blueprint for your application

Introduction to Alfresco Explorer

The Alfresco Enterprise Content Management product is bundled and shipped along with two web-based applications. One is called **Alfresco Explorer**, which was formerly known as the "Web Client". In this chapter we will go through the high-level overview of Alfresco Explorer. The other web-based application is called **Alfresco Share**, which enables collaboration. *Chapter 10, Alfresco Administration Operations Using Alfresco Share,* of this book has a detailed description of Alfresco Share.

By using any web browser you can connect to the Alfresco Explorer application. You will be able to manage users, security, content, business rules, and everything related to your enterprise content stored in Alfresco through Alfresco Explorer.

In the rest of the book, wherever the web client configuration files are referred to, consider them as Alfresco Explorer related configuration files.

Logging in to Alfresco as an administrator

To begin, if Alfresco was installed by using the Tomcat or JBoss bundle, access the Alfresco Explorer from `http://localhost:8080/alfresco`. Access the Alfresco Explorer in the portal from `http://localhost:8080/portal` and navigate to Alfresco Explorer from the page menu, and then maximize the portlet.

If you have started Alfresco for the first time, then Alfresco will create the initial database content that is required to manage content. The first time you use Alfresco, your username will be `admin` and your password will be `admin`. You can change the admin password once you log in. Depending on your installation, you may have a choice of languages in the language drop-down menu. This book assumes that your selected language is English.

Screen layout

Once you log in, you will see the **My Alfresco** dashboard. You can browse through the Alfresco Explorer by clicking on the **Company Home** link provided at the top. A typical Alfresco Explorer page is shown in the following screenshot. Let us examine various sections of the Alfresco Explorer layout.

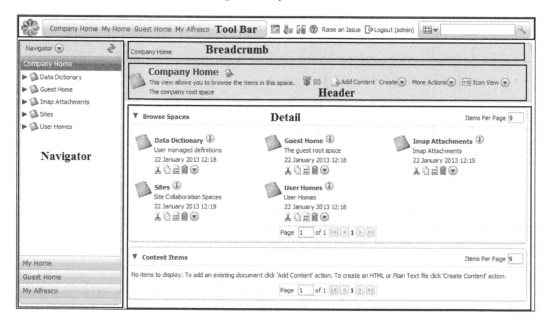

Toolbar

Tool Bar at the top provides the following information:

- Logo
- Links to home spaces and the **My Alfresco** dashboard
- Administration Console icon (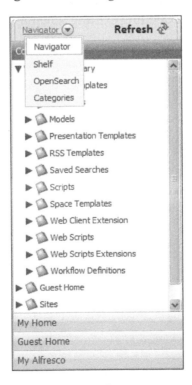) to perform system administration functions
- User options icon ( ) to change your options and settings
- Icon to hide or show the shelf
- Help button ( ) to launch online help
- **Raise an Issue** link to submit bug reports to Alfresco
- **Login** and **Logout** options
- Search box with basic and advanced search options

Navigator

The **Navigator** window is used to display the Navigator tree view, which consists of **Shelf**, **OpenSearch**, and **Categories** browsing as shown in the following screenshot:

Navigator tree view

The **Navigator** provides a tree view of the entire repository hierarchy including folders and subfolders. There is also a **Refresh** button, as shown in the previous screenshot, to refresh the navigator tree view with the latest files.

Shelf

The **Shelf** includes clipboard, recent spaces, and shortcuts:

- **Clipboard**: It is useful to cut or copy content, and to paste in multiple spaces. Clipboard also facilitates the creation of links to actual content items or spaces.

- **Recent Spaces**: It provides the list of recently visited spaces, thus useful when you want to go back to a specific space with one click. The information in the recent spaces is going to be refreshed every time you log in to Alfresco Explorer.

- **Shortcuts**: These are similar to favorites. You can create shortcuts to your frequently visited spaces.

OpenSearch

The **OpenSearch** is Alfresco's implementation of open-standards-based search API for sharing of search results, and extending existing schemas such as ATOM and RSS.

The execution of searches is supported via HTTP requests and responses. For example, the keyword search shown in the previous screenshot can also be executed via an HTTP request as follows:

```
http://localhost:8080/alfresco/service/api/search/keyword?q=alfresco
```

More details about **OpenSearch** are covered in *Chapter 12, Search in Alfresco*, of this book.

Categories logical view

Alfresco content can be categorized to be part of one or more categories. The **Categories** window provides a logical navigation of content as per the category hierarchy:

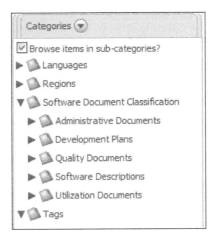

Breadcrumbs

Breadcrumbs help you navigate through various spaces. Typically breadcrumbs provide paths to parent spaces.

Header

The **Header** screen provides information about the current space, number of business rules applied to the current space, options to create content, menu actions to manage content, and options to use various views to display the information in the current space.

Detail

The **Detail** screen provides information about the subspaces and contents that are a part of current space.

You can click on icon or title of a space or content item in the **Detail** screen to access the information.

Actions are listed as icons for each space or content. Additional action items will be listed if you click on the arrow icon ().

Administration Console

The **Administration Console** in Alfresco Explorer is useful to perform all the system-administration tasks. You can access the **Administration Console** by clicking on the administration console icon in the toolbar as shown in the following screenshot. This icon is visible and accessible only to the users with admin privileges. Refer the following screenshot to view the list of administration functions that can be performed by the system administrator:

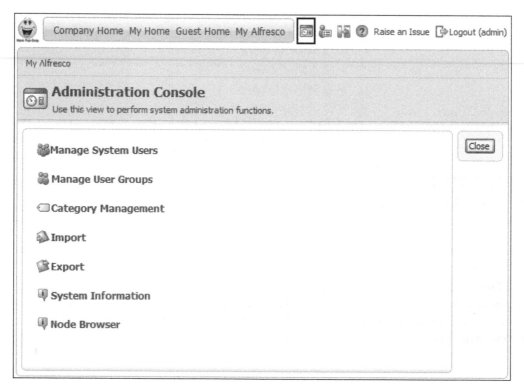

Users and groups management

You can add and delete users, and update user information using the **Manage System Users** functionality. When you first install Alfresco, there will be two users, namely admin and guest, created by the installer. You can create new users using this functionality.

The **Manage User Groups** functionality is useful to create groups of users and subgroups within the groups. Groups are useful to provide authorization to access the content.

Category management

Categorization allows content information to be classified in a number of different ways. This aids searching of content. Categories can be edited only by the administrator. Categories can have subcategories, and content can be linked to one or more categories.

Data management

Export and **Import** functionality is useful for bulk extracting and loading of personal, departmental, or team information, from one location to another location, within the repository or to another repository. **Import** and **Export** functionality is covered in detail in *Chapter 14, Administering and Maintaining the System*.

System information

The **System Information** functionality is useful to view session information and the HTTP header information. The content in Alfresco is stored in industry standard **Java Content Repository (JCR)**, where every folder and file is represented as a **node**. The subfolders are represented as branches of a node, which are nodes itself. **Node Browser** functionality is useful to navigate through the entire repository through nodes and subnodes. More details on **Node Browser** are covered in *Chapter 14, Administering and Maintaining the System*.

Getting started with content creation

The remaining chapters of the book cover the content creation, management, and delivery aspects of Alfresco in detail. In this section you will be introduced to the key terminology, and you will get a basic understanding of content creation in Alfresco.

Creating Space

Alfresco space is a folder with additional properties such as business rules and security. Similar to a folder, space can hold subspaces and any type of content. To create space within a space, click on the **Create** icon in the header, and then click on the **Create Space** link as shown in the following screenshot:

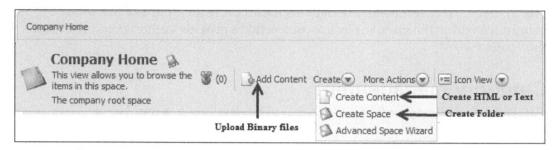

The **Create Space** wizard will be displayed as shown in the following screenshot. **Name** is a mandatory property (as you can notice a small star next to the label), whereas **Title** and **Description** are the optional properties. You can associate an icon to this space. Fill up the information and click on the **Create Space** button to create the space:

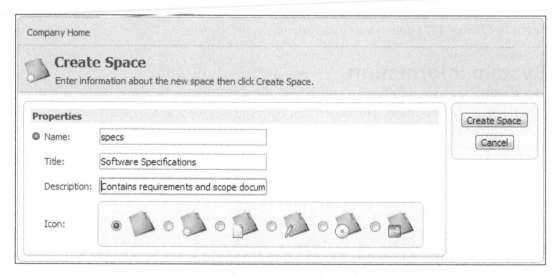

Each space supports various actions such as **Delete**, **Copy**, and **Paste All**, as shown in the following screenshot. For each logged-in user, the actions for a specific space will be different based on the security permissions. For example, if you do not have permissions to delete on a space, you will not see the **Delete** link or icon in the **More Actions** menu.

Creating content

In Alfresco, content is any kind of document, such as a Microsoft Office file, Open Office file, PDF, HTML, XML, text, image, audio, or video file.

Each content item is made of two main elements — the content itself and the information about the content called as metadata or properties. By default each content item will have the properties such as title, description, and author, and the audit trail information such as creator, creation date, modifier, and modification date. Additional properties can be added as needed.

To add a document in a space, click on the **Add Content** link in the header, as shown in the first screenshot in the *Create Space* section. To create HTML or text content in a space, click on the **Create** icon and click on the **Create Content** menu link as shown in the first screenshot in the *Create Space* section.

Every content item supports various actions such as **Delete**, **Update**, **Cut**, and **Copy** as shown in the following screenshot. For each logged-in user, the actions for a specific content will be different, based on the security permissions.

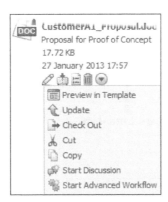

Creating a link to content

A link (or shortcut) to content is a special type of file that serves as a reference to another file. This is similar to the symbolic links commonly used in Unix-like operating systems. A link only contains a symbolic path to content stored elsewhere in the Alfresco repository. Thus, when a user removes a link, the file to which it points remains unaffected.

There might be situations where you need to have the same file in two spaces. For example, you might want to have a product datasheet in the engineering department space as well as in the marketing department space. Instead of creating two copies of the same file, you can keep one copy at one place and create links to the target file in other spaces.

If the target of a link is removed, all symbolic links would also be removed. Conversely, removing a symbolic link has no effect on its target.

Perform the following process to create a link to content:

1. Identify the target document and click on the **Copy** action (as shown in the previous screenshot).

2. The document will be placed in the clipboard as shown in the following screenshot.

3. Go to the space where you would like to create the link to the content.

4. Click on the **Paste content as Link** icon (🗒) in clipboard to create link as shown in the following screenshot:

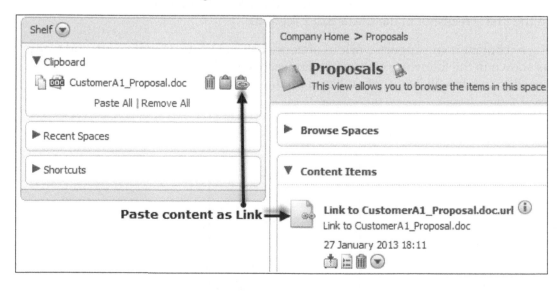

My Alfresco dashboards

In the Alfresco Explorer user interface, the **My Alfresco** area is known as the **dashboard**. You can construct your own dashboard page from a list of preconfigured components available out of the box.

Choosing My Alfresco Dashboard as start location

The start location is the first page that will be displayed immediately after you log in to the Alfresco Explorer. You can choose your start location using the user profile icon (⬛) as shown in the following screenshot. Once you log in to the Alfresco Explorer, the first page you will see is the page that you have chosen as start location.

To select the My Alfresco dashboard as your starting page, click on user options icon in the top menu and select **My Alfresco** as your start location. Next time when you log in, My Alfresco Dashboard will be displayed as your personal home page. You can also view this dashboard page by clicking on the **My Alfresco** menu item at the top.

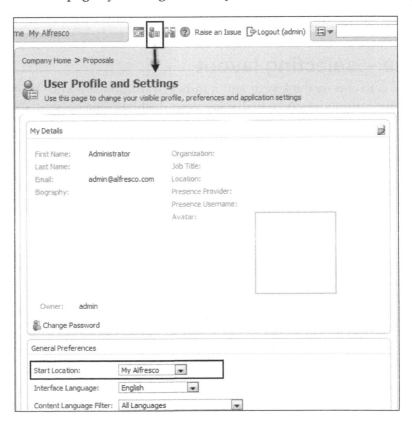

Configuring a personal dashboard using wizard

If you click on the **My Alfresco** link provided in the toolbar menu, you will see a default dashboard, which contains useful information for the beginners. Using the dashboard wizard, you can configure the dashboard layout and dashboard components (also known as **dashlets**). The dashboard configuration is very specific to your personal requirements. The dashboard configuration settings you choose will be stored in the database. Every time you log in to Alfresco Explorer, you will see your personal dashboard as the homepage.

To start configuring your dashboard, click on the **Configure** icon given in **My Alfresco Dashboard** as shown in the following screenshot. The **Configure Dashboard Wizard** will open up (as shown in the first screenshot in the next section) allowing you to select the dashboard layout and dashlets.

Step one – selecting layout

The first step is to choose the layout and number of columns for your dashboard view. There are four styles given to display your dashlets. The options are pictorially represented in the following screenshot:

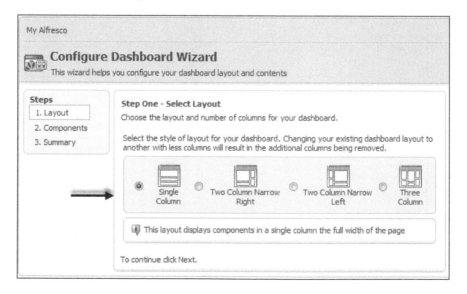

Select the style of layout for your dashboard. Changing your existing dashboard layout to another with less number of columns will result in the additional columns being removed.

As an example, select the **Two Column Narrow Right** option to display your dashboard components in two columns with a narrow right-hand column. Click on the **Next** button to move to the next step of selecting dashboard components.

Step two – selecting components

Based on the number of columns you selected in the previous step, you need to add components to each column as shown in the following screenshot. Notice the list of available dashboard components. These dashboard components are also called dashlets as they display certain information in small windows similar to portal's portlets. Also you can sequence the dashlet using the **+** and **-** buttons given.

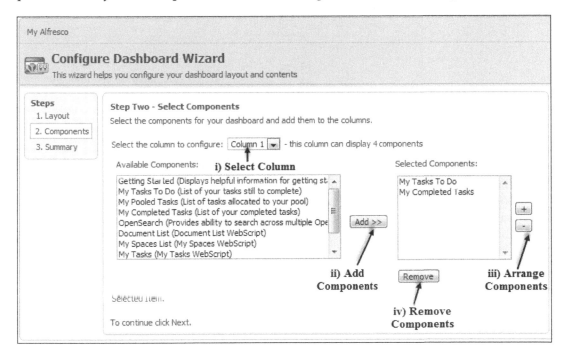

Select the following components for **Column1**:

- **My Tasks To Do**: Lists all the tasks assigned to you and are pending
- **My Completed Tasks**: Lists all the tasks completed by you

Select the following component for **Column2**:

- **My Spaces List**: Lists all the documents and spaces created by you

Click on the **Next** or **Finish** button to save your selection. The selection is effective immediately, as you can see the dashboard with your selections as shown in the following screenshot:

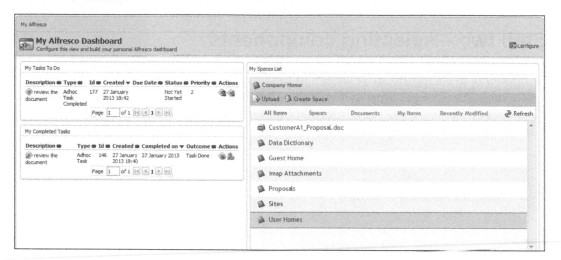

Starting with basic configuration

Now that you have planned your implementation, you can start configuring Alfresco as per your business needs. This section covers basic configuration settings such as e-mail server, look and feel, and multilingual support, as required before using the system.

Extending Alfresco configuration

Alfresco configuration items are completely exposed as XML files, so you can override the default out-of-the-box Alfresco configuration items by customizing individual configuration items.

Alfresco ConfigRoot folder

The default configuration files for Alfresco are in the application WAR file. When the server starts, the files are expanded to `<configRoot>`, which is either:

JBoss: `<JBOSS_HOME>/server/default/tmp/deploy/tmp*alfresco-exp.war/ WEBINF/classes` or

Tomcat: `<TOMCAT_HOME>/webapps/alfresco/WEB-INF/classes`

The default configuration files, maintained by Alfresco, are contained in the `tomcat/webapps/alfresco/WEB-INF/classes/alfresco` folder. The repository properties file (`repository.properties`) in this folder defines some of the core system properties including the following properties:

- `dir.root`: This is the folder (`alf_data`) where the binary content and Lucene indexes are stored. It is relative by default, but should be pointed to a permanent, backed-up location for permanent data storage.
- `db.*`: These are the default database connection properties.

The web client configuration files are located in web client `*.xml` files. Examine the other configuration files in the `tomcat/webapps/alfresco/WEB-INF/classes/alfresco` folder.

Alfresco extension folder

You can override or extend the Alfresco configuration by placing the custom configuration files in the `<extension>` folder. If you have downloaded one of the bundles, you will find the sample files at the following location:

- **JBoss**: `<alfresco>/jboss/server/default/conf/alfresco/extension`
- **Tomcat**: `<alfresco>/tomcat/shared/classes/alfresco/extension`

Configuration approach

When Alfresco starts, it reads all the default configuration files, and then reads the customized configuration items (in the `extension` folder). So, depending upon the type of item, the customization either extends, or overrides the default configuration item.

The following example extends the advanced search form. The first file contains the default configuration. This file can be found in the folder from the path `tomcat/webapps/alfresco/WEB-INF/classes/alfresco/web-client-config.xml`.

```
<alfresco-config>
...
...
  <config evaluator="string-compare" condition="Advanced Search">
    <advanced-search>
      <custom-properties>
        <meta-data aspect="rma:filePlan"
```

```
                                  property="rma:recordCategoryName" />
                <meta-data aspect="rma:filePlan"
                               property="rma:recordCategoryIdentifier" />
                <meta-data aspect="rma:record"
                                    property="rma:recordIdentifier" />
                <meta-data aspect="rma:record"
                                         property="rma:orginator" />
            </custom-properties>
          </advanced-search>
        </config>
    ...
    ...
    </alfresco-config>
```

The web client configuration file in the `extension` folder (located at `tomcat/ common/classes/alfresco/extension/web-client-config-custom.xml`) adds an additional property called `cm:effectivity` to the advanced search form.

```
        <alfresco-config>
          <config evaluator="string-compare" condition="Advanced Search">
            <advanced-search>
              <custom-properties>
                <meta-data aspect= "cm:effectivity" property="cm:to" />
              </custom-properties>
            </advanced-search>
          </config>
        </alfresco-config>
```

Web client configuration files can contain configuration that either augments the standard configuration or replaces it.

Replacement is performed at the `config` level by adding a `replace= true` attribute to the configuration element, for example:

```
        <config evaluator="xx" condition="yy" replace="true">
```

Any configuration found within a section marked this way will replace any configuration found in the Alfresco maintained files. For example, if you wanted to replace the list of languages shown in the login page, you could add the following code:

```
        <config evaluator="string-compare" condition="Languages"
            replace="true">
            <languages>
                <language locale="fr_FR">French</language>
```

```
        <language locale="de_DE">German</language>
    </languages>
</config>
```

On the other hand if you just wanted to add French to the list of languages, you would add the following code:

```
<config evaluator="string-compare" condition="Languages">
    <languages>
        <language locale="fr_FR">French</language>
    </languages>
</config>
```

Whenever you make changes to these configuration files in the `extension` folder, you need to restart Alfresco to see the effect of the changes.

Alfresco also provides the **Web Client Administration** console to dynamically deploy the web client configuration. With dynamic deployment there is no need to restart the server. More details about the dynamic approach are provided in *Chapter 7, Extending Alfresco Content Model*.

Packaging and deploying Java extensions

If your customization only consists of Alfresco configuration files or properties files, that is, `web-client-config-custom.xml` or `webclient.properties`, then you can place the customization files in the `extension` folder.

However, if you are changing the Java source code, the process is a little different. Java classes are typically packaged within a `.jar` file; this then has to go in the web application's `WEB-INF/lib` folder. If you have Java code, you are more than likely going to have at least one other file as part of your extension, that is, configuration files. These too can be contained within the `.jar` file, simply package them within the `.jar` file in the `alfresco/extension` folder.

Another alternative is to add your `.jar` file to the `alfresco.war` file. In JBoss, if you deploy a web application as a WAR file, the application gets exploded to a temporary folder each time the application server starts. Thus there is nowhere to copy the `.jar` file to. One solution is to use an exploded deployment. Create a folder called `alfresco.war` under the `deploy` folder and extract the contents of `alfresco.war` (the file) into it. Then copy your `.jar` file to `deploy/alfresco.war/WEB-INF/lib` and restart JBoss.

Installing the enterprise license file

If you have installed the enterprise version of Alfresco, then you have to install the enterprise license file. Otherwise by default the Alfresco enterprise software expires in 30 days after installation.

Get the `.lic` file from Alfresco. Copy the `.lic` file to the `shared/classes/alfresco/extension/license` folder (for example, for Tomcat it is `tomcat/shared/classes/extension/license`). With fresh installation you don't have the `license` folder, you need to create the folder. Once in place, restart the Alfresco server. Information about the license being set will be visible in the logs; also the license file is renamed with `.installed`. The **Administration Console** within Alfresco also gives details of the license status.

Changing the default administrator password

Administrator is the super user of the system. The administrator user ID is `admin`, and the password is also `admin`. The following are the different ways to change the default administrator password

- At the time of installation using Installer setup wizard
- Updating the web client configuration file in the `extensions` folder with the following code:

  ```
  <admin>
      <initial-password>admin</initial-password>
  </admin>
  ```

- Log in to Alfresco as admin user and change the password

Configuring the content store

Alfresco stores the content (binary files) and search indexes in file system. By default, on Windows platform, this location is the `<tomcat_install>/alf_data` folder.

You can manage the file system storage locations by editing the `alfresco-global.properties` file in the `tomcat/shared/classes/` folder. The main property to edit is `dir.root`, which points to the file repository location.

If these properties are not listed in your `alfresco-global.properties` file, then copy these properties from the `tomcat/webapps/alfresco/WEB-INF/classes/repository.properties` file into the `tomcat/shared/classes/alfresco-global.properties` file and edit accordingly.

For example:

```
dir.root=C:/Alfresco/alf_data
```

 You must use forward slashes for all operating systems

The best practice is to use an absolute path such as `./alf_data` to avoid confusion.

Configuring logfiles

Logfiles hold very important runtime system information. For Tomcat installation, the logfiles are located at `<install_folder>` itself. Tomcat application server creates a logfile per day. The current logfile is named `alfresco.log` and at the end of the day, the logfile will be backed up as `alfresco.log.YYYY-MM-DD` (for example, `alfresco.log.2008-12-22`).

You can configure the logfile by creating a new custom `log4j.proprties` file in the `tomcat/shared/classes/alfresco/extension` folder and make your logger entries. Your filename should always end with the suffix `-log4j`, for example `xxx-log4j.properties`. Custom `log4j` file overrides the default configuration provided in the `log4j.properties` file in `tomcat/webapps/alfresco/WEB-INF/classes`.

The following is the sample logger entry in the custom `log4j` file.

```
log4j.logger.org.alfresco.util.exec.RuntimeExec=debug
```

You can set the level of logging as either `info`, `debug`, or `error`, based on the amount of information you need (for example, `log4j.logger org.alfresco.web=info`). For example, the option `debug` will provide you very detailed information; however, it creates performance issues in high traffic installations.

Configuring default logos

While using the Alfresco Explorer, you would have noticed the Alfresco logo appearing in login page, and in web client toolbar as shown in the following screenshots. You can configure custom logos as per your branding requirements.

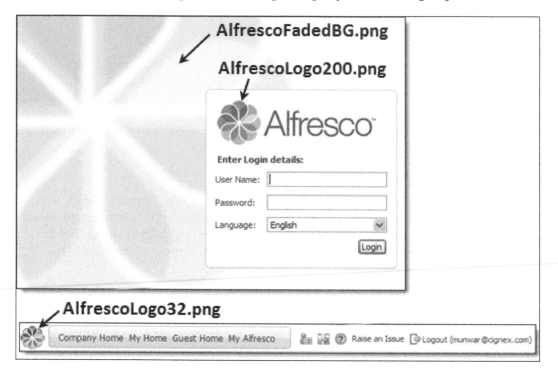

All the logos that appear in the web client application are kept in the logo's folder in the file system. In Tomcat installation, the logo's folder is `<install_folder>\tomcat\webapps\alfresco\images\logo`.

Examine some of the logos in this folder:

- `AlfrescoLogo32.png`: This is the site logo. This logo is displayed always at the top-left corner of the Alfresco Explorer. This logo is 32 pixels wide and 30 pixels high.

- `AlfrescoLogo200.png`: This is the login page logo. This logo is displayed in the login page in the login window along with username and password. This logo is 200 pixels wide and 60 pixels high.

- `AlfrescoFadedBG.png`: This is the login page background logo. This is the blurred logo displayed as background image in the login page. This logo is 428 pixels wide and 422 pixels high.

To customize these logos, first rename the existing logos to `AlfrescoLogo32_OLD.png`, `AlfrescoLogo200_OLD.png`, and `AlfrescoFadedBG_OLD.png` respectively, for backup purposes. Create three new logos with the original names with the same sizes. For example, a custom site logo with the filename as `AlfrescoLogo32.png` (32 x 30 pixels size).

Now your Alfresco application displays new custom logos, instead of the default old ones. In some browsers you might not be able to see the new logos due to the fact that the old logos are cached in the browser. Refresh the browser cache to view the new logos in Alfresco Explorer.

Customizing the look and feel using CSS

Cascading Style Sheets (CSS) files define how to display HTML elements, in other words, the look and feel of Alfresco Explorer. The font size, font color, background color, font style, text alignment, and table structure, everything is controlled by the CSS files.

The CSS files are located in the file system `<install_folder>\tomcat\webapps\alfresco\css` folder. You can customize the look and feel by changing the values in the `main.css` file. For example, you can customize the title look and feel by editing the following block in the `main.css` file:

```
headbarTitle
  {
    color: #003366;
    font-size: 11px;
    font-weight: bold;
    margin-bottom: 5px;
  }
```

 It is a good practice to back up the `main.css` file before making any changes to it.

Directly modifying the files in Alfresco WAR folder is not a good way. As part of best practice you should deploy any changes to Alfresco using the **AMP (Alfresco Module Package)** file. With the use of AMP, it gets easier to revert back any changes. More details about packaging the files in AMP and deploying AMP file is provided at `https://wiki.alfresco.com/wiki/AMP_Files`.

Configuring multilanguage support

You can configure Alfresco to support various languages such as:

- Chinese
- Dutch
- English
- French
- German
- Italian
- Japanese
- Russian
- Spanish

The support for other languages is being developed. The beauty of a true open-source development is that most of these language packs are developed and donated by community users.

The following are the steps to configure a specific language support for your Alfresco application:

1. Download Alfresco language packs from Alfresco add-ons site, http://addons.alfresco.com/search/node/language. (Alfresco's official language translations are managed by the collaborative tool CrowdIn (http://crowdin.net/project/alfresco).)

2. Copy the required language packs to the `tomcat/shared/classes/alfresco/messages` folder in the file system.

3. Edit the `web-client-config-custom.xml` file in the `extensions` folder and include the following XML code to configure the specific languages:

```
<!-- English is the default language.  Add additional languages to
   the list in the login page -->
  <config evaluator="string-compare" condition="Languages">
    <languages>
      <language locale="de_DE">German</language>
      <language locale="es_ES">Spanish</language>
      <language locale="fr_FR">French</language>
      <language locale="it_IT">Italian</language>
      <language locale="ja_JP">Japanese</language>
    </languages>
  </config>
```

4. Restart Alfresco.

Alfresco web client login screen displays all the configured languages in the drop-down list. The languages appear in the login option and will be in the same order as they are defined in the configuration file. Select the language of your choice as shown in the following screenshot:

Configuring subsystems

Subsystems, as the term suggests, are independent components embedded within Alfresco. Each subsystem wraps a functional module of Alfresco, for example, authentication function is designed as one of the subsystems in Alfresco. Each subsystem has its own separate **Spring Application Context** and configuration file, which leverage us to start, stop, or configure the subsystem without affecting the main server. Subsystem can have multiple instances of implementation.

A few main subsystems are as follows:

- Authentication
- File server
- Audit
- Third party
- Email

Each subsystem has category and type:

- **category**: It describes functionality of the subsystem, for example, email.
- **type**: It should be a name for the specific implementation of subsystem. For example, authentication has various types of implementations, such as `ldap` and `kerberos`. Subsystem with single implementation defines `default` as type.

Default configuration of subsystem is located at `<install_folder>\tomcat\ webapps\alfresco\WEB-INF\classes\alfresco\subsystem\<category>\<type>`.

For example, all files for authentication subsystem with LDAP will be located at `<install_folder>\tomcat\webapps\alfresco\WEB-INF\classes\alfresco\ subsystem\Authentication\ldap`.

Each subsystem folder mainly has `*-context.xml` and `*.properties` configuration files. These files will be loaded by the subsystem's application context.

Subsystem works as an abstract system, it hides its implementation. In Alfresco, main server accesses the subsystem by mounting them. This is achieved with declaration of bean with the `ChildApplicationContextFactory` class. Instance of this class encloses the Spring Application Context of subsystems.

For example, GoogleDocs subsystem is mounted to main server using the following bean definition in the `bootstrap-context.xml` (`<install_folder>\tomcat\ webapps\alfresco\WEB-INF\classes\alfresco`) file. The `id` of the bean is the category of subsystem:

```
<bean id="googledocs" class="org.alfresco.repo.management.subsystems.
ChildApplicationContextFactory" parent="abstractPropertyBackedBean">
        <property name="autoStart">
            <value>true</value>
        </property>
    </bean>
```

You would have folder with name as `category` within subsystems `<install_ folder>\tomcat\webapps\alfresco\WEB-INF\classes\alfresco\subsystem\ googledocs`.

Extending any subsystem

For extending the subsystem you can perform the following steps as per your requirements:

- For configuration of any subsystem properties, add your changes in the `alfresco-global.properties` file at `<install_folder>\tomcat\shared\ classes`, or this can be done via JMX, which you will learn in *Chapter 14, Administering and Maintaining the System*. After change in the `alfresco-global.properties` file, restart Alfresco.

- In case you need a separate properties file for each subsystem, place your properties file at `<extension>/subsystems/<category>/<type>/<id>/ *.properties`. Let's take the example of FileServer subsystem. It doesn't have multiple implementations, so `type` and `id` of such system is `default`. We place our files at `<extension>/subsystems/fileServers/default/ default/custom-fileserver.properties`.

- To extend any configuration create a custom context file and place it at `<extension>/subsystems/<category>/<type>/<id>/*-context. xml`. For file servers subsystem, any configuration of beans would go into `<extension>/subsystems/fileServers/default/default/custom- fileserver-context.xml`.

Configuring the audit subsystem

Your content could be one of your most valuable assets. Based on the regulatory and compliance requirements, you might want to have a full audit trail and accountability of user activities in your content management system. Auditing subsystem helps you to achieve this in Alfresco. All user and system activities are logged and made available through the server auditing system.

Auditing system has the following main components:

- **Data Producer**: This component defines components which would generate data that might be used for auditing, irrespective of whether it would be stored or not.

- **Audit Filter**: This component filters out the data generated by Data Producer for auditing based on the filter parameters. We can configure these filters.

- **Data Extractor and Generator**: This component extracts the filtered data and generates it in a format required to be stored.

Let's learn how we can configure audit.

Enable audit

To enable auditing, add the following highlighted property in the `alfresco-global.properties` file.

```
audit.enabled=true
```

(This property enables the audit framework in Alfresco, which is by default enabled.)

`audit.alfresco-access.enabled=true`

This property controls the generation of the audit data, which can be viewed from Alfresco Explorer and Share. It is by default disabled.

Configure Audit Filters

Once the audit Data Producers generate the data for any event, filters are applied to either accept or reject the event. The following is a sample filter configured out of the box in the `repository.properties` files at `<alfresco>/tomcat/webapps/alfresco/WEB-INF/classes/alfresco`:

```
audit.filter.alfresco-access.default.enabled=true
audit.filter.alfresco-access.transaction.user=~System;~null;.*

audit.filter.alfresco-access.transaction.type=cm:folder;cm:content;st
:site
audit.filter.alfresco-access.transaction.path=~/sys:archivedItem;~/
ver:;.*
```

Each filter has the list of regular expressions separated by a semicolon. As per the previous setting, events generated for any content or folder, not under path archive and version, would be recorded. List of expressions for each property is evaluated from left to right, which allows filtration of various combinations of audit data.

To override any filter, copy the respective property in `alfresco-global.properties` and make the changes are per your need. Sample configuration is as shown in the following line of code:

`audit.filter.alfresco-access.transaction.user=.*`

Here we are accepting audit data generated by any user.

View audit trail

To view the audit trail of any content from Alfresco Explorer, locate the content and use the **Preview in Template** button, and select the show_audit.ftl template from the drop-down list. The following screenshot shows sample audit trail of content:

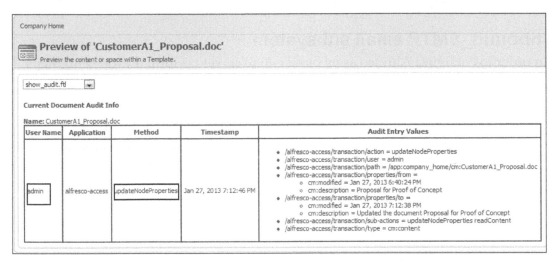

Configuring the email subsystem

Alfresco provides various notifications to the users during the content management process. You need to configure Alfresco to use an existing e-mail server to send outbound e-mails. Similarly you can also use Alfresco as an e-mail server itself for all the inbound e-mails.

Outbound_SMTP email subsystem

Follow the given steps to configure Alfresco repository to send e-mails from an SMTP server:

1. Edit the tomcat/shared/classes/alfresco/extension/alfresco-global.properties file.

2. Add the following property and modify it as per your required value as follows (you can delete any unmodified property, because it will retain the default value from tomcat/webapps/alfresco/WEB-INF/classes/subsystems/email/OutboundSMTP/outboundSMTP.properties):

   ```
   mail.host=<the name of your SMTP host>
   mail.port=<the port that your SMTP service runs on
                                   (the default is
   25)>
   ```

```
        mail.username=<the username of the account you want e-mail
  to be sent from >
        mail.password=<the password>
        mail.from.default=<the default FROM email address>
```

3. Restart Alfresco.

Inbound_SMTP email subsystem

In order to configure Alfresco as inbound e-mail server perform the following steps:

1. Edit the `tomcat/shared/classes/alfresco/extension/alfresco-global.properties` file.

2. Add the following property and modify it as per your required value as follows (you can delete any unmodified property, because it will retain the default value from `tomcat/webapps/alfresco/WEB-INF/classes/subsystems/email/InboundSMTP/inboundSMTP.properties`):

    ```
    email.server.port= provide port of your email server(default 25)
       email.server.domain= provide domain address of your email
    server
    ```

3. Restart Alfresco.

Also there are other settings in the file such as blocked list and allowed list, which can be configured as per your needs.

Configuring IMAP

Alfresco supports IMAP protocol. With IMAP, e-mail applications such as outlook and thunderbird can connect and interact with Alfresco. In order to enable IMAP in Alfresco perform the following steps:

1. Edit the `tomcat/shared/classes/alfresco/extension/alfresco-global.properties` file.

2. Add the following property and modify it as per your required values:

    ```
    imap.server.enabled=true <Enable or disable the imap>
    imap.server.port=143 <Imap server port>
    imap.server.host=x.x.x.x <IP address of Alfresco server. Don't
    give value as localhost>
    ```

3. Restart Alfresco.

Once the IMAP is enabled, you can connect to Alfresco using any e-mail client. There would be an `inbox` folder created, where you can directly place your e-mails.

Configuring the FileServers subsystem

One of the unique strengths of Alfresco is the ability to access the repository through a variety of interfaces such as FTP, WebDav, and CIFS. These interfaces are referred to as the **virtual file system**.

To customize the default FTP and CIFS file server configuration values, you must override the values in the `alfresco-global.properties` file. CIFS and FTP are enabled by default. For any configuration of fileservers bean, use the subsystem extension mechanism.

Configuring CIFS

In order to configure CIFS perform the following steps:

1. Edit the `tomcat/shared/classes/alfresco/extension/alfresco-global.properties` file.

2. Add the following properties and modify it as per your requirements. You can delete any unmodified property, because it will retain the default value from `tomcat/webapps/alfresco/WEB-INF/classes/subsystems/fileServers/default/file-servers.properties`:

   ```
   cifs.enabled=true
   cifs.serverName=${localname}A
   cifs.domain=<domain/workgroup of the server optional property>

   cifs.tcpipSMB.port=445
   cifs.netBIOSSMB.sessionPort=139
   cifs.netBIOSSMB.namePort=137
   cifs.netBIOSSMB.datagramPort=138
   ```

   TCP and NETBIOS property can be changed to non-privileged ports. These properties are required for non-Windows machines.

3. Restart Alfresco.

Configuring File System Transfer Receiver

Many a times we have requirement where we need to transfer content from repository to any remote file system. Alfresco provides this facility to transfer content from Alfresco repository to any target, such as remote file system.

Perform the following steps to configure **File System Transfer Receiver** on external file system, where you want to transfer the content.

1. Download the Alfresco specific version ZIP bundle for File System Transfer Receiver.

2. Extract the ZIP bundle. The ZIP bundle has the transfer receiver associated files and embedded Tomcat. It runs as standalone application.

3. Edit the following property as per your needs in the `ftr-launcher.properties` file located at `<FSTR Dir>/classes`:

    ```
    ftr.tomcat.portNum=<FSTR tomcat port (default 9090)>
    ```

4. Execute the following command to start the File System Transfer Receiver system:

    ```
    java -jar file-transfer-receiver.jar
    ```

Once the File System Transfer Receiver is started, your remote file system can now receive the files transferred from Alfresco.

Setting up a multi-tenant environment

Multi-tenancy (**MT**) is a software architecture where a single instance of the software runs on a **software-as-a-service** (**SaaS**) vendor's servers, serving multiple-client organizations (tenants). With a multitenant architecture, a software application is designed to virtually partition its data and configuration so that each client organization works with a customized virtual application instance.

Alfresco ECM can be configured as a true single-instance multi-tenant environment. The Alfresco instance is logically partitioned in such a way that it will appear to each tenant that they are accessing a completely separate instance of Alfresco.

Enabling multi-tenancy

Multi-tenancy comes preconfigured in Alfresco but disabled. It gets enabled on creation of first tenant.

The default Alfresco admin user can be considered as the "super tenant". All tenants can be administered by this super tenant admin user with the **Tenant Administration Console**.

Log in to Alfresco Explorer (`http://<servername>:<port>/alfresco`) using the admin user ID and password. The URL to the tenant administration console is `http://<Alfresco Explorer URL>/faces/jsp/admin/tenantadmin-console.jsp`, which is `http://localhost:8080/alfresco/faces/jsp/admin/tenantadmin-console.jsp`, as shown in the following screenshot:

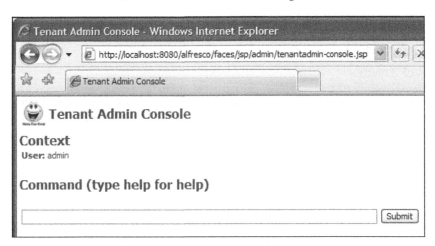

To test the multi-tenancy features, create a tenant account using **Tenant Admin Console**.

```
create funcorp.com pwmike /usr/tenantstores/funcorp
```

Where `funcorp.com` is the domain, `pwmike` is the tenant administrator's password, and `funcorp` is the name of tenant store. Now `admin@funcorp.com` will be the administrator for the tenant account `funcorp.com`.

There are few limitations of multi-tenancy. Multi tenancy is not supported when we use SOLR with Alfresco. CIFS, Record Management, LDAP authentication, and IMAP doesn't support multi-tenancy.

High availability

In real-time scenarios, we have large-scale system where high availability of the system becomes a must. System should be available with minimum downtime. Alfresco provides high availability with clustering. **Cluster** is collection of multiple instance of Alfresco, each known as node. With simple configuration we can achieve clustering of nodes. The following components of Alfresco need to be synchronized across each cluster:

- Database
- Content Store
- Lucene Indexes
- Level 2 cache

Let us consider a scenario where we have two separate web applications accessing the same repository (database and content store). Each web application has its own local indexes and cache. Refer to the following diagram:

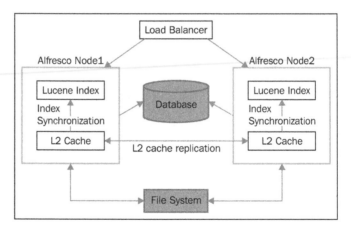

Perform the following steps to set up such clustering:

1. Install Alfresco following the steps mentioned in *Chapter 2, Installing Alfresco*. Make sure clock times on both the servers are in sync.

2. Set common database property in the `alfresco-global.properties` file for both nodes.

3. Set the `dir.root` property in `alfresco-global.properties` of both nodes pointing to shared content store location. Make sure shared content store is accessible from both nodes.

4. Make sure you are using `lucene`. Set the following properties as per your requirements in the `alfresco-global.properties` file:

```
dir.indexes=<Absolute path of indexes location>
index.subsystem.name=lucene (By default this is solr)
```

5. Set the cluster name and index synchronization properties in the `alfresco-global.properties` file. Each node in cluster should have same name. Alfresco uses this property to identify the nodes.

```
alfresco.cluster.name=<CLUSTERNAME>
index.recovery.mode=Auto
index.tracking.cronExpression= 0/5 * * * * ?
```

6. Set the `Jgroup` property. It allows to communicate between nodes using UDP or TCP protocol. By default it is UDP.

```
alfresco.jgroups.bind_address=<Server IP address>
alfresco.jgroups.bind_interface=<Network Interface>
```

7. Rename the file `ehcache-custom.xml.sample.cluster` located at `<alfresco>tomcat/shared/classes/alfresco/extension` to `ehcache-custom.xml`.

Verify the clustering by creating content on one node. It should be automatically synchronized on a second node.

Creating a blueprint for your application

Now that the configuration is done, the next step is to create the blueprint for your application. The **blueprint** is nothing but creating a skeleton application on Alfresco without the actual content. This includes the security framework, folder structure within Alfresco repository, categories for taxonomy, workflow, and business rules.

Enterprise intranet as a theme

Build intranet for your enterprise, where each department has its own space, document management and security, and business rules. All departments collaborate to create effective enterprise knowledge management portal.

This example solution is extended in all the chapters. Hence reading the chapters in the same sequence would help you to understand the features of Alfresco in a systematic manner. While reading each chapter, you will get the concepts of Alfresco, and at the same time you will be developing the solution. Though the extended sample is related to enterprise intranet, it is created in such a way that you would learn all the features of Alfresco.

Let us name your enterprise as **Have Fun Corporation**, which has the following groups of people:

- **Administrator**: Manages membership, groups, categories, security, business rules, workflow, and templates
- **Executive**: Has highest authority on the content and manages approvals
- **HR**: Manages corporate policy documents
- **Corporate communications**: Manages external PR, internal news releases, and syndication
- **Marketing**: Manages website, company brochures, marketing campaign projects, and digital assets
- **Sales**: Manages presentations, contracts, documents, and reports
- **Finance**: Manages account documents, scanned invoices and checks, and notifications
- **Engineering**: Collaborates on engineering projects, workflow, XML documents, and presentation templates

Features you are going to implement

These are the high-level features you are going to implement as a part of solution:

- **Security and access control**: Give decentralized control to each department to manage their own content and yet share with others.
- **Document Management**: Including version control, check-in and check-out, categorization, notifications, bulk upload, advanced search, and other features. Every group will use these features.
- **Space templates**: For engineering projects and marketing projects. Each engineering project will follow a standard structure, workflow, and security rules. Similarly each marketing project will follow specific workflow, transformation, and publishing rules.
- **Content transformations**: For marketing and sales material.
- **Imaging solution**: The finance group will use this feature to handle scanned invoices and checks.
- **Presentation templates including dashboard views**: The corporate communications group will use this to display news and latest PR files, the finance group will use this to have thumbnail views of scanned checks, and the engineering group will use this to display XML documents.

- **Automated business rules**: Each group uses it in a specific manner. For example, the HR group might send an e-mail notification to a specific group when a document is updated, the sales group will automatically convert a PPT to Flash, the finance group will trigger an approval process whenever a scanned check gets into the system, and so on.

Summary

Alfresco Explorer, one of the Alfresco's built-in web applications, provides an intuitive user interface, so that the beginners of the system can start using it without any specialized user training.

You have been introduced to the key terminology in Alfresco such as Alfresco Explorer, administrator console, space, content, category, aspects, actions, and rules.

When Alfresco starts, it reads all the default configuration files, and then reads the customized configuration items in the `extensions` folder. So, depending on the type of item, the customization either extends, or overrides the default configuration item. You have flexibility in choosing the database and membership framework of your choice. You can configure e-mail, multilanguage support, and look and feel of the application. The applications built on top of Alfresco are highly configurable, customizable, and extendible.

In the next chapter you will understand the concepts and the underlying framework behind the Alfresco security model and membership system.

4
Implementing Membership and Security

In this chapter you will understand the concepts and the underlying framework behind the Alfresco security model and membership system. The Alfresco security model is flexible and allows you to choose either a built-in security or an external security model defined by your organization via systems such as LDAP and Active Directory. You will understand various security models and learn to choose the one that is most suited to your enterprise's requirements. Alfresco membership system is highly scalable and can cater to hundreds and thousands of users and content managers.

By the end of this chapter you would have learned how to:

- Create, update, and delete users
- Group users, based on the activities they perform
- Search and locate users and groups
- Extend the security policy
- Secure spaces and individual content as per your organizational security requirements
- Choose a suitable security model
- Migrate existing users and groups to Alfresco

Alfresco membership and security model

A content management system requires a membership system for its users to access content, setup user preferences, and to allow its users to receive notifications and alerts. Members of the system can collaborate with other members by selectively sharing documents, and sharing ideas via discussion forums. Members can control and follow the business process through a workflow.

Traditional membership models address basic authentication (who can access) and authorization (what they can do). Alfresco extends this model by providing capabilities to manage groups and subgroups of members, member attributes, and member workspace, and provides a set of administrative tools to configure and control the membership.

Users and groups

Users are individual members, whereas groups are logical categorizations of users.

In Alfresco, a user is identified by a unique user ID, also known as login ID. The administrator is like a super user of the system. Alfresco identifies the registered users (users not logged in as guest). The name of such logged-in user is shown on the top right-hand corner of the Alfresco Explorer screen and left-hand corner of the Alfresco Share.

Alfresco groups, logically group a set of users in the system for security and collaboration purpose. A group can have any number of subgroups. There is a default group called EVERYONE, which represents all the users of the system.

A user can belong to more than one group and subgroup as shown in the following diagram. For example, the user **Mike ExecEngg** belongs to two groups: **Executive** and **Engineering**.

A group can have more than one user. For example, the **Sales** group in the following diagram contains two users: **Amit Sales** and **Candace Sales**.

A user belonging to a subgroup will automatically belong to the parent group. For example, **Chi EnggDoc** belongs to the **Engineering Documentation** subgroup, and thus automatically belongs to the **Engineering** group.

This is how a typical organization's hierarchy works. An employee belongs to a particular department or some times more than one department.

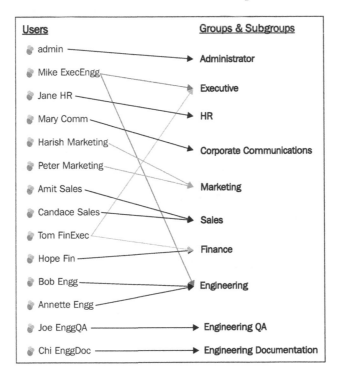

Permissions and roles

Permissions define access rights on spaces and content. Out-of-the-box Alfresco supports extensive permission settings on spaces and content. In Alfresco, users are assigned a set of permissions on a content, which would define user's access right and control user's actions on that content. Permission sets an association between user and content. More detailed description is provided in Securing your spaces and Securing your content sections of this chapter.

Permissions are identified by a string. A particular permission, for example ReadChildren, may be granted or denied to an authority: a user, group, administrator, owner, and so on. The children of a node will inherit permissions from their parents. So by default, the files within a folder will inherit their permissions from the folder. Permissions set on a node take precedence over permissions set on the parent nodes. Permissions inheritance may be turned off for any node.

A permission group is a convenient grouping of permissions such as Read made up of ReadProperties and ReadChildren. Each one of these permissions is applicable to node, space, space properties, subspace, content, content properties, and business rules. The following are typical permissions groups:

- Read
- Edit
- Add
- Delete

Roles are collections of permissions assigned to a user. Each role comprises of a set of permissions. Alfresco provides out-of-the-box support for the following roles:

- **Consumer**: This role can read content
- **Editor**: This role can read and edit content
- **Contributor**: This role can read and add content
- **Collaborator**: This role can read, edit and add content
- **Coordinator**: This role can read, edit, add and delete content (full access)

Alfresco roles and permissions may be extended to support your requirements, refer *Extending security permissions and roles* section in later part of chapter.

Authentication

Alfresco imposes authentication using the user name and password pair. Authentication is performed at the following entry points to Alfresco repository:

- Web client
- CIFS
- FTP
- WebDAV
- Web services
- Web Scripts
- Spring beans exposed as public services in Java

For example, a user can access Alfresco repository through Explorer program or another application can access Alfresco repository through web services protocol. No matter how a user or an external system connects to Alfresco, they all should go through the same authentication process to access data from the Alfresco repository.

How is security imposed in Alfresco?

Alfresco imposes authorization by assigning a role to a specific user or group for a specific space or content.

Spaces and content in Alfresco can be secured in a number of ways. By default, a space or content in Alfresco can be managed only by the owner who created it. For each space, you need to give specific roles (group of permissions) to specific users (or group of users) to set the permissions on that space. Subspaces may inherit parent space permissions. Security rules may be specified at the individual content level that may be different from security rules for its parent folder or space.

Refer to the previous figure, where users **Tom FinExec** and **Hope Fin** both belong to the **Finance** group. Let us say you have a space called Finance Department and you would like to give full access control to only people who belong to Finance group and give Read access to the people who belong to Sales and Executive groups.

As an administrator to Finance Department space, you can invite Finance group as Coordinator (full access) and Sales and Executive groups as Consumer (read access). Refer to the table given below which shows examples of space structure and roles assigned to specific groups and individual users on a space:

Space Title	Group	Assigned Role
Finance Department	Finance	Coordinator – Full Access
	Sales	Consumer - Only Read Access
	Executive	Consumer – Only Read Access
Company Policies	Human Resource	Coordinator – Full Access
	EVERYONE	Consumer - Only Read Access

Managing system users

You have to log in to Alfresco Explorer as an administrator (admin) to create accounts for each Alfresco user. Only users that belong to Administrators group can manage user accounts.

To add users, you need to know the user ID, password, and other details as listed in the following *Create new users* section.

In Alfresco, each user can have his/her individual space. Location and name for a space can be specified while creating a user account. The user for which a space is created becomes the owner of that space. As an owner, the user can have full access to his/her space.

Creating new users

It is a good practice to create all users in a single space called as **User Homes**.

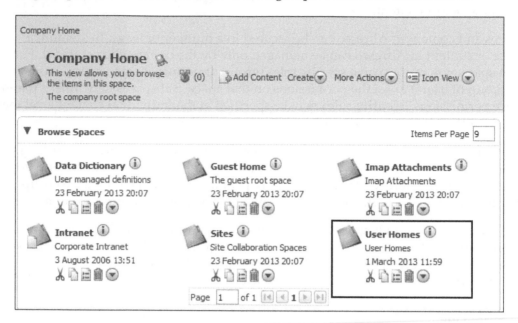

Before adding users, you will need to know the following details for each user:

- First Name
- Last Name
- Email ID (valid corporate email)
- Company ID (for customer extranet, this could be customer's company name)
- User name (login ID)
- Password
- Home space name (usually username)

Refer to the first figure for the list of users to be created for your intranet. Follow the given steps to create a user:

1. In any space, click on the **Administration Console** button provided in the top toolbar as shown in the following screenshot:

2. The **Administration Console** pane appears. Click on the **Manage System Users** link. The **Manage System Users** pane appears as shown in the previous screenshot.

3. In the header, click the **Create User** link (highlighted in the previous screenshot).

4. The first pane of the **New User Wizard** appears. This is the **Person Properties** pane, as you can see from the list of steps at the left of the pane.

5. For the user **Mike ExecEngg**, provide **Mike** as the **First Name**, **Exec Engg** as the **Last Name**, mike@localhost.com as the **Email**, and **Have Fun Corp** as the **Company ID**. In fact, you may also provide the employee ID in the **Company ID** field.

6. Click on the **Next** button to the right of the pane. The second pane of the **New User Wizard**. This is the **User Properties** pane, as you can see from the list of steps at the left side of the pane.

7. Choose **mike** (all lower case) for **User Name** and **Password**. Choose **Users Home** as the parent space and **mike** as the **Home Space Name**. Note that the username and password must be between 3 and 32 characters in length.

8. Click on the **Next** button to the right of the pane. The third pane which is the **Summary** pane for the **New User Wizard** appears.

9. Verify all the information and click on the **Finish** button to confirm.

 For every wizard in Alfresco, you need to click on the **Finish** button to confirm; otherwise, the information you provided earlier will be lost.

Similarly, create all the users (except admin, which is already created out-of-the-box) listed in the first figure.

 Do not proceed to the subsequent sections without creating the users first. Remaining sample solution is based on these users and the groups they belong to.

Searching for existing users in Alfresco Explorer

Alfresco provides a user-search tool to find a user by using their first name, last name, and/or username. Follow the given steps to search existing users:

1. In any space, click the **Administration Console** icon. The **Administration Console** pane appears.

2. Click the **Manage System Users** link. The **Manage System Users** pane appears.

3. In the search box, provide user's first name or last name to search. Alternatively, to see all users click the **Show all** button without providing any information in the search box.

The search results will be displayed as shown in the following screenshot. If there are many users in the system then the search will return multiple pages with pagination numbers.

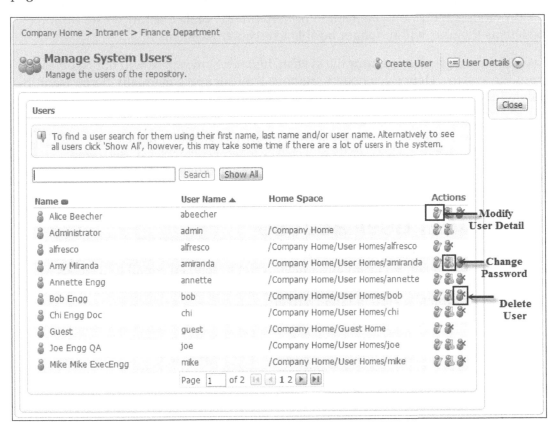

Modifying user details

Search for a system user as explained in the *Searching for existing users* section previously. To edit user detail information, click on the **Modify** icon, belonging to that user as shown in the previous screenshot.

The first pane of the **Edit User Wizard** appears. You can edit and make corrections as required and then click the **Finish** button to confirm.

Deleting a user

Search for a system user as explained previously in the *Searching for existing users* section. To delete user, click on the **Delete** icon, belonging to that user as shown in the previous screenshot. You need to be very careful while deleting a user from the system as the user will no longer be able to access the system.

Even if the user is deleted from the system, his/her home space will not be deleted from the system. Hence you need to remove the user space manually if you want the deleted user's content removed from the system.

 Alfresco provides a content recovery tool to recover the deleted content. However there is no way to recover the deleted user. Hence, you need to be careful while deleting a user from the system.

Individual user access

Once a user account is created by the administrator, user can log in to the system. The administrator can set up an automated script to send an e-mail to the user with the user ID and password information. You will know more about such e-mail notification template scripts in later chapters.

New user login and my homepage

Log in to Alfresco, by entering the following URL in your browser:
`http://server_name:8080/alfresco`

If you are already logged in as an administrator, log out by clicking on the **Logout** button, given in the top toolbar.

In the **User Name** text box enter your user name as **mike** and in the **Password** text box enter your password as **mike**.

 User **Mike ExecEngg** is created as a part of new user account in the earlier section.

Depending on your installation, you may have a choice of languages in the
Language drop-down menu. This example assumes that your selected language
is **English**. Click on the **Login** link and enter your credentials. Your home space
appears as shown in the following screenshot:

Updating the personal details and password

You can update your profile information and password by clicking on the user
options icon given at the top toolbar as shown in the following screenshot.

Click on the **edit personal profile** icon to update your name and user ID. Click on the
Change Password link to update the password.

Under general preferences block, select the **Start Location** as landing page once you
log in to Alfresco Explorer.

Managing user groups

Alfresco comes with two default user group called EVERYONE and ALFRESCO_ ADMINISTRATORS. The EVERYONE group logically includes all the system users irrespective of the groups they belong to. This is useful to give read access to EVERYONE on certain common spaces for example, HR Policies and so on. You can create and manage your own groups. In order to create groups, log in to Alfresco Explorer as an administrator. ALFRESCO_ADMINISTRATORS group by default includes admin user. If you want to give multiple users admin rights then add the users to this group.

Creating groups and subgroups

Before adding a group or subgroup (hierarchical groups), you will need to finalize group names. The group name (identifier) should be unique and cannot be changed once set.

Refer to the first figure for the list of groups to be created for your intranet. Follow the given steps to create a group:

1. In any space, click on the administration console icon. The **Administration Console** pane appears.

2. Click the **Manage User Groups** link. The **Groups Management** pane appears.

3. In the header, click **Create | Create Group**. In **Create Group Wizard** specify **Executive** as **Group Identifier**, the group used for all company executives. Click on **Create Group** button to confirm.

Similarly, create all the groups listed in the first screenshot except Administrator (which is already created out-of-the-box).

 Do not proceed to the subsequent sections without creating the groups. Remaining sample solution relies upon the existence of these groups for security and collaboration.

Click on the **Engineering** group and create two subgroups called **Quality Assurance** and **Documentation**.

Now you can see the groups at root level as shown in the following screenshot. You will notice that **Quality Assurance** and **Documentation** are not part of root-level groups, as they are subgroups under the **Engineering** group.

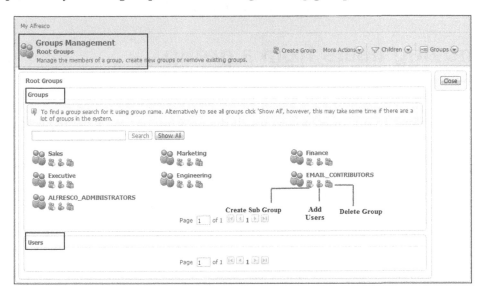

Adding users to a group

To add users to a group, click on the **Add Users** icon as shown in the above screenshot. The **Add User** dialog will pop up. You can search for the system users and add them to a group as shown in the next screenshot. Click on the **Finish** button to confirm the operation.

Add users to the newly created groups as explained in the first screenshot. For example, add user Jane HR to Human Resource group. Add user Mary Comm to Corporate Communications group. Similarly, add user Joe EnggQA to Quality Assurance subgroup of Engineering group, and so on.

Removing users from a group

Users can be removed from a group by clicking on the **Remove User** icon as shown in the following screenshot.

A user may belong to one or more groups. If the user got deleted from the system users list, then that user will be automatically removed from all the groups.

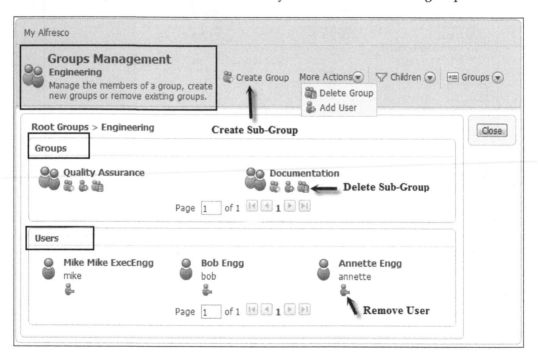

Extending security permissions and roles

Out-of-the-box Alfresco supports an extensive set of permissions to provide security controls. Alfresco supports a set of roles by grouping these permissions. The security permissions and roles can be extended. However, before extending the permissions and roles, you need to evaluate and understand existing permissions and roles and justify the decision for extending them.

Default permissions

Alfresco supports a number of permissions to access the spaces, content, their properties, and so on. The following are some of the permissions for spaces:

- `ReadProperties`: Read space properties
- `ReadChildren`: Read the content within a space
- `WriteProperties`: Update properties such as title, description
- `DeleteNode`: Delete space
- `DeleteChildren`: Delete content and subspaces within a space
- `CreateChildren`: Create content within a space

The following are some of the permissions for content items:

- `ReadContent`: Read file
- `WriteContent`: Update file
- `ReadProperties`: Read file properties
- `WriteProperties`: Update file properties such as title, description etc
- `DeleteNode`: Delete file
- `ExecuteContent`: Execute file
- `SetOwner`: Set ownership on a content item

A complete list of default permissions and roles is provided in Alfresco configuration `<config>\model\permissionDefinitions.xml` file.

Default roles

Roles are collections of permissions assigned to users. Roles can be applied to any space or individual content items. Subspaces can inherit permissions from parent space. The following table lists the default roles supported out-of-the-box by Alfresco:

Role	Permission
Consumer	Read spaces and content
Editor	Consumer + edit existing content
Contributor	Consumer + add new content
Collaborator	Editor + Contributor
Coordinator	Full Control

Creating a custom role

You can add a new custom role as per your security requirements. You will have to include custom role details in permissionDefinitions.xml, which is located at <config>\model\. For a Tomcat installation, you can find this file at tomcat\webapps\alfresco\WEB-INF\classes\alfresco\model\ permissionDefinitions.xml.

You need to define your own permissions group (say ReviewerRole) and assign permissions as shown below:

```
<permissionGroup name="ReviewerRole" allowFullControl="false"
                                            expose="true" >
  <includePermissionGroup permissionGroup="Read" type="sys:base" />
  <includePermissionGroup permissionGroup="AddChildren"
                                        type="sys:base"/>
  <includePermissionGroup type="cm:lockable"
                                permissionGroup="CheckOut"/>
</permissionGroup>
```

Once you make the changes to XML file, you need to restart Alfresco to see the new role added to the system.

Securing your spaces

Space can be secured by assigning a role to a specific user (or group) on that space.

Role refers to a set of permissions that can be applied to a folder.

Permissions are identified by a string. A particular permission, for example ReadChildren, may be granted or denied to an authority; a user, group, administrator, owner, and so on. The children of a node will inherit permissions from their parents. So by default, the files in a folder will inherit their permissions from the folder. Permissions set on a node take precedence over permissions set on the parent nodes. The inheritance of permissions may be turned off for any node. A permission group is a convenient grouping of permissions such as Read made up of ReadProperties and ReadChildren.

User roles on a space

Alfresco uses roles to determine what a user can and cannot do in a space. These roles are associated with permissions. The following table lists the allowed permissions for each role on a given space. User (or group) with Consumer role on a space can read all the content within that space. Similarly, a user (or group) with Contributor role on a space can create content within the space.

Permission	Consumer	Contributor	Editor	Collaborator	Coordinator
Read Content within space	X	X	X	X	X
Read Space Properties	X	X	X	X	X
Read Subspaces	X	X	X	X	X
Read Forums, Topics, Posts	X	X	X	X	X
Copy	X	X	X	X	X
Preview in Template	X	X	X	X	X
Create Content within space		X		X	X
Create Sub-Spaces		X		X	X
Create Forums, Topics, Posts		X		X	X
Reply to Posts		X		X	X
Start Discussion		X		X	X
Edit Spaces Properties			X	X	X
Add/Edit Space users			X	X	X
Delete Space users					X
Add/Edit Space rules			X	X	X
Delete Space rules					X
Cut Content/ Sub-Spaces					X
Delete Content/Sub-Spaces					X
Checkout Content			X	X	X
Update Content			X	X	X
Take Ownership					X

Inviting users to your space

You can grant permission for the users (or groups) to do specific tasks in your space. You do this by inviting users to join your space. Each role applies only to the space in which it is assigned. For example, you could invite a user (or group) to one of your spaces as an editor. You could invite the same user (or group) to a different space as a collaborator. That same user (or group) could be invited to someone else's space as a coordinator.

Follow the given steps to invite a group of users to your space:

1. Click on the **Company Home** menu link in the toolbar (top-left corner of the screen).

2. In the header click on the **Create | Create Space** link.

3. Create a new space called **Intranet**.

4. Within **Intranet** space create a subspace called **Finance Department**. Ensure that you are in the **Finance Department** space.

5. In the space header, click **More Actions | Manage Space Users**. The **Manage Space Users** pane appears as shown in following screenshot:

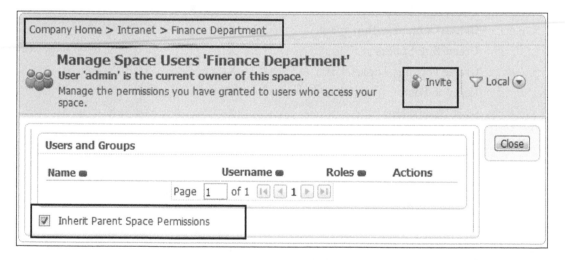

6. Leave the **Inherit Parent Space Permissions** option as checked (selected). When it is not selected, uninvited users cannot see the content item. Only invited users can see the content item, and can access it according to their assigned role.

7. In the header, click the **Invite** link. The Invite User Wizard pane appears.

8. Before continuing with your invitation, you can experiment with the Search feature. Select the **Groups** from the drop-down box and click on the **Search** button.

9. From the search results, select the **Finance** group, give **Coordinator** role and click on the **Add to list** button.

10. The finance group is added to the list of invitees.

11. As an administrator to the **Finance Department** space, you can invite the **Finance** group as coordinator (full access) and **Sales** and **Executive** groups as consumer (read access).

12. Click on the **Next** button to go to second pane where you can notify the selected users.

13. Do not select this option as you do not have to notify these selected users in this sample. Click on the **Finish** button to confirm.

Notice the permissions given to the groups on this space.

Defining and securing your spaces

In the previous example, you created a space called finance department and you gave coordinator role (full control) to finance group and gave consumer role (read access) to sales and executive groups.

Next, go to your **Company Home | Intranet** space and create spaces as given in the first column of the table below. Invite groups and assign roles as indicated in the second column of the table:

Space Name	Group (Assigned Role)	Individual (Assigned Role)
Executive and Board	Executive (Coordinator)	
Company Policies	HR (Coordinator)	
	EVERYONE (Consumer)	
Press and Media	Corporate Communications (Coordinator)	
	EVERYONE (Consumer)	
Marketing Communications	Marketing (Coordinator)	
	EVERYONE (Consumer)	
Sales Department	Sales (Coordinator)	Mr. CEO (Coordinator)
	Executive (Consumer)	

Space Name	Group (Assigned Role)	Individual (Assigned Role)
Finance Department	Finance (Coordinator)	
	Sales (Consumer)	
	Executive (Consumer)	
Engineering Department	Engineering (Coordinator)	Mrs. Presales (Coordinator)
	EVERYONE (Consumer)	

Securing your content

Content can be secured by assigning a role to a specific user (or group) on that content.

User roles for content

Alfresco uses roles to determine what a user can and cannot do with the content. These roles are associated with permissions. The following table shows each role and the permissions for that role for content:

Permissions	Consumer	Contributor	Editor	Collaborator	Coordinator
Read Content	X	X	X	X	X
Read Content Properties	X	X	X	X	X
Copy	X	X	X	X	X
Preview in Template	X	X	X	X	X
Start Discussion		X		X	X
Edit Content			X	X	X
Edit Properties			X	X	X
Apply Versioning			X	X	X
Apply Categorization			X	X	X
Checkout			X	X	X
Update			X	X	X
Take ownership					X
Cut					X
Delete					X

Inviting users to your content

Typically security and access control rules are defined at the space level. It is not advised to secure individual content item as it may become unmanageable with large number of files. It is the best practice to secure the parent space rather than securing the content itself. However, you can still control the access to a specific content item.

Follow the given steps to invite users to your content item:

1. Go to a space and add a file by clicking on the **Add Content** link.
2. Click on the **View Details** icon for the file to see the detailed view of the content.
3. From the right-hand side **Actions** menu, click on the **Manage Content** Users link, to assign users to this content item for collaboration.
4. Search and select a user and assign a **Collaborator** role to it.

Now the user can collaborate on the file.

 As part of good practice give permission to group and assign group to space.

Choosing a right security model for you

It is very important to choose a suitable security model at the beginning of Alfresco implementation. The authentication mechanism, user profile data storage, security settings, business rules, and so on are all based on the security model you choose.

Alfresco imposes authentication through user login ID and password. This is where you choose a security model such as Alfresco's built-in membership system, **NTLM (Windows NT LAN Manager)**, or **LDAP (Lightweight Directory Access Protocol)**. These security models are explained in detail in the subsequent sections of this chapter.

Alfresco imposes authorization by assigning a role to a specific user (or group) for a specific space (or content). This will be the same irrespective of which model you choose.

The security model you choose will be based on the requirements of your enterprise. Let us consider the following sample scenarios:

- Scenario 1: I would like to build an extranet as a standalone application to share documents with my customers. I have over 500 customers who will access the site, and I would like to control and manage the security. I need a flexible and highly scalable membership system.

  In this scenario, out-of-the-box Alfresco membership system would be able to solve the problem.

- Scenario 2: I work in the IT department of a large university. Over the years, the various departments have developed their own sites with local authentication and authorization. Our university has a directory-based central authentication system. How can I consolidate all the sites and provide a central point of authentication and authorization for all our subsites?

  In this scenario, it would make sense configuring Alfresco with LDAP for centralized identity management.

- Scenario 3: In my enterprise we have various systems such as customer support, ERP, proprietary content management systems, and open source ECM Alfresco. Our employees have different accounts on all these different systems and it is becoming unmanageable for us. We are looking at a single sign-on solution to access all our systems with one login ID and password.

  In this scenario Alfresco can be configured to use NTML to provide single sign-on.

Using the Alfresco out-of-the-box membership system

Alfresco out-of-the-box security includes the following functionality:

- User management
- Provision of user personal information
- User authentication
- Group management
- Ownership of nodes within the repository
- An extendable permission model
- Access control, to restrict calls to public services to authenticated users

Examples in this book are based on the out-of-the-box Alfresco security model.

Authentication Subsystem

Authentication Subsystem provides implementation of the entire security model supported by Alfresco. Following are the types of Authentication Subsystems:

Authentication Type	Description
alfrescoNtlm	Alfresco's built-in membership system
ldap	Authentication using LDAP like OpenLDAP
ldap-ad	Authentication using Active directory
kerberos	Authentication via Kerberos Realm
passthru	Authentication via windows domain server or external servers
external	Any external authentication system

The advantage of a Subsystem is that, with only simple property configuration we can activate or de-activate any authentication mechanism.

Authentication chain

Many organizations have multiple authentication servers. So there are requirement where you need to integrate all the authentication system with Alfresco. For that, Authentication Subsystem provides chaining mechanism. One instance of Alfresco can have more than one user source. However the sequence in which these user data sources are chained is important. When user logs into the system, Alfresco checks for authentication in the same sequence as shown in the following figure.

`authentication.chain` property in the `alfresco-global.properties` file specifies the authentication chain. Default authentication in chain is NTLM.

```
authentication.chain=alfrescoNtlm1:alfrescoNtlm <instance name : type
of authentication. It is same as like we create instance of any class
in Java>
```

We would learn in later part of chapter how we can add LDAP or other authentication mechanism in chain.

Configuring LDAP for Centralized Identity Management

LDAP evolved from X.500 OSI Directory Access Protocol. LDAP directory is the central authentication engine for the enterprise, and serves as yellow pages for user access, and profile information. The biggest advantage of LDAP is that your enterprise can access the LDAP directory from almost any computing platform, using any one of the increasing numbers of readily available LDAP-aware applications. In fact, LDAP is finding much wider industrial acceptance because of its status as an Internet standard.

You can use LDAP with any directory server, such as iPlanet, Novell's eDirectory, Microsoft's Active Directory, or OpenLDAP. If you are planning to implement an LDAP directory in your organization, you may consider OpenLDAP, Active Directory, or eDirectory. OpenLDAP is a stable and widely accepted open-source directory server.

LDAP configuration with Active Directory

Active Directory supports LDAP-based authentication. It can also support authentication using JAAS + Kerberos and NTLM authentication. Only NTLM will give you a single sign-on solution. In configuring NTLM for a single sign-on section we will discuss for single sign-on. It is possible to use any authentication methods against an Active Directory server and extract user and group information via LDAP.

Let us consider a scenario, Have Fun Corporation Intranet requires a security model where employees of organization should authenticate via their central authentication AD server. There are some external users who will authenticate via Alfresco's built-in membership system. Now for this scenario we need to have both LDAP and Alfresco NTLM authentication in chain.

Follow the given steps to configure such security model.

1. Create a folder hierarchy `subsystems/Authentication/ldap-ad/ldap1` in `<Alfresco_Home>/tomcat/shared/classes/alfresco/extension`. ldap1 is the instance of ldap-ad type of Authentication.

2. Copy `ldap-ad-authentication.properties` at above created folder from `<WEB-INF/classes/alfresco/subsystem/Authentication/ldap-ad>`. Modify the properties to your required value as follows. All other properties can be kept as it is in the file.

   `ldap.authentication.userNameFormat=%s@domain.com` **< Map the user id entered by the user to passed through LDAP , the %s is replaced with whatever the user types in as their userid on the login screen.>**

```
ldap.authentication.java.naming.provider.url=ldap://ldap.domain.
com:389.<the name and port of your LDAP server, the standard port
for LDAP is 389 >
ldap.authentication.java.naming.security.authentication=simple<the
authentication mechanism you want to use>
ldap.authentication.java.naming.security.principal=admin <the
user that has read access to the group and people information to
be extracted from Active Directory server>
ldap.authentication.java.naming.security.credentials=secret.<the
password for the user defined above>
```

3. Ldap-ad doesn't support CIFS authentication, so we need to configure passthru. Create a folder hierarchy `subsystems/Authentication/passthru/passthru1` in `<Alfresco_home>/tomcat/shared/classes/alfresco/extension`.

4. Copy the below mentioned files in `passthru1` folder from `<WEB-INF/classes/alfresco/subsystem/Authentication/passthru>`.

    ° `passthru-authentication-context.properties`

    ° `ntlm-filter.properties`

5. Modify the following property as per your needs in `passthru-authentication-context.properties file`:

    ```
    passthru.authentication.servers=DOMAIN\\ldap.domain.com <Comma
    separated list of domain servers prefixed by domain name>
    passthru.authentication.guestAccess=false
    passthru.authentication.defaultAdministratorUserNames=Administrato
    r,alfresco<Default Admin Users>
    ```

6. Single sign-on is by default enabled. Set false in below property in `ntlm-filter.properties`.

    ```
    ntlm.authentication.sso.enabled=false<If this property is set to
    true, windows credentials would be used to authenticate>
    ```

7. Make sure below entry is done in Alfresco-global properties file to configure the authentication chain. Be default we have only NTLM in chain

    ```
    authentication.chain=ldap1:ldap-ad,passthru1-passthru,alfrescoNtlm
    1:alfrescoNtlm
    ```

8. Restart Alfresco. Now you can log in with both LDAP and Alfresco users.

This authentication mechanism sends user names and passwords in plain text. It is the most simple to set up. This is supported by both Active Directory and OpenLDAP.

LDAP synchronization

As now you have configured LDAP with Active Directory. The next step would be to extract information from Active Directory. This synchronization of people and groups between the Alfresco repository and LDAP is supported by scheduled jobs. These jobs extract the user or group information from the LDAP repository and create the appropriate information as an Alfresco import xml file. This file is then imported into the repository.

1. Open ldap-ad-authentication.properties file created while configuring AD. Modify the properties to the required value as follows. All other properties can be kept as it is in the file.

   ```
   ldap.synchronization.active=true
   ldap.synchronization.personQuery=(&(objectclass\=user)
   (userAccountControl\:1.2.840.113556.1.4.803\:\=5 12))
   ldap.synchronization.userSearchBase=dc\=<domain>,dc\=com
   <These two options combine to make the query to find people.
   Synchronize users of only specified domain>

   ldap.synchronization.groupQuery=(objectclass\=group)
   ldap.synchronization.groupSearchBase=dc\=<domain>,dc\=com
   <These two options combine to make the query to find groups.
   In the example above, you will find all objects of type group
   anywhere in the directory>

   ldap-synchronization.java.naming.security.principal=user@domain
   ldap.synchronization.java.naming.security.credentials=secret
   <User Credentials with Admin access for Synchronization>
   ```

2. If you want to set the Scheduler timings for Synchronization add below property in `alfresco-global.properties` file and modify as per your requirement

   ```
   synchronization.import.cron=0 0 0 * * ?
   ```

3. Ensure that your changes are saved. Start Alfresco.

On restarting, you will be able to log in, in to Alfresco repository with LDAP users.

Configuring NTLM for single sign-on

NT LAN Manager (NTLM) is an authentication protocol used in various Microsoft network protocol implementations, and is also used throughout Microsoft's systems as an integrated single sign-on mechanism.

NTLM authentication can be used to provide single sign-on to Alfresco. Using this protocol, the password that is sent over the network is made more secure than when using basic authentication. NTLM pass-through authentication can also be used to replace the standard Alfresco user database and instead use a Windows server/domain controller, or list of servers, to authenticate users accessing Alfresco. This eliminates the task of creating user accounts within Alfresco.

By using NTLM authentication, the web browser can automatically log on when accessing Alfresco and Alfresco WebDAV sites. When NTLM is configured, Internet Explorer will use your Windows logon credentials when requested by the web server. Firefox and Mozilla also support the use of NTLM; for these you will be prompted for the username/password details, which can then optionally be stored using the password manager. Opera web browser does not support NTLM authentication. If an Opera browser is detected, you will be sent to the usual Alfresco logon page.

Let us consider a scenario

SSO with Active Directory: The users who are inside the company network (who logged into Active Directory) should automatically be logged into Alfresco repository.

SSO with Active Directory

Follow the steps given below to integrate single sign-on. We need to use `passthru` authentication subsystem for SSO with Active Directory.

1. Follow Step 1 to Step 5 mentioned in previous section for configuring Active Directory with Alfresco.

2. Single sign-on is by default enabled in passthru and make sure that the property in `ntlm-filter.properties` file at `<Extension> subsystems/ Authentication/passthru/passthru1` is set to `true`.

   ```
   ntlm.authentication.sso.enabled=true<If this property is set to
   true, windows credentials would be used to authenticate>
   ```

3. Restart the alfresco server. If you are logged into Active Directory you will be able to automatically logged into Alfresco repository.

Migrate existing users to Alfresco

If you are planning to migrate an existing application to Alfresco, then you might want to migrate its existing users to Alfresco as well. If you use LDAP or NTLM-based security model, then you don't have to migrate the existing users to Alfresco. Instead, you can directly connect to those user sources from Alfresco. This model is always preferred as you can manage users and groups at one centralized location and access the user information in many applications.

This is applicable if you are using Alfresco out-of-the-box security model.

Understanding of user and group structure in Alfresco

Any user/group is stored as a node in Alfresco. Below actions are taken when we create a user in Alfresco.

- **Person Node**: A node of type person would be created, which would store all the details of the user like first name, last name, company ID, and so on.

- **User Node**: This node stores the user ID and password related information. This node would be created only when we use Alfresco to store Credentials of user.

- **Zone Association**: Each user or group are associated with two zones.

Zone is designed to distinguish users based on the source of the users. Zones are grouped into two categories Application and Authentication related Zone. The following diagram shows the type of Zone.

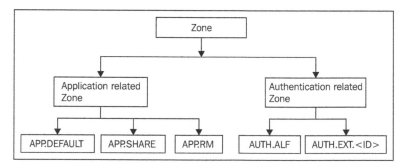

Application Related Zones divides the users based on application. All the users are by default added to **APP.DEFAULT** zone.

Authentication Related Zones divides users based on the source of user information. For example, Admin User in Alfresco belongs to **AUTH.ALF** Zone. Externally defined users will be added in the **AUTH.EXT.<ID>** Zone. This is useful in case where we have multiple LDAP chaining. At any point of time, user will belong to only one Authentication related Zone.

Using command-line scripts to bulk upload users

You can bulk upload users to Alfresco using command-line scripts. In order to bulk upload users, follow the given steps:

You have to create home folders for the users you are importing. Create `fredb` and `sues` folder inside the User Homes space.

Stop the Alfresco server.

1. You have to create a user data XML files in the specified path `<Alfresco_Home>` folder. Following are few sample code snippets for your reference:

    ○ `person.xml`: This would have the detail information about user. This xml would be responsible for creating the person node in alfresco.

    ```
    <cm:person view:childName="cm:person">
    <cm:userName>sues</cm:userName>
    <cm:firstName>Sue</cm:firstName>
    <cm:lastName>Sanderson</cm:lastName>
    <cm:email>sues@alfresco.org</cm:email>
    <cm:person>
    ```

    ○ `UserStore.xml`: This file would have the user ID and password related information. This xml would be responsible for creating the user node in Alfresco. Password has to be in MD5 encrypted format.

    ```
    <usr:user view:childName="usr:sues">
      <usr:username>sues</usr:username>
    <usr:password>209c6174da490caeb422f3fa5a7ae634</usr:password>
    <usr:enabled>true</usr:enabled>
    <usr:accountExpires>false</usr:accountExpires>
    <usr:credentialsExpire>false</usr:credentialsExpire>
    <usr:accountLocked>false</usr:accountLocked>
    ...
    ```

○ `Zone.xml`: This file would have the zone related information. This xml would be responsible for associating the user with the zones in Alfresco.

```
<view:reference view:pathref="sys:zones/cm:AUTH.ALF">
    <view:associations>
        <cm:inZone>
            <view:reference view:pathref="sys:people/
cm:sues" view:childName="cm:sues"></view:reference>
        </cm:inZone>
    </view:associations>
</view:reference>
```

2. Run a command-line script to upload the users given in the `person.xml`, `UserStore.xml`, and `Zone.xml` file. Change the path to `<Alfresco_Home>` folder and run the following commands. The syntax to call the script may change based on the operating-system platform. Here is a sample script that reads user data from `person.xml` file and uploads to Alfresco.

○ `java -cp "tomcat/webapps/alfresco/WEB-INF/lib/*;tomcat/webapps/alfresco/WEB-INF/classes;tomcat/lib/*;tomcat/endorsed/*;tomcat/shared/classes;tomcat/shared/lib/*" org.alfresco.tools.Import -user admin -pwd admin -store workspace://SpacesStore -path sys:system/sys:people -verbose person.xml`

○ `java -cp "tomcat/webapps/alfresco/WEB-INF/lib/*;tomcat/webapps/alfresco/WEB-INF/classes;tomcat/lib/*;tomcat/endorsed/*;tomcat/shared/classes;tomcat/shared/lib/*" org.alfresco.tools.Import -user admin -pwd admin -store user://alfrescoUserStore -path sys:system/sys:people -verbose UserStore.xml`

○ `java -cp "tomcat/webapps/alfresco/WEB-INF/lib/*;tomcat/webapps/alfresco/WEB-INF/classes;tomcat/lib/*;tomcat/endorsed/*;tomcat/shared/classes;tomcat/shared/lib/*" org.alfresco.tools.Import -user admin -pwd admin -store workspace://SpacesStore -path sys:system -verbose Zone.xml`

Bootstrapping the Alfresco repository with predefined user data

The Alfresco repository supports a bootstrap process, which is initiated whenever the repository is first started. The process populates the repository with information that is required upon first login such as system users, data dictionary definitions, and important root folders.

Detailed information about bootstrapping Alfresco repository is provided in *Chapter 14, Administering and Maintaining the System*.

Summary

The Alfresco membership framework is very secure, flexible, scalable, and customizable. Roles are collections of permissions assigned to users (consumer, contributor, editor, collaborator, and coordinator). You can manage system users and groups through the administration console. Security is imposed by assigning a role to a specific user or group for a specific space or content. Authentication is possible using Alfresco built-in membership system, NTLM, and LDAP. In the next chapter you would learn about how you can manage your documents in Alfresco.

5
Implementing Document Management

This chapter introduces you to the basic features of creating and managing content in Alfresco using Alfresco Explorer. With Alfresco, you can manage any type of document, such as HTML, text, XML, Microsoft Office documents, Adobe PDF, Flash, scanned image, media, and video files. You will also understand the concepts of creating and using categories and smart spaces. This chapter also focuses on the most important aspect of adopting a new enterprise content management system, which is migrating the existing data and using it effectively. In this chapter, you will learn various secure ways to share your content online using the syndication features.

By the end of this chapter, you will have learned how to:

- Create spaces and fill them with documents
- Automatically control the document versioning
- Lock, check-in, and check-out the documents
- Categorizing content so that you could facilitate search
- Access documents in the Alfresco repository from your web browser, or a networked drive, FTP, and WebDAV
- Recover deleted content
- Create and use space templates
- Migrate existing documents to Alfresco
- Create and use discussions on spaces and documents
- Enable RSS Syndication to share content

Managing spaces

A space in Alfresco is nothing but a folder, which contains content as well as sub-spaces. Space users are the users invited to a space to perform specific actions, such as editing content, adding content, discussing a particular document, and so on. The exact capability a given user has within a space is a function of their role or rights.

Consider the capability of creating a sub-space. By default, to create a sub-space, one of the following must apply:

- The user is the administrator of the system
- The user has been granted the Contributor role.
- The user has been granted the Coordinator role.
- The user has been granted the Collaborator role.

Similarly, to edit space properties, a user will need to be the administrator or be granted a role that gives them rights to edit the space. These roles include Editor, Collaborator, and Coordinator. For more information about user roles on a space, refer *Chapter 4, Implementing Membership and Security*.

Space is a smart folder

Space is a folder with additional features such as security, business rules, workflow, notifications, local search, and special views. These additional features which make a space a smart folder are explained as follows:

- **Space security**: You can define security at the space level. You can specify a user or a group of users, who may perform certain actions on content in a space. For example, on the **Marketing Communications** space in intranet, you can specify that only users of the marketing group can add the content and others can only see the content.

- **Space business rules**: Business rules, such as transforming content from Microsoft Word to Adobe PDF and sending notifications when content gets into a space can be defined at space level.

- **Space workflow**: You can define and manage content workflow on a space. Typically, you will create a space for the content to be reviewed, and a space for approved content. You will create various spaces for dealing with the different stages the work flows through, and Alfresco will manage the movement of the content between those spaces.

- **Space events**: Alfresco triggers events when content gets into a space, or when content goes out of a space, or when content is modified within a space. You can capture such events at space level and trigger certain actions, such as sending e-mail notifications to certain users.

- **Space aspects**: Aspects are additional properties and behavior, which could be added to the content, based on the space in which it resides. For example, you can define a business rule to add customer details to all the customer contract documents in your intranet's Sales space.

- **Space search**: Alfresco search can be limited to a space. For example, if you create a space called **Marketing**, you can limit the search for documents within the **Marketing** space, instead of searching the entire site.

- **Space syndication**: Space content can be syndicated by applying RSS feed scripts on a space. You can apply RSS feeds on your **News** space, so that other applications and websites can subscribe for news updates.

- **Space content**: Content in a space can be versioned, locked, checked-in and checked-out, and managed. You can specify certain documents in a space to be versioned and others not.

- **Space network folder**: Space can be mapped to a network drive on your local machine, enabling you to work with the content locally. For example, using CIFS interface, space can be mapped to the Windows network folder.

- **Space dashboard view**: Content in a space can be aggregated and presented using special dashboard views. For example, the **Company Policies** space can list all the latest policy documents which are updated for the past one month or so. You can create different views for Sales, Marketing and Finance departmental spaces.

Importance of space hierarchy

Like regular folders, a space can have child spaces (called sub-spaces) and sub-spaces can further have sub-spaces of their own. There is no limitation on the number of hierarchical levels. However, the space hierarchy is very important for all the reasons specified above in the previous section. Any business rule and security defined at a space is applicable to all the content and sub-spaces underlying that space by default.

In the previous chapter, you created system users, groups, and spaces for various departments as per the example. Your space hierarchy should look similar to the following screenshot:

A space in Alfresco enables you to define various business rules, a dashboard view, properties, workflow, and security for the content belonging to each department. You can decentralize the management of your content by giving access to departments at individual space levels.

The example of the intranet space should contain sub-spaces, as shown in the preceding screenshot. If you have not already created spaces as per the example given in the previous chapter, you must do it now by logging in as administrator. Examples used in the remaining chapters of this book refer to these spaces. Also, it is very important to set security (by inviting groups of users to these spaces) as explained in the previous chapter.

Editing a space

Using a web client, you can edit the spaces you have added previously. Note that you need to have edit permissions on the spaces to edit them, as explained in the previous chapter.

Editing space properties

Every space listed will have clickable actions, as shown in the following screenshot:

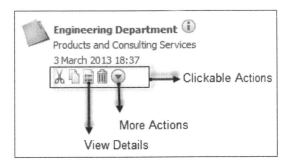

These clickable actions will be dynamically generated for each space based on the current user's permissions on that space. If you have copy permission on a space, you will notice the copy icon as a clickable action for that space. On clicking the **View Details** action icon, the detailed view of a space will be displayed, as shown in the next screenshot:

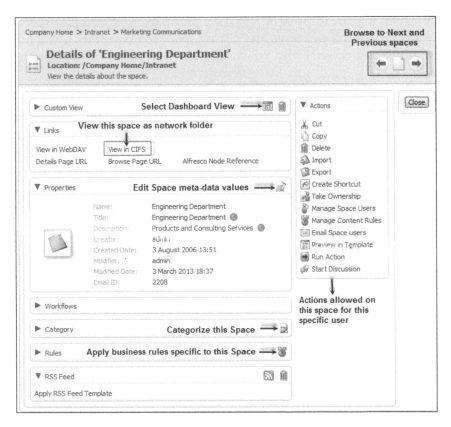

The detailed view page of a space allows you to select a dashboard view for viewing and editing existing space properties, to categorize the space, to set business rules, and to run various actions on the space, as shown in the preceding screenshot.

To edit space properties, click on the **Edit Space Properties** icon, shown in the preceding screenshot. You can change the name of the space and other properties as needed.

Deleting space and its contents

From the list of space actions, you can click on the **Delete** action to delete the space. You need to be very careful while deleting a space as all the business rules, sub-spaces, and the entire content within the space will also be deleted.

Moving or copying space by using the clipboard

From the list of space actions, you can click on the **Cut** action to move a space to the clipboard. Then you can navigate to any space hierarchy, assuming that you have the required permissions to do so, and paste this particular space, as required.

Similarly, you can use the **Copy** action to copy the space to some other space hierarchy. This is useful if you have an existing space structure (such as a marketing project or engineering project), and you would like to replicate it along with the data it contains.

The copied or moved space will be identical in all aspects to the original (source) space. When you copy a space, the space properties, categorization, business rules, space users, entire content within the space, and all sub-spaces along with their content will also be copied.

Creating a shortcut to a space for quick access

If you need to frequently access a space, you can create a shortcut (similar to the **Favorite** option in Internet browsers) to that space, in order to reach the space in just one click. From the list of space actions, you can click on the **Create Shortcut** action to create a shortcut to the existing space. Shortcuts are listed in the left-hand side shelf.

Consider a scenario where after creating the shortcut, the source space is deleted. The shortcuts are not automatically removed as there is a possibility for the user to retrieve the deleted space. Refer to the *Recovering deleted content* section in this chapter for more details. What will happen when you click on that shortcut link in the **Shelf**? If the source space is not found (deleted by user), then the shortcut will be removed with an appropriate error message.

Choosing a default view for your space

There are four different out-of-the-box options available (as shown in the screenshot overleaf). These options support the display of the space's information:

- **Details View**: This option provides listings of sub-spaces and content, in horizontal rows.

- **Icon View**: This option provides a title, description, timestamp, and action menus for each sub-space and content item present in the current space.

- **Browse View**: Similar to the preceding option, this option provides title, description, and list of sub-spaces for each space.

- **Dashboard View**: This option is disabled and appears in gray. This is because you have not enabled the dashboard view for this space. In order to enable dashboard view for a space, you need to select a dashboard view (Refer to the icon shown in the preceding screenshot).

Sample space structure for a marketing project

Let us say you are launching a new marketing project called **Product XYZ Launch**. Go to the **Company Home | Intranet | Marketing Communications** space and create a new space called **Product XYZ Launch** and create various sub-spaces as needed. You can create your own space structure within the marketing project space to manage content. For example, you can have a space called **02_Drafts** to keep all the draft marketing documents and so on.

Managing content

Content could be of any type, as mentioned at the start of this chapter. By using the Alfresco web client application, you can add and modify content and its properties. You can categorize content, lock content for safe editing, and can maintain several versions of the content. You can delete content, and you can also recover the deleted content.

This section uses the space you have already created as a part of your **Intranet** sample application. As a part of sample application, you will manage content in the **Intranet | Marketing Communications** space. Because you have secured this space earlier, only the administrator (admin) and users belonging to the **Marketing** group (**Peter Marketing** and **Harish Marketing**) can add content in this space. You can log in as **Peter Marketing** to manage content in this space.

Creating content

A web client provides two different interfaces for adding content. One can be used to create inline editable content, such as HTML, text, and XML, and the other can be used to add binary content, such Microsoft office files and scanned images.

You need to have either administrator, contributor, collaborator, or coordinator roles on a space to create content within that space. For more information about user roles on a space, refer to *Chapter 4, Implementing Membership and Security*.

Creating text documents – HTML, text, and XML

To create an HTML file in a space, follow these steps:

1. Ensure that you are in the **Intranet | Marketing Communications | Product XYZ Launch | 02_Drafts** space.

2. On the header, click on **Create | Create Content**. The first pane of the **Create Content** wizard appears. You can track your progress through the wizard from the list of steps at the left of the pane.

3. Provide name of the HTML file, select **HTML** as **Content Type** and click on the **Next** button. The **Enter Content** pane of the wizard appears, as shown in the next screenshot. Note that **Enter Content** is now highlighted in the list of steps at the left of the pane:

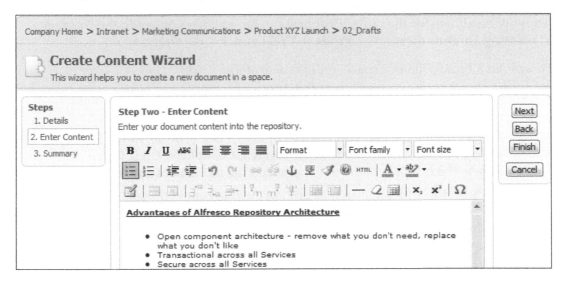

4. You can see that there is a comprehensive set of tools to help you format your HTML document. Enter some text, using some of the formatting features.

5. If you know HTML, you can also use the HTML editor by clicking on the **HTML** icon. The HTML source editor is displayed. Once you update the HTML content, click on the **Update** button to return to the **Enter Content** pane in the wizard, with the contents updated.

6. After the content is entered and edited in the **Enter Content** pane, click on **Finish**. You will see the **Modify Content Properties** screen, which can used to update the metadata associated with the content.

7. Give some filename with .html as extension. Also, you will notice that then **Inline Editing** checkbox is selected by default. Once you are done with editing the properties, click on the **OK** button to return to the **02_Drafts** space, with your newly created file inserted.

You can launch the newly created HTML file by clicking on it. Your browser launches most of the common files, such as HTML, text, and PDF. If the browser could not recognize the file, you will be prompted with the windows dialog box containing the list of applications, from which you must choose an application. This is the normal behavior if you try to launch a file on any Internet page.

Uploading binary files – Word, PDF, Flash, Image, and Media

Using a web client, you can upload content from your hard drive. Choose a file from your hard disk that is not an HTML or text file. I chose `Alfresco_CIGNEX.docx` from my hard disk for the sample application. Ensure that you are in the **Intranet** | **Marketing Communications** | **Product XYZ Launch** | **02_Drafts** space.

To upload a binary file in a space, follow these steps:

1. In the space header, click on the **Add Content** link. The **Add Content** dialog appears.

2. To specify the file that you want to upload, click **Browse**. In the **File Upload** dialog box, browse to the file that you want to upload. Click **Open**. Alfresco inserts the full path name of the selected file in the **Location** textbox.

3. Click on the **Upload** button to upload the file from your hard disk to the Alfresco repository. A message informs you that your upload was successful, as shown in the following screenshot.

4. Click **OK** to confirm.

5. Modify the **Content Properties** dialog appears. Verify the pre-populated properties and add information in the textboxes. Click **OK** to save and return to the **02_Drafts** space.

The file that you uploaded appears in the **Content Items** pane. Alfresco extracts the file size from the properties of the disk file, and includes the value in the size row.

Editing content

You can edit the content in Alfresco in three different ways: by using the **Edit Online**, **Edit Offline**, and **Update** actions. Note that you need to have edit permissions on the content to edit them, as explained in the previous chapter.

Online editing of HTML, text, and XML

HTML files and plain text files can be created and edited online. If you have edit access to a file, you will notice a small pencil (**Edit Online**) icon, as shown in the following screenshot:

Clicking on the pencil icon will open the file in its editor. Each file type is edited in its own WYSIWYG editor. Once you select to edit online, a working copy of the file will be created for editing, whereas the original file will be locked, as shown in the next screenshot.

The working copy can be edited further as needed by clicking on the **Edit Online** button. Once you are done with editing, you can commit all the changes to the original document by clicking on the **Done Editing** icon.

For some reason, if you decided to cancel editing of a document and discard any changes, you can do that by clicking on the **Cancel Editing** button given below. If you cancel editing of a document, the associated working copy will be deleted and all changes to it since it was checked out will be lost.

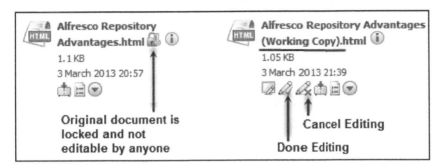

The working copy can be edited by any user who has edit access to the document or the folder containing the document. For example, if user1 created the working copy and user2 has edit access to the document, and then both user1 and user2 can edit the working copy.

Consider a scenario where user1 and user2 are editing the working copy simultaneously. If user1 commits the changes first, then the edits done by user2 will be lost.

Hence, it is important to follow best practices in editing the working copy. Some of these best practices are listed here for your reference:

- Securing the edit access to the working copy to avoid multiple users simultaneously editing the file
- Saving the working copy after each edit to avoid losing the work done
- Following the process of allowing only the owner of the document edit the working copy. If others need to edit, they can claim the ownership
- Triggering the workflow on working copy to confirm the changes before committing

Offline editing of files

If you wish to download the files to your local machine, edit it locally, and then upload the updated version to Alfresco, then you might consider using the **Edit Offline** option (pencil icon).

Once you click on the **Edit Offline** button, the original file will be locked automatically and a working copy of the file will be created for download. Then you will get an option to save the working copy of the document locally on your laptop or personal computer.

If you don't want to automatically download the files for offline editing, you can turn off this feature. In order to achieve this, click on the **User Profile** icon in the top menu, and uncheck the option for **Offline Editing**, as shown here:

The working copy can be updated by clicking on the **Upload New Version** button. Once you have finished editing the file, you can commit all the changes to the original document by clicking on the **Done Editing** icon. Or you can cancel all the changes by clicking on the **Cancel Editing** button.

Uploading updated content

If you have edit access to a binary file, you will notice the **Update** action icon in the drop-down list for the **More actions** link. Upon clicking on the **Update** icon, the **Update** pane opens. Click on the **Browse** button to upload the updated version of the document from your hard disk. It is always a good practice to check out the document and update the working copy rather than directly updating the document. Checking the file out avoids conflicting updates by locking the document, as explained in the previous section.

Content actions

Content will have clickable actions, as shown in the upcoming screenshot. These clickable actions (icons) will be dynamically generated for a content based on the current user's permissions for that content. For example, if you have copy permission for the content, you will notice the **Copy** icon as a clickable action for that content.

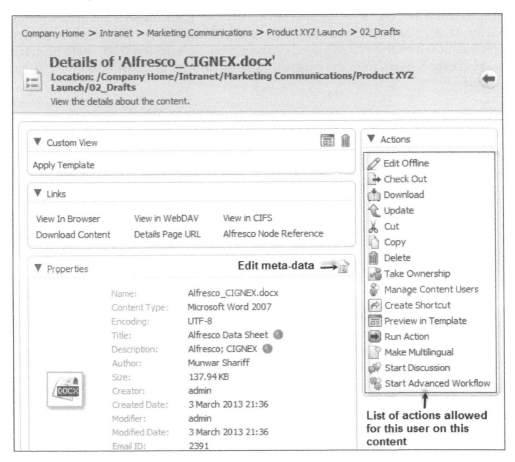

Deleting content

Click on the **Delete** action, from the list of content actions, to delete the content. Please note that when content is deleted, all the previous versions of that content will also be deleted.

Moving or copying content using the clipboard

From the list of content actions, as shown in the preceding screenshot, you can click on the **Cut** action to move content to the clipboard. Then, you can navigate to any space hierarchy and paste this particular content as required.

Similarly, you can use the **Copy** action to copy the content to another space.

Creating a shortcut to the content for quick access

If you have to access a particular content very frequently, you can create a shortcut (similar to the way you can with Internet and Windows browser's **Favorite** option) to that content, in order to reach the content in one click. From the list of content actions, as shown in the preceding screenshot, you can click on the **Create Shortcut** action to create a shortcut to the existing content. Shortcuts are listed in the left-hand side **Shelf**.

Managing content properties

Every content item in Alfresco will have properties associated with it. Refer to the preceding screenshot to see the list of properties, such as **Title**, **Description**, **Author**, **Size**, and **Creation Date**. These properties are associated with the actual content file, named Alfresco_CIGNEX.docx.

The content properties are stored in a relational database and are searchable using **Advanced Search** options.

What is Content Metadata?

Content properties are also known as **Content Metadata**. Metadata is structured data, which describes the characteristics of the content. It shares many similar characteristics with the cataloguing that takes place in libraries. The term "Meta" derives from the Greek word denoting a nature of a higher order or more fundamental kind. A metadata record consists of a number of predefined elements representing specific attributes of content, and each element can have one or more values.

Metadata is a systematic method for describing resources, and thereby improving access to them. If access to the content will be required, then it should be described using metadata, so as to maximize the ability to locate it. Metadata provides the essential link between the information creator and the information user.

While the primary aim of metadata is to improve resource discovery, metadata sets are also being developed for other reasons, including:

- Administrative control
- Security
- Management information
- Content rating
- Rights management

Metadata extractors

Typically, in most of the content management systems, once you upload the content file, you need to add the metadata (properties), such as title, description, and keywords to the content manually. Most of the content, such as Microsoft Office documents, media files, and PDF documents contain properties within the file itself. Hence, it is double the effort, having to enter those values again in the content management system along with the document.

Alfresco provides built-in metadata extractors for popular document types to extract the standard metadata values from a document and populate the values automatically.

This is very useful if you are uploading the documents through FTP, CIFS, or WebDAV interface, where you do not have to enter the properties manually, as Alfresco will transfer the document properties automatically.

Editing metadata

To edit metadata, you need to click the **Edit Metadata** icon (⬚) in content details view. Refer the **Edit Metadata** icon shown in the screenshot, which shows a detailed view of the Alfresco_CIGNEX.docx file. You can update the metadata values, such as **Name** and **Description** for your content items. However, certain metadata values, such as **Creator**, **Created Date**, **Modifier**, and **Modified Date** are read-only and you cannot change them. Certain properties, such as **Modifier** and **Modified Date** will be updated by Alfresco automatically, whenever the content is updated.

Adding additional properties

Additional properties can be added to the content in two ways. One way is to extend the data model and define more properties in a content type. More information is provided in *Chapter 7, Extending Alfresco Content Model*.

The other way is to dynamically attach the properties and behavior through **Aspects**. By using aspects, you can add additional properties, such as **Effectivity**, **Dublin Core Metadata**, and **Thumbnailable**, to the content. More information is provided in *Chapter 6, Implementing Business Rules*.

Library services

Library services are the common document management functions for controlling the users with permissions to create multiple instances of a document (versioning) and the users with access a document to make changes (checking-in/out).

Versioning

So far, you have learned about creating spaces, adding files, and editing them. You might have more than one person who can edit a document. What if somebody edits a document, and removes a useful piece of information? Well, you can use versioning features to avoid such issues.

Versioning allows history of previous versions of a content to be kept. Content needs to be versionable for versions to be kept. You can enable versioning in four different ways:

- **Individually**: To enable versioning for an individual content item, go to the **View Details** page and click on the **Allow Versioning** link. The screenshot on the next page illustrates the way to enable versioning on an individual content item.

- **Using Smart Spaces**: A business rule can be set for a space to allow versioning of all the content or selective content within that space. More information about this is provided in *Chapter 6, Implementing Business Rules*.

- **By Type**: By default, versioning is disabled for all content types in the Alfresco content model. Versioning can be enabled for a specific content type in the Alfresco content model, irrespective of the location of the content. More information about this is provided in *Chapter 7, Extending Alfresco Content Model* of this book.

- **Globally**: Alfresco can be configured globally to enable versioning for all the content throughout the site. More information about this is provided in *Chapter 7, Extending Alfresco Content Model*.

Enable versioning for the sample file you have already uploaded to the system. Go to the **Intranet | Marketing Communications | Product XYZ Launch | 02_Drafts** space and view details of the `Alfresco_CIGNEX.docx` file. Click on the **Allow Versioning** link to enable versioning, as shown in the following screenshot, and you will immediately notice that a version with 1.0 is created:

Auto Versioning

Auto versioning can be enabled by editing the content properties and selecting the **Auto Version** checkbox.

If auto versioning is enabled, then each **Save** of the content results in an incremented version number when edited directly from repository. Each **Update** (upload) of content also results in an incremented version number. If auto versioning is not enabled, version number is incremented only when content is checked in.

Check In and Check Out

By using the versioning feature, you can ensure that all the changes made to a document were saved. You might have more than one person who can edit a document. What if two people edit a document at once, and you get into a mess with two new versions. To resolve this issue, you'll need the library services.

Library services provide the ability to check out a document, reserving it for one user to edit while others can only access the document in a read-only mode. Once the necessary changes are made to the document, the user checks in the document and can either replace the original or create a version of the original.

Check Out locks the item and creates a working copy, which can be edited (content and details). **Check In** replaces the original item with the working copy and releases the lock.

Checking out documents

Ensure that you are in the **Intranet | Marketing Communications | Product XYZ Launch | 02_Drafts** space. For checking `Alfresco_CIGNEX.docx`, click on the **More Actions** button and then click on the **Check Out** action.

You can either check out the file in the current space or to any other predefined space. As best practice, it is recommended to check out the working copy in the user's own Home Space. For the current example, choose to check out the file to the **In the current space** option and click on the **Check Out** button. You will return to the **02_Drafts** space.

You will notice two copies of the same document. The original version of the file has a lock. This indicates that no one else can check out this file until you have checked it in again. The original version of the file can't be edited (no pencil icon) or cannot be checked out (no **Check Out** icon). The desired effect of all these features is that you cannot edit a checked-out file deliberately or accidentally.

You can only update the working copy. The checked-out file has **Working Copy** inserted in the filename. The working copy can be edited and checked in.

Checking in the working copy

Update the working copy `Alfresco_CIGNEX (Working Copy).docx` file. Updating the document is explained earlier in this chapter in the *Upload updated binary file* section. After you update the working copy, you can check in by clicking the **Check In** button.

Once you click on the **Check In** action, you will see the **Check In** dialog window. If you have only made minor changes to the file, you will check the **Minor Change** checkbox. By selecting the **Minor Change** checkbox, you will be able to increment only the number after the decimal (from 1.1 to 1.2); otherwise, you will increment the number before the decimal (from 1.0 to 2.0). Type your notes in **Version Notes**, which is a very important documentation to help understand the differences between various versions of the document.

There will no longer be a working copy of the document. Notice the latest modification timestamp of the original document. If you click on the **View Details** action and scroll down to **Version History**, you will see that the history has been updated, as shown in the following screenshot:

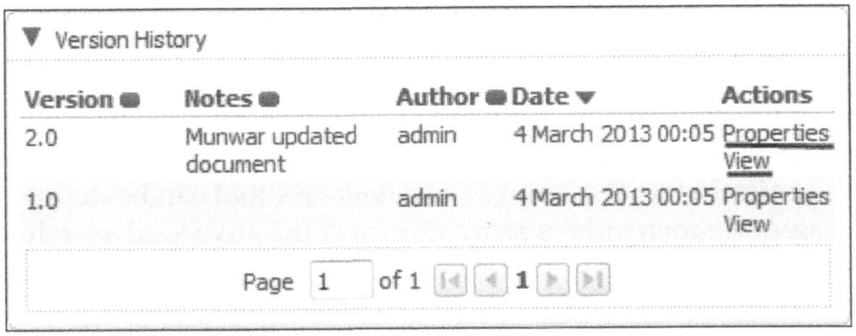

▼ Version History				
Version ●	Notes ●	Author ●	Date ▼	Actions
2.0	Munwar updated document	admin	4 March 2013 00:05	Properties View
1.0		admin	4 March 2013 00:05	Properties View
		Page 1 of 1 |◀ ◀ 1 ▶ ▶|		

At the time of writing this book, reverting back to older versions of the content is not supported in the user interface. The work around is to download the desired older version and upload it again as the current version. The "revert" feature is available in the Alfresco Java API for programmatically reverting to the version of the content needed. If you are a programmer, please refer Alfresco's API called **VersionService** and **revert** method for more details.

For a checked-out content, the version is updated when content is checked in. Version number is incremented from the content version number that was checked out.

Undo Check Out to unlock a document

Now that you can use library services, you might still have questions such as, how long does a file remain checked-out? Can we see who checked it out and when? And who can cancel the lock?

A document remains in the checked-out state (locked) forever, until the working copy is checked in or somebody cancels the checked-out status from the working copy. To cancel check out, locate the working copy of the document and click on the **Cancel Editing** button. This action will delete the working copy and release the lock, as if the checkout had not happened.

The owner of the document, or a coordinator, or an administrator can unlock the document by executing the **Cancel Editing** action on the working copy. Other users, who have read access to the space, can still see the working copy of the document but they can never edit or check in the document.

You can enable auditing on Alfresco repository, and find out the audit trail information, such as who locked the content and when. More information about the auditing is covered in *Chapter 14, Administering and Maintaining the System.*

Categorizing content

Categorization helps information to be classified in a number of ways. Various technologies use various terminologies, such as hierarchies, taxonomies, and ontology for the same concept.

In Alfresco, all of the content can be linked to one or more categories. Categories are defined and managed by administrators only. Categories can have subcategories and there is no limitation on the number of categories that can be defined, or depth of hierarchy. Categorization aids in searching, and the advanced search form in Alfresco allows you to search the content filtered by various categories.

Managing categories

Follow these steps to create two new categories called **Technology** and **Products** for your example application:

1. In any space, click on the **Administration Console** icon in the top toolbar. The **Administration Console** pane appears.

2. Click on the **Category Management** link. The **Category Management** pane appears. Notice the existing categories, such as **Software Document Classification**, **Regions**, and **Languages**.

3. In the header, click on the **Add Category** link to create a new category.

4. As an example, create a new category called **Open-Source Products**. Under that new category, create few subcategories, such as **Alfresco** and **Plone**.

You can add additional categories and subcategories, and can edit the existing categories.

Adding categories to content

In order to categorize content, you need to have either an administrator, or an editor, or a collaborator, or a coordinator role, on that content.

To enable categorization for an individual content item (say `Alfresco_CIGNEX.docx`), go to the **View Details** page, and click on the **Allow Categorization** link. Click on the **Change Category** icon to apply categorization to the content.

You will see the **Modify categories** dialog, as shown in the screenshot on the next page. Apply two different categories to the content. Click on the **OK** button to confirm. You will notice these two categories associated with your document in the **View Details** page:

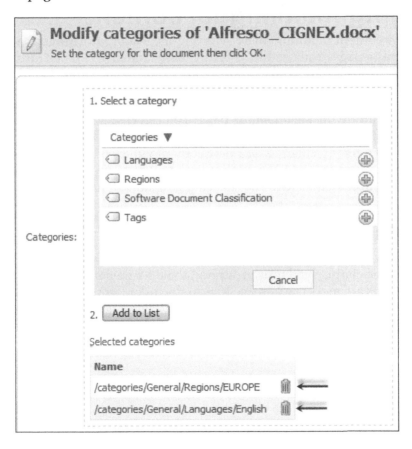

Searching content by category

Categorization helps to narrow down a search or filter the search results. From the earlier example, we will search for the marketing documents, with a text called **Content**, and categorized under **Open Source Products | Alfresco**.

Click on the **Advanced Search** link from the drop-down list of the search menu. From the form options, click on the **Show me results in the categories** pane. Click on the **Click here to select a category** link. Select **Open Source Products | Alfresco** as an option and provide text in the **Look For** textbox and then click on the **Search** button.

Managing multilingual content

You can make content multilingual by selecting the **Make Multilingual** action under the **View Details** page. You need to select the base language (**Pivot Translation**) and optionally add other translations.

Once multilingual support is added to a file, you will notice the **Multilingual Content Info** window in **View Details** page. You can change the properties, such as **Pivot Translation** by clicking on the **Edit** button. You can add translations with file and without a file. In either case, a new content will be created with the selected language. Clicking on the **Add Translation** link will open up the dialog box, enabling you to upload a file with the selected language translation.

Versions of multilingual content

At the time of writing this book, Alfresco's multilingual support is very basic. It is equivalent to associating (and thus grouping) the documents. All the latest versions of the documents are associated as one logical document group, as shown in the next screenshot. The latest version of the English document could be 1.0, the German translated version could be 1.1, whereas the Japanese version could be 2.0.

When you click on the **Manage Multilingual Content** link in the **View Details** page of the base (English) version of the document, you will notice the following screen:

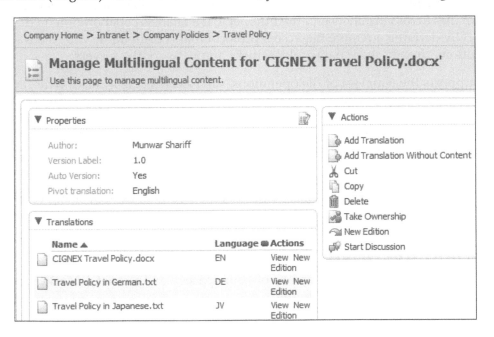

Multilingual files are associated to each other, and for all other purposes they are treated as separate files within Alfresco. They can have different versions, different metadata, different categorization, and different workflow processes. All of these translated files will show up in the **Search** result, if they match the search criteria.

Deleting multilingual content

You can't delete the base file if it has translated files available. In our example shown above, the content with base language English (with the icon **EN**) has two translations available for German (with the icon **DE**) and Japanese (with the icon JA). You will notice that you cannot delete the base English version. However, you can delete the translated versions. If a particular content does not have translated content, then it can be deleted.

Using network drives to manage content

Out-of-the-box installation comes with web client, where you can connect to the Alfresco repository through a web-based application. Apart from a web client, Alfresco supports various client applications to access repository content using protocols, such as FTP, WebDAV, and CIFS.

CIFS

Microsoft's **Server Message Block (SMB)**, is the standard way for computer users to share files across intranets and the Internet. CIFS enables collaboration on the Internet by defining a remote file-access protocol that is compatible with the way applications already share data on local disks and network file servers.

CIFS supports the usual set of file operations, such as open, close, read, write, and seek. CIFS also supports file and record lock and unlocking. CIFS allows multiple clients to access and update the same file while preventing conflicts by providing file sharing and file locking. CIFS servers support both anonymous transfers and secure, authenticated access to named files.

Using CIFS, you can map an existing Alfresco space as your local filesystem folder. You will be able to bulk upload files to server and edit them directly using your desktop applications.

Mapping the drive

As an example, you will now map one of your spaces, say **Intranet | Marketing Communications**, as your local folder:

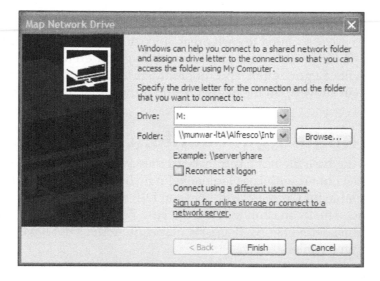

To map a space in Windows Explorer as a network drive, follow these steps:

1. In Windows Explorer, click on the **Tools | Map Network Drive** link. The **Map Network Drive** dialog appears, as shown in the preceding screenshot.

2. Select an unused drive letter (say **M** for the **Marketing Communications** space).

3. In the **Folder** textbox, type \\AlfrescoServerNameA\Alfresco\ Intranet\Marketing Communications. Please note that you have to append capital letter "A" at the end of your machine name. The syntax is \\YourMachineNameA\alfresco\YourSpaceName.

4. Click **Finish**. As the space is secured, the system will prompt for your authentication.

5. Type your Alfresco username and password when prompted.

Another easy way of mapping your space as a network folder in your local filesystem is by using a web client. Go to the space and click on the **Open Network Folder** icon, as shown in the following screenshot:

Once a space is mapped as a network folder, you can browse the space as if it is your local folder. You can drag and drop files into Alfresco folders.

FTP

FTP is useful to transfer files from your local filesystem to the remote server. Using any FTP client, you can connect to Alfresco server as if it were a FTP site and upload and retrieve files.

If you are connecting to a space, all of the rules are applied and all of the permissions are enforced. If versioning is enabled, then content will be versioned regardless of how it is updated.

Execute the following commands to use FTP via the Windows DOS prompt to upload a file from the local hard disk to your **Intranet | Marketing Communications | Product XYZ Launch | 02_Drafts** space:

```
> ftp localhost
Login as: admin/admin
> ls
> cd Alfresco
> ls
> cd Intranet
> ls
> cd Marketing*
> cd Product*
> cd 02_Drafts
> put c:\press2A.txt
> ls
```

Verify that the text file is now in the Alfresco repository. Similarly, you can use any FTP client application to connect to the Alfresco repository and access files.

WebDAV

WebDAV is primarily designed for editing and managing files on remote Web servers in a structured way. For example, an application such as Adobe Photoshop can directly open a file in the Alfresco content repository and edit it. This gives you the flexibility of using your own favorite editor to edit the content on the Alfresco server.

If you are connecting to a space, all of the rules are applied and all of the permissions are enforced. If versioning is enabled, then content will be versioned regardless of how it is updated.

If you have a WebDAV client, then you can access the Alfresco server by using the `http://<Your_Alfresco_Server_URL_Port>/alfresco/webdav/` URL

 You can only edit the content and you can't edit the metadata of the content using CIFS, FTP, or WebDAV access.

Recovering deleted content

When you delete an item (content or space) in Alfresco, the item will not be deleted from the server; but is moved to a temporary store called **Archive Space Store**. This gives you a chance to recover the items that were deleted earlier. Deleted item will be in the temporary store forever, until you decide to either recover or purge the deleted item. This feature is available to administrators through the **Manage Deleted Items** action.

To test these features, log in as a user or administrator, create a couple of dummy files in any space and delete them. Click on the **User Profile** Icon (🗎) on the top menu item and then click on **Manage Deleted Items**. The **Manage Deleted Items** pane appears.

You can list all of the deleted content by clicking on the **Show All** button. You can also search the deleted items by name, content, date, or person deleted, using search options provided. Select the item that you deleted earlier and click on the **Recover Listed Items** icon. You will notice that the item has been recovered to the original space.

When an item is recovered, it will be removed from the archive space store and moved to the original space, from where it was deleted.

Purged items are deleted forever and cannot be recovered. Since the deleted items will be in the temporary store forever, it is best practice to purge them periodically. It is also recommended to take regular backups of your data. More information about maintenance and backup is provided in *Chapter 14, Administering and Maintaining the System*.

Data Dictionary and space templates

The **Company Home** space is the root space that contains the sub-spaces, such as **Data Dictionary**, **Guest Home**, and **Users Home Spaces**.

The Data Dictionary space

The **Data Dictionary** space contains the following sub-spaces. The scripts and the templates contained in these spaces are covered in detail in the further chapters of this book. For the time being, note that the **Data Dictionary** space is a shared resource. All of the scripts and templates provided in the **Data Dictionary** space can be defined by the administrators and used by the users.

- **Email Templates**: Contains e-mail templates for notifying users of an invite to a space or document, and for sending notifications to users from a rule or an action. E-mail templates are written in the **Freemarker** template language and will have the .ftl file extension.

- **Messages**: Contains message files that are part of content model. Message files are nothing but property files that contain the multilingual messages to be displayed. One of the ways of customizing the messages is to include them in the <extension>/messages folder. However, it requires Alfresco to be restarted. The message files added to this space do not require restarting Alfresco.

- **Models**: Contains custom model files. As explained earlier, the model files added to this space do not require restarting Alfresco. More information about model files is provided in *Chapter 7, Extending Alfresco Content Model*.

- **Presentation Templates**: Contains presentation templates that are useful to consolidate and view content in different ways. Presentation templates are written in the FreeMarker template language and will have the .ftl extension.

- **RSS Templates**: Contains RSS templates, which are useful to provide RSS feeds on spaces. More information about RSS templates is provided in *Chapter 10, Alfresco Administration Operations Using Alfresco Share*.

- **Saved Searches**: Contains prebuilt queries, which are saved by user from the search results page. Each user will have their private saved searches. This space will also contain all the saved searches, which are publicly shared by the users.

- **Scripts**: Contains JavaScript files that are used to perform certain operations on content.

- **Space Templates**: This contains space structure that can be used as templates to create new spaces. Any space can be saved as a space template for future re-use of a space structure and data. More about space templates is covered in the following section.

- **Web Client Extension**: Contains dynamic web client customizations. This newly added space simply provides an additional source for loading and overriding the web client configuration.

- **Web Forms**: Contains Alfresco **Web Content Management (WCM)** web form definition files.

- **Web Scripts**: Contains new custom web scripts. Web Scripts are explained in details in *Chapter 9*, *Integrating External Applications with Alfresco*.

- **Web Scripts Extensions**: Contains the web script files to override the existing web script files.

- **Workflow Definitions**: Contains workflow definition files. The custom workflow files added to this space do not require restarting Alfresco.

Space templates for re-usable space structure

In the earlier sections, you created a marketing project for launching a new product in the **Company Home | Intranet | Marketing Communications | Product XYZ Launch** space. Let us assume that you are going to launch many such products in future, and each product will need a similar structure of documents. For example, your product launch space has marketing templates, draft documentation, and approved marketing collateral. Also, each product will have a hierarchy of spaces, security settings, business rules, notifications, and workflows.

Instead of having to repeatedly create the same structure for each product launch, you can maintain a **Product Launch Template** and keep on replicating it for every new product. Thus, all the work you that do manually can be done in a few seconds simply by using such template.

Creating new space template for re-use

Follow these steps to create your own space template using an existing space structure:

1. Log in as the admin and go to the **Company Home | Data Dictionary | Space Templates** space.

2. Click on the **Create | Advanced Space Wizard** link. The **Create Space Wizard** pane appears.

3. Click on the **Based on an existing space** radio button option and then on the **Next** button to go to the second pane, titled **Space Options**.

4. Browse and select the **Company Home | Intranet | Marketing Communications | Product XYZ Launch** space. Click on the **Next** button to go to the **Space Details** pane.

5. In the **Space Details** pane, give an appropriate title (such as **Product Launch Template**) to your space template and click on the **Finish** button to confirm.

6. You will notice a new space template called **Product Launch Template** in the **Company Home | Data Dictionary | Space Templates** space. Examine the space structure.

Using an existing space template to create a new space

You can re-use the **Product Launch Template** space template to create new marketing projects. To create a new marketing project, ensure that you are in the **Company Home | Intranet | Marketing Communications** space, and follow these steps:

1. In the space header, click on **Create | Advanced Space Wizard**.

2. The first pane of the **Create Space Wizard** pane appears. Click on the **Using a template** radio button option and click on the **Next** button.

3. The **Space Options** pane of the wizard appears.

4. Choose **Product Launch Template** and click on the **Next** button.

5. The **Space Details** pane of the wizard appears. Specify your new project name and click on the **Finish** button to confirm.

6. You can now browse around your new space and you will notice that the space contents were identical to that of the template space.

Discussions on spaces and documents

Alfresco provides a special type of space called **Discussion forums** for collaboration. You can leverage the extensive security framework to provide access to these spaces to promote collaboration. You can also set up inter-departmental collaboration using spaces, allowing multiple people to work on documents within a particular space.

Using the collaborative features, the author of a document can invite others to work on the document and participate in the general discussions about the document.

Discussion forums for collaboration

A discussion forum is a web-based facility for holding discussions, also commonly referred to as Internet forums, web forums, message boards, discussion boards, discussion groups, bulletin, or simply forums.

In Alfresco, a **forum space** is a special space that can contain other forum spaces or forums (discussion forums). A forum is essentially a space composed of a number of member-written topics, each entailing a discussion or conversation in the form of a series of member-written replies. The replies can be posted by group members as defined by the administrator or in some cases anonymously or in case of secure forum, by registered members only. These topics remain saved on the website for future reading indefinitely or until deletion by a moderator.

To summarize, you can have one or more forum spaces in Alfresco. Each forum space can have one or more forums. Each forum can have one or more topics. Each topic can have one or more replies. All the forums, topics, and replies are searchable.

Forum space

A forum space contains discussion forums. As an example, create a forum space in the **Engineering Department** space, as follows:

1. Log in to the Alfresco web client and go to the **Company Home | Intranet | Engineering Department** space.

2. Using the **Create** menu drop-down list, choose **Advanced Space Wizard**.

3. The **Create Space Wizard** window will pop up with multiple steps. From the options, select the **From scratch** option and click on the **Next** button situated at the right-hand side of the screen.

4. You will see a window for step 2 to select space options. Choose **Forum Space** and click on the **Next** button to view step 3.

5. In step 3, provide a name to your forum (say **Engineering Discussions**) and click on the **Finish** button.

Creating discussion forums in the forum space

You can create other forum spaces or discussion forums within a forum space.

Go to the forum space created above, named **Engineering Discussions**. When you click on the **Create** drop-down menu at the top, you will notice the options for creating forum spaces, or forums. Click on the **Create Forum** action and create few forums, for example a forum named **Alfresco Technology Forum**.

Creating topics in the forum

You can create various topics within a discussion forum. Topics are a type of content item such as a plain-text item.

Click on a forum (say **Alfresco Technology Forum**) and click on the **Create Topic** button to create a topic for discussion.

Replying to topics

Users, who have access to this topic, can reply with messages. Users can also reply to the replies. There is no limitation on the number of replies. As an administrator, you can edit or delete a particular topic or a post (reply).

Departmental forums and security

Forums and topics are types of spaces, and they are governed by the same permissions as all spaces. Users may be invited to forums and topics with certain roles.

The following table explains the roles and permissions with the forums:

Role	Permission
Consumer	Copy/view details (of the forum and its topics).
Editor	All the permissions of Consumer, plus can edit posts (within topic).
	Can also edit details of forum and topics.
Contributor	All the permissions of Consumer, plus create topic with forum.
	Can post to topic/post reply within a topic.
Coordinator	All the permissions of Consumer plus create topic.
	View/edit details of forum and topics.
	Manage space users of forum and topics.
	Post to topic and cut/delete topic.
	Post reply/edit post.

The following table explains the roles and permissions with topics:

Role	Permission
Consumer	Copy/View.
Editor	Consumer permissions plus may edit post.
	Edit details of topics.

Role	Permission
Contributor	Consumer permissions, plus may post to topic/post reply within a topic.
Coordinator	Consumer permissions plus may post to topic.
	Post reply.
	Edit a post.
	Delete a post.

When the **Inherit parent space permissions** option is disabled, no user can view the discussions unless explicitly invited. Even the Coordinators of the forum cannot see the topic. For those invited, they have the access rights, as stated above, corresponding to their role.

Defining forums for groups within a department

By setting the appropriate security, each group within a department can have a discussion forum and each project can have a separate discussion forum specific to that project. As a sample exercise, go to the **Company Home | Intranet | Engineering Department | ProjectA** space, delete the **Discussions** space, and create **Discussions** as a forum space. Create few project-specific discussion forums and topics. Invite various users to participate in discussions by giving them the **Contributor** role on the discussion forum. Test this by logging in as various users and by participating in discussions.

Inter-department collaboration using spaces

You can use the existing security framework to allow groups and individuals to access certain spaces and collaborate on content.

Managing space users

As an owner of a space, you can invite other users to your space to view, add, or edit content. On any space, the **More Actions | Manage Space Users** link shows a list of users that have permission to work on content in that space. You can click on the **Invite** link to invite the individual users or groups and assign them appropriate permissions. More details about securing a space are provided in *Chapter 4, Implementing Membership and Security.*

Space collaboration using e-mails

All the users who have access to a space can communicate using e-mails. In order to send an e-mail to the users in a space, click on the **More Actions | View Details** link and click on the **Email Space Users** action. The **Email Space Users** pane appears.

Groups and individual users who have access to this space will be listed as e-mail **Message Recipients**. You can choose to e-mail the entire group or only certain users in the group by expanding the group icon.

Starting a discussion on a specific space

You can start discussion on a specific space directly by clicking on the **Start Discussion** action, provided in actions menu, as shown in the following screenshot:

Once the discussion is started, you will see a discussion forum icon to view the discussions on the space.

Content collaboration

Similar to the collaboration on a specific space, you can collaborate on individual content items as well. You can start discussion on a specific document directly by clicking on the **Start Discussion** action provided in actions menu.

 It is always good practice to start discussion on a document in the workflow process. It enables various people to make, review comments, and capture all the review data as the document goes through various approval steps.

Owner invites individuals to collaborate on content

As an owner of the content, you can give the **Editor** role to another individual to edit the content. In the content's **View Details** screen, the **Manage content users** action shows a list of users that have permission to work on content.

The process is similar to that of space collaboration. However, the invited users should have proper roles on the content and the parent space.

RSS syndication

In order to share the information in a space with external systems as RSS feeds, you need to enable **RSS Feed** on that space.

Go to details page of the **News** space and click on the enable RSS syndication icon, as shown in the following screenshot:

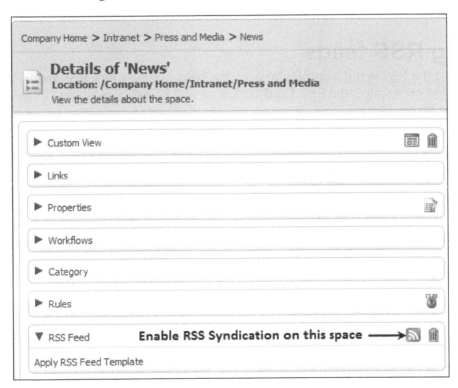

A new window pops up enabling you to select the RSS template to be applied to the space as an RSS feed. RSS templates are custom scripts that determine the content to be shown as feeds. Alfresco ships with built-in standard RSS template called RSS_2.0_recent_docs.ftl, which renders a valid RSS2.0 XML document, showing the documents in the current space created or modified in the last 7 days. Choose the default RSS template from the drop-down menu and select the **OK** button.

In order for the anonymous users to view the news feeds, they must have read permission on news space. It means, the **Guest** (anonymous) user must have **Consumer** role (READ access) on this space for the RSS feed to be publicly viewable.

This can be achieved using the **Manage Space Users** dialog, and inviting the **Guest** user into the **News** space.

[It is very important to ensure that the guest user has consumer role on the space to view RSS feeds of that space.]

Using RSS feeds

Let us test the RSS syndication features on the **News** space. Once **RSS feeds** are enabled on a space, the **RSS Feed Link** icon will be listed, as shown in the following screenshot:

By clicking on **RSS Feed Link**, you can view the RSS feeds of the **News** space in the web browser. You can view the RSS feeds of the **News** space in any RSS feeds-enabled web browser or RSS browser.

Version 7.0 of Microsoft Explorer has built-in RSS feeds viewer. You can receive content automatically by subscribing to a web feed and specifying the interval, at which Internet Explorer will check the website for updates. To view your feeds, click on the **Favorites Center** button, and then click on the **Feeds** link. This allows you to subscribe to feeds with Internet Explorer, and read them in other programs, such as e-mail clients.

RSS Templates

The news information that is displayed as an RSS feed is controlled by the RSS template used. RSS templates are custom scripts written in the FreeMarker template language. All of the RSS templates in Alfresco are located in the **Company Home | Data Dictionary | RSS Templates** space.

You can either customize the existing template by editing it or add a new RSS template by clicking on the **Add Content** link provided, as shown in the preceding screenshot.

Migrating existing content into Alfresco

If you want your Enterprise Content Management initiative to be successful, you need to make sure that you can move the existing content into the new system. Most of the enterprises will have content in the form of files (in local or shared hard disks), e-mail attachments, fax (invoices) and scanned images. It is very important to move the content to a centralized and highly scalable content repository such as Alfresco.

Alfresco being a powerful content management system for the enterprise supports various ways to migrate existing content in the enterprise.

Drag-and-drop content to the network drive

You can use drag-and-drop (bulk upload) content from your local hard disks to Alfresco server using options such as CIFS, FTP, or WebDAV. Refer the *Use network drives to manage content* section in this chapter to know how to move content from your hard disk to Alfresco server.

The issue with this approach is that you will have to manually update the metadata (properties) of the content.

Using web services to migrate content

Alfresco provides very rich web services API using which you can transfer your files as well as metadata to the Alfresco server.

Alfresco also provides RESTful Web Services (known as Web Scripts) using which you could migrate the content easily. RESTful Web Script is a very suitable and flexible solution to integrate Alfresco with any other application, and most likely the best solution among all other available options. More information about Web Scripts is provided in *Chapter 9, Integrating External Applications with Alfresco*.

With the web services approach, the content along with properties, associations, and security settings can be migrated efficiently.

Bulk import tools

There are many free and paid tools available in the market for bulk importing content into Alfresco. This is very useful when you are setting up the Alfresco document management system for the first time and would like to move massive amount of documents into Alfresco.

Alfresco provides an unsupported version of the Bulk Import tool for bulk importing content with versions and metadata into a repository from the Alfresco server's file system. For more details, refer the wiki at `http://wiki.alfresco.com/wiki/Bulk_Importer`.

This tool supports two kinds of bulk import:

- **Streaming import**: Files are moved into the repository content store by copying them in during the import.

- **In-place import**: Files are assumed to already exist within the repository content store, so no copying is required. This can result in a significant improvement in performance.

 This tool is a modified fork of an earlier version of the Bulk Filesystem Import Tool hosted on Google Code at `http://code.google.com/p/alfresco-bulk-filesystem-import`.

Summary

You can customize Alfresco features, such as smart spaces, library services, and security, to implement your enterprise document management requirements. Various interfaces, such as web client, CIFS, FTP, and WebDAV can be used to manage content in the Alfresco repository. You can enable discussions on spaces and individual documents to collaborate. You can enable RSS syndication to share information with external systems or users. Also, we understood various ways of migrating your existing content into Alfresco using free tools and web services.

6

Implementing Business Rules

So far, we have learned how to manage system users, user groups, space management, content management, check in and check out of documents, versioning of documents, and bulk upload using network uploads. In this chapter, we will learn about defining and using business rules as per custom business requirements.

By the end of this chapter, we will cover following areas:

- Automatically organize documents into specific spaces for bulk uploads
- Sequencing of business rules
- Run time-consuming business rules in the background
- Control document versions on specific documents in specific spaces
- Categorization of documents based on names
- Document event-driven e-mail notifications
- Document Transformation in various formats
- Dynamically add custom properties to documents based on the location
- Configure business rules as scheduled actions to run periodically
- Extend business rules using customized JavaScript files

Using business rules on spaces

You can leverage Alfresco's rules engine to define and deploy business rules based on your business needs, which does not require any programming expertise. You can choose to use a business rule from built-in rules or create your custom one. Business rules can be applied to the entire content or a specific content within a space, based on the conditions used in configuration. This section explains how a real-time business requirement can be achieved with business rules and the steps for business rule configuration.

Organizing documents automatically

In the previous chapter, we have learned to upload many documents (bulk upload) from your local folder to an Alfresco repository. However, each time we end up manually moving them to specific spaces to organize them inside the repository.

Let us consider a business scenario, where your finance department receives thousands of documents every day in an electronic format from various customers, vendors, and internal departments. Your finance department receives checks from customers in the form of scanned images, invoices from vendors in the form of PDF documents, and contracts and other documents from various departments in the form of Microsoft Word documents. They would like to upload them to the Alfresco repository and automatically organize them into various spaces, which are shown in the following screenshot:

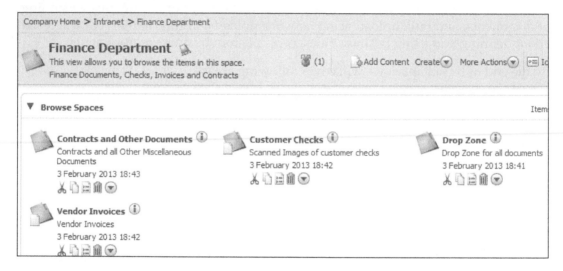

You can consider getting all these documents as bulk upload in to a **Drop Zone** (a space that is mapped as a network folder). If the document name contains Check (say Client1Check_7003.jpg), then move it to the **Customer Checks** space. If document name includes Invoice (say Vendor2Invoice_20060815.pdf), then move it to the **Vendor Invoices** space and for all other documents (say Project3Contract.doc) to the **Contracts and Other Documents** space. We will define a business rule that is triggered as soon as a document gets into the **Drop Zone**; it examines the filename and moves it to an appropriate space as defined above.

This example uses the space called **Finance Department**, which you have already created as a part of your Intranet sample application. As you have secured this space earlier, only administrator (`admin`) and users belonging to **Finance** group (`Tom FinExec` and `Hope Fin`) can add content in this space. We will use the **Tom FinExec** user to manage content in this space. Login as **Tom FinExec** and go to the **Company Home | Intranet | Finance Department** space and create the following four sub-spaces, as shown in the preceding screenshot:

- **Drop Zone**
- **Customer Checks**
- **Vendor Invoices**
- **Contracts and Other Documents**

Go to the **Drop Zone** space and follow the steps given below to define business rules on the **Drop Zone**. Click on the **More Actions** menu and select **Manage Content Rules**. It will display the **Content Rules** page, as shown here:

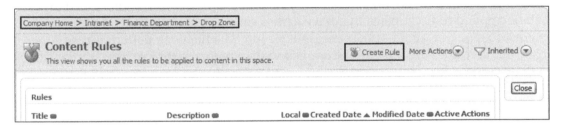

Clicking on the **Create Rule** link (as shown in the screenshot) opens the **Create Rule Wizard** window that is divided into four steps. The first step is to define the condition for selecting the documents, second step is to define the action, third step is to define when the rule should run, and the fourth step is to confirm and commit the business rule.

In the **Step One** window, we will see the **Select Condition** drop-down list, which displays all of the built-in conditions. We will examine all these conditions in later sections of this chapter. From the **Select Condition** drop-down list, select **Name contains value condition**.

Click on the **Set Values and Add** button to set the condition values, which allows you to set filename pattern, as shown in the following screenshot:

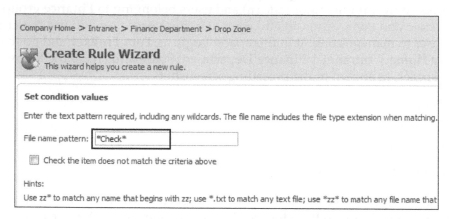

Select ***Check*** as the filename pattern. This means that this rule will be applied on any document which has Check anywhere in its name. For example, this rule will be applied to documents that have names such as Client1Check_7003.jpg, Check7003.jpg or 20060815Client1Check.jpg. The filename pattern is case insensitive, so the rule will also be applied to documents that have cHeCk anywhere in their name.

In the preceding screenshot, you can notice the checkbox which says **Check the item does not match the criteria**, to define the criteria which do not match this file pattern. This allows you to define the opposite criteria, that is, when Check is not found within the filename string. For this example, do not select this checkbox. Click on the **OK** button to confirm the condition.

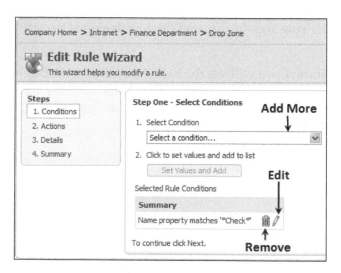

Selected Rule Conditions contain the **Summary** section, as shown in the preceding screenshot. You can edit the rule condition using the **Edit** (pencil) icon, and you can delete the rule condition using the **Remove** icon.

You can define as many conditions as you like by selecting the condition, and then clicking on the **Set Values and Add** button. All of the conditions have to be met to apply actions of the rule. Clicking on the **Next** button will take you to the **Step Two Actions** window.

In **Step Two**, you will notice that the **Select Action** drop-down list displays all the built-in actions. We will examine all these actions in the later sections of this chapter. From the **Select Action** drop-down list, select the **Move** action.

Click on the **Set Values and Add** button to set the action values. In the **Set action values** window, click on the **Click here to select the destination** link to select the destination space, which will display spaces, as shown in following screenshot:

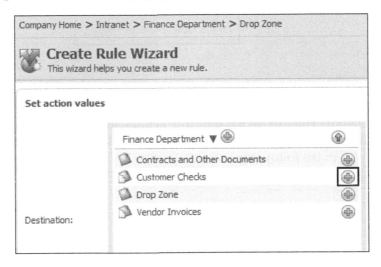

Select the **Customer Checks** space as the destination for the selected documents. Click on the **OK** button to confirm the action value:

Selected Rule Actions will be shown in the **Summary** section, as shown in the preceding screenshot. You can define multiple actions the same way we define multiple conditions. Clicking on the **Next** button will take you to the **Step Three** window, as shown in the following:

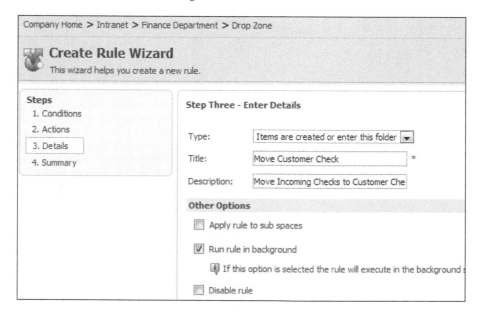

In the **Step Three** window, notice the business rule triggering options in the **Type** drop-down list. These triggering conditions will be applied on the **Drop Zone**, which is generated either via a web client, the Web Services API, or a protocol such as CIFS, WebDAV, and FTP. Alfresco comes with a property called `policy.content.update.ignoreEmpty`, which controls the execution behavior of a rule. Before Alfresco 4.1.2, the default value was `false`, but now it is `true`. It means if the node is empty, then the rule is not going to trigger at all. You can override this value in the `alfresco-global.properties` file.

- **Items are created or enter this folder**: Rule will trigger when a document is created, copied, moved, added, or dropped from the **Drop Zone** space.

- **Items are deleted or leave this folder**: Means this rule is triggered when a document is deleted or cut (to move to another space) from the **Drop Zone** space.

- **Items are updated**: Means this rule is triggered when a document in **Drop Zone** is updated.

Select the **Items are created or enter this folder** type and give a meaningful **Title** and **Description** to your rule. You can set various **Other options** for these triggering actions.

- **Apply rule to sub spaces**: Rule will be applied to **Drop Zone** and all of its sub-spaces.

- **Run rule in background**: Rule will be executed as a separate background process.

- **Disable rule**: Rule will be defined but not activated.

Select the **Run rule in background** checkbox, leaving the other checkboxes unselected as shown in the preceding screenshot. Clicking on the **Next** button will take you to the **Step Four** window, which displays a summary of the rule.

Click on the **OK** button in the **Summary** window to confirm the rule. You will notice that the rule is now listed for the **Drop Zone** space, as shown in the following screenshot. You can make changes to the existing business rule by clicking on the **Edit Rule** icon, as shown in the following screenshot:

Now follow the steps and similarly create another new rule in the **Drop Zone** space to move all of the documents that have "Invoice" (***Invoice***) in their name, to the **Vendor Invoices** space.

Define a third business rule in the **Drop Zone** space, which moves all the documents, other than **Checks** and **Invoices**, to the **Contracts and Other Documents** space. While selecting the condition, you have to select two conditions, as indicated in the following screenshot, to eliminate the previous two conditions and select all of the other documents. All the remaining steps are similar to those for the previous rules.

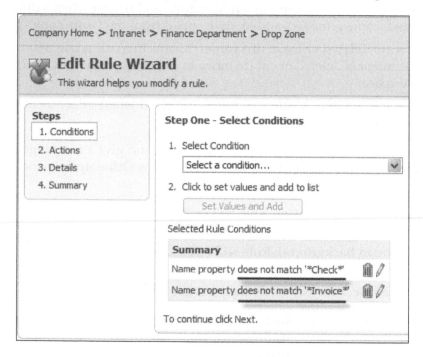

Once you are done with defining the rules, the **Content Rules** window for **Drop Zone** should display all the three rules, as shown in the following screenshot. This is an example how to set the rules based on the name property of the document. You can think of other useful scenarios that might be applicable to your business.

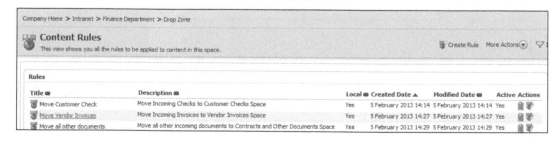

Now test the business rules set by you, by adding documents in the **Intranet |
Finance Department | Drop Zone** space. On your personal computer, create files
to test your business rules and choose filenames that match your business rules.
For example, create three files named `Client1Check_7003.jpg` (a scanned check),
`Vendor2Invoice_20060815.pdf` (a vendor invoice), and `Project3Contract.doc`
(a contract document). Drag and drop them to **Drop Zone**.

You will notice that the file containing "Check" has moved to the **Customer Checks**
space, the file containing "Invoice" has moved to the **Vendor Invoices** space, and the
third file has moved to the **Contracts and Other Documents** space automatically.
Current logged-in users must have a write permission to the targeted space in order
to successfully run this rule.

Running rules in the background

Typically, business rules are needed to run in real time, but in some business scenarios
that have complex or time-consuming processes might need to run in the background.
Consider a business rule that transforms 25 megabytes of Microsoft Word document
to PDF, sending e-mail notifications to hundreds of people, and so on. With Alfresco's
support of background rule processing, a user could continue with other tasks while
the rules are being executed in parallel in background. This allows users to continue
their actual work while the background processes execute in parallel.

Refer to the earlier screenshot (under the section describing **Step Three**), where
the rule has been selected to run in the background. The rule will execute in the
background, so the results may not appear immediately.

Dynamically adding properties to a document

In the previous chapter, you have edited the properties for each document. Those
properties are the default properties on every document. There might be situations
where you need additional properties for all of documents in a particular space. One
option is to change the Alfresco content model to include additional properties of a
document, but with this approach, all the documents in the repository will inherit
these properties. This will lead to overhead on the storage.

Another option is to define a business rule on a space to assign additional properties dynamically to all or a certain set of documents. Consider the example provided in the previous section, where the **Finance Department** space has various sub-spaces. Let us say you need to track the effective date and expiration date for all the documents in these sub-spaces. There is a built-in aspect called **Effectivity**, which adds two properties to a document namely `effective date` and `expiration date`.

An **Aspect** in Alfresco represents a collection of properties and as well as the behavior. Alfresco provides a set of Aspects to be readily used. Apart from these, you can also define your own aspects as per your business requirements. More details about changing the data model and defining custom aspects are covered in *Chapter 7, Extending Alfresco Content Model*.

Follow these steps to add the **Effectivity** aspect to all the documents in the **Finance Department** space:

1. In the **Finance Department** space, go to **More Actions | Manage Content Rules**.

2. Click on the **Create Rule** link, and you will see the **Create Rules Wizard**.

3. In the **First Step** window, from the **Select Condition** drop-down list, select **All Items**, and click on the **Add to List** button. Then click on the **Next** button.

4. In the **Step Two** window, from the **Select Actions** drop-down list, select **Add aspect**, and click on the **Set Values and Add** button. Select the **Effectivity** aspect and click **OK**. Then click on the **Next** button.

5. In the **Step Three** window, select **Items are created or enter this folder Type** and provide appropriate **Title** and **Description** for this rule. Select the **Apply rule to sub-spaces** checkbox to apply this rule to all the documents within the sub-spaces as well. Now, this rule will be applicable to all sub-spaces, including **Customer Checks**, **Vendor Invoices**, and **Contracts and Other Documents**.

6. Finish the rule.

Test this business rule by adding a document in the **Contracts and Other Documents** sub-space of the **Finance Department** space. You will notice two additional properties dynamically added to the document, as shown in the following screenshot:

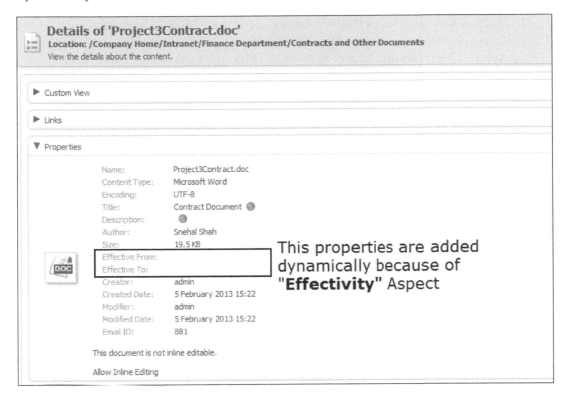

Automatic versioning of documents

In Alfresco, version control is disabled by default. It is a tedious job to enable versioning for each document if you have thousands of documents.

One option to enable versioning is to customize the Alfresco content model to enable versioning for every document. But this approach might be inefficient if you do not want to enable versioning for all the documents of same type. In the preceding example, **Drop Zone** is a temporary space; the **Customer Checks** space contains the scanned images of checks; we do not need versioning in such spaces, same case is for **Vendor Invoices**. The documents in the **Contracts and Other Documents** space require versioning support. Hence, it makes sense to enable versioning only for the documents in the **Contracts and Other Documents** space.

Follow these steps to enable versioning for all the documents in the **Contracts and Other Documents** space:

1. Go to the **Finance Department | Contracts and Other Documents** space.

2. Follow the same steps that we followed for the earlier **Effectivity** example, where we added the **Effectivity** aspect. Only change is to select a **Versionable** aspect instead of **Effectivity** in step 2.

3. Finish the rule.

Now versioning is enabled automatically for all the documents in the **Contracts and Other Documents** space. Test this business rule by adding a document to this space, and then verifying that the document now has a version history.

Sending notifications to specific people

E-mail notification is a powerful feature where specified people can be notified immediately on certain events in the content management system. You can notify people when documents are added to specific spaces or when changes are made to certain documents.

Let us say that in your organization, the Sales Group is responsible for following up on contracts with the customers. Follow these steps to send e-mail notifications to all of the people in Sales Group when a document in the **Contracts and Other Documents** space is updated.

1. From the **Company Home | Intranet | Finance Department | Contracts and Other Documents** space, we will create a new rule using the **Create Rules Wizard**. Follow the same steps that we followed earlier for other rules.

2. In the **Step One** window, from the **Select Condition** drop-down list, select **All Items** and click on the **Add to List** button. Then click on the **Next** button.

3. In the **Step Two** window, from the **Select Actions** drop-down list select **Send email**, and click on the **Set Values and Add** button.

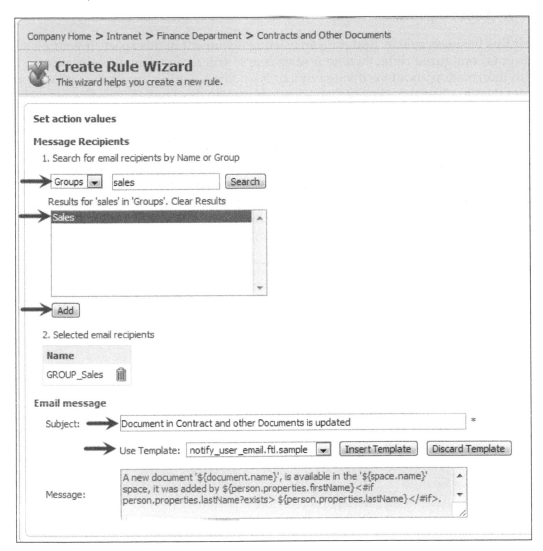

You will notice a **Set action values** window, as shown in the screenshot. Select the **Sales Group** as e-mail recipients. Use the built-in template called **notify_user_email.ftl.sample** and click on the **Insert Template** button. Give an appropriate subject for the e-mail.

4. In the **Step Three** window, select the **Items are updated Type**, to send notification on every document update.

5. Finish the rule.

Test this business rule by updating an existing document in this space. If your e-mail server is configured right, then your sales people will receive e-mail notifications with information about the document that is updated. Setting up your e-mail server is detailed in *Chapter 3, Getting Started with Alfresco* of this book.

Chaining all of the business rules

You can have as many business rules as required on a specific space. In a space, all the rules defined locally in that space, as well as all the rules inherited from the parent spaces, will be applied. For example, the **Contracts and Other Documents** space contains two local rules and one inherited rule (from its parent **Financial Department** space), as shown in the following screenshot:

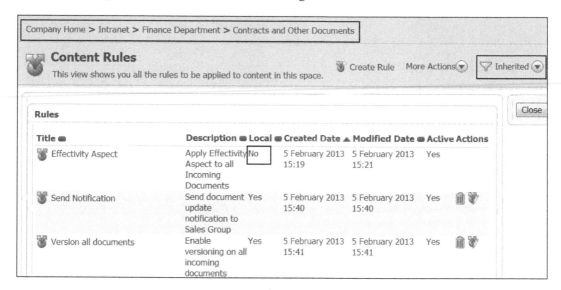

When a document is added to the **Contracts and Other Documents** space, it is automatically versioned due to the **Version all documents** local rule and two additional properties are added to the document due to the **Effectivity to all documents inherited** rule (from its parent space). When the document is updated, then the **Send notifications to Sales Group** local rule will be executed.

Hence, you can define business rules at spaces and sub-spaces and chain them together in a sequence to solve your business problem. For example, consider the following sequence of operations when a document titled `ProjectXYZ_Contract.doc` is dropped in the **Company Home | Intranet | Finance Department | Drop Zone** space:

1. Due to the business rules defined in **Drop Zone**, the document `ProjectXYZ_Contract.doc is` automatically moved to the **Finance Department | Contracts and Other Documents** space.

2. Due to the **Effectivity** rule defined in the parent **Finance Department** space, two properties (**Effective From** and **Effective To**) are added to the `ProjectXYZ_Contract.doc` document.

3. Due to the **Versioning** aspect rule defined in the space, the document `ProjectXYZ_Contract.doc` is automatically versioned.

However, there are certain things that you need to remember when applying multiple rules on a space.

The **Items are created or enter this folder** rule will not be applicable to the documents that are already present in that space prior to creating the rule. A rule will be applicable only to the documents that are added after the rule is created.

- If a space has more than one rule, all the rules will be executed in sequence.
- The rules defined in the parent spaces (with the **Apply rule to sub-spaces** option selected) will also be executed in the current space.

The **Items are created or enter this folder** rule in a space will be triggered when a document is uploaded to the space no matter how it is uploaded to alfresco repository of any available options such as Web Client, Web Services API, FTP, WebDAV, or CIFS.

Built-in business rules

You can leverage the built-in business rules by applying them on appropriate spaces. You have already used some of them in the previous sections. This section will provide you complete information about built-in business rules and the Alfresco rules wizard.

How these business rules work?

Alfresco's underlying framework supports the latest technology called **Aspect-Oriented Programming**, which is useful to change the behavior of the server dynamically without making changes to the code. Business rules leverage this technology so that you can define them at any space in Alfresco, and change the behavior of the system.

The Alfresco server follows a process to execute business rules:

- Whenever a document is added or updated to the space or removed from a space, Alfresco server checks whether that space or the parent spaces have any business rule to execute based on the triggering event type and business rule condition is satisfied.
- Then the server executes the action defined in the business rule.

The Alfresco Business **Rule Wizard** contains a sequence of screens (as **Steps**) to capture the following:

- The condition to apply the rule
- The action to be performed as a result
- The type of Event which triggers the action
- The summary of the business rule to commit

The screens and the built-in features are described in this section.

How the conditions are checked?

The first step in the **Rule Wizard** is to select the content items to apply the rule. The following can be checked against the content item:

- Does it have a particular name pattern?
- Is it in a particular category?
- Is it of a specific type or format?
- Does it have a particular aspect?
- Does it have a particular tag?
- Does a property have a specific text or date or text value?

You can define any number of conditions to select the content items. A content item must meet all the conditions to be selected.

You can also select a **Composite Condition**, where you can specify a number of conditions that can be combined by a logical "OR". This means that a content item must meet at least one of the conditions to be selected.

The following screenshot illustrates a composite condition where a content item will be selected if any of the conditions specified in summary section is true:

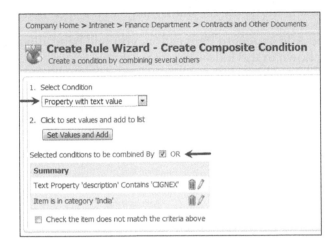

What actions are executed?

The second step in the **Rule Wizard** is to define the list of actions to be executed as a result. The following is the list of built-in actions to select from:

- **Add aspect**: Add additional properties and behavior to document
- **Add simple workflow**: Add approve and reject workflow
- **Check in**: Check in the document
- **Check out**: Check out the document to a space
- **Copy**: Copy the document to a space
- **Copy item to a folder in a web project**: Copy the document in web project's folder
- **Execute script**: Execute a JavaScript as an action
- **Extract common metadata fields**: Extract document metadata
- **Import**: Import as content package
- **Link to category**: Link document to a specific existing category
- **Move**: Cut document from the current space and move to specified space
- **Remove an aspect**: Remove property or set of properties from the document

- **Send an email**: Send e-mail notifications to specific users or groups of users

- **Specialize type**: Define the content type for the document

- **Transform and copy content**: Transform content say from DOC to PDF and move the resultant file to the specified space

- **Transform and copy image**: Transform and resize image say from JPG to PNG format and move the resultant image to the specified space

When you select the **Add aspect to item** action, you will have a list of built-in aspects to choose from, as shown in the following screenshot:

Each aspect has a different meaning, which are as follows:

- **Classifiable**: Enable **Categorization** so that the categories can be linked to the document.

- **Complianceable**: Add a compliance property called **Remove after** to the document.

- **Dublin Core**: Add Dublin core metadata to the document. Dublin core metadata includes properties such as **Publisher**, **Contributor**, **Subject**, and **Rights**.

- **Effectivity**: Add **Effectivity** properties called **Effective From** and **Effective To** to the document.

- **Email Alias**: Add a property called **Email Alias** to the document or space.

- **Emailed**: Add a set of properties called **Email Data** to the document. This is useful to capture the e-mail information when document is attached to an e-mail.

- **Index Control**: Allows controlling indexing using the **Is Indexed** and **Is Context Indexed** properties
- **Summarizable**: Add a property called **Summary** to the document.
- **Taggable**: Add a dynamic, taggable property to the document.
- **Templatable**: Enable the template view.
- **Versionable**: Enable versioning.

You can select one or more aspects to be applied as actions on the same document. For example, a document can have the **Effectivity** aspect as well as the **Taggable** aspect, as shown here:

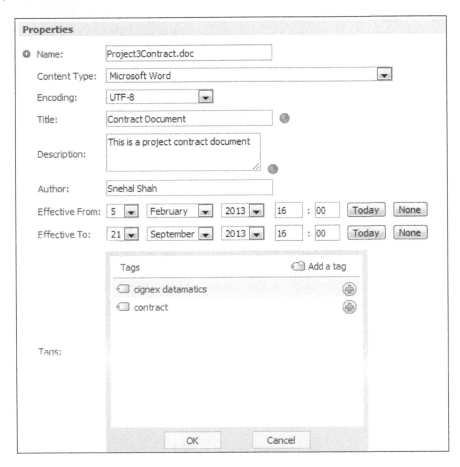

When are these rules triggered?

The third step in the **Rule Wizard** is to define the triggering event types. The rules are triggered by something happening and specified by the **Type** field as follows:

- **Items are created or enter this folder**: Content created or copied or moved into the space

- **Items are deleted or leave this folder**: Content either deleted or moved

- **Items are updated**: Content updated in the space

Applying actions to individual content

In any business, there will always be exceptions and there will be situations where you need to apply certain business rules to a specific document only. You can execute an action on a specific document directly without defining business rules on the space. This helps if you want to execute certain actions on an ad-hoc basis to specific documents.

The actions for content are invoked from the **View Details** page of a content item by clicking on the **Run Action** link in the **Actions** box. You are allowed to choose from the range of actions. You can also aggregate actions into a sequence that is applied in one go.

Removing an aspect from a content

You have applied the **Versionable** aspect to all the incoming documents in the **Finance Department | Contracts and Other Documents** space. Consider a scenario where you would not want a specific document to be versioned but all other documents to be versioned. The following are the steps for you to remove the **Versionable** aspect from a specific document:

1. Select a document in the **Finance Department | Contracts and Other Documents** space and go to the **View Details** page.

2. From the **Actions** box, click on the **Run Action** link, as shown in the following screenshot:

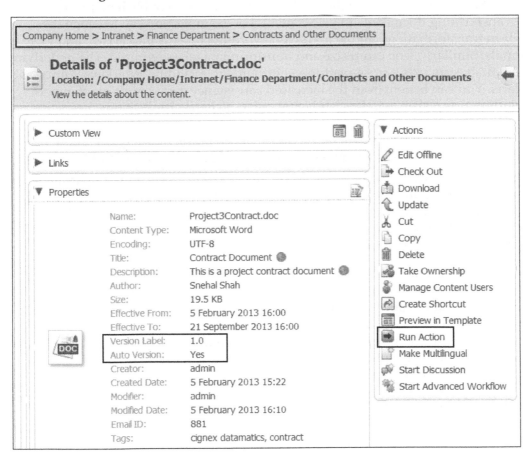

3. The **Run Action Wizard** window will show up. From the **Select Action** drop-down list, choose the **Remove aspect** action.

4. Click on the **Set Values and Add** button.

5. From the **Set action values** window, choose the **Versionable** aspect, and then click **OK**.

6. Once you complete executing the action, you will notice that the properties related to versioning have been removed and the document no longer maintains versions.

Similarly, for a specific document, you can use the **Run Action** option to execute actions, such as sending e-mail notifications, adding aspects, and executing scripts.

Handling content transformations

Content transformation simplifies and accelerates the web publishing process by transforming documents to web content. For example, you can leverage the built-in transformations engine to convert Word documents into HTML and PDF formats. Similarly, you can resize and transform images as required. The underlying technology supports a cross-platform environment, including Windows, Linux, and Solaris. You can benefit from the increased consistency across multiple channels, including print, Web, wireless, and other content-centric applications.

Transforming a Word document to PDF

Consider the following scenario as a staff member of the Marketing Department. You want to keep the source document in Microsoft Word format for editing, but you would like to send a PDF version of the document for publishing it on the website, and ensure that updating source document should update the transformed PDF document.

This section uses the space you have already created as a part of your Intranet sample application in *Chapter 5, Implementing Document Management*. As a part of the sample application, you will manage content in the **Intranet | Marketing Communications** space. As you have secured this space earlier, only administrator (**admin**) and users belonging to the **Marketing** group (**Peter Marketing** and **Harish Marketing**) can add content in this space. You can login as Peter Marketing to manage content in this space.

The following are the steps for you to transform and copy a Word document from the **Approved** space to a PDF document in the **Final** space:

1. Go to the **Company Home | Intranet | Marketing Communications | Switch to open source ECM | 04_Approved** space.
2. Follow the steps for creating a new rule and start a new **Create Rules Wizard**.
3. In the **Step One** window, from the **Select Condition** drop-down list, select **content of the mime type**, and click on the **Set Values and Add** button.

4. From the **Set condition values** window (shown in the following screenshot), choose **Microsoft Word** as the required source format, and click **OK**. Then click on the **Next** button:

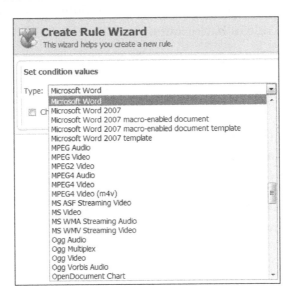

5. In **Step Two** window, from the **Select Actions** drop-down list, select **Transform and copy content**, and click on the **Set Values and Add** button.

6. From the **Set action values** window (shown in the following screenshot), choose **Adobe PDF Document** as the required format, and choose the **05_Final** space as the destination space to copy the transformed PDF document:

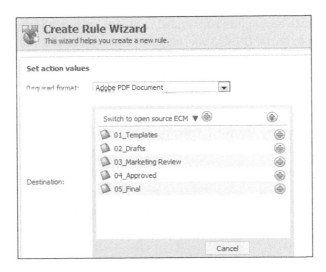

7. In the **Step Three** window, select **Items are created or enter this folder Type** and provide appropriate **Title** and **Description** for this rule. You can also select **Update Type**, if you would like to create the destination PDF document whenever you update the source Word document.

8. Select the **Run rule in background** checkbox and finish the rule.

Now, transformation is enabled automatically for all of the Microsoft Word documents in this space. Whenever a Word document is uploaded or moved to the **04_Approved** space, a PDF version of the document will be created in the **05_Final** space.

Test this business rule by adding a Word document to this space and testing the PDF document in the **05_Final** space.

Resizing and transforming images

Consider a scenario where you would like to keep the source image in PNG format and publish a fixed size (say 200 x 200 pixels), JPEG version of the image on the website.

PNG is an extensible file format for the lossless, portable, well-compressed storage of raster images. Indexed-color, grayscale, and true color images are all supported, plus an optional alpha channel for transparency.

Joint Photographic Experts Group (JPEG) is a compression method standardized by ISO. The JPEG compression format was standardized by ISO, and JPEG images are widely used on the Web. The amount of compression can be adjusted to achieve the desired trade-off between file size and visual quality. Progressive JPEG is a means of reordering the information so that, after only a small part has been downloaded, a hazy view of the entire image is presented rather than a crisp view of just a small part. It is part of the original JPEG specification, but was not implemented in web browsers until rather later on, around 1996. It is now fairly widely supported.

The following are the steps for you to transform and resize an image from PNG format to JPEG format:

1. Go to the **Company Home | Intranet | Marketing Communications | Switch to open source ECM | 04_Approved** space.

2. Follow the steps for creating a new rule and start a new **Create Rules Wizard**.

3. In the **Step One** window, from the **Select Condition** drop-down list, select **Items with the specified mime type**, and click on the **Set Values and Add** button.

4. From the **Set condition values** window, choose **PNG Image** as the required source format, and click **OK**. Then click on the **Next** button.

5. In the **Step Two** window, from the **Select Actions** drop-down list, select **Transform and copy image to a specific space**, and click on the **Set Values and Add** button.

6. From the **Set action values** window (shown in the following screenshot), choose **JPEG Image** as the required format. In the **Options** box, provide the resize options as **-resize 200x200**. Choose the **05_Final** space as the destination space to copy the transformed image:

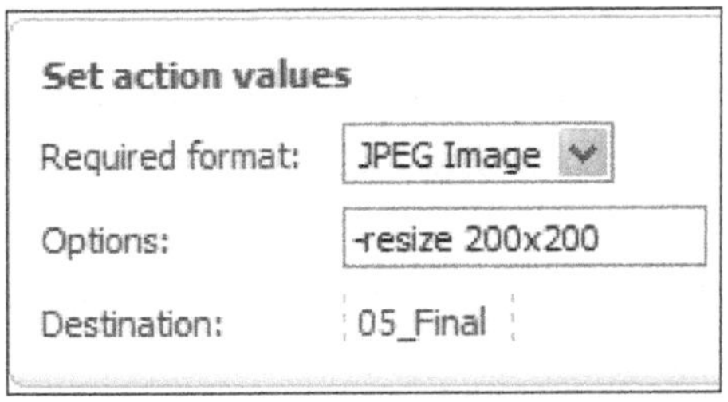

Set action values

Required format:	JPEG Image
Options:	-resize 200x200
Destination:	05_Final

7. In the **Step Three** window, select the **Items are created or enter this folder Type**, and provide appropriate **Title** and **Description** for this rule.

8. Select the **Run rule in background** checkbox and finish the rule.

Test this business rule by adding a PNG image to the **04_Approved** space and testing the resized JPEG image in the **05_Final** space.

OpenDocument Format

OpenDocument Format (ODF) is an Open XML-based file format suitable for office applications. ODF is an open format for saving and exchanging office documents such as memos, reports, books, spreadsheets, databases, charts, and presentations.

The goal of ODF is to deliver an application-independent format that is vendor-neutral. This helps you to view, use, and update documents in the future when you no longer have software bought many years ago. You will have an advantage of your content being shared across governments, and citizens, or multiple departments and organizations.

Alfresco's Virtual File System offers a simple shared drive interface to any office application. Microsoft Office and Open Office users alike can save or drag content into intelligent **Drop Zones**, where rules and actions transparently convert incoming content into the ODF vendor-neutral format.

The ability to share documents across organizations without being tied to the technology, strategy, pricing, and decisions of a single supplier is critical for businesses and government agencies today. The ability to access content without having a format and technology imposed on all users is equally important. Alfresco's ODF Virtual File System addresses these key issues.

Converting Microsoft Office documents to ODF

The example in this section uses the **Intranet | Marketing Communications** space to create and test the ODF Virtual File System. The following are the steps for you to convert a Microsoft Word document to an ODF office document:

1. Go to the **Company Home | Intranet | Marketing Communications** space.

2. Create a space called **Marketing Documents** and create two sub-spaces under that space called **Inbox** and **ODF Virtual File System**.

3. Go to the **Company Home | Intranet | Marketing Communications | Marketing Documents | Inbox** space.

4. Follow the steps for creating a new rule and start a new **Create Rules Wizard**.

5. In the **Step One** window, from the **Select Condition** drop-down list, select **Items with the specified mime type**, and click on the **Set Values and Add** button.

6. From the **Set condition values** window, choose **Microsoft Word** as the required source format, and click **OK**. Then, click on the **Next** button.

7. In the **Step Two** window, from the **Select Actions** drop-down list, select **Transform and copy content**, and click on the **Set Values and Add** button.

8. From the **Set action values** window (shown in the following screenshot), choose **OpenDocument Text (OpenOffice 2.0)** as the required format, and choose the **ODF Virtual File System** space as the destination space to copy the converted document:

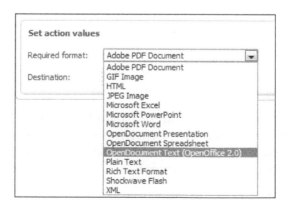

9. In the **Step Three** window, select **Items are created or enter this folder Type**, and provide appropriate **Title** and **Description** for this rule.

10. Select the **Run rule in background** checkbox and finish the rule.

Whenever a Microsoft Word document is uploaded or moved to the **Inbox** space, an ODF version of the document will be created in the **ODF Virtual File System** space.

Add a second business rule to the **Inbox** space, which converts the incoming Microsoft Excel documents to an **OpenDocument Spreadsheet** format, and copies it to the **ODF Virtual File System** space.

Add a third business rule to the **Inbox** space, which converts the incoming Microsoft PowerPoint documents to an **OpenDocument Presentation** format, and copies it to the **ODF Virtual File System** space.

The business rules on the **Inbox** space should be as shown in the following screenshot:

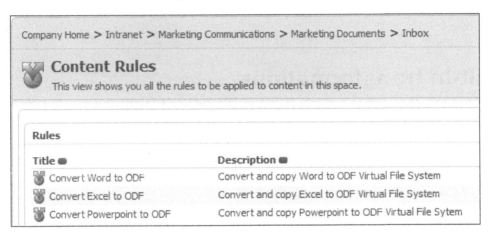

Test the business rules by copying Microsoft Word, Microsoft Excel, and Microsoft PowerPoint documents into the **Inbox** space. You should see the converted documents in the **ODF Virtual File System** space, as shown in the following screenshot:

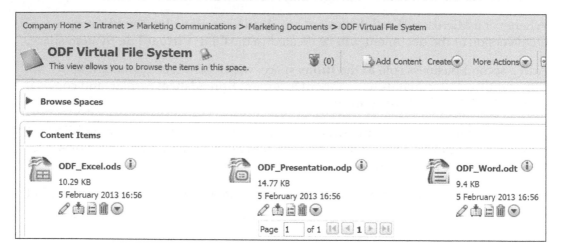

Built-In transformations

You can apply the built-in content transformations in a variety of ways. For example, your marketing department might want to keep the source presentation in Microsoft PowerPoint format, and publish the Flash version of the presentation on the website.

Try out the following transformations:

- Microsoft PowerPoint to Flash
- HTML to PDF
- HTML to JPEG image
- PDF to Text Document

Try out various document and image transformations available out of the box. In order to achieve this transformation, OpenOffice must be configured, as mentioned in *Chapter 2, Installing Alfresco*.

Executing JavaScript as business rules

The built-in rules might not be sufficient to address all your business requirements. You can execute a JavaScript as an action in your business rule. If you need even more flexibility, you can write business rules in custom JavaScript files and execute them as actions.

Using built-in JavaScript as actions

You can execute a JavaScript by selecting **Execute script** as an action in the **Rules Wizard**. The **Rules Wizard** displays the list of built-in JavaScript, such as:

- `alfresco docs.js.sample`: Search and log all the docs containing Alfresco text

- `append copyright.js.sample`: Append the copyright line to text or HTML files

- `backup.js.sample`: Simple document backup script

- `backup and log.js.sample`: Back up files and log the date and time

- `example test script.js.sample`: Example of various API calls

- `start-pooled-review-workflow.js`: Starts the Pooled Review and Approve workflow

- `test return value.js.sample`: Return a value from a script — for the command servlet

Extending business rules with custom JavaScript

The **Rules Wizard** lists all the JavaScript files that are available in the **Company Home | Data Dictionary | Scripts** space. You can extend your business rules by writing your own JavaScript files and placing them in this space so they are visible to the **Rules Wizard**.

This is a very powerful feature. Consider the following scenario. Let us say your Finance Department has received a contract with a dollar amount as one of the properties. You can trigger JavaScript code that updates an external financial system with the information extracted from the document.

Consider another example, where your HR group maintains certain corporate forms and policies that are time bound, that is, which expire after some time. The example in this section uses the **Company Policies** space to execute JavaScript code as a business rule. The JavaScript verifies the **Effective To** property of all the content items in space and moves the expired content to the **Archived** space.

Setting up the Corporate Forms Space

To set up a corporate space to implement the example mentioned above, go to the **Company Home | Intranet | Company Policies** space. Create a space called **Corporate Forms** and create two sub-spaces under that space called **In Use** and **Archived**.

- The **In Use** space contains forms that are actively in use by the corporation
- The **Archived** space contains forms that are no longer used

Go to the **Company Home | Intranet | Company Policies | Corporate Forms** space and create a business rule to add the **Effectivity** aspect to all of the incoming documents in the sub-spaces. Refer the section titled *Dynamically add properties to a document* in this chapter.

Now go to the **Company Home | Intranet | Company Policies | Corporate Forms | In Use** space and add a few sample documents. For each document in the **In Use** space, you will notice that two additional properties, namely **Effective From** and **Effective To**, are present. Update the **Effective From** and **Effective To** properties of the documents, making sure that some documents are expired as of today, so that they are ready to be moved to the **Archived** space. Refer to the following screenshot for more details:

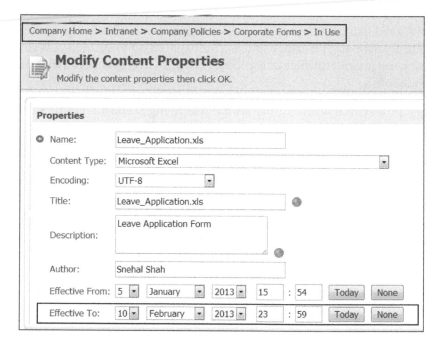

Creating custom JavaScript

Create a JavaScript file called `chapter6_archive_expired_content.js` in your personal computer with the following code. The script verifies the content in the **Intranet | Company Policies | Corporate Forms | In Use space** and moves the expired content (where the **Effective To** property value is less than or equals to today's date) to the **Archived** space:

```
// ------------------------------------------------------------
// Name: chapter6_archive_expired_content.js
// Description: Moves expired content to Archived space
// ------------------------------------------------------------
var activeFolder   = companyhome.childByNamePath("Intranet/Company
Policies/Corporate Forms/In Use");
var archivedFolder = companyhome.childByNamePath("Intranet/Company
Policies/Corporate Forms/Archived");

if(activeFolder != null)
{
    var i=0;
    var today = new Date();

    activeChildren   = activeFolder.children;
    activeTotal      = activeChildren.length;

    for(i=0; i<activeTotal;i++)
    {
        child = activeChildren[i];
        if(child.properties["cm:to"] <= today)
        {
            child.move(archivedFolder);
        }
    }
}
```

Go to the **Company Home | Data Dictionary | Scripts** space and click on the **Add Content** link and upload the `chapter6_archive_expired_content.js` file that you have created. You will need administrative rights to access **Data Dictionary** and its sub-spaces.

Executing custom JavaScript as an action

You can apply a business rule on a space in two different ways. One way is to create a business rule and another way is to execute the action manually as the **Run Action** command. For this example, let us follow the latter approach:

1. Go to the **Company Home | Intranet | Company Policies | Corporate Forms | In Use** space.

2. Go to the **View Details** page of the **In Use** space by clicking on the **More Actions | View Details** menu.

3. From the **Actions** box, click on the **Run Action** link.

4. The **Run Action Wizard** window will show up. From the **Select Action** drop-down list, choose the **Execute a script** action.

5. Click on the **Set Values and Add** button.

6. From the **Set action values** window, choose the `chapter6_archive_expired_content.js` script, and click **OK**.

7. Once you complete executing the rule, you will notice that all the expired documents in the **In Use** space have been moved to the **Archived** space.

 Note that the script uses the full path of spaces and hence it can be executed from any space.

Try creating another custom JavaScript that moves the effective content (the **Effective To** property value should be greater than today's date) from the **Archived** space to the **In Use** space. Test the custom script by applying it on the **Archived** space content. This is useful when you edit the form in the **Archived** space and make it effective again.

JavaScript API

The Alfresco JavaScript API allows script writers to develop JavaScript compatible files that access, modify, and create Alfresco repository Node objects. By using the API script, writers can find nodes (via XPath), walk node hierarchies, perform searches (including Lucene fulltext searches), examine and modify the value of node properties, and modify the aspects applied to a node. In addition, scripts can create new files and folder objects and copy/move/delete nodes. All the usual Alfresco security and ACL permissions apply.

As JavaScript is a standard language, there are many web resources, online tutorials, and books to help developers in writing JavaScript files. It is suggested that potential script writers read up on JavaScript resources before starting to script the Alfresco repository.

The `example test script.js.sample` JavaScript file in the **Company Home | Data Dictionary | Scripts** space lists examples of various Alfresco API calls.

The following are some of the objects available to scripts by default in the root scope:

Named object	Description
companyhome	The Company Home node.
userhome	The current user's Home Space node.
person	The Node representing the current user's Person object.
space	The current space node (If any). Note that for a script executing from a rule, the space object will be the space that the rule resides in.
document	The current document.
script	The node representing the script itself.
search	A host object providing access to Lucene and Saved Search results.
people	A host object providing access to people and groups in Alfresco.
session	Session related information (`session.ticket` for the authentication ticket).
classification	Read access to classifications and root categories.

 A detailed description about the Alfresco 4.0 JavaScript API is provided at `http://wiki.alfresco.com/wiki/4.0_JavaScript_API`.

Scheduled actions

Alfresco provides a way to execute these actions automatically at a specified time as well. This would be helpful in use cases, such as periodically checking document status, or generate reports, or execute business rules and notify certain users.

Alfresco supports **Scheduled actions** so that you could configure certain actions to run at certain time automatically. A scheduled action is made up of three parts:

- A cron expression: Defines the time
- A query template: Generates a query to select set of nodes (space and documents)
- An action template: The action to be executed

The query could be of any type like a document has an aspect, it was created in the last month, it is due in the next month, it is in a category, and so on.

Example to archive expired content

We have considered a scenario where the HR group maintains certain corporate forms and policies that are time bound, that is, which will expire after some time. In the earlier example, you manually ran the script. In this section, you are going to create a scheduled action, which executes the custom JavaScript `chapter6_archive_expired_content.js` automatically, every 15 minutes.

You need to create a schedule action XML configuration file in your extensions folder to specify the scheduled time and the custom JavaScript. You will find the scheduled action sample file `scheduled-action-services-context.xml.sample` in the following location:

- **JBoss**: `<alfresco>/jboss/server/default/conf/alfresco/extension`
- **Tomcat**: `<alfresco>/tomcat/shared/classes/alfresco/extension`

This file has many good sample scheduled actions for your reference. Copy the scheduled action sample file as `scheduled-action-services-context.xml` in the same folder, and edit the file as follows:

```xml
<?xml version='1.0' encoding='UTF-8'?>
<!DOCTYPE beans PUBLIC '-//SPRING//DTD BEAN//EN'
    'http://www.springframework.org/dtd/spring-beans.dtd'>

<beans>
    <!--
    Define the model factory used to generate object models
    suitable for use with freemarker templates.
    -->
    <bean id="templateActionModelFactory" class=
"org.alfresco.repo.action.scheduled.FreeMarkerWithLuceneExtensionsMod
elFactory">
        <property name="serviceRegistry">
            <ref bean="ServiceRegistry"/>
        </property>
    </bean>
    <!--
    Example Chapter 6 : Action Definition
    Action is to execute the "Company Home > Data Dictionary >
     Scripts > chapter6_archive_expired_content.js" script
```

```
    -->

    <bean id="chapter6_runScriptAction" class=
"org.alfresco.repo.action.scheduled.SimpleTemplateActionDefinition">
        <property name="actionName">
            <value>script</value>
        </property>
        <property name="parameterTemplates">
            <map>
                <entry>
                    <key>
                        <value>script-ref</value>
                    </key>
        <value>\$\{selectSingleNode('workspace://SpacesStore',
'lucene', 'PATH:"/app:company_home/app:dictionary/app:scripts/
cm:chapter6_archive_expired_content.js"' )\}</value>
                </entry>
            </map>
        </property>
        <property name="templateActionModelFactory">
            <ref bean="templateActionModelFactory"/>
        </property>
        <property name="dictionaryService">
            <ref bean="DictionaryService"/>
        </property>
        <property name="actionService">
            <ref bean="ActionService"/>
        </property>
        <property name="templateService">
            <ref bean="TemplateService"/>
        </property>
    </bean>

    <!--
    Example Chapter 6 : The query and scheduler definition
    Query    - No specific query is used
    Scheduler - Run the script for every 15 minutes
    Action   - Call chapter6_runScriptAction defined above
    -->
    <bean id="chapter6_runScript" class=
"org.alfresco.repo.action.scheduled.CronScheduledQueryBasedTemplateAct
ionDefinition">
        <property name="transactionMode">
            <value>UNTIL_FIRST_FAILURE</value>
```

```
        </property>
        <property name="compensatingActionMode">
            <value>IGNORE</value>
        </property>
        <property name="searchService">
            <ref bean="SearchService"/>
        </property>
        <property name="templateService">
            <ref bean="TemplateService"/>
        </property>
        <property name="queryLanguage">
            <value>lucene</value>
        </property>
        <property name="stores">
            <list>
                <value>workspace://SpacesStore</value>
            </list>
        </property>
        <property name="queryTemplate">
            <value>PATH:"/app:company_home"</value>
        </property>
        <property name="cronExpression">
            <value>0 0/15 * * * ?</value>
        </property>
        <property name="jobName">
            <value>jobD</value>
        </property>
        <property name="jobGroup">
            <value>jobGroup</value>
        </property>
        <property name="triggerName">
            <value>triggerD</value>
        </property>
        <property name="triggerGroup">
            <value>triggerGroup</value>
        </property>
        <property name="scheduler">
            <ref bean="schedulerFactory"/>
        </property>
        <property name="actionService">
            <ref bean="ActionService"/>
        </property>
        <property name="templateActionModelFactory">
            <ref bean="templateActionModelFactory"/>
```

```
            </property>
            <property name="templateActionDefinition">
              <ref bean="chapter6_runScriptAction"/>
              <!-- This is name of the action (bean) that gets run -->
            </property>
            <property name="transactionService">
                <ref bean="TransactionService"/>
            </property>
            <property name="runAsUser">
                <value>System</value>
            </property>
        </bean>
    </beans>
```

Restart the Alfresco server to ensure that the configuration changes are effective. Now go to the **Company Home | Intranet | Company Policies | Corporate Forms | In Use** space, and add few sample documents. For each document in the **In Use** space, update the **Effective To** date property in such a way that these documents will be moved to the **Archived** space at specified time. Note that the custom JavaScript executes every 15 minutes to move the effective documents to the **Archived** space.

XML configuration file for scheduled actions

Note that the `scheduled-action-services-context.xml` file has two blocks of XML configuration.

The first block, which starts with `<bean id="chapter6_runScriptAction"`, defines the action. This is where you specified the custom JavaScript to be executed. The important things to consider are as follows:

- `actionName`: The name of the action (the bean name for the implementation).
- `parameterTemplates`: A map of names and value templates. These are action-specific.

The second block, which starts with `<bean id="chapter6_runScript"`, contains the query and scheduler definitions. This is where you specified the time interval to execute custom JavaScript every 15 minutes. The important things to consider are as follows:

- `transactionMode`: The transaction mode to be used.
    - `ISOLATED_TRANSACTIONS`: For each node, the action is run in an isolated transaction. Failures are logged.
    - `UNTIL_FIRST_FAILURE`: For each node, the action is run as an isolated transaction. The first failure stops this.

- ○ ONE_TRANSACTION: The actions for all nodes are run in one transaction. One failure will roll back all.

- queryLanguage: The query language to be used.

- stores: A list of stores to query (currently only one store is supported).

- queryTemplate: The template string to build the query.

- cronExpression: The cron expression to define when the query runs.

- jobName: The name of the scheduled job.

- jobGroup: The group for the scheduled job.

- triggerName: The name for the trigger.

- triggerGroup: The group for the trigger.

- runAsUser: The user with whose identity the action will run.

- templateActionDefinition: The bean that defines the action.

The cron expression

A cron expression is of six or seven text fields that are separated by whitespace.

 A detailed description about the cron expression can be found at http://wiki.alfresco.com/wiki/Scheduled_Actions.

Field Name	Position	Mandatory	Allowed Values	Special Characters
Seconds	1	Yes	0-59	, - * /
Minutes	2	Yes	0-59	, - * /
Hours	3	Yes	0-23	, - * /
Day of Month	4	Yes	1-31	, - * ? / L W
Month	5	Yes	1-12 or JAN-DEC	, - * /
Day of Week	6	Yes	1-7 or SUN-SAT	, - * ? / L #
Year	7	No	empty, 1970-2099	, - * /

An explanation to special characters is provided in the following table:

*	All values.
?	No specific value.
-	This is used to specify a range. 1-5 in day of the week field would mean, "on days 1, 2, 3, 4 and 5". 0-11 in the hour's field would mean "each hour in the morning".
,	A list of values. In the minutes field, 0,15,30 would mean, "when the minute is 0, 15, or 30". In the day field, MON, TUES would mean, "on Mondays and Tuesdays".
/	After a value specifies increments. In the minutes field, 0/15 is equivalent to 0,15,30,45; */15 is equivalent to */15; and 10/15 is equivalent to 10,25,40,55.
L	Last.
W	The nearest week day.
LW	The last week day of the month.
#	The nth day of the week.

Summary

Business rules make a space smart. Rules are very powerful and flexible to address most of your business requirements. You can leverage the **Rules Wizard** to use the built-in rules as well as custom rules to address client specific scenarios. You can have the rules as scheduled actions and can be extended using custom JavaScript files. The best practice is to document the business rules, as they could affect the entire site globally. In the next chapter, you will learn about flexibility of Alfresco to extend content model with various possible options.

7
Extending Alfresco Content Model

In the previous chapters you were able to create content that had standard properties such as name, description, author, and so on . You were able to add aspects such as Effectivity and Dublin Core to the content using business rules. What if you need to have specific custom properties as per your business needs, custom content that handles the data, and business rules in a way to suit your business needs? Alfresco content model is highly configurable and easily extendable as per your business requirements. In this chapter, we will understand the process for customizing the content model. We will define our own custom properties and custom content type to extend the capabilities of as per business application needs.

By the end of this chapter you will have learned how to:

- Configure a custom content model
- Define and add custom aspect (set of properties)
- Define and use your custom content models
- Define associated documents for your custom content types
- Define constraints for your custom properties
- Preview content using custom presentation templates
- Enable dynamic customization of models without requiring a restart of the Alfresco server

Custom configuration

The Alfresco repository enables support for the storage, management, and retrieval of content. The content may range from coarse-grained documents to fine-grained snippets of information such as XML elements. The Alfresco repository supports a rich Data Dictionary where the properties, associations, and constraints of content are present to describe the structure of such content.

The Repository Data Dictionary is by default pre-populated with definitions that describe common content constructs such as folders, files, and metadata schemes. However, the data dictionary is extensible, it allows the repository to manage new types of content since each business application will have its own content requirements. This chapter explains the main concepts behind the Data Dictionary, such as how to define new types of content and use them in an application.

The following table contains the description of some of the key terms used:

Key term	Description
Property	A metadata which describes the content. For example, Author is a property which specifies the person who authored the content.
Content	Binary file along with a set of properties (metadata)
Association	Relationship between content items
Constraint	Constraints control the input property values. For example, you can specify the author name to be not more than 40 characters.
Aspect	A collection of properties and also defines the behavior.
Content Type	Provides a structure to create content. The structure includes the nature of content, properties, aspects, constraints, and associations.

Configuration files for default content model

The core Alfresco configuration files are present in the application war file and get expanded out once the server starts. This location, referred to as `<configRoot>`, varies depending on the environment that Alfresco runs in.

- **JBoss:** `<JBOSS_HOME>/server/default/tmp/deploy/tmp*alfresco-exp.war/WEB-INF/classes`
- **Tomcat:** `<TOMCAT_HOME>/webapps/alfresco/WEB-INF/classes`

A content model is a collection of related content types and aspects. The default configuration files for the content model maintained by Alfresco are contained in **<configRoot>** | **alfresco** | **model** folder.

The Alfresco repository also comes with several domain models described as following:

- `contentModel.xml`: It describes the content domain model such as Folder, File, Person, Category, and Dublin Core
- `systemModel.xml`: It describes system-level Repository concepts
- `applicationModel.xml`: It describes Alfresco application model
- `dictionaryModel.xml`: It describes the dictionary meta model
- `bpmModel.xml`: It describes the business process model
- `cmisModel.xml`: It describes the CMIS model definitions

Dictionary meta model contains data type definitions for basic types of property. Using this model, a developer can create new or extend existing property using Java classes.

Several other models to support the implementation of services are defined by the repository such as user management, versioning, actions, advanced workflow, collaboration, calendar events and rules. You can examine the other configuration files in the `<configRoot>/alfresco` folder.

You should not modify the default content models located in the `<configRoot>/alfresco` folder. This will break the Alfresco upgrades.

In the next section, we will go through the correct mechanism for adding custom content models in Alfresco.

Configuration files for Custom Content Model

Alfresco is built on Spring, which is the leading platform to build and run enterprise Java applications. Alfresco configuration and customization concepts are based on Spring framework.

For more information about Spring, refer http://www.springsource.org/.

You can override or extend the Alfresco content model by placing the custom configuration files in a folder. This location, referred to as `extension`, varies depending on the environment that Alfresco runs in.

- **JBoss**: `<JBOSS_HOME>/server/default/conf/alfresco/extension`
- **Tomcat**: `<TOMCAT_HOME>/shared/classes/alfresco/extension`

When you install Alfresco, the sample custom-content files are copied to `extension` folder for your reference. You can also examine the sample custom-configuration files in `extension` folder.

The steps to define a custom model in `extension` folder are as follows:

1. Create a custom model Spring context file.
2. Create a custom model definition file.
3. Create a custom web client configuration file.

The custom model Spring context file informs Spring how to bootstrap or load the custom model definition file. The custom model definition file defines your custom content types, aspects, and associations. The custom web client configuration file contains information to display these custom content types, aspects, and associations. The relationship between these files is shown as follows:

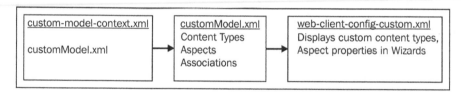

Custom model context file

The custom model context file defines a Spring bean which will be used to bootstrap the definition of your custom model. It lists one or more custom model files. This will be loaded on server startup.

Create a custom model context file and name the file as `<your-custom-model-name>-context.xml`, for example `intranetModel-context.xml`. It is very important for you to note that Alfresco server recognizes the context files that end with `-context.xml`. This is a default behavior of Alfresco to read files ending with `-context.xml` to set up the context and load related spring beans.

The following is the content of custom-model-context.xml.sample file in the extension folder. Note that the custom model context file defines customModel.xml as the custom model file.

```xml
<?xml version='1.0' encoding='UTF-8'?>
<!DOCTYPE beans PUBLIC '-//SPRING//DTD BEAN//EN'
    http://www.springframework.org/dtd/spring-beans.dtd'>

<beans>

    <!-- Registration of new models -->
    <bean id="extension.dictionaryBootstrap"
          parent="dictionaryModelBootstrap"
          depends-on="dictionaryBootstrap">
        <property name="models">
            <list>
                <value>alfresco/extension/model/customModel.xml</value>
            </list>
        </property>
    </bean>

</beans>
```

Custom model file

- Custom model file contains the definitions for the custom content types, aspects, and content associations.

A copy of customModel.xml file already exists in extension folder. Please copy the customModel.xml file to <extension>/model folder. If you examine the customModel.xml file, you will notice a custom namespace for all the variables called custom. XML Namespaces provides a method to avoid element name conflicts. Hence every custom variable will have a prefix custom in this file as follows:

```xml
<namespace uri="custom.model" prefix="custom"/>
```

Custom web client configuration file

A copy of web client configuration file web-client-config-custom.xml already exists in extension folder. This web client configuration file ensures that the custom content types and aspects are visible in Alfresco web client application. In this file, you can also override the default web client configuration provided out-of-the-box.

Hierarchy of configuration files

The hierarchy of configuration files is shown as follows:

```
<configRoot>/alfresco (folder)         <extension> (folder)
-> xyz-context.xml (files)             -> xyz-context.xml (files)
-> web-client-config-xyz.xml (files)   -> web-client-config-custom.xml (files)
-> model (sub-folder)                  -> model (sub-folder)
   -> xyzModel.xml (files)                -> xyzModel.xml (files)
```

During the start up, Alfresco server reads the configuration files in the following order:

1. Context files and then the model files in the `<configRoot>/alfresco` folder.

2. Context files in the `<extension>` folder and model files as per the configuration in context file. In our case, it is from `<extension>/model` sub folder.

3. Web client configuration files in the `<configRoot>/alfresco` folder.

4. Web client configuration files in the `<extension>` folder.

Custom aspect

Let us assume that your sales people would like to track all their proposals related to a customer. They would like to search the documents and execute business rules based on the customer details. They would like to capture the following customer details for all the documents in sales department space:

- Customer name
- Contact name at customer place
- Contact person's phone number
- Project identification number internally allocated
- Is this a new customer?

You can extend the Alfresco content model to include the properties listed above as an aspect. Aspect definition can contain associations along with properties. Associations are covered in a later section called *Custom associations*. This aspect can be applied to sales department space.

When do you need a custom aspect?

The Alfresco content model is designed to be extensible. You can introduce custom properties to your objects in two different ways. One way is to create a custom aspect called `Customer Details` and dynamically attach it to the documents in a specific space. The custom aspect would define the required properties. The other way is to create a custom content type called `Proposal Document` and define all the required properties on the type itself. The process of creating custom content types is explained in detail in the next section of this chapter.

The following are the advantages of having custom aspect over custom content type:

- Flexibility: By having a custom aspect will give you flexibility to add additional set of properties to the documents in specific spaces. For example, you can define these additional properties to the documents in Customer Checks spaces.

- Efficiency: Since these properties are applied selectively to certain documents in certain spaces only, you will consume limited storage in relational database for these properties.

- Behavior: A custom aspect can introduce new behavior for objects. Using Spring's aspect oriented support, you can define new beans which intercept content-related events and handle them according to your exact needs.

- Extension: A custom aspect can extend other aspect. It also gives you a flexibility of overriding some of the properties of parent aspect.

The following is the disadvantage of having custom aspect over custom content type:

- Dependency: You cannot define the dependency with other aspects. For example if you want the Effectivity aspect to always be associated with customer details aspect, you need to make sure you attach both the aspects to the documents.

Steps to add a custom aspect

The following process needs to be followed to add a custom aspect to the Alfresco content model:

- Define the custom properties and type of properties
- Extend the Alfresco content model with custom aspect
- Configure web client application for custom aspect
- Restart Alfresco to make sure the new changes are effective

Each one of these steps is explained in detail in the following sections:

Defining a custom aspect

You need to define the name of the custom aspect and the properties. For each property you need to define the type of the property. Some of the property types are listed in the following table. For complete listing of property types, please refer `<configRoot>/Alfresco/model/dictionaryModel.xml`.

Property data type	Description
text	Any string or name
content	Binary Document
int	Integer or Number
long	Big integer
float	Number with decimal values such as interest rate 7.5
date	Year, Month, and Day
datetime	Timestamp
Boolean	true or false
category	Reference to a category within a classification
path	URL Path

You may consider calling your custom aspect as `Customer Details` with the following properties:

Property name	Property label	Property type	Mandatory	Default value
CustomerName	Customer Name	text	No	None
CustomerContactName	Customer Contact Name	text	No	None
CustomerContactPhone	Customer Contact Phone	text	No	None
CustomerProjectID	Customer Project ID	Int	No	None
NewCustomer	New Customer	boolean	No	true

Extend content model with custom aspect

Now that you have identified your custom aspect and the properties, the next step is to extend the Alfresco content model with the XML representation of your custom aspect.

Go to the `extension` folder and rename `custom-model-context.xml.sample` file as `custom-model-context.xml`. Now examine the contents of `custom-model-context.xml` file that includes the name of custom content model file, `customModel.xml`.

Open the `customModel.xml` file and add your custom aspect as follows before the last line `</model>`.

```
<aspects>

    <!-- Definition of new Content Aspect: Customer Details -->
    <aspect name="custom:CustomerDetails">
        <title>Customer Details</title>
        <properties>
            <property name="custom:CustomerName">
                <title>Customer Name</title>
                <type>d:text</type>
                <protected>false</protected>
                <mandatory>false</mandatory>
                <multiple>false</multiple>
            </property>
            <property name="custom:CustomerContactName">
                <title>Customer Contact Name</title>
                <type>d:text</type>
            </property>
            <property name="custom:CustomerContactPhone">
                <title>Customer Contact Phone</title>
                <type>d:text</type>
            </property>
            <property name="custom:CustomerProjectID">
                <title>Customer Project ID</title>
                <type>d:int</type>
            </property>
            <property name="custom:NewCustomer">
                <title>New Customer</title>
                <type>d:boolean</type>
                <default>true</default>
            </property>
        </properties>
    </aspect>

</aspects>
```

A property can have various elements as shown in the following table:

Property element	Description
Property name	Unique ID of the property along with namespace.
Title	This element will act as label to display a meaningful name for the property.
Type	Specifies the data type of the property such as text, int, and date.
Protected	If this element is set to `true`, then it becomes a read-only property in Alfresco web client. Default value is `false`, which means users can edit the properties in web client.
Mandatory	If this element is set to true, then the value has to be either set or entered by the user before saving it. Default value is `false`, which means the property is optional.
Multiple	If this element is set to `true`, then the property can have multiple values set. Default value is `false`.
Default	Provides the given default value to the property.

Localizing the model using message resources

Every Property, Data Type, Aspect, and Association defined as a model has a title and description. To support localization of a model, Alfresco allows augmenting the model XML values with Locale specific values. This can be achieved by registering a Java Resource Bundle for each language variant.

The Alfresco models (System, Content, Application, and Dictionary) are each packaged with a default Resource Bundle. Refer the file `content-model.properties` located at `<TOMCAT_HOME>\webapps\alfresco\WEB-INF\classes\alfresco\messages`.

The key structures within each Resource Bundle are:

- `<model_prefix>_<model_name>.[title|description]`
- `<model_prefix>_<model_name>.<model_element>.<element_prefix>_<element_name>.[title|description]`

Structure details are as follows:

`<model_prefix>`	The namespace prefix used in model
`<model_name>`	Name of a Model
`<model_element>`	One of type, aspect, property, association, datatype
`<element_prefix>`	Element namespace prefix
`<element_name>`	Element Name

 For more information on localization configuration for model, refer `http://wiki.alfresco.com/wiki/Data_Dictionary_Guide#Registering_a_Model_Resource_Bundle`.

Configuring a web client for custom aspect

The content model is extended with custom aspect called `Customer Details`. You need to make sure the web client program recognizes this new custom aspect and displays it in the web based interface. In order to make this happen you need to configure the web client file `web-client-config-custom.xml` in `extension` folder.

Open the `web-client-config-custom.xml` file and add the following XML code before the last line `</alfresco-config>`.

```
<!-- Lists the custom aspect in business rules Action wizard -->
<config evaluator="string-compare" condition="Action Wizards">
   <aspects>
      <aspect name="custom:CustomerDetails"/>
   </aspects>
</config>
```

This code ensures that the new aspect called `Customer Details` is listed in the business rules **Set action values** page as shown in screenshot under the section *Using custom aspect as business rule*.

Open the `web-client-config-custom.xml` file and add the following XML code before the last line `</alfresco-config>`.

```
<!-- Displays the properties in view details page -->
<config evaluator="aspect-name" condition="custom:CustomerDetails">
   <property-sheet>
      <separator name="sepCust1" display-label="Customer Details"
component-generator="HeaderSeparatorGenerator" />
      <show-property name="custom:CustomerName"/>
      <show-property name="custom:CustomerContactName"/>
```

```
            <show-property name="custom:CustomerContactPhone"/>
            <show-property name="custom:CustomerProjectID"/>
            <show-property name="custom:NewCustomer"/>
      </property-sheet>
</config>
```

This code ensures that the properties added to the content due to `Customer Details` aspect will be displayed in content's view details page as shown in screenshot under the section *Using custom aspect as business rule*. The `separator` tag defined above is useful to group these properties and to separate them from the other list of properties in the property sheet by creating a bar with label Customer Details.

Now, restart Alfresco to make sure the changes are effective.

Using a custom aspect as a business rule

Now that the `Customer Details` aspect is available you can use it to add to your documents as if this aspect is available to you out-of-the-box.

You can define a business rule to include customer details dynamically to all the documents in a space. Consider the example provided earlier where `Sales Department` needs to maintain the customer details for all their proposals. Follow the given steps to add `Customer Details` aspect to all the documents in **Sales Department | Proposals** space.

1. Go to the **Company Home | Intranet | Sales Department** space and create a subspace for proposals called **Proposals**.

2. Ensure that you are in the **Company Home | Intranet | Sales Department | Proposals** space.

3. In the **Proposals** space click the **More Actions | Manage Content Rules**.

4. Click on the **Create Rule** link and you will see the **Create Rules Wizard**.

5. In **Step One**, select **Condition** drop-down list, select **All Items**, and click on the **Add to List** button. Then click on the **Next** button.

6. In **Step Two**, select **Actions** drop-down list, select **Add** aspect to item, and click on the **Set Values** and **Add** button.

7. In **Set action values** pane, select **Customer Details** aspect as shown in the following screenshot and then click **OK**. Finally click on the **Next** button.

8. In **Step Three**, select the **Inbound** option from the **Type** drop-down list, provide appropriate name and description for this rule.

9. Check **Apply rule to sub spaces** option and then click **Finish** to apply the rule.

Test this business rule by adding a document in the **Proposals** space. You will notice five additional properties dynamically added to the document. Add some meaningful customer data and click the **OK** button.

Navigate to the document and click on the **View Details** icon to view the details page. You will notice that the properties added to the document due to custom aspect are visible in the details page of the document as shown in the following screenshot:

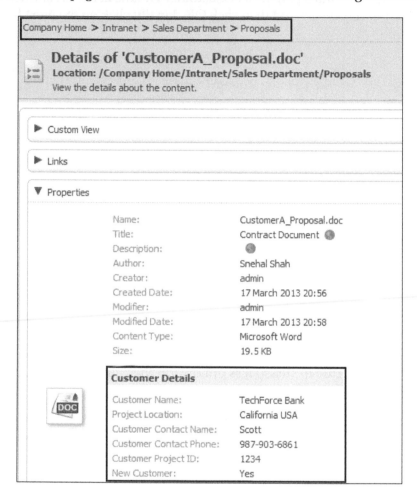

Similarly create a business rule on **Company Home | Intranet | Financial Department | Customer Checks** space to add customer details to all the incoming checks as shown in the following screenshot. Add an image file (scanned customer check) to this space and notice that the check has additional properties as per the customer details aspect.

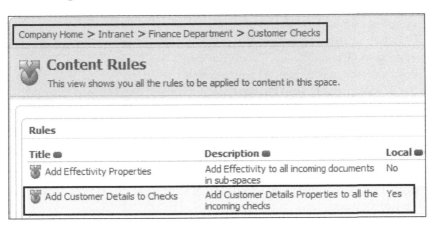

Constraints

A Constraint controls the input value of a property. Constraints can be used to validate the input values and to ensure certain predefined values for the properties. Constraints are defined separately from content types and aspects and referenced within a property type definition.

Constraint types

Alfresco provides four types of constraints out-of-the-box as follows. Apart from these, the custom constraints can be defined using Java Programming language.

- **REGEX**: ensures that a property value matches a regular expression pattern
- **LIST**: ensures that a property value is picked up from the list of predefined values
- **MINMAX**: ensures that the given property value falls within a defined numeric range
- **LENGTH**: ensures that the given property value falls within a defined character length range

REGEX

The following REGEX expression ensures that the property `filename` does not match the defined regular expression pattern. This constraint thus ensures that the file name value entered does not contain the specified special characters.

```
<constraint name="custom:filename" type="REGEX">
    <parameter name="expression">
        <value><![CDATA[[^\"\*\\\>\<\?\/\&\;]+]]></value>
    </parameter>
    <parameter name="requiresMatch">
        <value>false</value>
    </parameter>
</constraint>
```

LIST

The following LIST constraint restricts the property `officelocation` value to a predefined list of values:

```
<constraint name="custom:officelocation" type="LIST">
    <parameter name="allowedValues">
        <list>
            <value>California USA</value>
            <value>New Jersey USA</value>
            <value>London UK</value>
            <value>Ahmedabad India</value>
            <value>Singapore</value>
        </list>
    </parameter>
</constraint>
```

MINMAX

The following MINMAX constraint restricts the property `age` value to a predefined value:

```
<constraint name="custom:age" type="MINMAX">
    <parameter name="minValue">
        <value>1</value>
    </parameter>
    <parameter name="maxValue">
        <value>100</value>
    </parameter>
</constraint>
```

LENGTH

The following LENGTH constraint restricts the property `password` value to a predefined character length (between 6 characters and 10 characters length):

```
<constraint name="custom:password" type="LENGTH">
    <parameter name="minLength">
        <value>6</value>
    </parameter>
    <parameter name="maxLength">
        <value>10</value>
    </parameter>
</constraint>
```

Applying a constraint

To apply a constraint, it has to be referred from within a property definition.

Let us add few constraints to the existing Customer Details aspect which we created earlier in this chapter.

Go to the `extension` folder and open the `customModel.xml` file and add or change the following lines highlighted (bold). In the following model, we add two constraints named `custom:office_list`, to provide a predefined list of office locations and `custom:name_length`, to restrict the character length in a name. Apply the `name_length` constraint to `CustomerName` property and `office_list` constraint to a new property called Project Location.

```
<namespaces>
    <namespace uri="custom.model" prefix="custom"/>
</namespaces>

<constraints>
<constraint name="custom:office_list" type="LIST">
    <parameter name="allowedValues">
        <list>
            <value>California USA</value>
            <value>New Jersey USA</value>
            <value>London UK</value>
```

```xml
                <value>Ahmedabad India</value>
                <value>Singapore</value>
            </list>
        </parameter>
</constraint>

<constraint name="custom:name_length" type="LENGTH">
        <parameter name="minLength">
            <value>3</value>
        </parameter>
        <parameter name="maxLength">
            <value>20</value>
        </parameter>
</constraint>
</constraints>

<types>
  ..........
</types>

<aspects>

    <!-- Definition of new Content Aspect: Customer Details -->
    <aspect name="custom:CustomerDetails">
        <title>Customer Details</title>
        <properties>
            <property name="custom:CustomerName">
                <title>Customer Name</title>
                <type>d:text</type>
                <protected>false</protected>
                <mandatory>false</mandatory>
                <multiple>false</multiple>
                <constraints>
                    <constraint ref="custom:name_length"/>
                </constraints>
            </property>

            <property name="custom:ProjectLocation">
```

```
        <title>Project Location</title>
        <type>d:text</type>
        <constraints>
          <constraint ref="custom:office_list"/>
        </constraints>
      </property>

      <property name="custom:CustomerContactName">
        <title>Customer Contact Name</title>
        <type>d:text</type>
      </property>

      <property name="custom:CustomerContactPhone">
        <title>Customer Contact Phone</title>
        <type>d:text</type>
      </property>

      <property name="custom:CustomerProjectID">
        <title>Customer Project ID</title>
        <type>d:int</type>
      </property>

      <property name="custom:NewCustomer">
        <title>New Customer</title>
        <type>d:boolean</type>
        <default>true</default>
      </property>
    </properties>
  </aspect>

</aspects>
```

In the `<extension>/web-client-config-custom.xml` file, include the new property `ProjectLocation`, under the `CustomerDetails` aspect.

Restart Alfresco to make sure the changes are effective. Now log in to web client application to test the constraints you have added to `Customer Details` properties.

Go to the **Company Home | Intranet | Sales Department | Proposals** space and view details of one of the existing documents. Edit the properties and type the customer name value with more than 20 characters and click on the **OK** button. You will see the following message as the LENGTH constraint applied on Customer Name property:

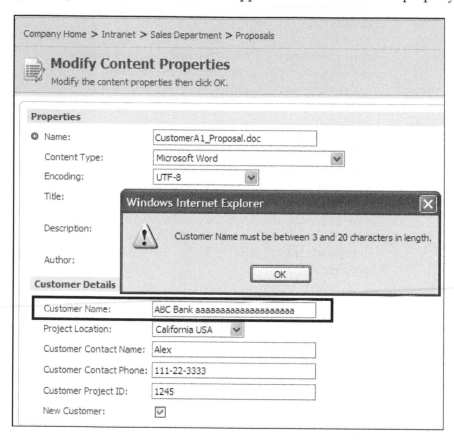

You will notice the list of allowed values for Project Location property due to LIST constraint as shown in the following screenshot:

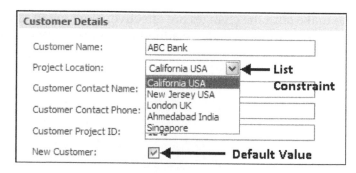

Advanced property sheet configuration

When configuring properties for end user display using web client property sheet window, you can control what labels to be shown for a specific language. You can also control how the properties can be viewed and edited.

Display labels

By default the property labels are taken from the `<title>` value of the property element as given in the content model file. Alternatively it is possible to override this with the display-label attribute in the `web-client-config-custom.xml` file.

However, the property labels displayed are not internationalized (for various languages). In order to achieve internationalized display labels, use `display-label-id` attribute in the `web-client-config-custom.xml` file shown as follows:

```
<property-sheet>
    ------------
    <show-property name="size" display-label-id="size" />
```

The label text will be displayed based on the language selected by the user when they log in to Alfresco Explorer. For example, for English users, the label will be displayed as Size and for Spanish users the label will be displayed as tamaño.

All the label IDs and labels used in Alfresco Explorer are defined in `<config>/messages/webclient.properties` file. To support the labels for a specific language, you need to have the language specific properties file. For example, the properties file for German language labels is `webclient_de_DE.properties`.

You can add your custom label ids and label text for specific languages in `webclient.properties` file in the `<extension>/messages` folder.

Conditional display of properties

By default all the properties are displayed when reading and editing the property information. To prevent a property from appearing when editing the property sheet, add the `show-in-edit-mode` attribute with a value of `false` shown as follows:

```
<property-sheet>
    ------------
    <show-property name="size" display-label-id="size" show-in-edit-
mode="false" />
```

Similarly to prevent a property from appearing when reading the property sheet, add the `show-in-view-mode` attribute with a value of `false`.

Converters

Converters allow you to display actual values of the properties with desired format. For example, if you want to display the property called size in a particular format (number of bytes), then you have to use the converters. There are built-in converters shown in the following code. For the list of available converters, refer `<config>/web-client-config-properties.xml` file. You can also write your own custom converters using Java language.

```
<property-sheet>
    ------------

    <show-property name="size" display-label-id="size" converter="org.
alfresco.faces.ByteSizeConverter" show-in-edit-mode="false" />
```

Component generators

In web client application, the property sheet will render the control appropriate for the property type. To assign a control other than the default to a property, you have to use the `component-generator` attribute. For example, the following component generator creates a bar with tag Customer Details to separate the properties and to group them under a specific tag.

```
<config evaluator="aspect-name" condition="custom:CustomerDetails">
    <property-sheet>
        <separator name="sepCust1" display-label="Customer Details"
component-generator="HeaderSeparatorGenerator" />
```

The following are some of the built-in generators:

- `MimeTypeSelectorGenerator`: Useful to list select mime type
- `MultilingualTextAreaGenerator`: Useful to show text box
- `SpaceIconPickerGenerator`: Useful to list select icon for a space

There are built-in generators as the ones we just saw. You can also write your own custom generators using Java language. Refer Alfresco wiki page `http://wiki.alfresco.com/wiki/Component_Generator_Framework` to implement a custom component generator.

Custom content type

Let us say your Corporate Communications group would like to create press releases and execute certain business rules if the content is of type press release. They would like to have the additional properties listed as follows:

- PR Person's Name
- PR Person's Email
- PR Person's Phone
- PR Released Date
- Content to be automatically versioned for every update

When do you need a custom content type?

Earlier in this chapter you have understood the advantages and disadvantages of having custom aspect over a custom content type. You need a custom content type if that type of content has some significance for you such as in the case of press release. You will be able to add Press Release content in any space anywhere as you like without going through the hassle of applying all kinds of business rules on spaces. Similarly with custom content type you will be able to execute business rules based on the content type. For example, you can send notifications to certain people when a Press Release is created.

Steps to add a custom content type

The following process needs to be followed to add a custom content type to Alfresco content model. You must restart the Alfresco server after following the given steps:

1. Define custom content type, properties, and mandatory aspects
2. Extend content model with custom content type
3. Configure web client for custom aspect

Defining a custom content type

You may consider calling your custom content type as `Press Release` with the properties as shown in the following table:

Property type	Property name	Property label
text	PRName	PR Person Name
text	PREmail	PR Person Email
text	PRPhone	PR Person Phone
Int	PRDate	PR Released Date

Extending content model with a custom content type

The next step is to extend the Alfresco content model with the XML representation of your custom content type.

Open the `customModel.xml` file and add the following XML code before the `aspects` block:

```xml
<types>

    <!-- Definition of new Content Type: Press Release -->
    <type name="custom:pressrelease">
        <title>Press Release</title>
        <parent>cm:content</parent>
        <properties>
            <property name="custom:PRName">
                <title>PR Person Name</title>
                <type>d:text</type>
            </property>
            <property name="custom:PREmail">
                <title>PR Person Email</title>
                <type>d:text</type>
            </property>
            <property name="custom:PRPhone">
                <title>PR Person Phone</title>
                <type>d:text</type>
            </property>
            <property name="custom:PRDate">
                <title>PR Released Date</title>
                <type>d:date</type>
```

```
        </property>
      </properties>
    </type>

  </types>
```

Configuring a web client for custom content type

You need to make sure the web client program recognizes this new custom content type and displays various dialog screens in web-based interface. In order to make this happen you need to configure the web client file `web-client-config-custom.xml` in extension (`<alfresco_install_folder>\tomcat\shared\classes\alfresco\extension`) folder.

Open the `web-client-config-custom.xml` file and add the following lines of code that are highlighted.

```
    <!-- Lists the custom aspect and custom content type in business
rules Action wizard -->
    <config evaluator="string-compare" condition="Action Wizards">
      <aspects>
        <aspect name="custom:CustomerDetails"/>
      </aspects>
      <subtypes>
        <type name="custom:pressrelease"/>
      </subtypes>
    </config>
```

This code ensures that the `Press Release` content is shown in Business Rules Action wizard.

Add the following XML code just before the block that we just saw. This code ensures that the press release content type is listed when you create new content.

```
    <config evaluator="string-compare" condition="Content Wizards">
      <content-types>
        <type name="custom:pressrelease" />
      </content-types>
    </config>
```

Add the following XML code just before the block that we just saw. This code ensures that the properties are available to edit in **edit properties** window for press release content.

```
<config evaluator="node-type" condition="custom:pressrelease">
  <property-sheet>
    <show-property name="mimetype"
      display-label-id="content_type"
      component-generator="MimeTypeSelectorGenerator" />
    <show-property name="size"
      display-label-id="size"
      converter="org.alfresco.faces.ByteSizeConverter"
      show-in-edit-mode="false" />
    <show-property name="custom:PRName" />
    <show-property name="custom:PREmail" />
    <show-property name="custom:PRPhone" />
    <show-property name="custom:PRDate" />
  </property-sheet>
</config>
```

After making changes to the configuration files, restart Alfresco.

Adding a custom content type

The new content type called `Press Release` is now available to add anywhere you like. On your personal computer, create a sample press release in HTML format and save it as `PressRelease1.html` file. Follow the given steps to upload your `Press Release` content:

1. Go to **Company Home | Intranet | Press and Media** space and create a subspace called **Press Releases**.

2. Ensure that you are in the **Company Home | Intranet | Press and Media | Press Releases** space.

3. In the space header, click the **Add Content** link. The **Add Content** dialog appears.

4. To specify the file that you want to upload, click on the **Browse** button. In the **File Upload** dialog box, browse to the file you have created earlier on your personal computer (`PressRelease1.html`) and click the **upload** button.

5. A message informs you that your upload was successful as shown in the screenshot on the next page.

6. Select **Press Release** as **Type** from the drop-down list.

7. Click the **OK** button to confirm.

8. A **Modify Content Properties** dialog box appears as shown in the screenshot on the next page.

9. The **Name, Tile, Description,** and **Author** properties are basic properties populated by default. **Auto Version** is a mandatory aspect that was attached to the press release content. The properties **PR Person Name, PR Person Email, PR Person Phone,** and **PR Released Date** are part of press release content. Also notice that **Edit Inline** is checked for HTML content. Fill up appropriate data for properties.

10. Click on the **OK** button to save and return to the **Press Releases** space.

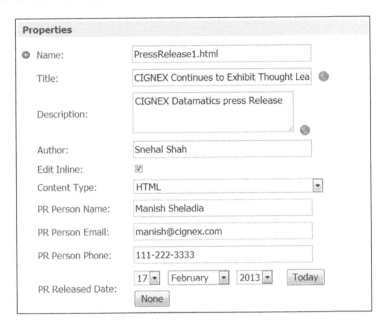

Creating Press Release as HTML Content

You can also create Press Release as HTML content in web client directly without uploading the file from your personal computer. To create an HTML file in a space, follow the given steps:

1. Ensure that you are in the **Company Home | Intranet | Press and Media | Press Releases** space.

2. In the header, click **Create | Create Content**. The first pane of the **Create Content Wizard** appears as shown in the following screenshot:

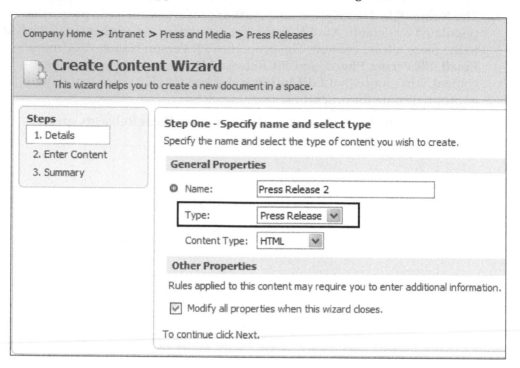

3. You need to provide **Name** of the HTML file, select **HTML** as **Content Type**, and click the **Next** button.

4. The **Enter Content** pane of the wizard will appear. You can enter some sample press release text using the text formatting features.

5. After the content is entered and edited in the **Enter Content** pane, click on **Finish**.

6. You will see **Modify Content Properties** screen to update metadata associated with the content as shown in the screenshot under the section **Add Custom Content Type**.

7. You can modify properties as required and click on the **OK** button. You can preview the newly created **Press Release** by clicking on it.

Creating business rules targeting custom content type

You can create a business rule targeting custom content type. For example, you can send notifications to concerned people when a press release is added. While creating the business rule select **content of type or sub-types** as condition, Click on the **Set Values and Add** button to set the condition. This will pop up a dialog box for setting condition values as shown in the following screenshot and select the **Press Release** option as **Type**.

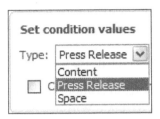

Custom associations

You can associate content within Alfresco repository with one or more content items. An association enables content to be related to other content.

Alfresco supports two types of associations. The first type is **reference association** where you refer other content items within a content item. For example you can associate a legal agreement document with master contract document. Hence you can refer to the associated master contract document, whenever you review the legal agreement. In reference association if you delete one of the documents, the other document will not be deleted.

The second type of association is **child association** where content (such as space) contains other content items. The child association is employed when the child of the association should not exist when the source goes away. It is a similar concept of cascaded delete in relational database or deleting a folder in Microsoft Windows Explorer. If you delete the parent then all their children that have parent as primary will be deleted. The association engine of Alfresco allows using secondary parents for managing multiple parenthoods to avoid redundancy of nodes.

You can create your own custom associations as per your business requirements. The process of creating and using custom associations is explained in this section.

When do you need an association?

Reference associations are very useful in various business applications. Let us say in your engineering department space, if you have a `testing` `document` you might want to associate it with an appropriate `requirements` `document`. Similarly you might want to refer some documents in your `Press` `Release`. Association is required if you want to refer or include some other content within your content.

Defining custom association

As an example, we will create two associations to the `Press` `Release` custom content type. The first one is the reference association called `Press` `Release` `Image`, which refers to an image within Alfresco repository. The second association is called `Press` `Release` `Files`, which refers to one or more files within Alfresco repository.

In order to define these associations in content model, open the `customModel.xml` file and insert the highlighted XML code within Press Release content type definition as shown in the following code. For `Press` `Release` `Files` association, the option `<many>` is set to `true` to indicate more than one reference file.

```xml
<!-- Definition of new Content Type: Press Release -->
<type name="custom:pressrelease">
    <title>Press Release</title>
    <parent>cm:content</parent>
    <properties>
        <property name="custom:PRName">
            <title>PR Person Name</title>
            <type>d:text</type>
        </property>
        <property name="custom:PREmail">
            <title>PR Person Email</title>
            <type>d:text</type>
        </property>
        <property name="custom:PRPhone">
            <title>PR Person Phone</title>
            <type>d:text</type>
        </property>
        <property name="custom:PRDate">
            <title>PR Released Date</title>
            <type>d:date</type>
        </property>
    </properties>
    <associations>
        <association name="custom:PRImage">
```

```
            <title>Press Release Image</title>
            <source>
                <mandatory>false</mandatory>
                <many>true</many>
            </source>
            <target>
                <class>cm:content</class>
                <mandatory>false</mandatory>
                <many>false</many>
            </target>
        </association>
        <association name="custom:PRFiles">
            <title>Press Release Files</title>
            <source>
                <mandatory>false</mandatory>
                <many>true</many>
            </source>
            <target>
                <class>cm:content</class>
                <mandatory>false</mandatory>
                <many>true</many>
            </target>
        </association>
    </associations>
    <mandatory-aspects>
        <aspect>cm:versionable</aspect>
    </mandatory-aspects>
</type>
```

It is very important to follow a specific sequence while defining the content model, otherwise Alfresco errors out while startup. First define parent, followed by properties, associations, and then mandatory aspects. It is best practice to modify the Alfresco content model definitions only by adding new definitions. It is also recommended that, one should not remove any existing model definition from Alfresco. Removal of existing custom definition would require you to remove all content referring to that content model from Alfresco repository.

You need to make sure the web client program recognizes these new custom associations in the web-based interface. Open the `web-client-config-custom.xml` file and insert the following lines of code that are highlighted:

```
<config evaluator="node-type" condition="custom:pressrelease">
    <property-sheet>
        <show-property name="mimetype"
          display-label-id="content_type"
          component-generator="MimeTypeSelectorGenerator"/>
        <show-property name="size" display-label-id="size"
          converter="org.alfresco.faces.ByteSizeConverter"
          show-in-edit-mode="false" />
        <show-property name="custom:PRName" />
        <show-property name="custom:PREmail" />
        <show-property name="custom:PRPhone" />
        <show-property name="custom:PRDate" />
        <show-association name="custom:PRImage"/>
        <show-association name="custom:PRFiles"/>
    </property-sheet>
</config>
```

Using custom association

Go to the **Company Home** | **Intranet** | **Press and Media** | **Press Releases** space and upload an image and two text files to test the custom associations. Click on the **view details** icon of one of the press releases (HTML file) in the space which you have created earlier. Click on the **edit properties** icon to select the associations as shown in the screenshot on the next page.

For **Press Release Image** association, select the image you have uploaded earlier. Similarly for the **Press Release Files** association, select both the text files you have uploaded earlier. Click on the **OK** button to update the properties. In the view details page you will notice the files associated with the press release.

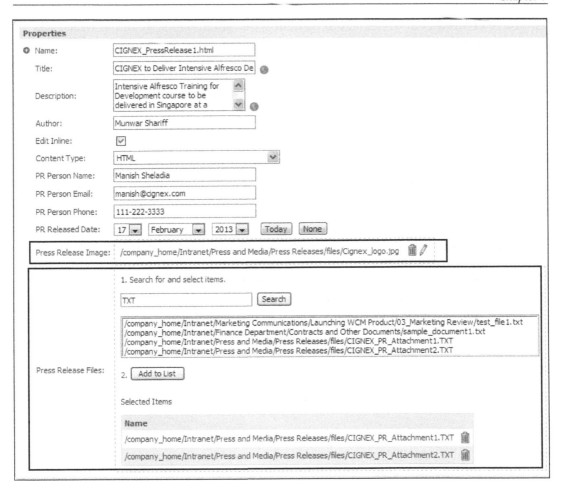

Presentation template for custom content type

The space **Company Home | Data Dictionary | Presentation Templates** contains presentation templates which are useful to consolidate and view content in various different ways. The presentation templates are written in Freemarker template language and will have .ftl extension.

You have created your own custom content type called `Press Release` which has the following things:

- Press release content in HTML format
- Properties about PR person details such as PRName, PREmail
- Press Release Image
- Related Files

You can create your own custom presentation template to preview the press release in a specific format as per your business requirements. The following are the steps to create your custom presentation template:

1. Create a file called `chapter7_PressReleaseTemplate.ftl` in your personal computer with the following code. This is Freemarker template code to display press release information in two columns. First column displays the image (associated with this press release) followed by the actual press release content in HTML format. The second column displays the properties (PR Contact details) followed by the list of associated files.

```
<#-- Shows Press Release content with Custom Properties,
Associated Image and Files -->

<H3> ${document.properties.name} </H3>
<HR>

<#if document?exists>
    <table>
      <tr>
        <td valign="top">
        <#if document.assocs["custom:PRImage"]?exists>
          <#list document.assocs["custom:PRImage"] as t>
                <img src="/alfresco${t.url}">
          </#list>
        </#if>

        <BR><BR>

        ${document.content}
        </td>
        <td valign="top">

            <B> PR CONTACT :</B> <BR>
            Contact: ${document.properties["custom:PRName"]} <BR>
            Email: ${document.properties["custom:PREmail"]} <BR>
```

```
      Phone: ${document.properties["custom:PRPhone"]} <BR>

   <BR>

      <B> Associated Files: </B>
   <#if document.assocs["custom:PRFiles"]?exists>
      <#list document.assocs["custom:PRFiles"] as t>
         <a href="/alfresco${t.url}"> ${t.name} </a> <BR>
      </#list>
   </#if>
   </td>
   </tr>

</table>
<#else>
   No document found!
</#if>
```

2. Go to the **Company Home | Data Dictionary | Presentation Templates** space and click the **Add Content** link and upload the chapter7_ PressReleaseTemplate.ftl file which you have created earlier as a new presentation template.

3. Go to the **Company Home | Intranet | Press and Media | Press Releases** space and make sure the content item you have created earlier as **Press Release** has all the properties filled up.

4. Use **Preview in Template** button and select the chapter7_ PressReleaseTemplate.ftl template from the drop-down list to display the press release as shown in the following screenshot:

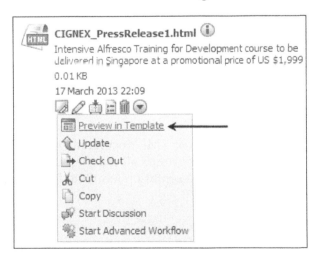

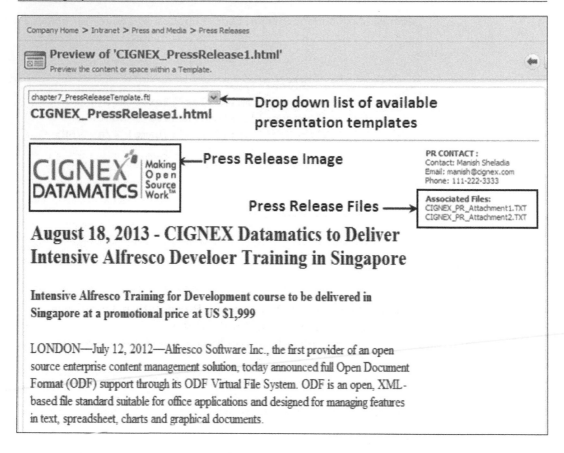

Association example

You can create various custom content types, aspects, and associations as per your business requirements.

Let us say you belong to a training department and would like to maintain the training material in Alfresco repository. As an example, create custom content types called the Book and the Chapters. In the content model, define the Book content type to have chapters as child associations.

Chapters are the actual text or HTML or XML documents which are version controlled. Book content type logically groups all the chapters using the child-association property. Create a presentation template for Book content to display all the chapters associated.

Dynamic models

You are able to customize Alfresco by using custom content types. These customizations are typically deployed via the `alfresco/extension` folder and require the Alfresco server to be restarted to take effect. Starting Version 2.9, Alfresco supports dynamic models to enable dynamic customization of models without requiring a restart of the Alfresco server.

Dynamic models are nothing but XML based model files, which are uploaded to Alfresco's repository in **Company Home** | **Data Dictionary** | **Model** space.

The following are the advantages of Dynamic models:

- Model file changes will not require any Alfresco Server Restart.

- Easy to maintain content & model files as they are stored in the repository.

- All the model files kept in `<extension>` folder will be considered active and will be loaded by Alfresco. However you can activate and inactivate the dynamic models by keeping the model XML file in the repository.

- In multi-tenant setup the models defined in `<extension>` folder are available to all tenants. If you would like to have custom content types and aspects for a specific tenant only, then dynamic models is the best choice.

Creating a dynamic custom model

Creating dynamic custom model is same as creating regular custom model. As an example create a custom content type with two properties. Create a file named `dynamicModel1.xml` on your personal computer with the following content.

```
<?xml version="1.0" encoding="UTF-8"?>

<!-- Dynamic Model -->

<model name="dynamic:dynamicModel" xmlns="http://www.alfresco.org/
model/dictionary/1.0">

    <!-- Optional meta-data about the model -->
    <description>Dynamic Model</description>
    <author></author>
    <version>1.0</version>

    <imports>
        <!-- Import Alfresco Dictionary Definitions -->
        <import uri="http://www.alfresco.org/model/dictionary/1.0"
prefix="d"/>
```

```
        <!-- Import Alfresco Content Domain Model Definitions -->
        <import uri="http://www.alfresco.org/model/content/1.0"
prefix="cm"/>
    </imports>

    <!-- Introduction of new namespaces defined by this model -->
    <!-- NOTE: The following namespace dynamic.model should be changed
to reflect your own namespace -->
    <namespaces>
        <namespace uri="dynamic.model" prefix="dynamic"/>
    </namespaces>

    <types>

        <!-- Definition of new Content Type: Model1 -->
        <type name="dynamic:Model1">
            <title>Dynamic Model ONE</title>
            <parent>cm:content</parent>
            <properties>
                <property name="dynamic:property11">
                    <title>Dynamic Property 11</title>
                    <type>d:text</type>
                </property>
                <property name="dynamic:property12">
                    <title>Dynamic Property 12</title>
                    <type>d:text</type>
                </property>
            </properties>
        </type>

    </types>

</model>
```

Deploying a custom model

Deploying a custom model is as simple as uploading the model file to a specific space in Alfresco. Log in to Alfresco Explorer and go to **Company Home** | **Data Dictionary** | **Model** space. Upload the dynamicModel1.xml file.

Activating and inactivating a custom model

By default, the model will not be active unless the **Model Active** checkbox is selected during the upload. To activate a previously inactive model, select **View Details** and then select the **Modify** properties icon. In the **Modify Content Properties** page, select the **Model Active** checkbox.

Similarly to inactivate a custom model, unselect the **Model Active** checkbox.

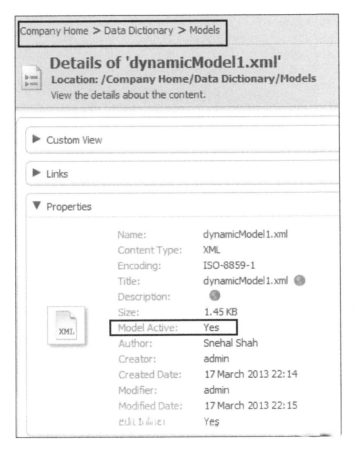

Updating a custom model

You can directly edit or update the XML model file. If the model is active then it will be reloaded. If the file is checked-out then the working copy will be ignored until such time that the file is checked in.

Dynamic web client

Dynamic web client configuration file will have the same name as custom web client configuration file. For example, create `web-client-config-custom.xml` file with the following content to support the dynamic content type created earlier.

```
<alfresco-config>

    <config evaluator="string-compare" condition="Content Wizards">
        <content-types>
            <type name="dynamic:Model1" />
        </content-types>
    </config>

    <config evaluator="node-type" condition="dynamic:Model1">
        <property-sheet>
            <show-property name="mimetype" display-label-id="content_
type"
                            component-generator="MimeTypeSelectorGenerat
or" />
            <show-property name="dynamic:property11" />
            <show-property name="dynamic:property12" />
        </property-sheet>
    </config>

    <!-- Lists the custom content type in business rules Action wizard
-->
    <config evaluator="string-compare" condition="Action Wizards">
        <subtypes>
            <type name="dynamic:Model1"/>
        </subtypes>
    </config>

</alfresco-config>
```

Deploying web client customizations

Deploying a dynamic web client configuration is as simple as uploading it to a specific space in Alfresco. Log in to Alfresco Explorer and go to **Company Home | Data Dictionary | Web Client Extension** space. Upload the `web-client-config-custom.xml` file.

The custom configuration will not be applied until it is explicitly reloaded (refer to the following section) or when the server is restarted.

Reloading web client customizations

If the `web-client-config-custom.xml` file has been added, edited, or updated, it can be dynamically reloaded by using the web client configuration console via the following link:

```
http://<server>:<port>/alfresco/faces/jsp/admin/webclientconfig-
console.jsp
```

This has a single command `reload` which will cause the web client configuration to be reloaded.

Dynamic models in a Multi-tenancy environment

Alfresco supports multi-tenancy architecture where a single instance of the software serves multiple client organizations (tenants). *Chapter 14, Administering and Maintaining the System* contains information about setting up Alfresco for a multi-tenant environment.

When configured for multi-tenant environment, Alfresco virtually partitions its data and configuration so that each client organization works with a customized virtual application instance. By default, the models defined in `<extension>` folder are available to all tenants.

If you would like to custom content types and custom aspects for a specific tenant only, then dynamic models is the best choice.

To test this out, create a few tenant accounts (say TenantA and TenantB) as per the instructions given in *Chapter 14, Administering and Maintaining the System*. Log in as a specific tenant administrator (say TenantA) and create a dynamic content type and use it. Now log in as a different tenant administrator (say TenantB) and you will notice that the dynamic content type created by TenantA is not available to TenantB.

Summary

Alfresco content model is highly extensible. The custom aspects provide you flexibility to add an additional set of properties to the documents in specific spaces. You can customize the content model to suit your business needs. Using content associations you can relate one document with one or more documents. You also understood the benefits of a newly added feature called Dynamic models for dynamic customization of models without requiring a restart of the Alfresco server. In the next chapter, you will learn an important feature called Workflow using Activity and JBPM engine. This is one of the main features which will give you flexibility to fully automate your complex business processes.

8
Implementing Workflow

Workflow is the automation of a business process, during which documents are passed from one participant to another for action, according to a set of procedural rules. Every content management system implementation will have workflow requirements. For some companies, workflow could be a simple approval process and for some companies it could be a complex business process management. Workflow provides ownership and control on the content and processes. In this chapter, you will understand the basic out-of-the-box workflow capabilities of Alfresco and the ways to extend it as per your business requirements.

By the end of this chapter, you will have learned how to:

- Enable simple workflow on documents
- Create e-mail templates and set e-mail notifications
- Extend workflow with multiple approval steps
- Implement advanced workflow using Activiti
- Create custom Activiti workflows
- Dynamically deploy workflow via the Activiti Console
- Create and deploy the workflow task dialog.
- Create and deploy the workflow resource bundle
- Start Advance Workflow
- Assign documents and properties to the workflow
- Assign workflow task to the users

Introduction to the Alfresco workflow process

Alfresco includes two types of workflows out-of-the-box. One is the **Simple Workflow** that is content-oriented, and the other is the **Advanced Workflow** that is task-oriented.

The Simple Workflow process in Alfresco is the movement of documents through various spaces. It's simple in that each workflow definition is restricted to a single state. Multiple states are represented by loosely tying multiple workflow definitions. Loose coupling is achieved by attaching a workflow definition to a space and a workflow instance to a content item. A content item is moved or copied to a new space at which point a new workflow instance is attached based on the workflow definition of the space. A workflow definition is unaware of other related workflow definitions.

The Advanced Workflow process is task-oriented, where you create a task, attach documents to be reviewed, and assign it to appropriate reviewers. You can track the list of tasks assigned to you and the tasks initiated by you. You can change the status of the tasks, reassign the tasks to other users, and cancel a task. You can send various notifications to all the parties involved and track the tasks to closure. Alfresco provides this level workflow ubiquitously throughout its entire product. The same robust workflow capabilities are available in DM, RM, and throughout our applications, including Alfresco Share.

Alfresco provides two advanced workflow engines: **JBPM** and **Activiti**. You can use out-of-the-box features provided by both the workflows or you can create your own custom advanced workflow as per the business processes of your organization using the JBPM or Activiti workflow engine.

Simple Workflow

For example, consider a purchase order that moves through various departments for authorization and eventual purchase. To implement simple workflow in Alfresco, you will create spaces for each department and allow documents to move through various department spaces. Each department space is secured allowing only users of that department to edit the document and to move it to the next departmental space in the workflow process.

The workflow process is so flexible that you could introduce new steps for approval into the operation without changing any code.

Out-of-the-box features

The simple workflow is implemented as an aspect that could be attached to any document in space through a business rule. Workflow can also be invoked on individual content items as actions.

Workflow has two steps—one for approval and one for rejection. You can refer to the screenshot on the next page where workflow is defined for the documents in a space called **Review Space**. Users belonging to the **Review Space** can act upon the document. If they reject, then the document moves to a space called **Rejected Space**. If they approve, then the document moves to a space called the **Approved space**. You can define the names of the spaces and the users on the spaces as per your business requirements.

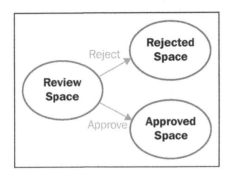

Defining and using Simple Workflow

The process to define and use Simple Workflow in Alfresco is as follows:

- Identify spaces and set security on those spaces
- Define your workflow process
- Add workflow to content in those spaces accordingly
- Select the e-mail template and people to send e-mail notifications
- Test the workflow process

As an example, let us define and use a simple workflow process to review and approve the engineering documents in your Intranet. Go to the **Company Home | Intranet | Engineering Department** space and create the **ProjectA** space using an existing **Software Engineering Project** space template. For more information about creating a space using an existing space template, refer *Chapter 5, Implementing Document Management*.

Identifying spaces and security

If you go to the **Company Home | Intranet | Engineering Department | ProjectA | Documentation** space, you will notice the following sub-spaces:

- **Samples**: This space is to store sample project documents. Set the security on this space so that only managers can edit the documents and others can copy the documents from this space.

- **Drafts**: This space contains initial drafts and documents of **ProjectA** that are being edited. Set security in such a way that only a few selected users (such as **Engineer1, Engineer2**—as shown in the next screenshot) can add and edit documents in this space.

- **Pending Approval**: This space contains all of the documents under review. Set security so that only the Project Manager of **ProjectA** can edit the documents.

- **Published**: This space contains all the documents that are approved and visible to others. Nobody should edit the documents while they are in the **Published** space. If you need to edit a document, you need to retract it to the **Drafts** space and follow the workflow process, as shown here:

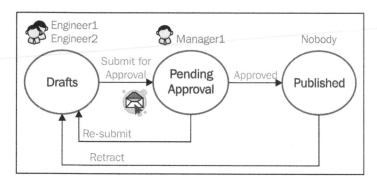

Set the security on these sub-spaces as required. For more information about securing spaces, refer *Chapter 4, Implementing Membership and Security.*

Defining the workflow process

Now that you have identified the spaces, the next step is to define your workflow process. The preceding screenshot illustrates the spaces and the workflow.

We will add workflow to all of the documents in the **Drafts** space. When a user selects the **Approve** action called **Submit for Approval** on a document, the document moves from the **Drafts** space to the **Pending Approval** space.

We will add workflow to all of the documents in the **Pending Approval** space. When a user selects the **Approve** action called **Approved on a document**, the document moves from the **Pending Approval** space to the **Published** space. Similarly, when user selects the **Reject** action called **Re-submit on a document**, it moves from the **Pending Approval** space to the **Drafts** space.

We will add workflow to all the documents in the **Published** space. When a user selects the **Reject** action called **Retract on a document**, it moves from the **Published** space to the **Drafts** space.

You can have as many review steps (spaces) as needed and you can choose the workflow action names as per your business' requirements.

Adding a simple workflow to items

Now that you have defined your workflow process, the next step is to add workflow to the documents in these spaces.

To add workflow to the **Drafts** space, follow these steps:

1. Ensure that you are in the **Company Home | Intranet | Engineering Department | ProjectA | Documentation | Drafts** space.
2. Click on **More Actions | Manage Content Rules**.
3. Click the **Create Rule** link and you will see the **Create Rules Wizard**.
4. In **Step One**, from the **Select Condition** drop-down list, select the **All Items** option, and click on the **Add to List** button. Click the **Next button**.

5. In **Step Two**, from the **Select Actions** drop-down list, select the **Add simple workflow to item** option, and click the **Set Values and Add** button. A **Set action values** dialog window appears, as shown in the next screenshot:

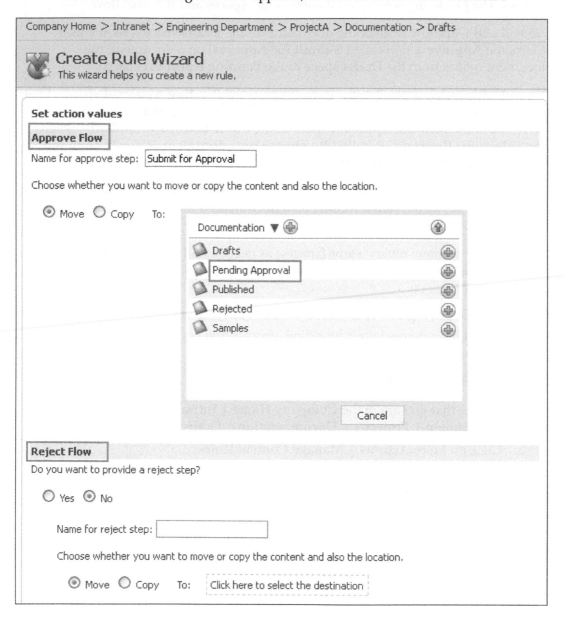

6. In the **Approve Flow** section, provide a workflow step name of **Submit for Approval**, and move the content to the **Pending Approval** space. This is as per your workflow design, as shown in the screenshot under the *Identify spaces and security* section for the **Drafts** space.

7. The workflow for the **Drafts** space does not require a "reject" step. Hence, select the option **No** for **Reject Flow**.

8. Click **OK**, and then click on the **Next** button.

9. In **Step Three**, select **Type** as **Items are created or enter this folder**, and provide an appropriate name and description for this rule. Finish the rule.

Similarly, create workflow for the **Pending Approval** space as per the design shown in the screenshot under the *Identify spaces and security* section. Remember that this space has both the **approve step** and **reject step** options, as shown here:

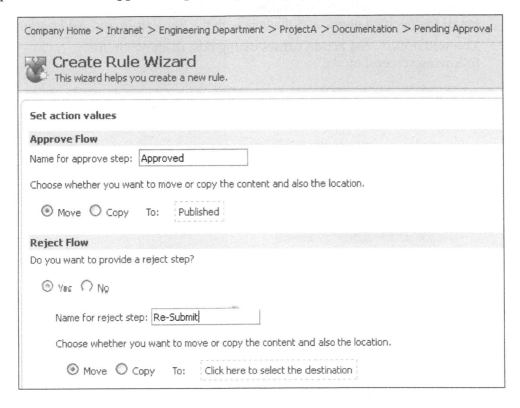

Next, create a workflow for the **Published** space as per the design shown in the screenshot under the *Identify spaces and security* section. Remember that this space has only the **approve step** option, which moves the content to the **Drafts** space upon retract. Provide **retract** as the name for the **approve step** option.

Sending a notification to the manager for approval

You can send a notification by e-mail to the Project Manager whenever a document is pending approval. Follow these steps to send an e-mail notification to the Project Manager of **ProjectA**, when a document gets into the **Pending Approval** space:

1. Ensure that you are in the **Company Home** | **Intranet** | **Engineering Department** | **ProjectA** | **Documentation** | **Pending Approval** space.

2. Click on the **More Actions** | **Manage Content Rules** link.

3. Click the **Create Rule** link and you will see the **Create Rule Wizard**.

4. In **Step One**, from the **Select Condition** drop-down list, select the **All Items** option, and then click on the **Add to List** button. Next, click on the **Next** button.

5. In **Step Two**, from the **Select Actions** drop-down list, select the **Send an email to specified users**, and then click on the **Set Values and Add** button.

6. You will notice a **Set action values** dialog box, as shown in the following screenshot:

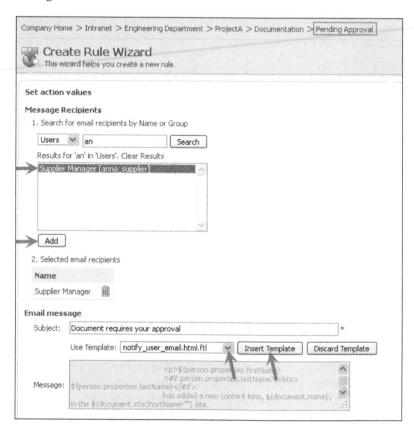

7. Search for and select the Project Manager's name as the e-mail recipient and click on the **Add** button. Provide an appropriate subject for the e-mail. As an e-mail message, you can either provide your own text or use the built-in e-mail template (**notify_user_email.ftl**), as shown in the preceding screenshot.

8. Click **OK** and then click on the **Next** button. Select the **Type** as **Inbound**; provide appropriate name and description for this rule.

9. Finish the rule.

Testing the simple workflow

To test the workflow process, go to the **Drafts** space and upload a sample document. You will notice the available workflow actions in **more actions** drop-down menu, as shown here. When you click on the **Submit for Approval** action, the document will be moved automatically to the **Pending Approval** space, as per the workflow rule:

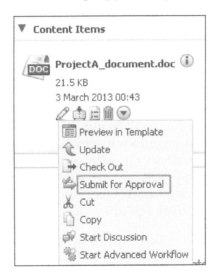

When the document moves into the **Pending Approval** space, two business rules will be applied.

One business rule is to send an e-mail notification to the Project Manager, indicating him or her that the document is pending approval. If your e-mail server is configured right, then the Project Manager will receive e-mail notifications with information about the document.

The second business rule is the workflow on all the incoming documents to this space. When the Project Manager logs in, he or she will notice the workflow actions in the **more actions** drop-down menu, as shown in the following screenshot:

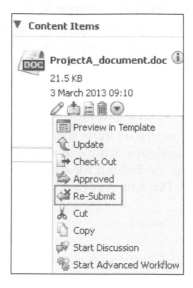

If the Project Manager is fine with the document, then he/she can click on the **Approved** action and the document will be moved to the **Published** space automatically. If the Project Manager requires more details, or is not satisfied with the document, then he/she can click on the **Re-submit** action to send the document to the original author to edit and re-submit it. In this situation, the document will be moved to the **Drafts** space automatically. Once the document is in the **Drafts** space, the workflow process starts all over again.

Select the **Approved** action and notice that the document is moved to the **Published** space. When the document is in **Published** state, it is typically visible to all the required employees, as it has already been reviewed and approved. You can retract the document to the **Drafts** space (as shown in the next screenshot) for further edits and approvals:

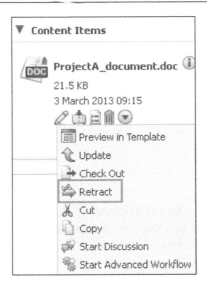

E-mail notification templates

For e-mail notifications, you can either use your own e-mail message or use a standard e-mail notification template (as shown in the screenshot under the *Sending a notification to the manager for approval* section). You can also create your own e-mail templates to re-use them wherever required. For more details about the Data dictionary and templates, please refer to *Chapter 5, Implementing Document Management*.

The **Company Home | Data Dictionary | Email Templates** space contains various e-mail templates. The e-mail templates are written in the FreeMarker template language and will have the .ftl extension. The following are the steps to create your e-mail template. For more details about Data dictionary and templates, please refer to *Chapter 5, Implementing Document Management*.

Create a file named chapter8_notify_pending_approval_email.ftl in your personal computer with the following code. This is FreeMarker template code, which includes the details of the document and the author to send them to the reviewer. Replace Your Title, Your Company Name, and other details as required:

```
<#-- Sends email to people when a document is pending approval -->

A document titled '${document.name}' is pending your approval in the
'${space.name}' space.

You can view it through this link:
```

```
http://<server-name>:<port>/alfresco${document.url}

Please review and approve it as soon as possible.

Best Regards

'${person.properties.firstName}<#if person.properties.lastName?exists>
${person.properties.lastName}</#if>'
Your Title
Your Company Name
Your Signature
```

Go to the **Company Home | Data Dictionary | Email Templates** space, and click on the **Add Content** link and upload the chapter8_notify_pending_approval_email.ftl file that you have created earlier.

The e-mail template is now ready to be used. You can go back to the e-mail notification business rule created on the **Pending Approval** space, and edit it to include the new email template that you have created.

Advanced workflows using Activiti

Simple workflows are good to implement content-oriented workflow processes. However, there are certain limitations of the simple workflow, which are as follows:

- Unable to create multistate workflow definitions
- Restricted to one or two exit transitions (approve, reject)
- Unable to define parallel workflows
- Reliance on folder structure for multistage workflow and action triggering
- No notion of a task or assignment

To resolve these limitations, Alfresco has embedded two advanced workflow engines: the **JBoss Business Process Management (JBPM)** engine and **Activiti** into its core.

JBPM was the default workflow engine prior to the release of Alfresco 4.0. It is still included in the current release of Alfresco to support the older versions and upgrades.

Activiti is the default advanced workflow engine for the current version of Alfresco; Activiti is the product from Alfresco (the company).

The rest of the chapter will focus only on the Activiti workflow engine.

Activiti is an open source, light-weight workflow engine. Its core is the **Business Process Model and Notation (BPMN)** 2 process engine. It can run in any Java application, on server, on cloud, and on a cluster environment. Activiti is responsible for managing the processes that are deployed, instantiating and executing processes, persisting process state and metadata to a relational database, and tracking task assignment and task lists. Workflows are described with "process definitions", using an XML-based language BPMN 2.0.

BPMN 2.0 is a standard developed by the **Object Manage Group (OMG)**. Its primary goal is to provide businesses with a notation for understanding their business procedures by all the stakeholders, from business analysts, to technical developers, to business people who manage these processes. Thus, BPMN bridges the gap between the business process design and the process implementation.

Out of the box features

The Advanced Workflow process is task-oriented, where you create a task, attach documents to be reviewed, and assign it to appropriate reviewers. It can also be implemented using business rules.

There are five advanced workflows available out of the box: Ad-hoc task-based workflow:

- **Ad-hoc task-based workflow**: Assign tasks to your colleague on an ad-hoc basis.
- **Group Review and Approve workflow**: Assign tasks to a group of your colleagues for review and approval.
- **Parallel Review and Approve workflow**: Assign task to your multiple colleagues for review and approval.
- **Pooled Review and Approve workflow**: Assign tasks to your multiple colleagues for review and approval. One colleague can take ownership of the task at a time for completing it, or once reviewed returning it to the pool to be claimed by another colleague associated with the task
- **Review and Approve workflow**: Assign tasks to your colleague for review and approval.

The following is an example to give you a better understanding of the concept:

The **RajComp** Company got a project from the **United Nations Organization (UNO)**. For this project, they have to send a request for a proposal to the client. The Project Manager asks the Team Leader to prepare a RFP document, and send it back within a week to the manager for approval. The Project Manager will review the document and can approve to send it the UNO or reject to make some corrections.

For this example, create a **RajComp** space in the **Company Home**. Create **Zoe Bull** and **Zarina Macaro** as the users. For more information about creating a space and users, refer to *Chapter 4, Implementing Membership and Security*, and *Chapter 5, Implementing Document Management*.

The following screenshot explains the process of creating a **Review** and **Approve** based workflow. **Zarina Macaro** prepares the RFP document and starts the workflow by providing the important information such as **Due Date** to complete the task, **Priority** of the task, and the **Notification** information and assign the document to **Zoe Bull** for **Review** and **Approve**. Please follow these steps to configure an ad-hoc workflow:

1. Click the document's **More Actions** button, and then click on the **Start Advanced Workflow** link, as shown in this screenshot:

2. This wizard lists all the available workflows, including the custom workflow processes. From the list of available workflows, select the **Adhoc Task** option and click on the **Next** button:

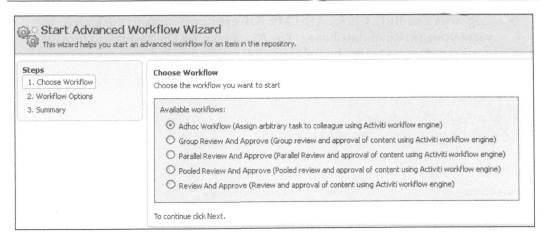

3. You will see the **Workflow options** pane of the **Start Adhoc Task Workflow Wizard**, as shown in the next screenshot. Provide a meaningful **Description** for the task and choose the **Priority** and the **Due Date**. Select the **Notify Me** checkbox to receive notifications on various workflow status updates on the document.

4. From the list of users, search for **Zoe Bull** and assign her the task. You can also add the additional resources (documents) to this workflow task by clicking on the **Add Resource** button, as shown in the next screenshot. This helps if you want to send a set of documents as one bunch for approval. Once you fill up the entire relevant information, click on the **OK** button to start the workflow process.

5. Log in as **Zoe Bull**. Click on the **My Alfresco** menu link in the toolbar to view your personal dashboard. The **My Tasks To Do** dashboard lists all your pending tasks, as shown in the following screenshot:

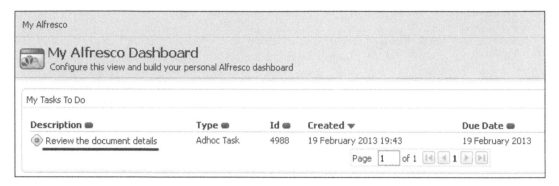

6. Click on link shown in the preceding screenshot. To complete the task, set **Status** as **Completed** and click on the **Task Done** button.

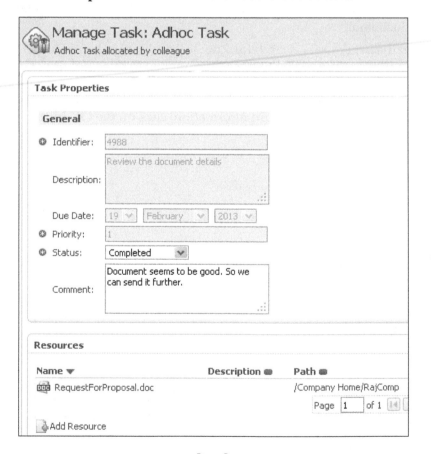

Creating custom advanced workflows

You can define and deploy your own task-oriented Activiti workflows in the Alfresco repository. However, you need to follow a particular format to define your workflow and a particular process to deploy it in Alfresco.

Process definition

The Activiti process definition consists of different elements and properties. The elements supported are events, tasks, and gateways. These elements are connected by "sequence flows". The properties supported are user assignment, variables, form key, and listener.

Process definition can be implemented using the Activiti process designer that supports BPMN 2.0 or hand crafted using an XML editor.

Activiti BPMN 2.0 Process Designer

Install the Activiti BPMN 2.0 Process Designer plugin for Eclipse by pointing Eclipse to `http://activiti.org/designer/update/`, as shown in the following screenshot:

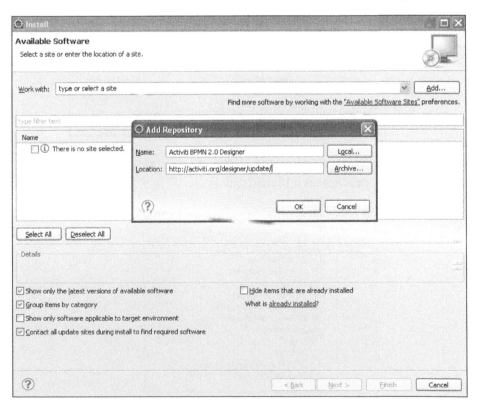

Create new Activiti project by right clicking on the project, select **New | Others | Activiti Project**, and then create an Activiti diagram by right-clicking on the project, select **New | Others | Activiti Diagram**. The Activiti Designer creates a .bpmn file when creating a new Activiti diagram. The .bpmn file when opened with the Activiti Designer Editor provides a graphical modeling canvas and palette, and when opened with an XML editor shows BPMN 2.0 XML elements of the process definition:

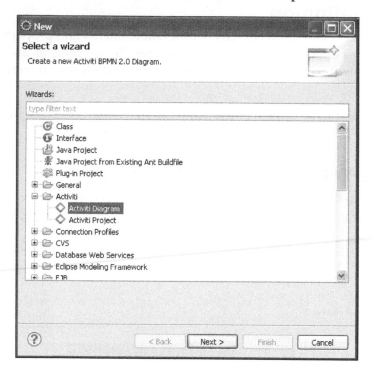

Save the .bpmn file as **MyFirstActivitiWorkflow.bpmn**. Now, you are all set to start drawing the business process on a blank canvas:

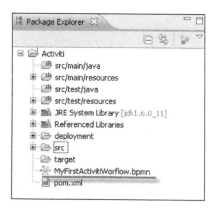

My first Activiti workflow sample

Create **MyFirstActivitiWorkflow**, which consists of a start event, a review task (Alfresco User Task), and an end event. After dragging and dropping these elements from the palette and connecting them with sequence flows, the diagram would look like this:

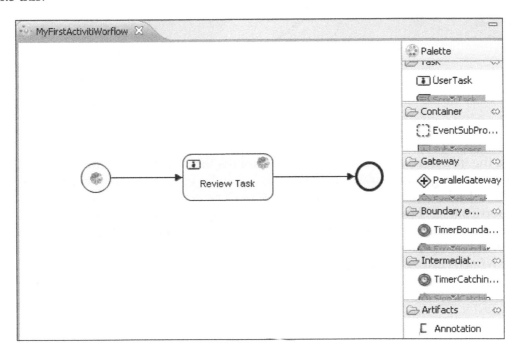

Now, the user who initiates the workflow should be able to select a reviewer to assign the review task. For that, the start event should be mapped to a type in the workflow content model that can hold the user, this is done by setting the **Form key** attribute to a type in the workflow content model that has mandatory aspect as **bpm:assignee**. Here the start event and the user task that I have used are the Alfresco start event and Alfresco user task respectively. These elements have predefined types.

Open the **Properties** view, click on the start event and select the
wf:submitReviewTask type from the drop-down, as shown in the following
screenshot; the **wf:submitReviewTask** type exists in workflowModel.xml:

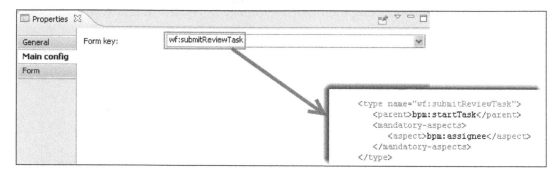

Once the initiator selects an assignee and submits the workflow, the **Review Task**
should be assigned to an assignee. For this, open the **Properties** view, click on the
Review Task, and specify **Assignee** for the performer type, and **${bpm_assignee.**
properties.userName} for the Expression. The assignee should be able to approve or
reject it. For this, the **Review Task** should be mapped to a type in the content model
where it has the property with values **Approve** or **Reject**. Here it is mapped to a
type **wf:activeReviewTask** that exist in workflowModel.xml, as shown in the
following screenshot:

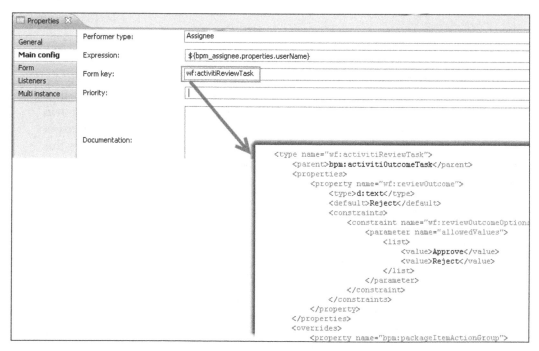

Here is the XML representation of **MyFirstActivitiWorkflow**:

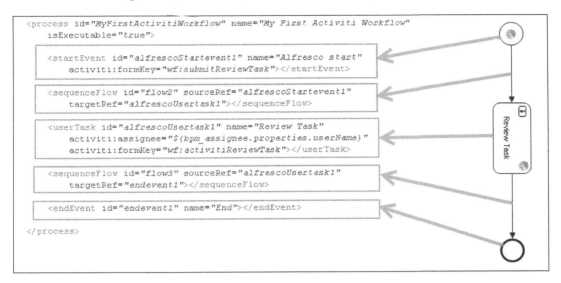

```
<process id="MyFirstActivitiWorkflow" name="My First Activiti Workflow"
    isExecutable="true">

    <startEvent id="alfrescoStartevent1" name="Alfresco start"
        activiti:formKey="wf:submitReviewTask"></startEvent>

    <sequenceFlow id="flow2" sourceRef="alfrescoStartevent1"
        targetRef="alfrescoUsertask1"></sequenceFlow>

    <userTask id="alfrescoUsertask1" name="Review Task"
        activiti:assignee="${bpm_assignee.properties.userName}"
        activiti:formKey="wf:activitiReviewTask"></userTask>

    <sequenceFlow id="flow3" sourceRef="alfrescoUsertask1"
        targetRef="endevent1"></sequenceFlow>

    <endEvent id="endevent1" name="End"></endEvent>

</process>
```

Once the **MyFirstActivitiWorkflow** process definition file is complete, the next step is to create and deploy the task model, make Alfresco Explorer UI configuration and localization. As I have used out-of-the-box form keys, **wf:submitReviewTask** and **wf:activitiReviewTask**, which already exist in workflowModel.xml, it saves my time by not creating and deploying task model, make Alfresco Explorer UI configuration and localization. We will look at these steps later.

The next step is to deploy the **MyFirstActivitiWorkflow** process definition file. Process definitions can be deployed either using the Activiti workflow, Explorer Workflow Console, Spring, or Dynamic Deployment, by creating the process definition file in **Company Home | Data Dictionary | Workflow Definitions** space. I will deploy the **MyFirstActivitiWorkflow** process definition using Spring. Later in this chapter, I will show how to deploy the process definition using the Activiti Workflow Console.

Create a new Spring context file called `myfirstactivitiworkflow-workflow-context.xml` and add a workflow deploy bean in it, like this:

```xml
<beans>
    <bean id="myfirstactivitiworkflow.workflowBootstrap" parent="workflowDeployer">
        <property name="workflowDefinitions">
            <list>
                <props>
                    <prop key="engineId">activiti</prop>
                    <prop key="location">alfresco/extension/workflows/MyFirstActivitiWorkflow.bpmn20.xml</prop>
                    <prop key="mimetype">text/xml</prop>
                    <prop key="redeploy">false</prop>
                </props>
            </list>
        </property>
    </bean>
</beans>
```

Copy `myfirstactivitiworkflow-workflow-context.xml` to the TOMCAT_HOME/shared/classed/alfresco/extension location and copy the **MyFirstActivitWorkflow** process definition to **TOMCAT_HOME/shared/classed/alfresco/extension/workflows**. Note that in the current Activiti version (5.9), the `.bpmn` extension is not supported as a deployment artifact for a procession definition. It supports the `.bpmn20.xml` extension. Thus, rename `MyFirstActivitiWorkflow.xml` to `MyFirstActivitiWorkflow.bpmn20.xml`. Now everything is ready. Restart Alfresco, log in, and initiate an advance work on any content, you will see **MyFirstActivitiWorkflow** in the workflow selection page:

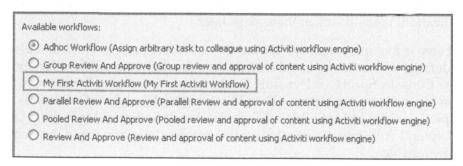

Activiti workflow basics

Let's look at some of the important elements and features of Activiti:

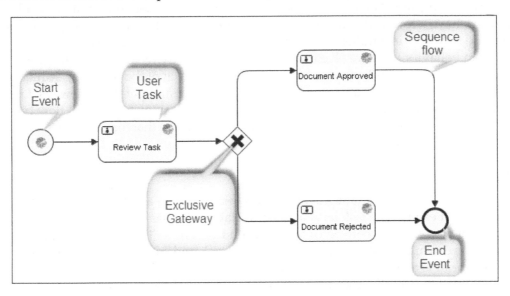

Events

Events are used to model something that happens during the lifetime of a process. A start event indicates where a process starts. An end event signifies the end of a process. The other events supported by Activiti are **None Start Event**, **Timer Start Event**, **Message Start Event**, **Error Start Event**, **None End Event**, **Error End Event**, and **Cancel End Event**. There are other several events of the type **Boundary Events** and **Intermediate Catching Events** supported by Activiti.

Tasks

Tasks can be of type user task or script task. User tasks are assigned to users (human performer) and script tasks are generally created to perform some kind of operation against the Alfresco repository.

Gateways

Gateways can be exclusive, parallel, or inclusive. Exclusive gateways are used to implement conditional flow in conjunction with conditional sequence flows. Parallel gateways have a fork and join behavior. Fork behavior is where all outgoing sequence flows are followed in parallel, creating one concurrent execution for each sequence flow. Join behavior is where all concurrent executions arriving at the parallel gateway wait in the gateway until an execution has arrived for each of the incoming sequence flows. Inclusive gateways are a combination of exclusive and parallel gateways. Like exclusive gateways, inclusive gateways are used to implement conditional flow but the main difference is that the inclusive gateway can take more than one sequence flow, like parallel gateways.

Variables

There are two types of variables available: process variables and task variables. The variables that exist at the task level are task variables. The task variables are not available across tasks or between a task and condition flow. The process variables are ones that are available across tasks or between a task and condition flow. To make the task variable available across tasks or between a task and condition flow, you will first need to copy the variable to the process execution level. This can be done by implementing a `TaskListener` on a task completion. In this task listener, you can run Alfresco JavaScript code that copies the task variables to the process level. For example:

```
execution.setVariable('wf_reviewOutcome',
task.getVariable('wf_reviewOutcome'));
```

Node Objects

In Activiti BPMN, Alfresco Node Objects are node references and associations of the Alfresco repository. The Alfresco Node Objects combined with the scripting capabilities of Alfresco JavaScript, help us to control the flow based on the repository metadata, as well as perform common repository automations using scripts as part of the workflow. **bpm_workflowDescription**, **bpm_workflowDueDate**, **bpm_package**, **initiator**, **initiatorhome**, **companyhome**, **logger**, **people**, **Groups** are some of the Node Objects available in Activiti.

User Assignment

As explained earlier, user tasks can be directly assigned to a user by defining the **humanPerformer** sub-element, which uses a **resourceAssignmentExpression** that actually defines a user. In the Activiti Process Designer, you can set the user task to a user, as shown in the following screenshot:

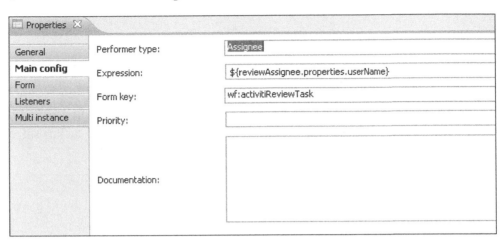

The XML representation of user assignment is as follows:

```
<humanPerformer>
    <resourceAssignmentExpression>
        <formalExpression>${reviewAssignee.properties.userName}</formalExpression>
    </resourceAssignmentExpression>
</humanPerformer>
```

You might have noticed that in **MyFirstActivitiWorkflow**, assigning a user task to a given user generated the XML as:

```
<userTask id="alfrescoUsertask1" name="Review Task"
    activiti:assignee="${bpm_assignee.properties.userName}"
    activiti:formKey="wf:activitiReviewTask"></userTask>
```

In the preceding XML, the assignee attribute, which is an Activiti custom extension, is exactly the same as using the humanPerformer construct.

Pooled assignment

User tasks can also be assigned multiple users or groups. The `candidateUser` attribute, which is an Activiti custom extension, or the `potentialOwner` construct can be used to assign user task to multiple users. The `candiateGroups` attribute, which is an Activiti custom extension, or the `potentialOwner` construct can be used to assign user task to groups.

Multi-instance tasks

Sometimes, you will want to have a task performed by all members of a group and not just by one user in a group. In such cases, Activiti offers you the possibility of creating a multi-instance task. With a multi-instance task, it is possible to create a task in the personal task list of a collection of users; this collection could come from one or more groups. In the Activiti Process Designer, a multi-instance task is set, as shown in the following screenshot:

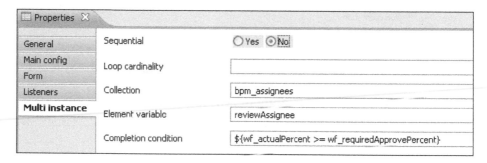

The generated XML looks like this:

```
<!-- For each assignee, task is created -->
<multiInstanceLoopCharacteristics isSequential="false">
    <loopDataInputRef>bpm_assignees</loopDataInputRef>
    <inputDataItem name="reviewAssignee" />
    <completionCondition>${wf_actualPercent >= wf_requiredApprovePercent}</completionCondition>
</multiInstanceLoopCharacteristics>
</userTask>
```

Listeners

Listeners are an Activiti extension to BPMN 2.0 that implements hook point inside the process definition, which is triggered by events that happens when the workflow is executed. There are two types of listeners: **execution** and **task**.

Task listeners can be configured only on a user task, while execution listeners can be configured on the process itself, as well as activities and transitions:

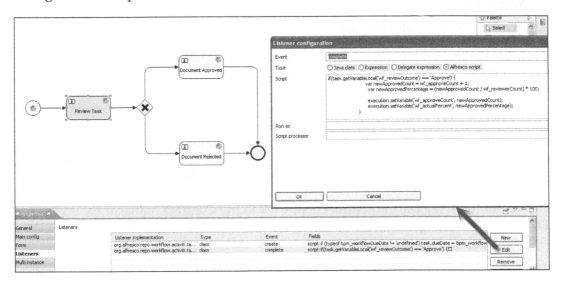

Form key

Each task in a workflow must correspond to a type in the workflow content model. These tasks have properties that the workflow and user interface can exploit to present and gather information from the user, change the behavior of the workflow, track the workflow, and so on. These tasks interact with the form system to provide the forms that the user sees in Alfresco Explorer and Share.

To specify the task, type the **Form key** attribute on the user task used:

To learn more about activity elements and features, refer
http://www.activiti.org/userguide/index.html.

Creating and deploying your custom Activiti workflow

As an example, we will configure one workflow. The use-case scenario is as follows:

Let us consider a fictitious business case. **Global Autoparts**, our fictitious organization, and supplier of car batteries, **Global Batteries**, another fictitious organization. Global Autoparts plans to purchase the car batteries from Global Batteries before which the terms and condition of the contract has to be approved by the Contract Manager, Supplier, and Product Manager. The required process is where the contract editor creates the contract and sends it to Contract Manager. Once the Contract Manager finds the contract complete and error free, then he/she simultaneously sends the contract both to the Supplier and the Product Manager for review. If both, the Supplier and Product Manager approve, then the process ends. If any one of them rejects, the contract goes back to the Contract Manager for review. The Contract Manager reviews the contract, modifies it, and sends it to the Supplier and the Product Manager and the process goes on.

For this example, create users **Supplier | anna_supplier, Product Manager | smith_pm, Contract Manager | john_cm**, and **Contract Editor | jim_editor**. Create a **Global Autoparts** space under **Company Home**. For more information on creating spaces and users, refer *Chapter 4, Implementing Membership and Security*.

After creating users and space, the next step is to lay out the process using the Activiti BPMN 2.0 Designer plugin for Eclipse.

Step 1 – creating and deploying the process definition

After dragging and dropping the events, tasks, and gateways, and connecting these by sequence flows, the layout looks like this:

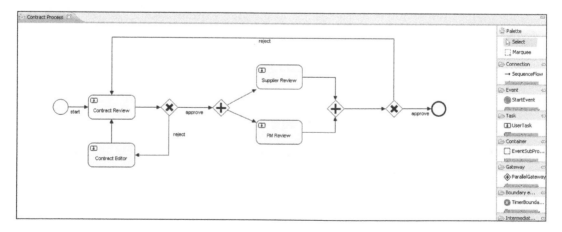

Defining the workflow's process

The Contract Editor creates the contract and starts the Contract Process workflow, on that, the start event is invoked. Once the Contract Editor submits the contract to the Contract Manager, the **Contract Review** task is created for the Contract Manager, which will be listed in the **My Task To Do** dashlet. The Contract Manager opens up the task and reviews the contract. If any further modifications are to be made to the contract, the Contract Manager rejects the task and the contract goes back to the Contract Editor. If the Contract Manager finds the contract complete, then he/she selects the Supplier and the Product Manager and submits the task. Here, a parallel gateway (Fork) is used so that the Supplier and the Product Manager gets the contract for review at the same time. Two tasks are created: one for the Supplier named **Supplier Review** (User Task), and another for the Product Manager named **PM Review** (User Task). Until and unless both the Supplier and Product Manager take the decision on the contract, the workflow doesn't proceed further, this is due to the **Supplier Review** task and the **PM Review** task being connected to a parallel gateway (Join). Once the decision has been taken by the Supplier and the Product Manager, the flow is moved to an exclusive gateway. Here the exclusive gateway is used because based on the decision taken by the Supplier and Product Manager, the flow has to be moved. If the Supplier and the Product Manager approve the contract, then the workflow ends. If one of the parties rejects, then the flow goes back to the **Contract Review** task, where the Contract Manager can review/modify the contract and send it back for review. The process goes on until both the Supplier and the Product Manager approve it.

Setting properties

Once the layout and process is defined, the next step is to set the properties of the required elements. The following tables list down the properties that have to be added for the different elements:

| Event/Task/ | Properties | |
Sequence flow	Main Config	Listener
Start Event (Event)	**Form key**: `cp:startTask`	

Event/Task/ Sequence flow	Properties	
	Main Config	**Listener**

Contract Review (User Task)	**Assignee:** ${cp_ cmAssignee. properties.userName}
	
	Form key : cp:reviewContract
		Event: create
		
		Java class: org.alfresco.repo. workflow.activiti.tasklistner
		
		Alfresco script: if (typeof bpm_ dueDate != 'undefined') task. dueDate = bpm_dueDate;
		
		    if (typeof bpm_priority != 'undefined') task.priority = bpm_priority;
		
		Event: complete
		
		Java class: org.alfresco.repo. workflow.activiti.tasklistner
		
		Alfresco script: execution. setVariable('cp_ supplierAssignee', task.getVariable('cp_ supplierAssignee'));
		
		    execution. setVariable('cp_pmAssignee', task.getVariable('cp_ pmAssignee'));
		
		    execution. setVariable('cp_cmAssignee', task.getVariable('cp_ cmAssignee'));
		
		    execution. setVariable('cp_ cmReviewOutcome', task. getVariable('cp_ cmReviewOutcome'));

Event/Task/ Sequence flow	Properties	
	Main Config	**Listener**
Supplier Review (User Task)	**Assignee**: ${cp_ supplierAssignee. properties.userName} **Form key**: cp:supplierReview	**Event**: create **Java class**: org.alfresco.repo. workflow.activiti.tasklistner **Alfresco script**: if (typeof bpm_ dueDate != 'undefined') task. dueDate = bpm_dueDate; if (typeof bpm_priority != 'undefined') task.priority = bpm_priority; **Event**: complete **Java class**: org.alfresco.repo. workflow.activiti.tasklistner **Alfresco script**: execution. setVariable('cp_ supplieReviewOutcome', task.getVariable(cp_ supplierReviewOutcome);
PM Review (User Task)	**Assignee**: ${cp_ pmAssignee. properties.userName} **Form key**: cp:pmReview	**Event**: create **Java class**: org.alfresco.repo. workflow.activiti.tasklistner **Alfresco script**: if (typeof bpm_ dueDate != 'undefined') task. dueDate = bpm_dueDate; if (typeof bpm_priority != 'undefined') task.priority = bpm_priority; **Event**: complete **Java class**: org.alfresco.repo. workflow.activiti.tasklistner **Alfresco script**: execution. setVariable('cp_ pmReviewOutcome', task.getVariable(cp_ pmReviewOutcome);

| Event/Task/ | Properties | |
Sequence flow	Main Config	Listener
Reject (Sequence flow8}	**Condition**: ${cp_supplierReviewOutcome == 'Reject' || cp_pmReviewOucome == 'Reject'}	
Approve (Sequence flow9)	**Condition**: ${cp_supplierReviewOutcome == 'Approve' && cp_pmReviewOucome == 'Approve'}	
Reject (Sequence flow12}	**Condition**: ${cp_cmReviewOutcome == 'Reject'}	
Approve (Sequence flow13)	**Condition**: ${cp_cmReviewOutcome == 'Approve'}	

 Download the process definition file (Contract Process.bpmn20.xml) from Packt's website.

After the process definition file is ready, the next step is to deploy the process definition file.

The new thing that has been implemented in this example when compared to **MyFirstActivitiWorkflow** is the custom types and added decision logic. The custom types created are almost the same as the ones used in **MyFirstActivitiWorkflow**, so I will leave that out. Let's look at the decision logic.

Adding the decision logic

The Contract Process has a decision based on the review outcome of the task that can be found at two places. One when based on the Contract Manager's review outcome, the contract is either sent to the Contract Editor or the Supplier and the Product Manager. The other one is when based on the Supplier and the Product Manager's review outcome, the contract is sent to the Contract Manager or the process ends.

For the first decision logic, in the **Contract Review** user task, the review out of the Contract Manager has been captured and set at the process level:

```
execution.setVariable('cp_cmReviewOutcome', task.getVariable('cp_
cmReviewOutcome'));
```

The next step is to add the code to the decision that will choose appropriate the flow based on the review outcome:

```
<sequenceFlow id="flow12" name="approve" sourceRef="exclusivegateway2"
targetRef="parallelgateway1">
    <conditionExpression xsi:type="tFormalExpression"><![CDATA[${
cp_cmReviewOutcome == 'Approve'}]]></conditionExpression>
  </sequenceFlow>

<sequenceFlow id="flow13" name="reject" sourceRef="exclusivegateway2"
targetRef="usertask4">
    <conditionExpression xsi:type="tFormalExpression"><![CDATA[${
cp_cmReviewOutcome == 'Reject'}]]></conditionExpression>
  </sequenceFlow>
```

For the second decision logic, in the **Supplier Review** and **PM Review** user tasks, the review outcome of the Supplier and Product Manager has been captured and set at the process level:

```
execution.setVariable('cp_supplierReviewOutcome', task.
getVariable('cp_supplierReviewOutcome'));
execution.setVariable('cp_pmReviewOutcome', task.getVariable('cp_
pmReviewOutcome'));
```

The next step is to add the code to the decision, which will choose the appropriate flow based on the review outcome:

```
< sequenceFlow id="flow8" name="approve" sourceRef="exclusivegateway1"
targetRef="endevent1">
    <conditionExpression xsi:type="tFormalExpression"><![CDATA[
${cp_supplierReviewOutcome == 'Approve' && cp_pmReviewOutcome ==
'Approve'}]]></conditionExpression>
  </ sequenceFlow>
  <sequenceFlow id="flow9" name="reject"
sourceRef="exclusivegateway1" targetRef="usertask1">
    <conditionExpression xsi:type="tFormalExpression"><![CDATA
[${cp_supplierReviewOutcome == 'Reject' || cp_pmReviewOutcome ==
'Reject'}]]></conditionExpression>
  </sequenceFlow>
```

Deployment

The process definition can be deployed using the Activiti Workflow, Explorer Workflow Console, or Spring. Here, I'm going to use the Activiti Workflow Console to deploy the process definition.

Right-click on the project in the package explorer and click on **Create deployment artifacts**:

A bar file is created that needs to be deployed using the Activiti Workflow Explorer:

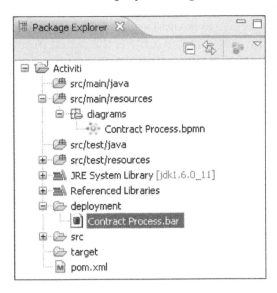

The Activiti Workflow Console is accessible to the administrator through a link in the Share Administrator console or by navigating directly to `http://localhost:8080/alfresco/activiti-admin`. From there, clicking on **Deployments | Upload New** will display the file upload dialog. Then browse to the folder where the `*.bar` file is created.

The process definition is deployed successfully and the bar file is displayed in the list. Once you click the bar file, two files are displayed at the right-hand side of the page: one with a `.bpmn20.xml` extension and the other with `.png`, as seen in the following screenshot. The `*.bpmn20.xml` file is the actual process definition file and the `*.png` file is the activity workflow diagram.

Alfresco currently supports the ability to manage workflow process definitions dynamically via the Workflow Console, assuming the definitions are using existing task models and messages. With the introduction of dynamic models, it is now possible to dynamically manage new workflow process definitions using new task models and messages and client configuration. In addition, it is also possible to deploy workflow definitions directly from a repository location.

Step 2 – creating and deploying the task model

For each task in the process definition (the **form key** attribute), it is possible to associate a task description. The description specifies the information that may be attached to a task, that is, properties (name and data type) and associations (name and type of associated object). A user may view and edit this information in the **Task** dialog within the Alfresco Explorer.

The task model is expressed as a content model, as supported by the data dictionary. To create a task model:

1. Create a new content model for the process definition.
2. Create a custom content type for each task.
3. Within each type, describe the properties and associations (information) required for that task.

The task model can be dynamically deployed without restarting the server.

Dynamically deploying the task models

Dynamic custom models are stored in the new **Models** space (**Company Home | Data Dictionary | Models**). This is a feature that enables dynamic customization of models without requiring a restart of the Alfresco server. This feature is provided from Alfresco Version 3.0.

Upload a custom XML model file to the **Models** space. By default, the model will not be active unless the **Model Active** checkbox is selected during the upload. To activate a previously inactive model, select **View Details** and then select the **Modify** properties icon. In the **Modify Content Properties** page, select the **Model Active** checkbox.

To deactivate a model, select **View Details** and then select the **Modify** properties icon. In the **Modify Content Properties** page, unselect the **Model Active** checkbox.

Deployment of model files can be achieved as an administrator using the `http://< server_name>:<port>/alfresco/faces/jsp/admin/repoadmin-console.jsp` URL.

Use the `activate model contractProcessWorkflowModel.xml` command. This command is used to set the repository model to active and load into runtime data dictionary.

Use the `deploy model alfresco/extension/ contractProcessWorkflowModel.xml` command. This command uploads models to the repository and load into runtime data dictionary. This will also set the repository model as active.

Follow these steps to dynamically deploy a model:

1. Go to **Company Home | Data Dictionary | Models**.

2. In the header, click on **Create Content**:

3. The **Create Content Wizard** is displayed, as shown in the following screenshot:

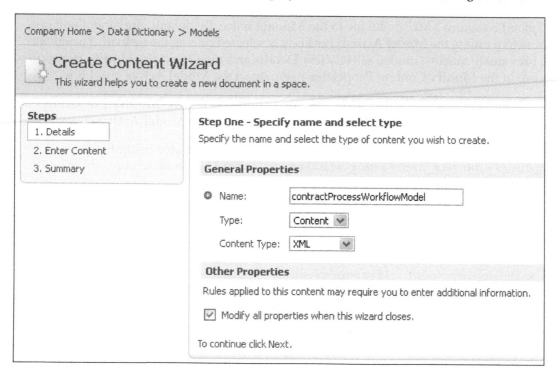

4. In the **Name** textbox, type contracrProcessWorkflowModel.

5. Select **XML** as the **Content Type**.

6. Click on the **Next** button to add content into the specified file.

7. Copy the following content into the content wizard, as shown in the screenshot:

 Download the `contractProcessWorkflowModel.xml` file from the Packt's website.

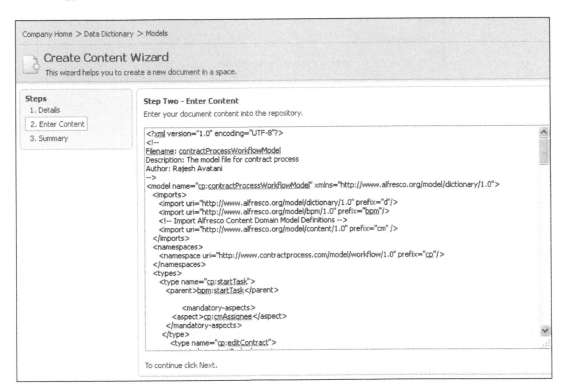

8. Click **Next** and click **Finish**.

9. Check the **Model Active** property, as shown in the following screenshot:

10. Click **OK**.

11. To verify the changes, log out/log in.

Step 3 – creating and deploying the workflow resource bundles

For a localized workflow interaction, it is necessary to provide the resource bundles containing UI labels for each piece of text that is exposed to the user. With the appropriate resource bundles, a single workflow instance may spawn tasks where the user interface for each task is rendered in a different language based on the locale of the user. The resource bundles can also be dynamically deployed without restarting the server.

Dynamically deploy the resource bundles

The associated message resource bundles are stored in the new **Messages** space (**Company Home | Data Dictionary | Messages**). Upload the custom resource bundle by uploading each of the message property files (for all locales) to the **Messages** space. The messages will not be applied until they are explicitly reloaded or when the server is restarted.

They can be dynamically reloaded by using the repo admin console via `http://<server-name>:<port>/alfresco/faces/jsp/admin/repoadmin-console.jsp`.

The `reload messages <resource bundle base name>` command will cause the message resource to be re-registered.

Follow these steps to create:

1. Go to **Company Home | Data Dictionary | Messages**.
2. In the header, click on **Create Content**.

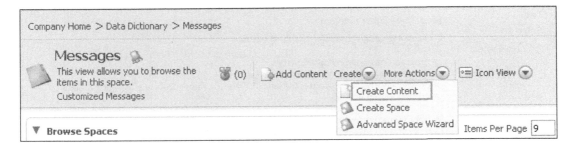

3. The **Create Content Wizard** is displayed, as shown in the following screenshot:

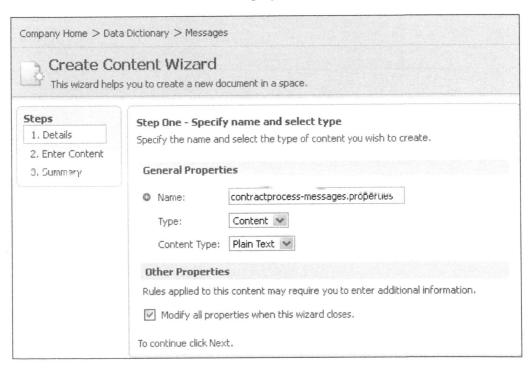

4. In the **Name** textbox, type `contractprocess-messages.properties`.

5. Select **Plain Text** as the **Content Type**.

6. Click on the **Next** button to add content into the specified file.

7. Copy the following content into the content wizard, as shown in the screenshot:

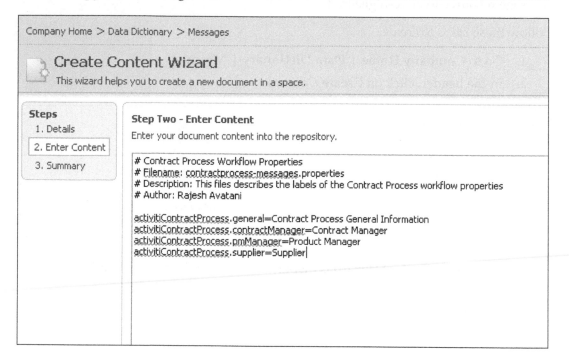

```
# Contract Process Workflow Properties
# Filename: contractprocess-messages.properties
# Description: This files describes the labels of the Contract
Process workflow properties
# Author: Rajesh Avatani

activitiContractProcess.general=Contract Process General
Information
activitiContractProcess.contractManager=Contract Manager
activitiContractProcess.pmManager=Product Manager
activitiContractProcess.supplier=Supplier
```

8. Click **Next** and click **Finish**. Finally, click **OK**.

9. The deployment of the property files can be achieved as an administrator using the `http://<server-name>:<port>/alfresco/faces/jsp/admin/repoadmin-console.jsp` URL.

10. Use the following command to deploy the file:

```
reload messages contractprocess-messages
```

11. To verify the changes, log out/log in.

Step 4 – creating and deploying the Alfresco Explorer Task dialogs

The **Start Workflow Wizard** uses an XML configuration to display the relevant controls to collect the data from the user. The **Manage Task** dialog uses the same approach to display the data it needs to collect. The Alfresco Explorer can also be dynamically deployed without restarting the server.

Dynamic Alfresco Explorer

Dynamic Alfresco Explorer customizations are stored in the new **Web Client Extension** space (**Company Home | Data Dictionary | Web Client Extension**). Upload a custom `web-client-config-custom.xml` file to the **Web Client Extension** space. The custom configuration will not be applied until it is explicitly reloaded or when the server is restarted. If the `web-client-config-custom.xml` file has been added, edited, or updated, it can be dynamically reloaded by using the Alfresco Explorer config console via `http://<server-name>:<port>/alfresco/faces/jsp/admin/webclientconfig-console.jsp`.

This has a single `reload` command, which will cause the Alfresco Explorer configuration to be reloaded.

Follow these steps to create:

1. Browse to the `web-client-config-custom.xml` file specified in the `tomcat/shared/classes/alfresco/extension` location.

2. Copy the following content into the file:

```
<config evaluator="node-type" condition="cp:startTask"
replace="true">
    <property-sheet>
        <separator name="sep1" display-label-
id="activitiContractProcess.general" component-generator="HeaderSe
paratorGenerator" />
        <show-property name="bpm:description" component-
generator="TextAreaGenerator"/>
        <show-property name="bpm:dueDate" />
        <show-property name="bpm:priority"/>
        <show-property name="bpm:status" />
        <show-property name="bpm:comment" component-
generator="TextAreaGenerator" />
```

```
            <separator name="sep2" display-label-id="users_and_roles"
component-generator="HeaderSeparatorGenerator" />
            <show-association name="cp:cmAssignee" display-label-
id="activitiContractProcess.contractManager" />
        </property-sheet>
      </config>


      <config evaluator="node-type" condition="cp:editContract"
replace="true">
        <property-sheet>
            <separator name="sep1" display-label-
id="activitiContractProcess.general" component-generator="HeaderSe
paratorGenerator" />
            <show-property name="bpm:description" component-
generator="TextAreaGenerator"/>
            <show-property name="bpm:dueDate" read-only="true"/>
            <show-property name="bpm:priority" read-only="true"/>
            <show-property name="bpm:status" read-only="true"/>
            <show-property name="bpm:comment" component-
generator="TextAreaGenerator" />

        </property-sheet>
      </config>


      <config evaluator="node-type" condition="cp:reviewContract"
replace="true">
        <property-sheet>
            <separator name="sep1" display-label-
id="activitiContractProcess.general" component-generator="HeaderSe
paratorGenerator" />
            <show-property name="bpm:taskId" />
            <show-property name="bpm:description" component-
generator="TextAreaGenerator"/>
            <show-property name="bpm:dueDate"/>
            <show-property name="bpm:priority"/>
            <show-property name="bpm:status" />
        <show-property name="cp:cmReviewOutcome" />
            <show-property name="bpm:comment" component-
generator="TextAreaGenerator" />
            <separator name="sep2" display-label-id="users_and_roles"
component-generator="HeaderSeparatorGenerator" />
            <show-association name="cp:supplierAssignee" display-
label-id="activitiContractProcess.supplier" />
        <separator name="sep2" display-label-id="users_and_roles"
component-generator="HeaderSeparatorGenerator" />
```

```
        <show-association name="cp:pmAssignee" display-label-
id="activitiContractProcess.pmManager" />
    </property-sheet>
  </config>

  <config evaluator="node-type" condition="cp:supplierReview"
replace="true">
    <property-sheet>
        <separator name="sep1" display-label-
id="activitiContractProcess.general" component-generator="HeaderSe
paratorGenerator" />
            <show-property name="bpm:taskId" />
        <show-property name="bpm:description" component-
generator="TextAreaGenerator" read-only="true"/>
        <show-property name="bpm:dueDate" read-only="true" />
        <show-property name="bpm:priority" read-only="true" />
        <show-property name="bpm:status" />
        <show-property name="cp:supplierReviewOutcome" />
        <show-property name="bpm:comment" component-
generator="TextAreaGenerator" />
    </property-sheet>
  </config>

  <config evaluator="node-type" condition="cp:pmReview"
replace="true">
    <property-sheet>
        <separator name="sep1" display-label-
id="activitiContractProcess.general" component-generator="HeaderSe
paratorGenerator" />
        <show-property name="bpm:taskId" />
        <show-property name="bpm:description" component-
generator="TextAreaGenerator" read-only="true"/>
        <show-property name="bpm:dueDate" read-only="true" />
        <show-property name="bpm:priority" read-only="true" />
        <show-property name="bpm:status" />
        <show-property name="cp:pmReviewOutcome" />
        <show-property name="bpm:comment" component-
generator="TextAreaGenerator" />
    </property-sheet>
  </config>
```

3. Deployment of Alfresco Explorer can be achieved as an administrator using the `http://<server-name>:<port>/alfresco/faces/jsp/admin/webclientconfig-console.jsp` URL.

4. Use the following command to deploy the file:

   `reload`

Step 5 – testing the workflow

Here are the steps to do so:

1. Login as `jim_editor`.

2. Upload a contract to **Company Home | Global Autoparts**. Click the contract's **More Actions** button and click on the **Start Advance Workflow** link.

3. Select **Contract Process** from **List of Predefined Workflows**. Click on the **Next** button.

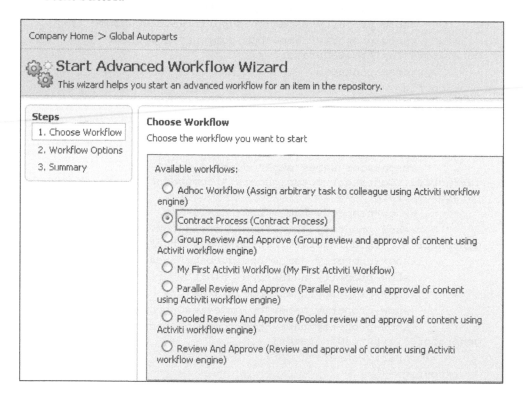

4. Add the **Contract Process General Information** and set **Contract Manager** as **john_cm** from the user list, and click on the **Finish** button:

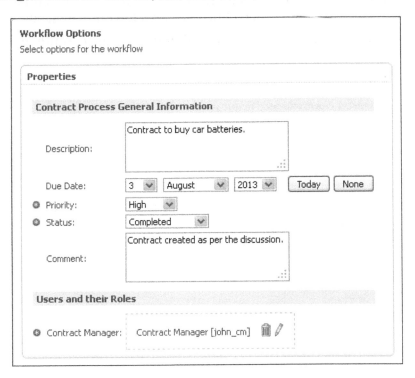

5. Now, logged in as contract manager john_cm, click on the **My Alfresco** menu in toolbar to view your dashboard, that is, **My task To Do**. Shortly we will be discussing the various workflow related dashboards. You will then notice that the review is assigned by the contract editor, jim_editor.

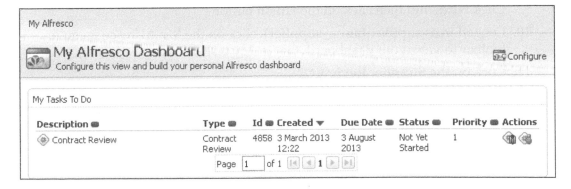

6. Click on the **Contract Review** task.

7. If no further modification is required to the contract by the contract editor, select **Approve** for **cmReviewOutcome** and add your comments.

8. Select **Supplier (anna_supplier)** and **Product Manager (smith_pm)**:

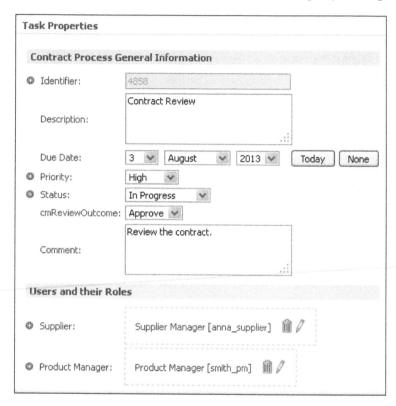

9. Click **Next**, and then click on the **Finish** button.

10. Logged in as supplier (**anna_supplier**), click on the **My Alfresco** menu in toolbar to view your dashboard, that is, **My task To Do**.

11. Click on the **Supplier Review** task.

12. Select **Approve** for the **supplierReviewOutcome** property and add your comments:

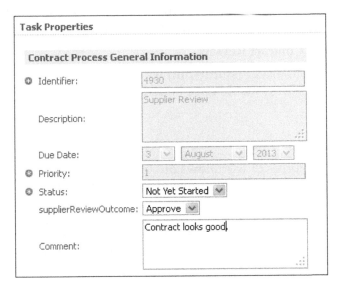

13. Click on the **Task Done** button.

14. Now logged in as the Product Manager (**smith_pm**), click on the **My Alfresco** menu in toolbar to view your dashboard, that is, **My task To Do**.

15. Click on the **PM Review** task.

16. Select **Reject** for the **pmReviewOutcome** property and add your comments:

17. As the Product Manager has rejected the contract, the contract is sent back to Contract Manager for review.

18. Logged in as Contract Manager (**john_cm**). Click on the **My Alfresco** menu in toolbar to view your dashboard, that is, **My task To Do**.

19. You will find **Contract Review**.

20. If the Product Manager (**smith_pm**) would have had to approved the contract, the process would have ended.

Summary

Alfresco includes two types of workflows out of the box. One is the simple workflow that is content-oriented, and the other one is the advanced workflow that is task-oriented.

The simple workflow feature of Alfresco enables you to define a simple approve-reject workflow for your documents. The e-mail templates and notification business rules are helpful to notify all the concerned people involved in the workflow process. You can also implement complex workflows by chaining the spaces with multiple approve and reject steps.

The complex task-oriented workflow requirements can be handled by Advanced Workflow features. Alfresco provides two workflow engines: Activiti and jBPM. You can create your own Activiti custom workflow using Activiti BPMN 2.0 Process Designer; dynamically deploy it using the Activiti Console. You can create a task, attach documents, and send it to multiple people for review. In the next chapter, we will talk about Alfresco integration with external applications.

9
Integrating External Applications with Alfresco

In the previous chapters, we have experienced the content management features of Alfresco as a standalone application. We have used the Alfresco Explorer which is a built-in web application to access and manage the content within Alfresco repository. However, in a real scenario, many customers integrated their own business applications with Alfresco in variety of ways. In this chapter we will focus on the various ways of integrating external applications with Alfresco to leverage the features of highly scalable and high performance content management system.

By the end of this chapter you would have learned about:

- Alfresco Integration Protocols
- Alfresco Web Script framework which provides RESTful web services for integration
- Various application integration examples including Liferay Portal, Drupal CMS, iPhone, and Facebook
- Alfresco Support for CMIS (Content Management Interoperability Service)

Alfresco content platform

Alfresco is architected in such a way that the repository services are separated from the user interface, thus giving infinite options to either embed or integrate with external applications. Alfresco repository can be embedded into customer application or it can be integrated with the customer application as shown in the following figure:

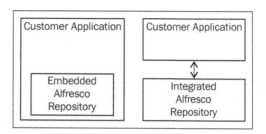

Embeddable Enterprise content management system

Alfresco Enterprise content management server is now available as a standalone embeddable option for OEM's. Alfresco was designed from the ground up to be embedded in modern architectures for the new world of enterprise software. It offers:

- A 100 percent Java WAR file that can be simply run in an application sever

- A system that can share the same JVM as the embedding application or be accessed remotely

- The most scalable standards-based JSR-170 repository

- An environment for rapid development with API sets for REST, Web Services, Java, JSR-170

The Alfresco Enterprise content management system enables OEM/ISV/VARs to focus core engineering resources on their product rather than building and maintaining a proprietary ECM system. Many customers including some of the largest software companies in the world have already "white-labeled" the Alfresco by embedding it in their core products.

Integrated enterprise content management system

At the time of writing this book, over 3000 enterprises in 180 countries adopted Alfresco for solving their business needs. The production applications include Portals, Media Publishing Sites, Extranets, Intranets, Mobile Applications, Public Static Websites, Dynamic Websites, Collaborative Frameworks, Social Networking Sites, Financial applications, Digital Asset Management, and Knowledge Management Systems.

These applications are written using various languages such as Java, PHP, .NET, Python, and Ruby on Rails; Runs on various platforms such as Microsoft Windows, Linux, Unix, Solaris, and IBM; Uses various databases such as Oracle, MySQL, Microsoft SQL, PosgresSQL, and DB2.

Alfresco has integration options independent of programming language, operating system, application server, and the underlying database.

The following figure illustrates some of the current production integrations with Alfresco:

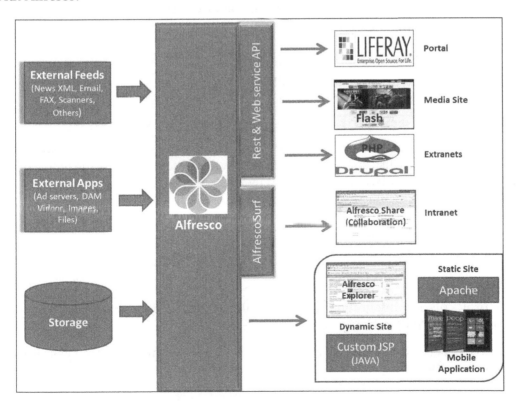

Various protocols to integrate

Alfresco offers the following protocols to integrate with the repository:

- **FTP**: Transfer files in and out of Alfresco repository through FTP protocol
- **CIFS**: Maps Alfresco repository as local drive
- **WebDAV**: Connects to Alfresco repository though HTTP based WebDAV protocol
- **Web Services API**: Provides Web Services support to connect to repository using Java, PHP, .Net based applications
- **Java API**: Connects to Alfresco using Java API
- **JCR API**: Connect using industry standard JCR API
- **RESTful Web Services**: Alfresco Web Scripts framework provides interface with zero installation of client software
- **Microsoft SharePoint Protocol**: Connects to Alfresco repository from Microsoft office applications
- **Alfresco Surf**: A collaborative web framework
- **CMIS**: Content Management Interoperability Service
- **RSS**: Syndication of content
- **OpenSearch**: Open Standards based search interface

Some of the options are explained as follows to give you an idea to explore further.

Using Web service as an integration solution

Web services is widely accepted and mostly used as an interpretability solution for any application. Alfresco also supports SOAP based web services to access the repository of the Alfresco. The web services provided by Alfresco is easy to understand and develop, accessible to almost all clients and languages, and mainly designed for accessing repository remotely by composite applications and business processes.

Using FTP, WebDAV, and CIFS protocols for integration

These protocols and integration options are already covered in *Chapter 5, Implementing Document Management*.

Alfresco can act as a FTP client as well a FTP Server. By default, Alfresco has support for this protocol.

WebDAV is basically used for editing and managing files on the remote web servers. If you have WebDAV client, you can access Alfresco with the URL:

```
http://localhost:8080/alfresco/webdev/
```

The **Common Internet File System (CIFS)** is an excellent way for achieving Desktop integration. Here you use Alfresco as a CIFS server to expose the repository and all the clients (users) would be able to map the repository as a normal windows drive (as Shared network drive).

RESTful web services

Alfresco provides Web Script framework which is based on REST architecture. Nowadays REST architecture has become popular and is widely used as an integration mechanism. RESTful Web Script is the very suitable and flexible solution to integrate Alfresco with any other application and most likely the best solution among all other available options. With the help of Web Scripts, you can easily access the repository of Alfresco and perform all the operations like searching of document, managing a document, and so on from outside the Alfresco also. For more details about Web Script, please refer the following section, in which we have explained the Web Script in detail with some examples.

Web Scripts

Web scripts are basically RESTful web services. Alfresco provides REST architecture based framework for web scripts.

You can achieve **model-view-controller (MVC)** pattern using Web Script to create your own application or API. You can create application which gets render using template language like FreeMarker. It may use Java or JavaScript based Web Script controller to access Alfresco repository and create data model to use it on front-end for generating user interface.

In this section we will talk about Web Script, implementation of Web Script, some Out-of-the box Web Script examples and some custom Web Script examples.

Understanding Web Scripts

A REST Web Script is simply a service bound to a URI and based on HTTP, so the technology that the external application is implemented in is irrelevant. This means that they are cross-platform and cross-language. You are not restricted to any programming language or development environment.

The Web Script framework lets you roll your own APIs, thereby allowing you to fine tune the remote APIs you expose to the external application. REST has proven itself to be simple, flexible, and extremely scalable and it provides a convenient bridge between any native application and the content management and easier content streaming than SOAP. Using Web Scripts, the Alfresco system now provides access to its repository services from anywhere, are easier to access content and workflow information. Web Scripts support access and update using standard HTTP methods and can be constructed using light-weight scripting languages including JavaScript.

By definition, REST-style Web services are resource-oriented services. You can identify and locate resources by a **Universal Resource Identifier (URI)**, and the operations that might be performed against those resources are defined by the HTTP specification. The core operations include GET, POST, PUT, and DELETE.

Web Script allows you to:

- Build custom URI-identified and HTTP accessible Content Management Web Services

- Turn your Alfresco repository into a content management powered HTTP Server

- Easily access, manage, and cross-link your content via a tailored RESTful API

You do not need any special tools or sound Java knowledge. All you need is your favorite text editor to generate the Web Script coding. No compilation, generators, server restarts, or complex installs are required.

With Web Scripts, we can either build our own RESTful interface using light-weight scripting technologies such as JavaScript and FreeMarker, allowing you to arbitrarily map any content in the repository to resources on the web, or we can use pre-built out-of-the-box Web Scripts that already encapsulate many of the mappings. Typically, Web Scripts are used for querying, searching, and accessing content within the repository.

Mainly there are two types of Web Scripts:

- **Data Web Script**: They encapsulate access and modification of content/data held in the repository therefore are provided and exposed only by the Alfresco Repository server. They provide a repository interface for client applications to query, retrieve, update, and perform processes typically using document formats such as XML & JSON. Out-of-the-box, Alfresco provides a series of Data Web Scripts such as. for tagging, activities, site management, and so on.

- **Presentation Web Script**: They allow you to build user interfaces such as a dashlet for Alfresco Explorer or Alfresco Share, a portlet for a JSR-168 portal, a UI component within Alfresco SURF, a website, or a custom Application. They typically render HTML (and perhaps include browser hosted JavaScript). Unlike Data Web Scripts, Presentation Web Scripts may be hosted in the Alfresco repository server or in a separate presentation server. When hosted separately, the Presentation Web Scripts interact with Data Web Scripts. Out-of-the-box Alfresco provides a series of Presentation Web Scripts for example, Portlets, Office Integration, SURF Components.

Implementing Web Scripts

Implementation of Web Script consists of mainly four parts.

1. Create a Web Script:

   You need to create 3 files for this example.

   - Description Document, which describes the URL that initiates the web script along with short name, description, output format, authentication and transactional needs.

   - Controller, optional JavaScript or JavaBean.

   - Rendering template (FreeMarker or xslt which will render the output in desired format XML/HTML/JSON and so on). In case of using Java-based controller extending `AbstractWebSctipt` class, creating template files becomes optional. If you extend `AbstractWebSctipt` class that means you can control request and response such like any other MVC framework.

2. Store the Web Script:

   There are 2 ways to store the Web Scripts in Alfresco

   - Store it in Executable content:

     - You can store web script files in **Company Home | Data Dictionary | Web Script Extensions**.

     - Create required folder structure under above path and then put web script files, description document, rendering template and controller script (if you have).

- ° Store it on classpath extension:
  - ° If you want to store it on File System, you need to store it under the directory, `<<alfresco_server>>/tomcat/shared/extension/templates/webscripts`. You can create desired folder structure inside the above mentioned directory and then put all the web scripts files there.

3. Register the Web Script:
   - ° Once you are done with storing required files of the Web Script, you need to register it to Alfresco.
   - ° For registering the Web Scripts stored in Alfresco Explorer, go to `http://localhost:8080/alfresco/service/index`. Click on the **Refresh Web Scripts** button. You will be able to see a message with how many web scripts were found and registered recently.
   - ° For registering the Web Scripts stored on File System, it requires the restart of the Alfresco server.

4. List the Web Scripts for external access:

   Now you can use the Web Script which we developed with the proper URL, you have mentioned in description document file. For example,

   `http://localhost:8080/alfresco/service/index/package/org/alfresco/portlets`

   Or else you can go to,

   `http://localhost:8080/alfresco/service/index` and then choose Browse by URL or Browse by Package and so on. and then select particular Web Script which we create.

Hello World example

As in above section, we have mentioned four parts of web script for implementation. We will take a Hello World example in this section and walk through all the four steps. In this example, we will just try to greet the use who is executing this Web Script.

1. Create a Web Script:

   Create `greeting.get.desc.xml` file with the detail of URL, authentication and all.

```
<webscript>
  <shortname>Welcome</shortname>
  <description>Polite greeting</description>
  <url>/sample/greeting</url>
```

```
<authentication>user</authentication>
</webscript>
```

Let's understand the meaning of tags added in the preceding code:

- `shortname`: It is a human readable name for the Web Script
- `description` (optional): It is brief documentation for the Web Script
- `url` (one or more): It is a URL Template using which Web Script can be called
- `authentication` (optional): It specifies the level of authentication needed prior to executing Web Script; It is important to understand that, if authentication level is not mentioned then it is considered as none. The following are the valid values of it:
  - `none`: specifies that no authentication is required
  - `guest`: specifies that at least guest authentication is needed
  - `user`: specifies that at least specified user authentication is required
  - `admin`: specifies that at least a named admin authentication is required

Here we don't require any controller as we are just displaying greeting message.

Create response template file for with output as `greeting.get.html.ftl` like,

```
Welcome ${person.properties.userName}
```

2. Store the Web Script:
   - We will store the 2 files in **Company Home | Data Dictionary | Web Script Extensions**.
   - Next, we will create folder structure like **org | Alfresco | sample** if it's not already there and then put the 2 files in this sample folder.

3. Register the Web Script:
   - To register the Web Script, go to `http://localhost:8080/alfresco/service/index`
   - Click on the **Refresh Web Scripts** button.

4. List the Web Scripts for external access:
   - Now you can access this Web Script with the help of specified URL:
   - `http://localhost:8080/alfresco/service/sample/greeting`

    ◦   When you hit this URL from browser, you will be able to see the greeting message as, **Welcome admin**, meaning your Web Script is working perfectly.

    ◦   This Web Script is authenticated as user and hence admin is the username.

Sample out-of-the-box portlet Web Scripts

Alfresco is providing some Out-of-the-box Web Scripts for portlet integration with JSR 168 portlets. Some of the examples for portlet Web Scripts are as follows:

Myspaces portlet

This Web Script displays the documents and spaces in the repository as a portlet. You can upload new documents in any spaces or you can also upload new documents in any space with the help of this Web Script.

URL: `http://<host>:<port>/alfresco/service/ui/`
`myspaces?f={filter?}&p={path}`

Example: `http://<host>:<port>/alfresco/service/ui/`
`myspaces?f=0&p=%2FCompany%20Home`

Document list portlet Web Script

This web script displays the documents available in the repository, you can filter those by particular type of document, also you can give path and query along with type of document as input parameters.

URL:

`http://<host>:<port>/alfresco/service/ui/doclist?f={filter?}&p={path?`
`}&q={query?}`

Example:

`http://<host>:<port>/alfresco/service/ui/doclist?f=0`

In the preceding example, the parameter `0` stands for all documents. You can also pass your path query to search in specific location in parameter `q` (For example, `q=PATH:"/app:company_home"`).

Web Script to list latest documents

This example shows how to integrate some external Java-based web-based application with Alfresco. Here we have one web application which displays the recently modified documents on the daily dose documents page. If the daily dose date of any document is greater than or equal to today, then this document should be listed on the daily dose page of the web application. All the documents are managed by alfresco repository and daily dose date will be one of the metadata for this document. Now we will generate a Web Script, which will be responsible to display these documents on the web application. This Web Script will return HTML output, which we can easily incorporate in the existing web application.

Daily dose integration Web Script detail

In the following table you can see description, end goal, and different conditions scenario for daily dose integration Web Script.

Description:	This web script is responsible for displaying the latest documents updated on daily basis on an external web application.
Links:	Home page of external application
Package:	recentdocuments.dailydose
Web script base URL:	/recentdocuments/dailydose/listDailyDose
Output:	HTML having following details of documents: • document title (with link) • type of document • author • expiration date
Conditions	Documents whose End Daily Dose Date is greater than or equal to current date
Controller	JavaScript as a controller, which will fetch the documents from the alfresco repository fulfilling above specified condition

Follow the given steps to create a Web Script:

1. Create a `listDailyDose.get.desc.xml`

   ```
   <webscript>
     <shortname>Listing of Daily Dose Document Through
     Webscript</shortname>
     <description>Contains the list of daily dose
     documents</description>
   ```

```
<url>/recentdocuments/dailydose/listDailyDose</url>
<authentication>guest</authentication>
<transaction>required</transaction>
</webscript>
```

2. Create a `listDailyDose.get.js` file, It will contain controller logic for Web Script,

```
var l_customerDocs =
companyhome.childByNamePath("CustomerDocuments");
model.m_documents_node=l_customerDocs;
```

3. Create a `listDailyDose.ftl.html` file. See the following code snippet:

```
<#list m_documents_node.children as cust_documents>
<#if (dateCompare(cust_documents.properties["CUST:EndDailyDoseDate
"],date)) == 1>
<tr>
<td>
<img src="${url.context}${cust_documents.icon32}"/>
</td>
<td align="center">
<a class="title" href="/alfresco/${cust_documents.url}">${cust_
documents.properties.name}</a>
</td>
<td> </td>
<td align="center"> ${cust_documents.properties["CUST:DocumentTy
pe"]}
</td>
<td> </td>
<td> ${cust_documents.properties.creator}</td>
<td> </td>
<#if cust_documents.properties["CUST:ExpirationDate"]?exists>
<td align="center">
${cust_documents.properties["CUST:ExpirationDate"]?date}
</td>
<#else>
<td> </td>
    </tr>
</#if>
</#list>
```

Let's understand the preceding code snippet:

As you see in controller code, m_documents_node stores nodes under CustomerDocuments. In template code you can see loop for children nodes. It displays the property for children nodes whose EndDailyDoseDate date match with current date you can find information about FreeMarker tags from `http://wiki.alfresco.com/wiki/FreeMarker_Template_Cookbook`

4. Store the Web Script:

    To Store this Web Script browse to **Company Home | Data Dictionary | Web Script Extensions** and create folder hierarchy named **recentdocuments | dailydose**. Store all the three files here.

5. Browse to the folder **Company Home | Data Dictionary | Models folder**. Add the `custModel.xml`. Make the model active by checking the Active property.

6. Browse to the folder **Company Home | Data Dictionary | Web Scripts Extensions**. Add the `web-client-config custom.xml`. Deployment of Alfresco Explorer can be achieved as administrator using the following URL: `http://localhost:8080/alfresco/faces/jsp/admin/webclientconfig-console.jsp`.

7. Use the following command to deploy the file:

    reload

 Download the `custModel.xml` and `web-client-config-custom.xml` from Packt publisher's book website.

8. Create a space called as CustomerDocuments in company home. Upload few documents in the folder. Apply the aspect Customer Document Details to all the documents. Register the Web Script. For registering, go to `http://<host>:<port>/alfresco/service/index`

    Click on the **Refresh Web Scripts** button. You will be able to see a message with how many web scripts were found and registered recently.

9. List the Web Scripts for external access:

    Now you can use the Web Script which we developed with the proper URL, you have mentioned in description document file. For our example URL is:

    `http://<host>:<port>/alfresco/service/index/uri/recentdocuments/dailydose/listDailyDose`

Please find below the screenshot of the daily dose page of web application which is generated with the use of above mentioned web script.

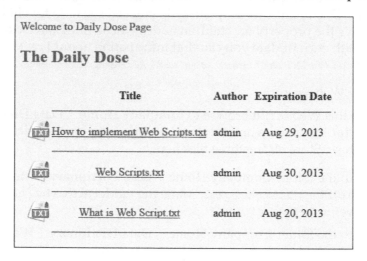

Integrating Web Script with an external Java application

You can call this http URL in the JSP of your web application and can embed the HTML output return by this Web Script in your JSP.

You can call Web Script in browser using the following code snippet.

```html
<html>
<title> The Daily Dose </title>
<body bgcolor="#edf6fc" text="blue">
<head bgcolor="#edf6fc"> Welcome to Daily Dose Page</head>
<H2 bgcolor="#edf6fc"> The Daily Dose</H2>
<iframe bgcolor="#edf6fc" width="60%" height="60%"frameborder=0
src="http://localhost:8080/alfresco/service/recentdocuments/dailydose/
listDailyDose"/>
</body>
</html>
```

Web Script to integrate document search

Since Alfresco could be used as content repository, it's a very suitable use case where we have external application, with any kind of rich user interface and we have a search interface incorporated which will search inside the content repository and displays the result based on some input parameters. You can also define some filtering criteria for searching the documents from the Alfresco.

In this example, we will search the documents in the Alfresco with some parameters like client name, keyword, and so on metadata of the documents. This will return XML/HTML output. You can process XML output in your application and orchestrate the UI layer. And if you want to display it as an HTML then you can use HTML output of the same Web Script, which you can directly incorporate in your application.

Document search Web Script detail

In the following table you can see description, end goal, and different conditions scenario for document search Web Script:

Description:	This Web Script is responsible for searching the documents from the repository based on some input parameters.
Links:	Home page of external application
Package:	custdocuments.searchDocs
Web Script base URL:	`/custdocuments/searchDocs.xml?keyword={keyword?}&amp;clientname={clientname?}`
	`/custdocuments/searchDocs?keyword={keyword?}&amp;clientname={clientname?}`
Input parameters:	Keywords
	client_name
Output:	XML/HTML (we will use free marker template language to generate XML/HTML file)
	• document title (with link)
	• type of document
	• author
	• expiration date
Conditions	None
Controller	We will have JavaScript as a controller, which will search the documents from the Alfresco repository based on the criteria specified in the Input parameters.

Following are the four parts of Web Scripts:-

Creating Web Scripts

Basically three files are required, Description Document, search `Docs.get.desc.xml` as,

```xml
<webscript>
  <shortname>
    Searching of Documents in the repository Through Webscript
  </shortname>
   <description>
    Searches the documents in the repository
  </description>
   <url>
  /custdocuments/searchDocs?keyword={keyword?}&amp;clientname={client
name?}
  </url>
   <url>
  /custdocuments/searchDocs.xml?keyword={keyword?}&amp;clientname={cl
ientname?}
  </url>
   <authentication>user</authentication>
   <transaction>required</transaction>
</webscript>
```

Controller, JavaScript, or JavaBean, in this example, we will use JavaScript. The JavaScript, `searchDocs.get.js` will contain code for searching documents. It searches provided parameters in Alfresco repository. As you see in the following code snippet, code for pagination is given first after that it checks for valid arguments. Once all the parameters are properly inserted, it creates query to find the documents and store the search result in a model.

```javascript
var l_folder = "app:company_home/cm:CustomerDocuments";
var l_search_docs = new Object();
if (args.startpage == undefined)
{
   l_search_docs.startPage = 1;
}
else
{
   l_search_docs.startPage = parseInt(args.startpage);
}
if (args.count == undefined)
{
   l_search_docs.itemsPerPage = 5;
}
```

```
else
{
    l_search_docs.itemsPerPage = parseInt(args.count);
}
l_search_docs.startIndex = (l_search_docs.startPage-1) * l_search_
docs.itemsPerPage;
l_search_docs.searchTerms ="";

if (args.keyword == null || args.keyword.length == 0) {
  status.code = 400;
  status.message = "\"keyword\" argument is null or undefined";
  status.redirect = true;
}
else if (args.clientname == null || args.clientname.length == 0) {
  status.code = 400;
  status.message = "\"clientname\" argument is null or undefined";
  status.redirect = true;
}
else
{
  l_search_docs.searchTerms = args.keyword;
  l_search_docs.clientName = args.clientname;
  query = buildSearchQuery();
  var results = search.luceneSearch(query);
  l_search_docs.results = results;
  l_search_docs.totalResults = results.length;
  l_search_docs.totalPages = Math.ceil(results.length / l_search_docs.
itemsPerPage);
  model.m_search_docs = l_search_docs;
}
function addQueryCriterion(param, value, isContained) {
  var valueStub;
  if (isContained) {
    valueStub = "*" + value + "*";
  }
  else {
    valueStub = value;
  }
  criterion = " AND @CUST\\:" + param + ":" + valueStub;
  return criterion;
}
function buildSearchQuery() {
      searchQuery = "PATH:\"//" + l_folder + "//*\"";
    if (args.keyword != null) {
```

```
        searchQuery += addQueryCriterion("Keywords", args.keyword, true);
    }

    if (args.clientname != null) {
      searchQuery += addQueryCriterion("ClientName", args.clientname,
true);
    }
    return searchQuery;
}
```

Rendering template, FreeMarker or xslt which will render the output in desired format XML/HTML/JSON and so on. we will use FreeMarker with HTML output in this example.

The FreeMarker template file `searchDocs.ftl.xml` as,

```
<?xml version="1.0" encoding="UTF-8"?>
<items>
  <#if m_search_docs.results?exists>
  <#assign count=0>
  <#assign index=0>
  <#list m_search_docs.results as l_result_document>
  <#if (index>=m_search_docs.startPage) &&              (index<m_
search_docs.startPage+m_search_docs.itemsPerPage)>
  <#assign count=count+1>
  <#assign curl=url.serviceContext>
  <item>
    <name>${l_result_document.properties.name}</name>
    <title>
      <#if l_result_document.properties.title?exists>
        ${l_result_document.properties.title}
      </#if>
    </title>
    <size> ${l_result_document.size} </size>
    <author>${l_result_document.properties.creator}</author>
    <clientname>                                <#if l_result_document.prop
erties["CUST:ClientName"]?exists>
      ${l_result_document.properties["CUST:ClientName"]}
    </#if>
    </clientname>
    <expirationdate>
    <#if l_result_document.properties["CUST:ExpirationDate"]?exists>
    ${l_result_document.properties["CUST:ExpirationDate"]?datetime}
    </#if>
    </expirationdate>
```

```
    <modificationdate>
    <#if l_result_document.properties["cm:modified"]?exists>
      ${l_result_document.properties["cm:modified"]?datetime}
    </#if>
    </modificationdate>
  </item>
  </#if>
  <#assign index=index+1>
  </#list>
  <#else>
    No results to display.
  </#if>
</items>
```

And the FreeMarker template file for HTML output, searchDocs.ftl.html as,

```
<html>
    <head>
        <title>Alfresco Search</title>
    </head>
    <body>
        <b>Search Results: </b>
        <#if m_search_docs.results?exists>
        <#assign count=0>
        <#assign index=0>
        Showing page <b>${m_search_docs.startPage}</b> of <b>${m_
search_docs.totalPages}</b> from <b>${m_search_docs.totalResults}</b>
results for Keyword : <b>${m_search_docs.searchTerms}</b> and
        Client: <b>${m_search_docs.clientName}</b>
        <br> <br>
        <table>
            <tr>
                <th> </th> <th> Name of Document </th>
                <th> </th> <th> Author </th>
                <th> </th> <th> Client Name </th>
                <th> </th> <th> Expiration Date</th>
            </tr>
            <#list m_search_docs.results as l_result_document>
                <#if (index>=m_search_docs.startIndex) && (index<m_
search_docs.startIndex+m_search_docs.itemsPerPage )>
                    <#assign count=count+1>
                    <#assign curl=url.serviceContext>
                        <tr>
                            <td>
```

```
                            <img src="${url.context}${l_result_
document.icon16}"/>Integrating External Applications with Alfresco
                        </td>
                        <td align="center">
                            <a class="title" href="/alfresco/${l_
result_document.url}">${l_result_document .properties.name}</a>
                        </td>
                        <td> </td>
                        <td> ${l_result_document.properties.creator}
</td>
                        <td> </td>
                        <td align="center">${l_result_document.
properties["CUST:ClientName"]} </td>
                        <td> </td>
                        <#if l_result_document.properties["CUST:Expira
tionDate"]?exists>
                            <td align="center"> ${l_result_document.pr
operties["CUST:ExpirationDate"]?d ate} </td>
                        <#else>
                            <td> </td>
                        </#if>
                    </tr>
                    <tr>
                        <td> </td>
                        <td> <HR> </td> <td> <HR> </td>
                        <td> <HR> </td> <td> <HR> </td>
                        <td> <HR> </td> <td> <HR> </td>
                        <td> <HR> </td> <td> <HR> </td>
                    </tr>
                </#if>
                <#assign index=index+1>
            </#list>
        </table>
        <br>
        <#if (m_search_docs.startPage > 1)>
            <a href="${url.service}?keyword=${m_search_docs.
searchTerms}&clientname=${m_search_docs.clientName}&startpage=0&cou
nt=${m_search_docs.itemsPerPage}">
        </#if>
            First
        <#if (m_search_docs.startPage > 0)></a></#if> |
        <#if (m_search_docs.startPage > 1)>
            <a href="${url.service}?keyword=${m_search_docs.
searchTerms} &clientname=${m_search_docs.clientName}&startpage=${m_s
earch_docs.startPage -1}&count=${m_search_docs.itemsPerPage}"></#if>
```

```
                    Prev
    <#if (m_search_docs.startPage > 0)></a></#if> |
    <#if (m_search_docs.startPage < m_search_docs.totalPages)>
        <a href="${url.service}?keyword=${m_search_docs.
searchTerms}&clientname=${m_search_docs.clientName}&startpage=${m_s
earch_docs.startPage +1}&count=${m_search_docs.itemsPerPage}"></#if>
            Next
    <#if (m_search_docs.startPage+1 < m_search_docs.totalPages)></
a></#if> |

    <#if (m_search_docs.startPage < m_search_docs.totalPages)>
        <a href="${url.service}?keyword=${m_search_docs.
searchTerms}&clientname=${m_search_docs.clientName}&startpage=${m_s
earch_docs.totalPages - 1}&count=${m_search_docs.itemsPerPage}"></#if>
            Last
    <#if (m_search_docs.startPage+1 < m_search_docs.totalPages)></
a></#if>
    <#else>
        <i>No results to display.</i>
    </#if>
</body>
</html>
```

Storing Web Scripts

To Store this Web Script browse to **Company Home | Data Dictionary | Web Script Extensions** and create folders named custdocuments. Store all the previous three files here.

 Download the files from Packt publisher's book website.

Register Web Scripts

Once you develop the Web Script, you need to register it to use. For registering, go to http://localhost:8080/alfresco/service/index.

Click on the **Refresh Web Scripts** button. You will be able to see a message with how many Web Scripts were found and registered recently.

Listing Web Scripts for external access

Now you can use the Web Script, which we developed with the proper URL, you have mentioned in description document file. For our example URLs are:

```
http://<host>:<port>/alfresco/service/custdocuments/searchDocs.xml?ke
yword={keyword?}&clientname={clientName?}
```

```
http://<server_name>:<port>/alfresco/service/custdocuments/searchDocs
?keyword={keyword?}&clientname={clientName?}
```

Calling Web Scripts from an external application

You can call this http URL in the JSP of your web application and can embed the HTML output return by this web script in your JSP. Or you can use the Web Script with XML output and process that returned XML in your application itself.

Please find the following screenshot for the XML output returned by this Web Script:

```xml
<?xml version="1.0" encoding="UTF-8"?>
<items>
                <item>
        <name>Web Scripts.txt</name>
        <title>

        </title>
        <size> 270 </size>
        <author>admin</author>
        <clientname>
            HaveFun
        </clientname>
        <expirationdate>
            Aug 30, 2013 1:59:00 PM
        </expirationdate>
        <modificationdate>
            Feb 10, 2013 2:30:04 PM
        </modificationdate>
        </item>
        <item>
        <name>What is Web Script.txt</name>
        <title>

        </title>
        <size> 41,956 </size>
        <author>admin</author>
        <clientname>
            HaveFun
        </clientname>
        <expirationdate>
            Aug 20, 2013 2:00:00 PM
        </expirationdate>
        <modificationdate>
            Feb 10, 2013 2:30:13 PM
        </modificationdate>
        </item>
</items>
```

Please find the following screenshot for the HTML output returned by this Web Script:

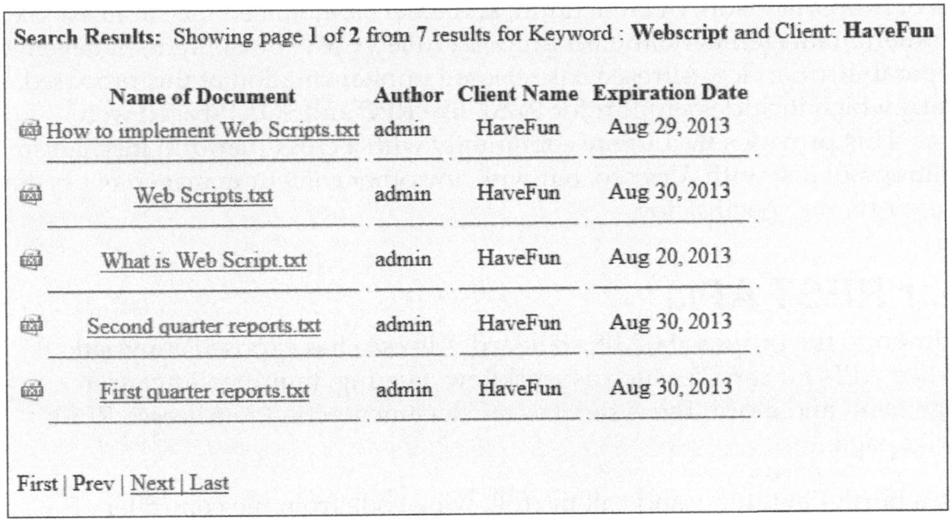

Search Results: Showing page 1 of **2** from 7 results for Keyword : **Webscript** and Client: **HaveFun**

Name of Document	Author	Client Name	Expiration Date
How to implement Web Scripts.txt	admin	HaveFun	Aug 29, 2013
Web Scripts.txt	admin	HaveFun	Aug 30, 2013
What is Web Script.txt	admin	HaveFun	Aug 20, 2013
Second quarter reports.txt	admin	HaveFun	Aug 30, 2013
First quarter reports.txt	admin	HaveFun	Aug 30, 2013

First | Prev | Next | Last

Various application integration examples

This section contains various production examples which are currently available. Hence, before developing integration with Alfresco, you can check these examples to evaluate if you could reuse any of them for your application.

Various available options

With Alfresco version 4.x, to use Alfresco with Liferay, there are different options. Some of them are explained in the following sections.

Using web service

Alfresco supports web service that offers way to access Alfresco repository from any remote application. There are list of web service that comes with Alfresco to access file and folder from remote application. You can also develop your custom web service to satisfy your requirement to access content in Alfresco.

Using the CMIS proposed standard

Alfresco, IBM, Microsoft, Documentum, and others announced the submission of a new content management standard proposal called CMIS or Content Management Interoperability Service. Alfresco has released implementation of this proposed standard which includes support for REST-like RPC and SOAP-based web services. This provides the Liferay community with a cross-platform mechanism of integrating not just with Alfresco, but with any other content management system that supports the specification.

Other REST APIs

In addition to the proposed CMIS standard, Alfresco has exposed a myriad of REST-like APIs for services such as workflow, tagging, thumbnailing, user management, and more. These services are documented in the Alfresco REST API wiki page.

Create a portlet in Liferay and call the following code from the controller of the portlet.

```
/* Initializing resource bundle to load property file */
ResourceBundle resource = ResourceBundle.getBundle(REST_BUNDLE);

/* Reading URL, user and password */
String _urlString = resource.getString(URL);
String _user = resource.getString(USER_NAME);
String _password = resource.getString(PASSWORD);
String _content = null;
try {
  // Prepare the request
  Request _request = new Request(Method.GET, _urlString);
  ChallengeResponse challengeResponse = new ChallengeResponse(Challeng
eScheme.HTTP_BASIC, _user, _password);
  _request.setChallengeResponse(challengeResponse);

  // Handle it using an HTTP client connector
  Client _client = new Client(Protocol.HTTP);
  Response _response = _client.handle(_request);

  // Write the response entity on the console
  if (_response.getStatus().isSuccess()) {
    if (_response != null) {
      _content = _response.getEntity().getText();
      System.out.println("Response output : \n"+_ouput);
```

```
    } else if (Status.CLIENT_ERROR_UNAUTHORIZED.equals(_response.
getStatus())) {
        System.out.println("TestRest.java: Unauthorized access");
    } else {
        System.out.println("TestRest.java: Unexpected status");
    }
} catch(IOException e) {
    // Handle exception
}
```

 Download the `TestRest.java` file from Packt publisher's book website.

Using your own API

You can write your own API for communicating Liferay with Alfresco.

This method consists on creating an API which communicates with Alfresco, this API is independent from Liferay, you can use it in a portlet, a servlet or a normal Java application and this API allows you to search, delete, send documents, and so on to Alfresco through web services.

For example, you can search in a space (filtering by one property) and you obtain a list with all the documents found. Then, in your Liferay Portlet you can work with that list as you prefer. The advantage is that allows you to have Liferay and Alfresco in different machines.

Integrating with Drupal

Drupal is a very powerful open source based web content management framework. It is developed using PHP language. More information about Drupal can be found at `http://www.drupal.org`.

Drupal-Alfresco is a good choice in scenarios where there is a significant amount of file-based content that requires services such as workflow, versioning, security, check-in/check-out, but needs to be shared in the context of a community. Alfresco acts as backend content repository and Drupal acts as front-end presentation layer. Here, Drupal really becomes equivalent in terms of where it sits in the architecture and the role it plays to traditional portals like Liferay or JBoss Portal.

Content from Drupal is harder for other systems to get to than if it sits in Alfresco. There are Drupal modules that make it easier to syndicate but Alfresco is built to expose content in this way. Once it is in Alfresco, content can be routed through Alfresco workflows, and then approved to be made available to one or more front-end Drupal sites. Content could come from a Drupal site, get persisted to Alfresco, routed around for editorial review, and then be made available.

Not all Drupal modules need to persist their data back to Alfresco. Things like comments and ratings will likely never need to be treated as real content. Instead of trying to persist everything you would either modify select modules to integrate with Alfresco or create new ones that work with Alfresco. For example, you might want to have Drupal stick file uploads in Alfresco instead of the local file system. Or, it might make sense to have a **send to Alfresco** button visible to certain roles that would send the current node to Alfresco.

You may also want to get some Drupal data from within Alfresco or want to tag objects using the same set of tags Drupal knows about, or maybe you want to do a mass import of Drupal objects into the Alfresco repository, all this is possible by integrating Alfresco and Drupal.

Following is a code snippet through which you can access your Alfresco through Drupal.

Hello world is the simple Web Script created in alfresco to test the Drupal Alfresco integration.

```
function data_from_webscript_block1() {
  $output = '';
  $url = 'http://<host>:<port>/alfresco/service/
   /facebook/helloworld';
  $http_result = drupal_http_request($url);
  if ($http_result->code == 200) {
    $doc = $http_result->data;
    $output .= $doc;
  }
  else {
    $msg = 'No content from %url.';
    $vars = array('%url' => $url);
    watchdog('data_from_webscript', $msg, $vars, WATCHDOG_WARNING);
    return t("The webscript is not accessible.");
  }
  return $output;
}
```

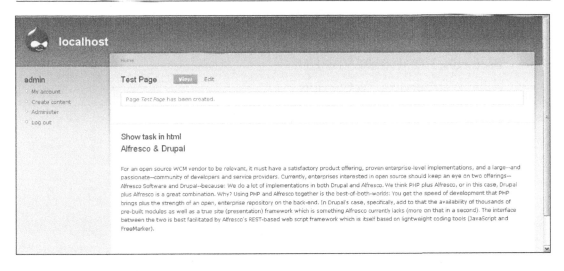

Recent version of Drupal support CMIS. Using CMIS support now it's possible to integrate Drupal with any content management repository which offers support of CMIS protocol. You can refer this link for more information `http://drupal.org/ project/cmis`.

Integrating with Adobe Flex

Providing a Flex-based client to access Alfresco content repository, can Improve user experience by delivering an easily customizable and highly-interactive interface, seamless integration in the user desktop and cross-platform.

There can be two approaches to this, the first approach uses custom Java services and the second one uses Alfresco Web Scripts (REST).

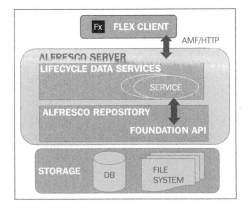

LiveCycle Data Services is Adobe server-side component that allows communication between Flex client and Java application. Several options to create an Alfresco client:

- Protocols: FTP, WebDAV, CIFS
- APIs: Web Services, Web Scripts
- Custom solution that uses the Alfresco Foundation API directly

Next steps could be to create an AIR application to leverage:

- integration with user's desktop
- Drag-n-Drop documents (inbound/outbound)
- Access file system
- Embedded SQL DB to provide offline functions

For more details on Alfresco and Flex integration, refer *Chapter 11, Customizing the User Interface*.

E-mail integration – MS Outlook, Lotus Notes, Novell, and Thunderbird

Using Third party product Alfresco can be configured as a Mail Server or a Mail Client Application. This makes for an effective e-mail management for users, who will benefit from the convenience and speed. The users can simply drag-and-drop emails directly into the Alfresco repository for automatic filing. Familiarity with the tools makes the interaction easy. The users can find and view documents and e-mails from the e-mail client or file system view. The document search is regardless of the document format. The user can configure rules based on which they can store and share outgoing e-mails

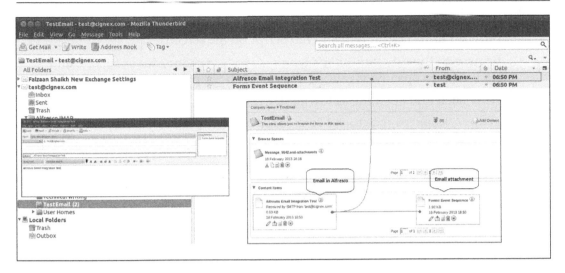

This can allow the organization to create a secure, auditable central store of information and correspondence that can easily demonstrate compliance with regulatory requirements and respond to requests for information. Information can be made available for everyone and duplication of data avoided. Enhanced productivity, facilitated and improved knowledge sharing and collaboration are all the by-products. Even if a staff member leaves, key information is readily available within the organization. A cross-team or cross-project view of all communications internally and with customers or other external parties is readily available.

Integrating with iPhone

We built a simple Alfresco navigator for iPhone. It is in fact an iPhone-friendly web client. This navigator is backed by three Web Scripts (one for DM space/doc navigation, one for WCM navigation and one for search) and leverages open source iUI package to provide looking-n-feel. The performance of the navigator is quite good on iPhone. The script shows different branches of a single DOM tree based on where you are and when you navigate down to a new space or web project directory it will add the new nodes to the tree. The capabilities of the navigator include: navigation of spaces, docs, web projects, preview of images, PDF's websites, search, and display posts and topics attached to the docs.

To install the package on your Alfresco, simply follow the given steps:

- Unzip `iui.zip` to `tomcat/webapps/alfresco/scripts`
- Import `iphone-navigator.zip` to Company Home | Data Dictionary | Web Scripts Extensions

- Open the URL: `http://<host>:<port>/alfresco/service/index` in your browser and click on refresh Web Script on the screen.

- Browse to the `Web Script package /org/alfresco/demo/iphone` and click on it to open Navigation (iPhone) Web Script.

- Now click and open the following URL:

    ```
    http://<host>:<port>/alfresco/service/iphone/
    navigation?p={path?}
    ```

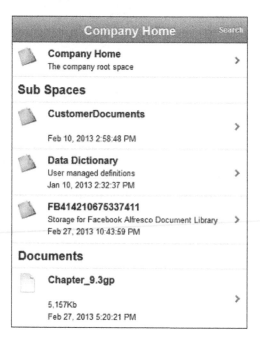

Download the `iui.zip`, `iphone-navigator.zip` file from Packt publisher's book website.

Alfresco Mobile application

Now a days Smartphone and tablet becomes very common in our day-to-day activity. Using them for accessing corporate content that you need to work with is not a bad idea. Alfresco now offers Mobile application to manage content from iOS and Android based smartphone and tablets. Using this facility now you can access your document totally free with help of these applications. Mobile application provides facilities to view, open, and edits documents, workflow initiation and complete functions, content collaborate, assign and monitor tasks, and achieve many other activities for mobile document sharing.

Document management and file sharing using iPad has become critical requirements for most companies; Alfresco Mobile is designed to address this challenges.

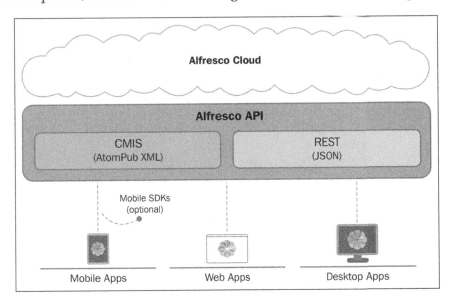

Such like web client and Alfresco share, Alfresco provides mobile SDK and API. It allows developers to build custom application for enterprise. The Alfresco Mobile SDK is an optional interface layer specifically for iOS and Android mobile app developers who wish to develop application, for more information about mobile SDK and API check `developer.alfresco.com`.

You can download free Alfresco application for Android based smartphone or tablets from `https://play.google.com/store/apps/details?id=org.alfresco.mobile.android.application` and for iOS based smartphones and tables from `https://itunes.apple.com/us/app/alfresco/id459242610?mt=8`

Alfresco now offers cloud based services as well. You can subscribe for cloud access and get 10 GB free space for evaluating cloud services. You can simply access cloud Alfresco site from your mobile application you installed.

Here are the steps to configure or access Alfresco application in mobile. You can install mobile application in your smartphone or tablet. Following are the simple steps to configure Alfresco instance with mobile application:

1. Open Alfresco mobile application. You will see the following screenshot with two options. If you already have cloud account, simply click on **Alfresco Cloud** button or sign-up for cloud access.

    If you have installed Alfresco on your server and want to access it from your mobile application, click on **Alfresco Server** button.

2. If you are accessing cloud space, you simply enter your username and password to access your files from mobile application. To access your Alfresco server, provide following detail of your and configure it to access it on mobile application.

3. Once you configured Alfresco server with your mobile application, You can access Alfresco content in your mobile.

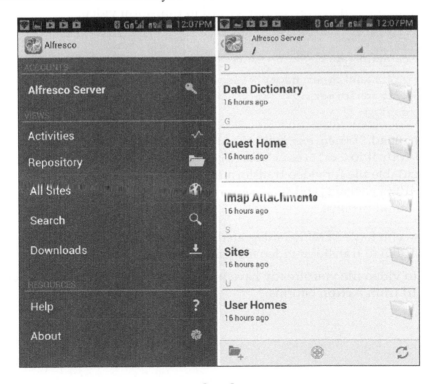

Integrating with FFMPEG video transcoder

FFMPEG is a very popular high performance video and audio transcoder. It is widely used various commercial tools to convert audio and video files from one format to another. It is basically a command-line interface. We can easily integrate any such command-line applications easily with Alfresco.

After Alfresco 4, FFMPEG integration come out-of-the-box. Based on your requirement you enable and configure it. In this section we will see steps to configure FFMPEG in Alfresco.

1. Go to `<<alfresco_server>>\tomcat\shared\classes\alfresco\extension` folder and rename the following two files:

   ○ `video-thumbnail-context.xml.sample` to `video-thumbnail-context.xml`

   ○ `video-transformation-context.xml.sample` to `video-transformation-context.xml`

2. Copy following code to `<<alfresco_server>>\tomcat\shared\classes\alfresco\extension\web-client-config-custom.xml` file to add MP4 file type in action wizard. You can also add as many mime-types you wish to add based on your requirement. Once you add any mime-type here, you will get it as an option from action wizard to transform video.

   ```
   <config evaluator="string-compare" condition="Action
   Wizards">
     <transformers>
       <transformer name="video/mp4"/>
     </transformers>
   </config>
   ```

3. Download `ffmpeg.exe` from `http://www.ffmpeg.org/download.html` and copy it to `<<alfresco_server>>\bin folder`. Alfresco will use this executable file for video transformation. If you are using Linux, Install FFMPEG package, and set appropriate path to make it executable from command prompt.

4. Now you have FFMPEG integrated with Alfresco. Let's see how we can use FFMPEG to transform video file using Alfresco.

5. Go to video file you already have uploaded in your repository, click on **view detail** from **Action** buttons.

6. Now click on **Run Action** link from left panel to start video transformation process. Select **Transform and copy content** action from the drop-down list as shown in the following screenshot and click on **Set value** and **Add button**.

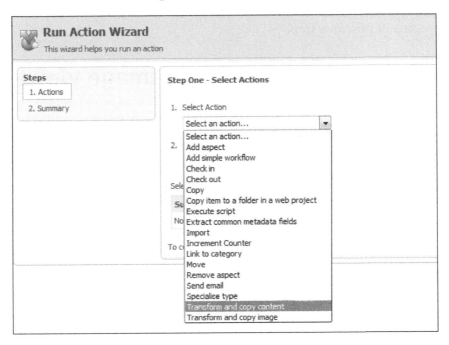

7. Select video type you want your source video to be converted. **MPEG4 Video** you see in options because the configuration you added in `web-client-config-custom.xml` file.

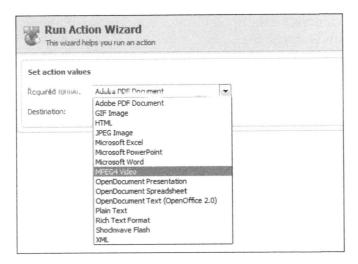

8. Select destination folder where you want to copy your transformed video then click on the **OK** button.

9. Now click on the **Next** button to see summary for action. Click on **Finish** to run video transformation. You can see transformed video in folder you selected in previous step.

Integrating with ViewOnePro image viewer

ViewOnePro is the world's first Java applet image viewer to be extendable with additional modules without user installation, offering support for additional file formats (PDF Module, Universal Viewing Module), and for additional viewer functionality (Annotations Module, Permanent Redaction Server Module, Document Streaming Server Module, and the Print Accelerator Module). ViewOnePro is a powerful in-browser viewer with ability to extend an applet's capabilities which represents a major breakthrough for web-based document management users.

To protect the integrity of your records for compliance, ViewOnePro provides viewing—and crucially not editing—access to the wide range of documents stored in your repository. To integrate ViewOnePro with Alfresco, follow the given steps:

1. Download ViewOnePro from `http://www.daeja.com`.

2. Extract the downloaded zip file and copy the `v1files` folder to `<<alfresco_ server>>/tomcat/webapps/alfresco` folder. This folder contains required JAR files and applet classes.

3. Now create your own presentation template specifying the applet tag for the applet ViewONE provided by viewOnePro package.

4. You also need to set some parameters for look and feel of the applet and available options for the applet like viewmode, pageButtons, fileMenus, and so on in this template file.

5. Template file will have extension `.ftl` similar to other FreeMarker template used by Alfresco. Following is the sample `v1preview.ftl` file.

```
<html>
  <body onLoad="setTimeout('delayer()', 500)">

    <APPLET CODEBASE="/alfresco/v1files"
    ARCHIVE="ji.jar, daeja1.jar, daeja2.jar, daeja3.jar"
    CODE="ji.applet.jiApplet.class"
    NAME="ViewONE"
    WIDTH="980"
    HEIGHT="980"
    HSPACE="0"
```

```
        VSPACE="0"
        MAYSCRIPT="true"
        ALIGN="middle">

        <PARAM NAME="cabbase" VALUE="viewone.cab">
        <PARAM NAME="ACMPreloadFile" value="ji">
        <PARAM NAME="fileMenus" value="false">
        <PARAM NAME="pageButtons" value="true">
        <PARAM NAME="draggingEnabled" value="true">
        <param name="viewmode" value="thumbsleft">
        <PARAM NAME="ACMRedirectTarget" value="_self">
        <PARAM NAME="ACMDownloadPrompt" value="true">
        <PARAM NAME="ACMUpdate" value="false">
        <PARAM NAME="JavaScriptExtensions" VALUE="true">

        <#assign counter = 1>

        <#list space.children as child>
        <#if child.isDocument >
          <#if child.mimetype = "image/gif" ||
child.mimetype="image/jpeg" ||
            child.mimetype="application/pdf" ||
child.mimetype="image/tiff">
          <param name="page${counter?string}"
value="/alfresco${child.url}">
            <#assign counter = counter + 1 >
        </#if>
      </#if>
      </#list>
    </APPLET>
    <script>
      function delayer()
      {
        ViewONE.setFileButtons(false);
        ViewONE.setAreaZoom (true);
      }
    </script>
    </body>
</html>
```

6. Upload this template file to **Company Home | Data Dictionary | Presentation Templates** folder.

7. To see the ViewOnePro functionality, you can apply this template as custom view on any spaces.

    1. For that, click on **More Actions** button of any space, you will have option for **Preview in Template** as shown in the following screenshot:

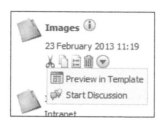

    2. In the next screen, you will be asked to choose template from available list of presentation templates, select your FTL presentation template file. In our case it will be `v1preview.ftl`.

8. Now you will be able to preview that space with ViewOnePro functionality. In our example we are using ViewOnePro for previewing images, so we will preview **Images** folder as shown in the following screenshot:

Integrating with Facebook social network application

Facebook is the most popular social network where people share content and connect with their friends, family, and businesses.

The integration will enable users of the Alfresco Enterprise Content Network to use Facebook to publish content. It is Alfresco's aim to make publishing and sharing enterprise content as simple and familiar as possible.

A large enough segment of any workforce is active on one web-based social network or another – if not Facebook, then MySpace, or LinkedIn, or one of the myriad boutique networks out there – to compel corporations to take them seriously as communication platforms.

Through the announced Facebook integration, Alfresco users can upload and share enterprise content with customers, fellow employees, and partners in a secure and audited way. Platform functionality includes application registration, Facebook authorization, and single sign-on, FBML support, and Facebook model support. The tools that are available to employees using the platform will be familiar if they are or have ever been users of Facebook. In the secure environment, they can upload documents; view My Documents, All Documents, or Recently Added Documents; and view documents from colleagues and friends through the Facebook newsfeed.

Now social networks websites like Facebook can easily be built up with Alfresco's REST-based web services. This results into emerging the enterprise content management capabilities with the social graph of Facebook integration. In this case study we will see how we can develop Alfresco Facebook Application with the help of Web Scripts. We will extend Web Scripts in such a way that will support Facebook capabilities. As we are suing Web Script Framework, we don't use any core development with Java, but will just use the scripting language.

Creating a new Facebook application

1. In this exercise we will create develop help world Web Script and display its output on Facebook's application page.

2. Let's create an app in Facebook by using the following steps:

3. Go to `http://developers.facebook.com/`.

4. Click on the **Apps** link, you see in header of page.

5. Click on **Create New App** button. It will open light-box to provide App name. Once you click on continue, it will present CAPTCHA for security get.

6. Now you will be able to see the various settings you need to configure for your application. Provide your **Web Script URL** in **Canvas URL** field.

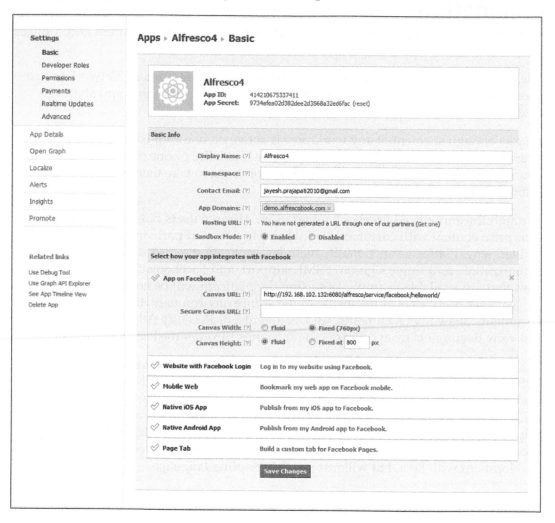

Enter the appropriate data and save. Provide proper application name that you can easily identify. Callback URL is required for forwarding requests to Alfresco from Facebook.

> Here all generated API key, Secret key, and Application ID randomly generated every time. So it would not be same, as I have in my previous screenshot. Also, /facebook/heloworld/ should match to URL provided for Alfresco. So the syntax would be http://<HOST>:<PORT>/alfresco/<WEBSCRIPT URL>.

Once you set up your application and submit it. You can see your application is created.

It is important to note that we need to pay attention more on the following properties: Application Name and Callback URL.

Registering a Facebook application with Alfresco

Once you run fresh alfresco to create appropriate folder structure described as follows:

1. Create folder named `Facebook<applicationID>` inside Company Home.

2. Go to following path, if folders don't exist create them.

   Data Dictionary | Web Scripts | com | Facebook | _apps.

3. Create app `<API_KEY>.js` file inside _apps folder. Please note that the API key is different in each case. Provide the following information in the file:

   ```
   // Facebook App: Alfresco Document Library

   app.id="414210675337411";

   app.secret="9734afea02d382dee2d3568a32ed6fac";
   ```

4. Now go to **Data Dictionary | Web Scripts** extension and create a hello world Web Script.

5. Create a file with the name `helloworld.post.desc.xml` and add the following code:

   ```
   <webscript>
   <shortname>Hello World</shortname>
   <url>/facebook/helloworld/</url>
   <format default="fbml"/>
   <authentication>user</authentication>
   </webscript>
   ```

6. Create `hellofriends.post.fbml.ftl` file and add the following code to generate output on apps page:

   ```
   <h1>Hello World</h1> <br/>
   <h4>This he my first hello world webscript to demonstrate
   Alfresco and Facebook integration.<h4>
   ```

   Now once all are setup, register your new web scripts to Alfresco.

7. Go to `http://<host>:<port>/alfresco/service/index` page and click on the **Refresh Web Scripts** button.

Now we are ready to run our application. Open new browser window and point App URL. In our case it will show the following output:

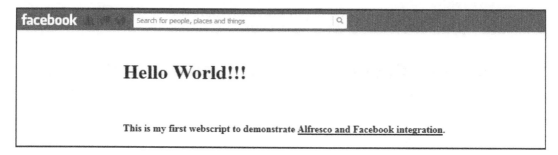

Managing Alfresco Content from within Microsoft Office

In *Chapter 2, Installing Alfresco* you learned about installing SharePoint protocol support in Alfresco. In this topic, you will learn use of SharePoint protocol to manage document from Microsoft office suit. Microsoft office suits provide word, excel, power point, and so on application. This applications are widely used in our day to day activity to create documents, reports, and so on. You will learn to leverage Alfresco repository to manage such document from Microsoft client application itself. You can perform all the following activities with help of SharePoint protocol.

Manage a document within Microsoft Word to,

- Create a Document Workspace
- Edit a contents (check-in and check-out)
- View a previous content version and then restoring the content to that version
- Add files to a Document Workspace

You can collaborate with colleagues for a document review to,

- Save document to the Document Workspace
- Customize the Document Workspace
- Manage the site membership by adding users; view and edit user profiles and change member roles
- Work with linked documents (local copies and site copies)
- Delete the Document Workspace

You can collaborate with colleagues around a meeting to,

- Create a Meeting Workspace
- View the workspace from Outlook
- Add and remove users from the Meeting Workspace
- Cancel a meeting
- Using Alfresco documents in Microsoft application is straightforward, you can follow the given steps to manage documents.

Creating a document workspace

Such like other workspace; you can create document workspace using Microsoft office applications. When you create workspace, it creates site in Alfresco share. Then after, whatever document you create gets managed within this site. Based on role and permission you provide to user on that site, document gets available to other users. In this topic we will see steps to create document workspace using Office-2007 version. For other version of Office, there could be variations in these steps.

1. Open Microsoft word, create document, add some text, and save it to local drive as **SSP.docx**.

2. Now click on **Microsoft office** button and select **Publish** option, then click on **Create Document Workspace** option.

3. Give name to workspace, let's give SSP at this point and provide URL of your workspace and click on **Create**.

    ```
    http://<alfresco server host>:<7070>/alfresco
    ```

    You may be, wondering why port is 7070, its SharePoint protocol port listening on your Alfresco instance. It is configured in `<<Affresco-server>>\tomcat\webapps\alfresco\WEB-INF\classes\alfresco\module\org.alfresco.module.vti\context\vti.properties`

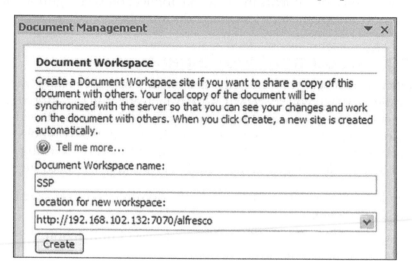

4. If you receive the following prompt with message, make entry of your Alfresco host as trusted site in internet explorer and make IE as default explorer.

5. Now it will prompt for login credentials, provide user name and password, and then click on **OK**. Word will create **Document Workspace** (Share site) and add **SSP.docx** on your desktop. Now you will see **Document Management** task pane. Office might prompt you to log in again. If it asks, provide the same user name and password.

6. Once you create document workspace, it will create site in Alfresco share with document workspace name.

Adding a document to document workspace

You can create folder structure as you want and add document to document workspace. You can follow the given steps to create folder and add document:

1. Open the **Document Management** task pane of the document SSP.docx and go to **Documents** tab. You will see file and folder which are currently available in your site document library folder.

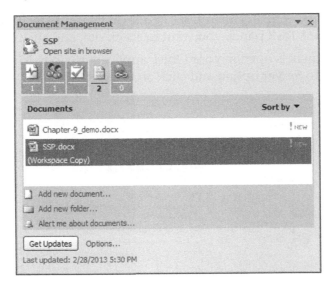

2. Click on **Add new folder** link and enter folder name (downloads) to create.

3. Go to the folder by clicking on name and click on **Add new document** link from bottom, Browse file you want to add to the site.

4. You can see uploaded file in Alfresco Share site.

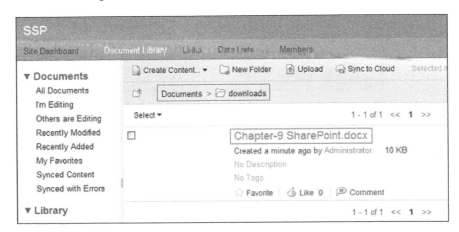

Check-in and Check-out document

You can edit document of Alfresco share site from Office application itself. You can check-out document and make changes you want. On check-out of document, it gets locked for other user so that no other users can change this document except you. You can follow the given steps to check-out the document.

Check-out document

1. Open the SSP.docx document, select document from **Document Management Task** panel, you want to check-out, and click on it to open.

2. Now document is open in your Office application. Go to **Microsoft office** button, go to **Server** option and click on **Check Out**

3. Once your document is checked out you can update the document. By the time you update the document, it get locked for other users so that no users other than you make change in document.

Check-in document

1. Once you are done with the changes in document, you can process to check-in the document. You can observe that in the **Document Management** panel in left side, you see link for check-in, click on **Check in**.

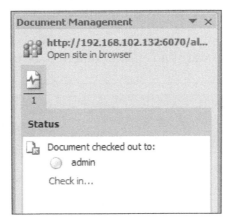

2. Once you click on check-in link, it will prompt dialog to provide comment, add appropriate comment. Now document locked from share site get released.

View version history

1. You can also see version history of particular document from Microsoft Office application. All you need to do is,

2. Open document from **Document Management Task** panel by clicking on the document name.

3. Go to **Microsoft office** button, select server option, and click on **view version history** menu item.

CMIS

Content Management Interoperability Services (CMIS) standard will define a domain model and set of bindings, such as Web Service and REST/ Atom that can be used by applications to work with one or more Content Management systems/ repositories.

The CMIS interface is designed to be layered on top of existing Content Management systems and their existing programmatic interfaces. It is not intended to prescribe how specific features should be implemented within those CM systems, nor to exhaustively expose all of the CM system's capabilities through the CMIS interfaces Rather, it is intended to define a generic/universal set of capabilities provided by a CM system and a set of services for working with those capabilities.

The following shows not only a typical requirement in a larger enterprise, but also to show off how the CMIS standard can enable content to be ubiquitous in enterprises.

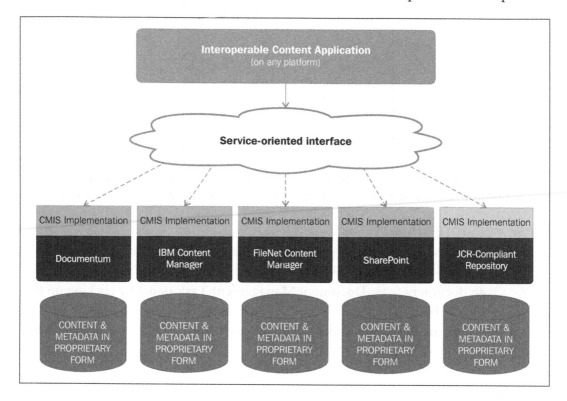

Just as the major database vendors standardized on SQL in the 1980's, today's leading ECM vendors have developed a draft specification with the goal of delivering and enabling interoperability across content repositories. The draft specification is backed by Alfresco, EMC, IBM, Microsoft, OpenText, Oracle, and SAP.

Alfresco leads the charge being the first vendor to provide a draft implementation of CMIS at such an early stage of the standard. In September 2008, Alfresco released the industry's first draft implementation of the CMIS specification. The company has also recently made available the CMIS Developer Toolbox, which includes a working implementation and contains resources to assist developers in the CMIS community to start creating portable content applications, based on the draft specification.

Scope of CMIS

To ensure that CMIS meets the previously-stated goal of allowing for the creation of rich ECM applications using this standard, here is the list of representative use cases that are accounted for in the CMIS capabilities, as well as some that were not targeted for CMIS v1. These are categorized into the following groups:

- **Core ECM use cases that are directly supported by the CMIS interfaces**: These are the fundamental ECM use cases that are common to most/all ECM applications today.

- **ECM applications and use cases that can be built on top of the CMIS interfaces**: These are examples of applications that can use the basic capabilities exposed via the CMIS interfaces to provide higher-level solutions to customer problems

- **Out-of-scope use cases for CMIS 1.0**: These are use cases/applications that, although in many cases are important for ECM scenarios, have been deemed out-of-scope for the initial version of the CMIS standard.

Core ECM Use Cases	ECM applications & use cases that c an be built on top of the CMIS interfaces	Out-of-scope use cases for CMIS 1. 0
Collaborative Content Creation	Workflow & business process management	Records management & compliance
Portals	Archival applications	Digital asset management
Mashups	Compound / Virtual documents	Web Content Management
	Electronic legal discovery	Subscription/ Notification Services

Alfresco CMIS implementation

CMIS exposes services for:

- Discovering Object Type definitions and other repository information (including which optional capabilities are supported by a particular Repository.)

- Creating, Reading, Updating, and Deleting objects

- Filing Documents into zero, one, or more Folders, if the repository supports the optional multi filing capability.

- Navigating and traversing the hierarchy of folders in the repository

- Creating versions of Documents and accessing a Document's version history

- Querying a repository to retrieve one or more objects matching user-specified search criteria including full-text search queries

Liferay integration using CMIS

CMIS is universal platform to get connected with any framework support CMIS. Liferay provide portlet for accessing repository using CMIS service. In this example, we will see integration of Alfresco repository and Liferay document library.

You need to make the following settings at Liferay side to access Alfresco repository:

1. Add the following two properties in `portal-ext.properties` file:

   ○ `session.store.password=true`: This property mean, password you enter during logging into Liferay get save in session as.

   ○ `company.security.auth.type=screenName`: When you set this property, it instructs Liferay to change login attribute to screen name.

2. Now you need to mount Alfresco repository to Liferay portlet.

   1. Go to Liferay **Control Panel | Documents and Media** portlet.

2. Select **Home** from left panel and click on the **Add** button to select the **Repository** option as you can see in the following screenshot:

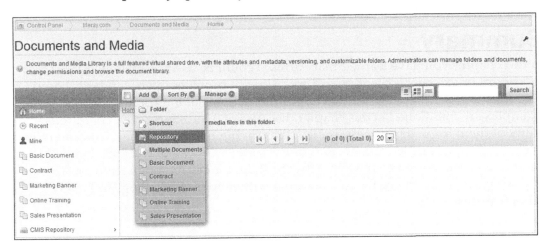

3. Fill-up the form to get connect with Alfresco CMIS. You need to select CMIS Repository (AtomPub) option for repository type and provide http://<host>:<port>/alfresco/cmisatom to AtomPub.

4. Once you save the settings, you will be able to see Alfresco repository content in Liferay portlet like following screenshot:

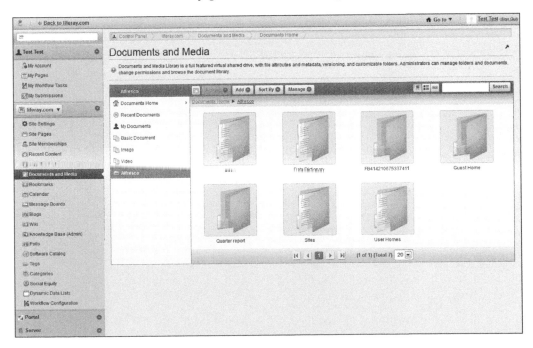

From Alfresco side you need to make sure that the user accessing this portlet must exist with same user and password in Alfresco.

Summary

In this chapter you have learned that Alfresco could be used as an embedded repository or external content repository. Alfresco provides open standards based protocols to integrate with external applications. Some of the application integration examples are mentioned in this chapter. Because of open source, you could reuse many of them for your business applications saving time and money. You can refer `http://docs.alfresco.com/4.0/index.jsp` for various integrations. In next chapter you will learn about using Alfresco share for collaboration features. You will see various use of site for collaboration with help of WIKI, Blog, and many other features.

10
Alfresco Administration Operations Using Alfresco Share

In this chapter, we will cover Alfresco Administrative operations that can be done via Alfresco Share. This chapter does not cover any administrative operations that are specific to Alfresco Share.

By the end of this chapter you will have learned how to:

- Manage users
- Manage groups
- Manage categories
- Manage social content publishing
- Manage fileservers
- Manage activity feed e-mails
- Manage the Alfresco license
- Manage replication jobs
- Manage search
- Manage deleted files
- Manage workflows
- Manage emails
- Google Docs integration

Alfresco Share

Alfresco Share is built on the Alfresco enterprise-class document repository and delivers out-of-the-box collaborative content management. It simplifies capturing, sharing, and retrieval of information across virtual teams. Team or project members can rapidly find relevant content, experts, look at past or similar projects, and keep on top of any relevant changes to make them more efficient.

Share is focused on Collaboration tasks and includes integration with popular blogging, wiki, and forum/discussion products out of the box. It provides a great interface into the more traditional document management library (think folders) as well. Keep in mind that all of the website's content and documents are still stored in the Alfresco repository. As such, they are secured, versioned, searchable, and auditable.

Share is an independent client application that accesses the repository through web scripts. It is built on the **Alfresco Surf** platform. Alfresco Share is a web application that runs on a machine that is separate from that of the repository.

Share provides a paradigm for creating collaborative applications by aggregating Surf components and incorporating new Surf components as they are developed. With Share, users can modify their workspaces to fit their collaborative requirements inside or outside the organization. Users can invite their peers to share and collaborate around the project and the content. With the addition of Share, Alfresco delivers a **Web 2.0** application that leverages Flash and AJAX with a polished interface, which any business person will enjoy.

Features like Document Libraries, Search, Activity Feeds, Virtual Teams, personalized dashboard, N-tier Architecture, and CMIS 1.0 support make it a really competent tool for collaborative content management.

For more details on collaboration using Alfresco Share, refer the *Alfresco Share* book published by *Packt Publishing*. The book can be found at `http://www.packtpub.com/alfresco-share-easy-collaboration-for-enterprises/book`.

Managing Alfresco using the Admin Console in Alfresco Share

Now, you can manage the administration operations using the Admin Console, which is a browser-based console. You can manage users and groups, e-mails, filesystems, categories, tags, social content publishing, activity feeds, replication jobs, workflows, deleted files, the Alfresco license, and search. The other things that you can do from the Admin Console are Integrating with Google Docs and search content and its properties using the Node Browser.

The **Admin Console** is visible to only an admin or a user who is a member of the **ALFRESCO_ADMINISTRATORS** group.

On the toolbar, expand the **+More** menu, and then click any of the admin tools or **More** in the **Admin Tools…** section. The **Admin Console** opens up.

Managing users

Using the **Users** tool, you can create, edit, delete, and disable user accounts, change user passwords, search user accounts, and manage a user's group membership.

Creating user accounts

The **Users** page allows you to create a user account. Follow these steps to create a user account:

1. Click **Users** in the **Admin Console**. You'll see the following page:

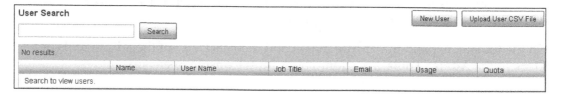

2. Click on **New User**.
3. Complete all the required user fields and click on **Create User**:

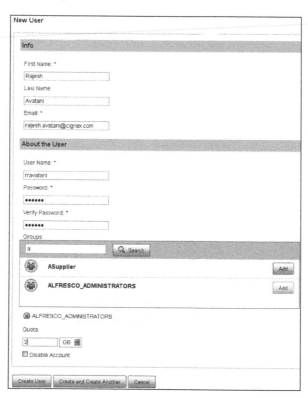

4. If you want to immediately create another user, click on **Create and Create Another**.

Editing user accounts

You can change a user's personal information, group membership, password, and enable/disable his/her account. Follow these steps to edit a user's account:

1. Click **Users** in the **Admin Console**.

2. Search a user and click on the user's name:

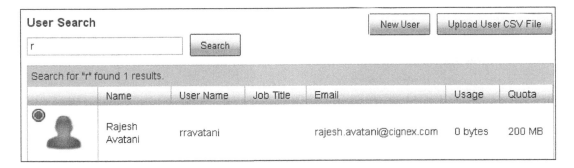

3. On the **User Profile** page, click on **Edit User**:

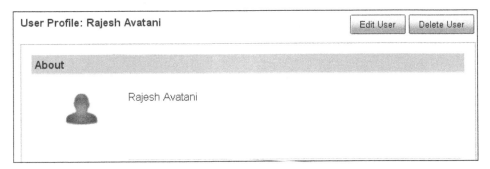

4. Edit the needed fields and click on **Save Changes**:

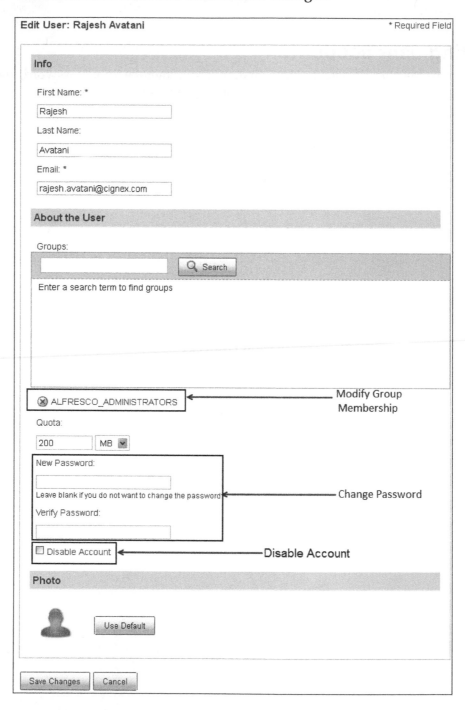

You can modify group memberships, change passwords, or disable the account.

On the **User Profile** page, the user account shows as disabled, and on **User Search** page the user displays in the search result list with a red dot, indicating that the account is disabled.

Deleting user accounts

Follow these steps to delete a user account:

1. Follow first two steps of the *Editing user accounts* section.

2. On the **User Profile** page, click **Delete User**.

Managing groups

Using the Groups tool, you can create, edit, delete, and search groups. You can also manage group memberships.

Creating groups

The **Groups** tool allows you create both top-level user groups and subgroups within the existing groups.

Top-level group

A top level group is at the top in the hierarchy of groups. You can create a subgroup within the top-level group. Follow these steps to create a top-level group:

1. Click **Groups** in the **Admin Console**. You'll see the following page:

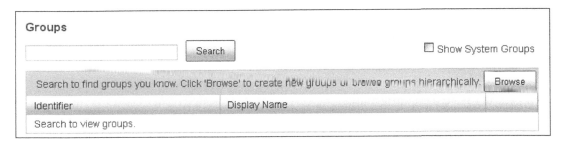

2. Click on **Browse,** and in the next screen click on the **New Group** icon:

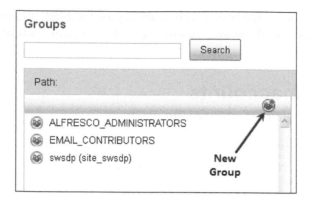

3. Add **Identifier** and **Display Name** and click on **Create Group**. If you want to create another group at the same level, then click on **Create and Create Another**:

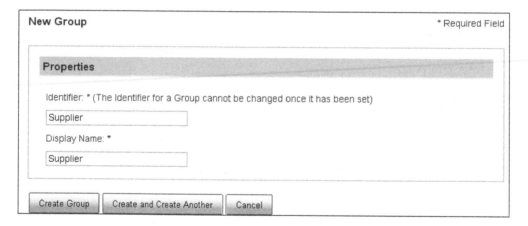

Subgroups

A group which is created within the top-level group is called a subgroup. Follow these steps to create a subgroup:

1. Click **Groups** in the **Admin Console**.
2. Click on **Browse**.

3. Select the group for which you want to create a subgroup, click on the **New Sub Group** icon:

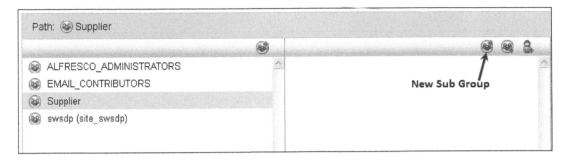

4. Add **Identifier** and **Display Name** and click on **Create Group**. If you want to create a group at the same level, then click on **Create and Create Another**.

Edit/delete groups

By deleting a top-level group, the subgroups within that group also get deleted. Follow these steps to edit or delete a group:

1. Click **Groups** in the **Admin Console**.
2. Click **Browse**.
3. Select the group that you want to edit or delete to display its available actions.
4. Click on the **Edit** icon to edit the group, or the **Delete** icon to delete the group:

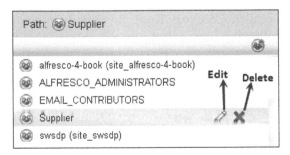

Managing group memberships

You can add users and groups within a group. Follow these steps to add a user and a group within a specific group:

1. Click **Groups** in the **Admin Console**.
2. Click on **Browse**.

3. Select the group you want to work with.

4. To add a user, click on the **Add User** icon in the pane. Search the user you want to add to the selected group. Click **Add**, located to the right of the user:

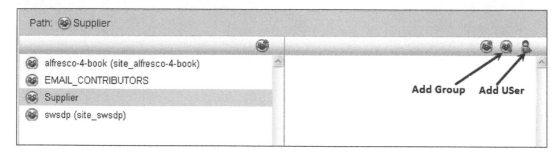

5. Similarly, to add a group, click on the **Add Group** icon in the pane. Search for the group you want to add to the selected group. Click **Add**, located to the right of the user.

Managing categories

The **Category Manager** page allows you to add, edit, and delete categories. Follow these steps to add/edit/delete categories:

1. Click **Category Manager** in the **Admin Console**.

2. The categories in the form of the tree structure are displayed in the **Category Manager** page.

3. The top level is called **Category Root**. By default, subcategories are listed, as shown in the following screenshot:

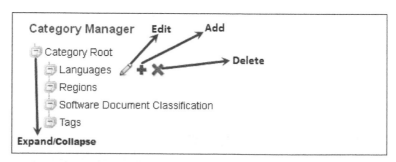

4. Click on the category icon to expand the list of categories.

5. When you hover over the category name, you will see the available actions, as shown in the preceding screenshot.

6. Click on the **Edit** icon to edit the category, **Add** icon to add the category, and similarly click on the **Delete** icon to delete the category.

Managing social content publishing

Social content publishing allows publishing the content from Alfresco to other social platforms, such as Facebook, LinkedIn, and so on.

Currently, the following out-of-the-box social platforms are supported:

- Facebook
- Flickr
- LinkedIn
- SlideShare
- Twitter
- YouTube

Creating channels

The **Channel Manager** page allows you to create a channel. Follow these steps to create a channel:

1. Click on **Channel Manager** in the **Admin Console**.
2. Click **New** and select the channel type from the drop-down:

3. On selecting the channel, it redirects you to the authorization page of the selected channel. Once the authorization is successful, the channel is created:

Setting channel permissions

Permissions can be set to users and groups for each publishing channel, either by inherited permissions or locally set permissions:

1. Click **Channel Manager** in the **Admin Console**.

2. Click **Permissions** of the desired channel, you'll see the **Manage Permissions** page:

3. To disable inherit permissions, click **Inherit Permissions**.

4. To add users/groups, click **Add User/Group**.

Authorizing channels

Once a channel has been created, it has to be authorized. Follow these steps for authorizing a channel:

1. Click **Channel Manager** in the **Admin Console**.

2. Click **Reauthorization** of the desired channel, you'll be redirected to the channel's authorization page.

3. Follow the instructions for authorizing the channel.

Deleting channels

The **Channel Manager** page allows you to delete a channel. Follow these steps to delete a channel:

1. Click **Channel Manager** in the **Admin Console**.

2. Click **Delete** of the desired channel, you'll be prompted with a dialog for confirmation:

3. Click **OK** to confirm. The channel is deleted and the channel icon is deleted from the channel management page.

Managing fileservers

The fileserver tool allows you to manage the properties for the CIFS and FTP servers.

1. Click **Fileservers** in the **Admin Console**. You'll see the following screen:

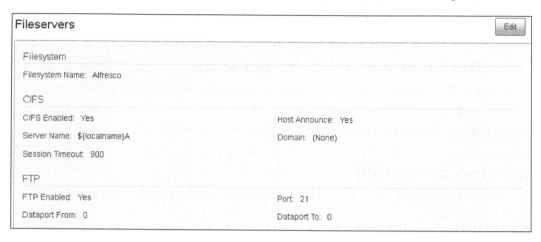

2. Click **Edit**.

3. You can update the flowing properties for the CIFS server:
    ° **CIFS Enabled**: This property allows enabling or disabling the CIFS server.

    ° **Host Announce**: This property makes the CIFS server show up in the Network Places.

    ° **Server Name**: This is the hostname for the Alfresco CIFS server that can be maximum of 16 characters and unique on the network.

    ° **Domain**: This property is to specify the domain or workgroup to which the server belongs.

    ° **Session Timeout**: This property allows setting the CIFS session timeout value in seconds.

4. You can update the following properties for the FTP server:
    ° **FTP Enabled**: This property allows enabling or disabling the FTP server.

    ° **Port**: This property allows setting the port that the FTP server listens for incoming connections on.

    ° **Dataport From** and **Dataport To**: You can set the range of ports for data ports. **Dataport From** allows setting the lower limit and **Dataport To** allows setting the higher limit.

Managing Activities Feed e-mails

The **Activities Feed** feature allows you to set activity e-mails. All the events that are listed in activity feed dashlet for those e-mail notifications are sent to the Administrator.

1. Click **Activities Feed** in the **Admin Console**. You'll see the following screen:

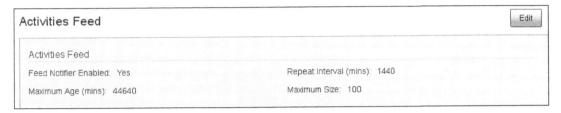

2. Click **Edit**.
3. You can update the flowing properties:
    *   **Feed Notifier Enabled**: To enable/disable activity e-mail notification for Activities Feed.
    *   **Repeat Intervals (mins)**: This property sets how often you will receive the Activities Feed notification e-mails. The default value is 1440, which means you will receive the notification every day.
    *   **Maximum Age (mins)**: This property sets the maximum age in minutes of the activity events listed in the Activities Feed notification e-mails. The default value is 44640, which means that the activities that are created within 31 days will be shown and those which are older than 31 days will not be shown.
    *   **Maximum Size**: This property sets the maximum activity events to be shown in Activities Feed notification e-mails.

4. After setting the properties, click **Save**.

> The full list of activity feed e-mail notifications can be found in the `share\WEB-INF\classes\alfresco\site-webscripts\org\alfresco\components\dashlets\activity-list.get.properties` file.

Managing Alfresco License

The **Alfresco License** tool helps you to view the Alfresco license details and load the license:

1. Click **License Descriptor** in the **Admin Console**.
2. Click **Edit**.

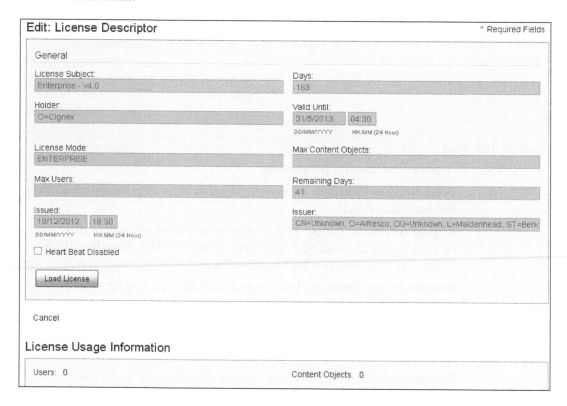

3. You can view the flowing properties:
    - **License Subject**: This property shows the installed version.
    - **Days**: This property shows the number of days this license is valid for.
    - **Holder**: This property shows the company/organization/individual name of the license holder.
    - **Valid Until**: This property shows when the license expires.
    - **License Mode**: This property shows the license type.
    - **Max Content Objects**: This property shows the maximum objects that can be present in Alfresco system.

- ° **Max Users**: This property shows the maximum users that can exist in Alfresco system.

- ° **Remaining Days**: This property shows the remaining number of days for the Alfresco license to expire.

- ° **Issued**: This property shows the date in which the license was issued.

- ° **Issuer**: This property shows the original location from where the license was issued.

- ° **Heart Beat Disabled**: This property shows if the license is allowed to send the repository statics to Alfresco.

- ° **Users**: This property shows the current number of users named in the Alfresco system. If the value of this property shows **0**, it means the license has no user restrictions.

- ° **Content Objects**: This property shows the number of content objects that currently exist in the Alfresco system.

4. To load a license, click **Load License**. But before that you need to copy your license file to the directory in which Alfresco is installed. Alternatively, you can copy the license file to the `<ALFRESCO_HOME>/tomcat/shared/classes/alfresco/extension/license` directory. If the `/license` sub-directory does not exist, you need to create it.

Managing Replication Jobs

The **Replication Jobs** tool allows you to manage and create the replication job where you can specify the content to be replicated, target location where the content should be replicated, and when the job should run.

Creating replication jobs

The **Replication Jobs** page allows you to create replication jobs. You can create any number of replication jobs as per your needs. Follow these steps to create a replication job:

1. Click **Replication Jobs** in the **Admin Console**.

2. In the **Jobs** section, click **Create Job**:

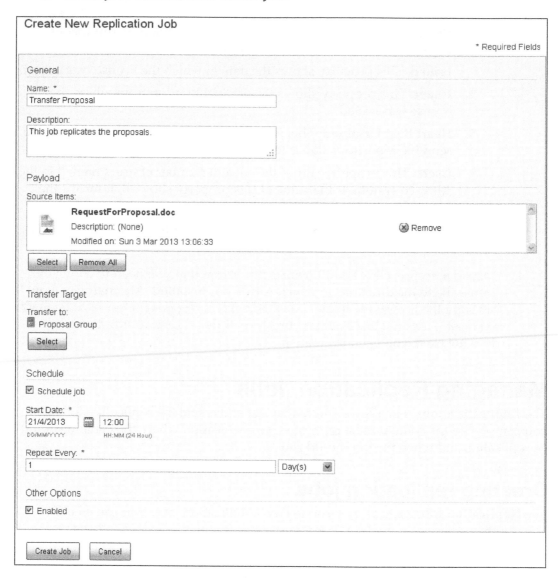

Create New Replication Job

* Required Fields

General

Name: *

Transfer Proposal

Description:

This job replicates the proposals.

Payload

Source Items:

RequestForProposal.doc
Description: (None)
Modified on: Sun 3 Mar 2013 13:06:33   ⊗ Remove

Select   Remove All

Transfer Target

Transfer to:
Proposal Group

Select

Schedule

☑ Schedule job

Start Date: *

21/4/2013   📅   12:00
DD/MM/YYYY   HH:MM (24 Hour)

Repeat Every: *

1   Day(s) ▾

Other Options

☑ Enabled

Create Job   Cancel

3. In the **Create New Replication Job** page, add the following properties:

    ○ **Name**: This property allows you to set the replication job's name.

    ○ **Description**: This property allows you to set the job's description. This is an optional property.

    ○ **Payload**: This property allows setting the content that needs to be replicated.

- ○ **Transfer Target**: This property allows you to set the target group where the content is to be transferred. The default group is available out-of-the-box under **Data Dictionary | Transfers | Transfers Target Group**. The additional groups can be created within the default group. A rule defined on the default group specializes the type of any folder created within it.

- ○ **Schedule Job**: Select the checkbox. The **Start Date** and **Repeat Every** properties shows up. Enter the date and time the job is to run and the repeat period for this job.

- ○ **Enable**: Select this checkbox if you want to run this job manually.

- ○ Click **Create Job**. The job appears highlighted in the job list. The job detail appears on the right-hand side of the page.

Editing replication jobs

You can update the replication job and also disable the job. Follow these steps to update/disable the replication job:

1. Click **Replication Jobs** in the **Admin Console**.

2. In the **Jobs** section, select the job you want to edit. On the right-hand side, the job details appear where you will find the **Edit** button. Click **Edit**.

3. Edit the properties required. If you want to disable the replication job, deselect the **Enabled** checkbox.

4. Click **Save**.

Deleting replication jobs

You can delete the replication job from the **Jobs** list. Once you delete the job, you cannot recover it. If you think you might need the job later, then disable it rather than deleting it. Follow these steps to delete a replication job:

1. Click **Replication Jobs** in the **Admin Console**.

2. In the **Jobs** section, select the job you want to edit. On the right-hand side, the job details appear where you will find the **Delete** button. Click **Delete**.

3. The confirmation message pops up, click **OK**.

Manually running a replication job

You can run the replication job manually any time. If you have scheduled a job, it will run at the appropriate time no matter you run the same job manually at any time. Follow these steps to run the replication job manually:

1. Click **Replication Jobs** in the **Admin Console**.

2. In the **Jobs** section, select the job you want to run. On the right-hand side, the job details appears, this is where you will find the **Run** button. This button will be enabled only if you have selected the **Enabled** checkbox under **Other Options** while creating the job. Click **Run**.

3. Click **Refresh**, the job execution status gets displayed.

Cancelling a running replication job

You can cancel the scheduled job or manual run job that is currently running. Follow these steps to cancel a replication job:

1. Click **Replication Jobs** in the **Admin Console**.

2. In the **Jobs** section, select the job that is currently running and which you want to cancel it. On the right-hand side, the job details appear where you will find the **Cancel Job** button. Click **Cancel Job**.

Managing Search

The **Search** tool allows you to select the search service that you want to use for searching content in Alfresco. The search services available are Lucene and Solr. This tool also allows you to set the Lucene and Solr properties.

Search services

The **Search Manager** page allows you to change the search service to be used in Alfresco. Currently, only Solr and Lucene search services are supported. Follow these steps to change a search service:

1. Click **Search Manager** under the **Search** section in the **Admin Console**.

2. In the **Search Manager** page, click **Edit**.

3. Select the search service from the drop-down:

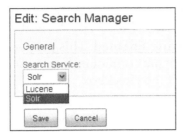

4. Click **Save**.

The Lucene search service

The **Lucene** page allows you to change the properties of the Lucene search service. Follow these steps to edit the Lucene search service properties:

1. Click **Lucene** under the **Search** section in the **Admin Console**.

2. In the **Lucene** page, click **Edit**:

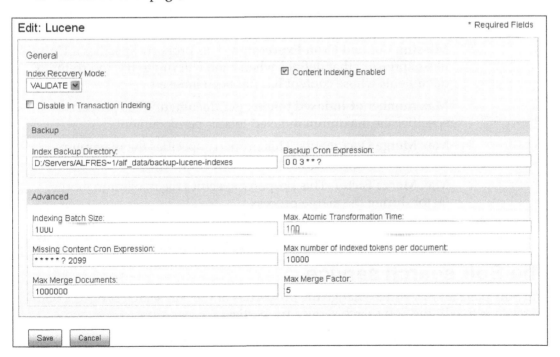

3. You can edit the following properties:

    ° **Index Recovery Mode**: This property allows you to select one of the options from **VALIDATE**, **AUTO**, and **FULL** for index recovery.

    ° **Content Indexing Enabled**: This property allows you to activate/deactivate content indexing. To activate content indexing, select the checkbox.

    ° **Disable in Transaction Indexing**: This property allows you to enable or disable in-transaction indexing.

    ° **Index Backup Directory**: This property specifies the default backup directory for the Lucene index.

    ° **Backup Cron Expression**: This property allows you to set the Unix-like expression, which specifies when the backup should occur.

    ° **Indexing Batch Size**: This property specifies the batch size of an index rebuild.

    ° **Max Atomic Transformation Time**: This property specifies the time, in milliseconds, to be taken for content transformation. If it takes more time, then the specified time, the content transformation will be done in the background. Increase the time to force the atomic content indexing.

    ° **Missing Content Cron Expression**: This property specifies a Unix-like expression that defines when a job will run to try and re-index documents whose content has not been indexed.

    ° **Max number of indexed tokens per document**: This property specifies the maximum indexed tokens per document.

    ° **Max Merge Documents**: This property specifies the maximum number of merged documents during the merge process.

    ° **Max Merge Factor**: This property specifies the maximum merge factor during the merge process.

4. After editing the required properties, click **Save**.

The Solr search service

The **Solr** page allows you to change the properties of the Solr search service. Follow these steps to edit the Solr search service properties:

1. Click **Solr** under the **Search** section in the **Admin Console**.

2. In the **Solr** page, click **Edit**.

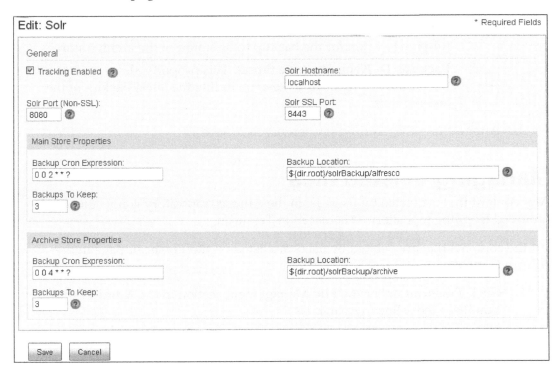

3. You can edit the following properties:
    ○ **Tracking Enabled**: This property allows you to enable or disable index tracking. To enable index tracking, select the checkbox.

    ○ **Solr Hostname**: This property specifies the host name on which the Solr server is running.

    ○ **Solr Port (Non-SSL)**: This property specifies the port number on which the Solr server is running.

    ○ **Solr SSL Port**. This property specifies the SSL port number.

    ○ **Backup Cron Expression (Main Store)**: This property allows you to specify when the backup should occur of the main store.

    ○ **Backup Location (Main Store)**: This property allows you to set the fullpath location for the backup to be stored of the main store.

    ○ **Backups To Keep (Main Store)**: This property allows you to set the number of backups to keep including the latest backup of the main store.

- ° **Backup Cron Expression (Archive Store)**: This property allows you to specify when the backup should occur of the archive store.

- ° **Backup Location (Archive Store)**: This property allows you to set the fullpath location for the backup to be stored of the archive store.

- ° **Backups To Keep (Archive Store)**: This property allows you to set the number of backups to keep including the latest backup of the archive store.

4. After editing the required properties, click **Save**.

Managing deleted files

Any content that is deleted by users from the Alfresco repository is not completely removed from the repository; it is placed in Trashcan.

All the contents that are deleted by users are listed on the **Trashcan** page in the **Admin Console**:

1. Click **Trashcan** under the **File Management** section in the **Admin Console**. You'll see the following page.

2. The content items are listed in the date order. To the right-hand side, you will find the **Recover** and **Delete** button for each content list. Click **Delete** to delete the content:

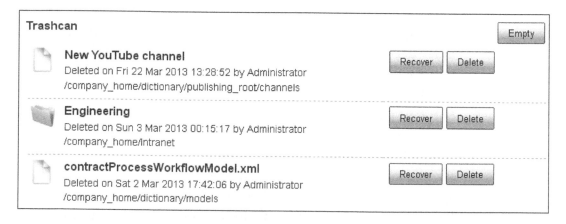

3. Click **Recover** to restore the item to its original place in the repository.

4. To empty the trash can, click **Empty** on the top-right section of the page.

Managing workflows

The **Workflow** tool in the Admin Console allows you to view the workflow engine properties and navigate to the Activiti Workflow Console for managing Activiti-based workflows and process definitions, which is explained in detailed in *Chapter 8, Implementing Workflow*.

Viewing the workflow engine properties

You can view both the Activiti and jBPM workflow engine properties. Click **Workflow** in the **Admin Console**. You'll see the following page:

```
Workflow

  Activiti Engine

  Enabled:  Yes                          Definitions Visible:  Yes

  Number Of Tasks:  6                    Number Of Definitions:  11

  Number Of Workflows:  6

  JBPM Engine

  Enabled:  No                           Definitions Visible:  No

  Number Of Tasks:  0                    Number Of Definitions:  0

  Number Of Workflows:  0


Activiti Tools

  Activiti Workflow Console
```

Activiti engine properties

You can view the following Activiti engine properties:

- **Enable**: This property shows that the Activiti workflow engine is enabled or disabled. By default, the Activiti workflow engine is enabled. To disable it, set the `system.workflow.engine.activiti.enabled` property to `false` in the `alfresco-global.properties` file.

- **Number Of Tasks**: This property specifies the number of Activiti-defined tasks that exist in the system.

- **Number Of Workflows**: This property specifies the number of Activiti workflows that exist in the system.

- **Definition Visible**: This property specifies whether the Activiti workflow definitions are visible or not.

- **Number Of Definitions**: This property specifies the number of Activiti definitions that exist in the system.

jBPM engine properties

You can view the following jBPM engine properties:

- **Enable**: This property shows that the jBPM workflow engine is enabled or disabled. By default, the jBPM workflow engine is disabled. To enable it, set the `system.workflow.engine.jbpm.enabled` property to `true` in the `alfresco-global.properties` file.

- **Number Of Tasks**: This property specifies the number of jBPM-defined tasks that exist in the system.

- **Number Of Workflows**: This property specifies the number of jBPM workflows that exist in the system.

- **Definition Visible**: This property specifies whether the jBPM workflow definitions are visible or not. To enable it, set the `system.workflow.engine.jbpm.definitions` property to `true` in the `alfresco-global.properties` file.

- **Number Of Definitions**: This property specifies the number of jBPM definitions that exist in the system.

Managing IMAP emails

The **Email (IMAP)** page allows you to set the IMAP properties to store user mailboxes in the Alfresco repository.

1. Click **Email (IMAP)** under the **Email** section in the **Admin Console**.

2. On the **Email (IMAP)** page, click **Edit**. You'll see the following page:

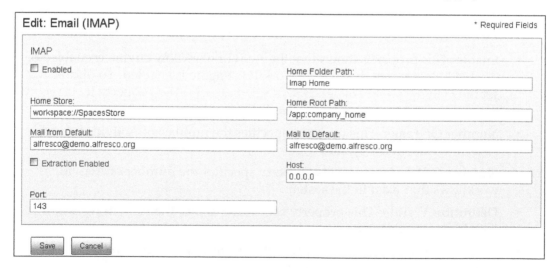

3. You can edit the following properties:

     ° **Enabled**: This property allows you to enable or disable the IMAP subsystem.

     ° **Home Folder Path**: This property specifies the name of the folder for the IMAP mount point.

     ° **Home Store**: This property specifies the default store of the IMAP mount point.

     ° **Home Root Path**: This property specifies the default location of the IMAP mount point.

     ° **Mail from Default**: This property allows you to set the default from-e-mail address.

     ° **Mail to Default**: This property allows you to set the default to-e-mail address.

     ° **Extraction Enabled**: This property allows you to enable or disable the incoming mail attachment as a separate document in the repository.

     ° **Host**: This property allows you to set the hostname of your IMAP server.

     ° **Port**: This property allows you to set the port.

4. After editing the required properties, click **Save**.

Google Docs integration

Google Docs integration allows you to store and edit the documents in Google Docs. To integrate Alfresco with Google Docs, you need to have a Google Docs account. Google Docs integration supports only Office 2003 formats. Follow these steps to integrate Alfresco with Google Docs:

1. Click **Google Docs** in the **Admin Console**, you'll see the **Google Docs** page.

2. Click **Edit**. You'll see the following page:

```
Edit: Google Docs

  General
  ☑ Enabled

  Username:                              Password:
  rajesh.avatani@gmail.com               •••••••••

  [ Save ]  [ Cancel ]
```

3. You can edit the following properties

   ° **Enabled**: This property allows you to enable/disable the Google Docs feature. Click this checkbox and also enter the username and password to enable the Google Docs feature.

   ° **Username**: This property allows you to enter the Google Docs username. This Google Docs username will be treated as an administrative Google Docs account. The users must add their personal Google Docs username in their own profile to access the shared documents in the Google administrative account.

   ° **Password**: This property allows you to set the password of the administrative Google Docs username.

> Google Docs integration supports `.doc`, `.xls`, and `.ppt` file extensions.

Summary

Alfresco administrative operations can be managed via Alfresco Share using the Admin Console.

The Admin Console provides you tools and pages to manage users, groups, categories, managing social content publishing, fileservers, activity feed e-mails, Alfresco license, replication jobs, search, deleted files, workflows, IMAP e-mails and Google Docs integration. It also provides you with operations that are specific to Alfresco Share, such as managing inbound and outbound e-mails and managing subscription to follow users, which are not covered in this chapter. In the next chapter, you will learn about customizing the Alfresco Explorer user interface.

11
Customizing the User Interface

The Alfresco Explorer user interface is designed to handle most of the common user interaction scenarios. However, each business application will have some specific user interface requirements. Alfresco allows you to configure certain user-interface elements, such as space icons, menu options, and the custom look and feel of a space. Of course, you can change the entire look and feel of the application using Java programming.

Each user of the system can have a personalized dashboard view. In this chapter, you will examine various options to customize the user interface, including custom dashlets (dashboard components). You will experience the power of FreeMarker in consolidating the content information and presenting it to the end users. FreeMarker is covered under the *Presentation templates* section later in this chapter. Alfresco Explorer is the default UI provided by the same web application to access the repository. Each customization of the Explorer must be tested very well before moving to the production environments.

The Alfresco Share delivers out-of-the box collaborative content management. You can configure certain user interface elements, such as dashlets, page components, and the custom look and feel of the space. For each user of the system you can provide a personalized dashboard view, a customized site dashboard, and customized components. You will find that this is mostly built using CSS, JavaScript, FTL, and XML files. Alfresco Share is out of the scope of this chapter.

In this chapter, we will learn how to:

- Configure space portal views
- Add custom icons to spaces
- Extend the action menu items

- Write custom dashlets
- Use webscript as dashlets
- Write custom templates to preview content
- Write custom templates
- Write custom JSPs
- Integration with external system

Configuring Alfresco Explorer

You can configure the look and feel of the Alfresco Explorer by simply editing the XML configuration file. You can change the look and feel of the Alfresco Explorer, change navigation elements, and modify the space views as per your organizational or departmental requirements.

Configuring views

This section gives you insight into the process of configuring various views in Alfresco.

Configuring space views

Every space can be viewed in the following four different ways:

- **Details View**: This provides detailed information about documents, as rows.
- **Icon View**: This provides icon, description, and modification time properties of the documents.
- **Browse View**: This provides information about sub-spaces.
- **Custom View**: This provides the custom view selected by the user for that space.

For Windows users, this is similar to having various view options for folders in the Windows Explorer. The **Details View**, **Icon View**, and **Browse View** are provided out of the box. **Custom View** is the customized view of that space, which is selected by the user.

The default view for a space is the **Icon View**. You can choose a specific view (say **Details View**) by selecting it from the drop-down list, as highlighted in the next screenshot. However, the selection is going to be saved only for that session, and the next time you log in to Alfresco web client, you will see the default view on the space. You can configure the default view for spaces, and you can also specify the number of items to be displayed in a page.

You can find the details about the default configuration in the file named `web-client-config.xml`, which is located in your configuration folder. To customize the default view, you need to update the `web-client-config.xml` file in the `extensions` folder. Go to the `extensions` folder (for Tomcat installation, it is in the following folder: `<alfresco_install_folder>\tomcat\shared\classes\alfresco\extension`. Here, you will have to edit the `web-client-config-custom.xml` file, and add the following XML block. If you want to display the details of all documents in your space (as shown in the screenshot on the previous page), then you can choose **View Details** as default. If you want to see more documents in a page, you can increase the number of documents displayed per page from `10` to `25`.

```
<config evaluator="string-compare" condition="Views">
      <!-- the views available in the client -->
  <views>
      <!-- default values for the views available in the client -->
    <view-defaults>
      <browse>
        <!-- allowable values: list|details|icons -->
```

```
        <view>details</view>
        <page-size>
        <list>10</list>
        <details>25</details>
        <icons>9</icons>
        </page-size>
      </browse>
    </view-defaults>
  </views>
</config>
```

 Deployment of Alfresco Explorer can be achieved as the administrator by using the URL: `http://serverip:port/alfresco/faces/jsp/admin/webclientconfig-console.jsp`.

Use the `reload` command to deploy the file.

Applying a Custom View on a space

A **Custom View** is a portal window that shows up on the top of each space, when a **Custom View** option is selected. This is useful to represent the content in a space in a specific manner, such as showing the recent documents and a summary of the documents. For example, you can apply a custom view on the **Finance Department | Checks** space to display a list of checks received in the past week.

This enables you to have an alternate view of spaces using templates. Other scenarios can be:

- Display the space and its sub-spaces (collapse the tree).
- Traverse the entire repository, displaying content whose date is effective.
- Show filenames of all the images, their thumbnails, and create HTML links to the actual images.
- Display summaries of the information within a space, such as the total number of documents, number of documents under review, the number of documents belonging to a category, and the number of documents published or approved.

Let us say you would like to see all of the documents in your home space that are either created or modified in the past week. Follow these steps given to apply a custom view on your home space:

1. Go to the space to which you would like to apply the custom view.
2. Using the **More Actions | View details** menu option, go to details page.

3. Click on the **Add Custom View** icon, as shown in the following screenshot, to select a custom view. The **Remove Custom View** icon (also shown in the following screenshot) is useful to remove an existing custom view on a space:

4. Clicking on the **Apply Template** link will open a window, as shown in the screenshot. You can select a template to be applied on the space as a **Custom View**. There are already some built-in templates provided for you for most generic use cases. You can also apply your own custom templates to this space. The process of adding a custom template is explained later in this chapter.

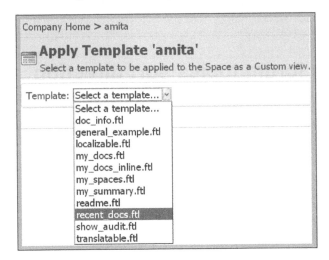

5. From the list of presentation templates, select the recent_docs.ftl template, which displays the list of documents in the current space that were either created or updated in the past week.

6. Once you select the presentation template, click on the **OK** button and close the **View Details** page. You will notice that the presentation template you have chosen is applied to the space as a **Custom View** (refer to the following screenshot):

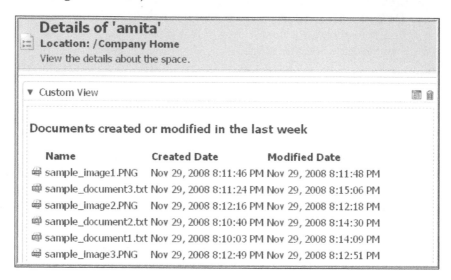

Configuring forum topics sort direction

By default, the topic view in the forums functionality lists the posts in descending order, that is, the last post is at the top of the list. If you wish to change this, add the following XML text to the `web-client-config-custom.xml` file. Also, you can define the number of posts listed per page.

```
<topic>
       <!-- allowable values: details|bubble -->
  <view>bubble</view>
  <sort-column>created</sort-column>
       <!-- allowable values: ascending|descending -->
  <sort-direction>ascending</sort-direction>
  <page-size>
    <bubble>5</bubble>
    <details>20</details>
  </page-size>
</topic>
```

Adding a custom icon to a space

To add another space icon to the list to choose from when creating a space, add the following to the `web-client-config-custom.xml` file:

```
<!-- Example of adding a custom icon to the Create Space dialog -->
<config evaluator="string-compare" condition="cm:folder icons">
  <icons>
    <icon name="space-icon-custom" path="/images/icons/
                                    space-icon-custom1.gif" />
  </icons>
</config>
```

A similar approach can be used to add icons for the forums space types (`fm:forums`, `fm:forum`, and `fm:topic`).

Once you add the custom icon names in the `web-client-config-custom.xml` file, you need to make sure the icons with the same filename are copied to the system icons folder. For an installation of Tomcat, the `icons` folder is at `<install_folder>\tomcat\webapps\alfresco\images\icons`. Also, for uniformity, ensure that all the icons are sized to 32 x 32 pixels.

As per the example, create a `.gif` file icon named `space-icon-custom1.gif` (32 x 32 pixels) and copy it to the `icons` folder. Once you reload the `web-client-config-custom.xml` file, you will notice the new icon when creating a space, as shown in the following screenshot:

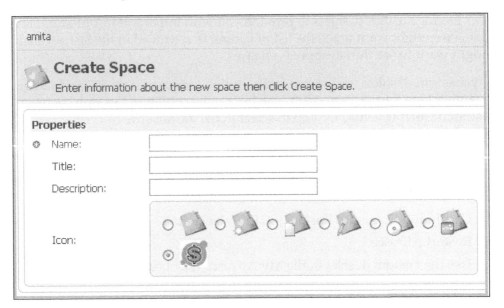

Configuring HTML links to appear in Alfresco Explorer

You can control certain HTML links that appear in the web client. For example, there is a small help icon in the menu on the top. By clicking on which, you can navigate to Alfresco's website. You can update the following lines in the web client configuration file to point help icon to your internal online help guide (if you have any). The URL to the client **Help** file is `<help-url>http://www.alfresco.org/help/webclient</help-url>`.

User-configurable dashboards

In the Alfresco Explorer user interface, the **My Alfresco** area is known as the **dashboard**. End users can construct their own dashboard page from a list of preconfigured components known as **dashlets**. As a developer, you can configure new components and make them available for selection by users when they are configuring their pages.

For more details about configuring your personal dashboard, refer *Chapter 3, Getting Started with Alfresco*.

Writing custom dashlets

There are certain dashlets provided to you out of the box. Since the dashboard is going to be a place where you can see all the dynamic information, you might consider having custom dashlets to provide you with important information. For example, you might want to see the list of contracts approved in the last seven days. You might want to see the latest press releases.

Usually, custom dashlets are written in a scripting language such as FreeMarker and called from a **Java Server Page (JSP)**. The JSP can be configured in web client so that the custom dashlet is visible for you to select in the dashboard.

The following steps are required to write and configure a custom dashlet:

1. Create a custom dashlet script.
2. Create a custom dashlet JSP (which internally uses dashlet script).
3. Configure the custom dashlet JSP in web client.
4. Restart Alfresco.
5. Use the custom dashlet in the **My Alfresco** dashboard.

Creating a custom dashlet script

As an example, write a custom dashlet script using the FreeMarker template language to display the latest press releases from the **Company Home | Intranet | Press and Media | Press Releases** space.

The dashlet script could be plain HTML text, FreeMarker template, JavaScript, or a JSP page. For this example, let us use a FreeMarker template.

Using the following code, create a file named chapter11_press_releases.ftl in your Alfresco configuration's templates folder. For the installation of Tomcat, the folder is <install_folder>\tomcat\webapps\alfresco\WEB-INF\classes\ alfresco\ templates.

```
<#----------------------------------------------------------------->
<#-- Name: chapter11_press_releases.ftl                         -->
<#--Displays a table of all the documents from a "Press Releases"-->
<#-- folder under Company Home/Intranet/Press and Media space   -->
<#-- NOTE: Obviously this folder needs to exist and             -->
<#--       the docs in it should have the title and content     -->
<#----------------------------------------------------------------->
<table>
  <#assign l_space = companyhome.childByNamePath["Intranet/Press and
                                      Media/Press Releases"]>
    <#list l_space.children as doc>
      <#if doc.isDocument>
      <tr>
        <td>
          <a class="title" href="/alfresco/${doc.url}">$
                                  {doc.properties.title}</a></td>
        </tr>
      <tr>
        <td style="padding-left:8px">
          <#if (doc.content?length > 500)>
            <small>${doc.content[0..500]}...</small>
          <#else>
            <small>${doc.content}</small>
           </#if>
          </td>
        </tr>
        <tr><td> <HR> </td></tr>
        </#if>
      </#list>
  </table>
```

Creating a custom dashlet JSP

Once the custom dashlet script is created in the `templates` folder, the next step is to create a custom dashlet JSP, which uses the custom dashlet script.

Create the `chapter11_press_releases.jsp` file with the following code and place the file in the dashlets folder. For a Tomcat installation, the folder is `<install_folder>\tomcat\webapps\alfresco\jsp\dashboards\dashlets`.

```
<%--
Name    : chapter11_press_releases.jsp
Purpose: Dashlet to display the latest press releases
--%>
<%@ taglib uri="/WEB-INF/repo.tld" prefix="r" %>
<%-- Note that this template is loaded from the classpath --%>
<r:template template="/alfresco/templates/chapter11_press_releases.
ftl" />
```

Configuring custom dashlet JSP in Alfresco Explorer

Now you need to configure the web client with the custom dashlet to make it visible in dashboard wizard.

Add the following code in the `web-client-config-custom.xml` file before the last XML tag, `</alfresco-config>`:

```
<config evaluator="string-compare" condition="Dashboards">
<!-- Dashboard layouts and available dashlets for the My Alfresco
                                                        Pages -->
  <dashboards>
    <dashlets>
<!-- Add additional dashlet for press releases -->
      <dashlet id="press-releases" label="Press Releases"
                       description="Lists Press Releases with URL"
          jsp="/jsp/dashboards/dashlets/chapter11_press_releases.jsp"
                                        allow-narrow="true" />
    </dashlets>
  </dashboards>
</config>
```

The following table describes each dashlet element used in the XML configuration:

Dashlet element	Description
Id	An ID string that uniquely identifies the dashlet.
Jsp	The JSP page to be used for the dashlet implementation.

Dashlet element	Description
`label` or `label-id`	The label text or label i18n message ID for the dashlet. This label is shown in the list of available components presented to the user in the Dashboard Configuration Wizard.
`description` or `description-id`	The description text or description i18n message ID for the layout. This description text is shown in the list of available components presented to the user in the Dashboard Configuration Wizard

Restarting Alfresco

To make the configuration changes effective, you need to restart Alfresco. The newly created custom dashlet example requires one or two press releases to be available in the **Company Home | Intranet | Press and Media | Press Releases** space. In *Chapter 7, Extending Alfresco Content Model*, you have created a few press releases in the **Company Home | Intranet | Press and Media | Press Releases** space.

Make sure you have at least two press releases created in the **Press Releases** space. Refer to the *Create press release as an HTML content* section in *Chapter 7, Extending Alfresco Content Model*.

Using the custom dashlet in the My Alfresco Dashboard

Click on the **My Alfresco** link provided in the toolbar menu to view the dashboard. Click on the **Configure** icon given in the **My Alfresco Dashboard** and the **Configure Dashboard Wizard** will display the custom dashlet in **Step Two**. Then, select the **Components** screen, as shown in the following screenshot:

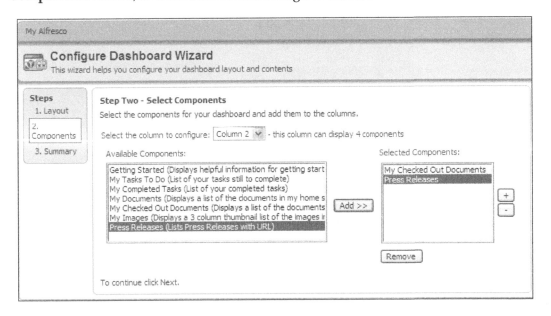

Select the **Press Releases** dashlet for **Column2**, as shown in the preceding screenshot. Once you finish the configuration, you will notice the custom dashlet in your dashboard, as shown in the following screenshot:

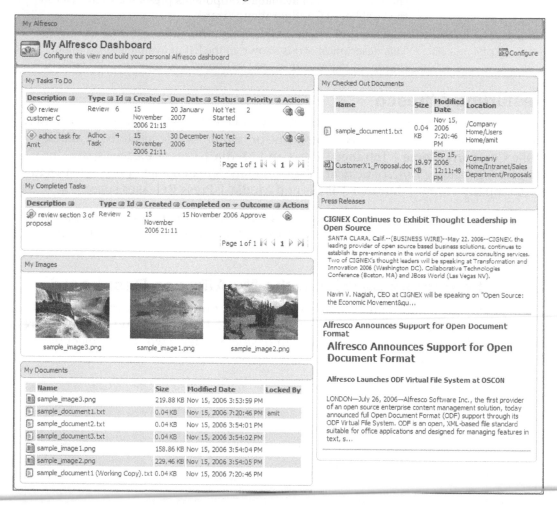

Using webscripts as dashlets

Alfresco provides a webscript feature as an easy way to interface other applications with the repository. In the previous module, we have seen how to customize a dashlet using FreeMarker templates. With the example that is given below, we will use webscript as a dashlet.

The following steps are required to configure a dashlet as webscripts:

1. Create a custom dashlet JSP.

2. Configure a custom dashlet JSP.

3. Configure a custom **My Spaces** dashlet in Alfresco Explorer.

Creating a custom dashlet JSP

Create a new JSP page called as `Chpater11-myspaces-webscript.jsp` with the following code in it and place the file in `dashlets` folder. For a Tomcat installation, the folder is `<install_folder>\tomcat\webapps\alfresco\jsp\dashboards\ dashlets`.

```
<%--
Purpose    : Dashlet to display the summary information of Home
Space
Created by: Snehal Shah
Created on: March 18, 2013
--%>
<%@ taglib uri="/WEB-INF/repo.tld" prefix="r" %>
http://localhost:8080/alfresco/service/ui/myspaces?f=0
<r:webScript scriptUrl="/wcs/ui/myspaces?f=0" />
```

Here, `<r:webscript>` is a built-in tag. In order to call webscript, put webscript URL in `scriptUrl` attribute of this tag. We have used an out of the box provided `myspaces` webscript URL in the preceding code.

Configuring the custom dashlet JSP

Add the following code in the `web-client-config-custom.xml` file before the last XML tag, `</alfresco-config>`:

```
<config evaluator="string-compare" condition="Dashboards">
    <!-- Dashboard layouts and available dashlets for the My Alfresco
Pages -->
    <dashboards>
    <dashlets>
        <!-- Add additional dashlet for press releases -->
      <dashlet id="MySpaces" label="MySpaces"
                description="Webscript Dashlet for My Spaces"
        jsp="/jsp/dashboards/dashlets/Chpater11-myspaces-webscript.jsp"
                        allow-narrow="true" />
    </dashlets>
    </dashboards>
</config>
```

Configuring the MySpaces dashlet

Configure the newly created **MySpaces** custom webscript dashlet in dashboard as we configured the JSP custom dashlet in **My Alfresco** dashboard, as shown in the following screenshot:

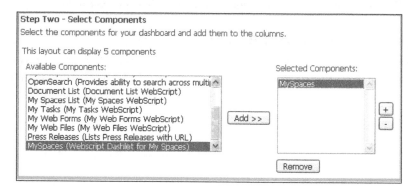

Custom dashlet

Once you configure the dashlet, you can see your webscript dashlet, as shown in the following screenshot:

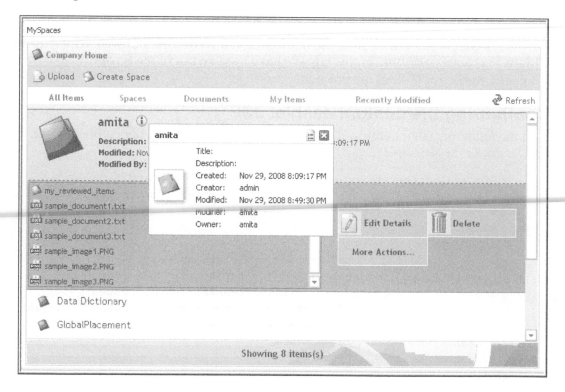

FreeMarker dashlet from the repository

Dashlet components can contain any selection of JSF components, including the template component. This means it is possible to use the results of a FreeMarker template as the dashlet contents. In the preceding example, you have used the FreeMarker template from the filesystem.

However, you can also use the FreeMarker template from your Alfresco Explorer's **Company Home | Data Dictionary | Presentation Templates** space.

To display a template stored in the repository, copy the `NodeRef` of the template file and create the page as follows, pasting your `NodeRef` value into the template attribute in this example:

```
<%@ taglib uri="/WEB-INF/repo.tld" prefix="r" %>
<r:template template="workspace://SpacesStore/
                              e4d1c727-e98b-11da-821a-936824f635fe" />
```

Presentation templates

The **Company Home | Data Dictionary | Presentation Templates** space contains both, built-in and custom presentation templates. A presentation template can be used to preview the content and to provide look and feel for the content. An example of presentation template is provided in *Chapter 7, Extending the Alfresco Content Model*, where a custom template is used to preview the press release content. Presentation templates are written in FreeMarker template language and will have an `.ftl` extension.

FreeMarker is an open source template engine. It is a generic tool to generate text output (anything from HTML to auto-generated source code) based on templates. FreeMarker is designed to be practical for the generation of HTML web pages following the **Model View Controller** (**MVC**) pattern. The idea behind using the MVC pattern for dynamic web pages is that you separate the content authors from the programmers. This separation is useful, even for projects where the programmer and the HMTL page author are the same person, as it helps to keep the application clear and easily maintainable.

In the following diagram, the content authors create document content in Alfresco. The programmers create the presentation template file with stylesheets, HTML code, and take care of the look and feel. The final content will be generated by the FreeMarker engine (which is embedded in Alfresco) by applying the presentation template on the document content, as shown in the diagram:

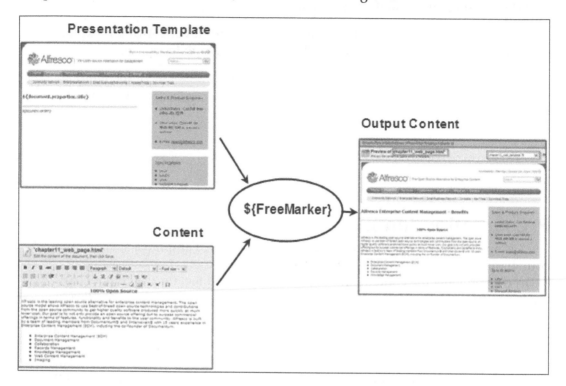

The FreeMarker template engine within Alfresco

The FreeMarker template engine is embedded within Alfresco. FreeMarker takes the Alfresco data model as input and generates text (HTML or XML) as output. FreeMarker also supports XSLT to translate XML content.

The Alfresco objects available to FreeMarker

The default model provides a set of named objects that wrap Alfresco node objects to provide a rich, object-oriented layer that is suitable for scripting usage. If you are accessing the templates through the web-client UI, then the following named objects are provided by default. Note that all the methods exposed by the FreeMarker template engine perform read-only operations. There is no method to modify, drop, or add contents in the repository:

Named object	Description
companyhome	The Company Home template node
userhome	The current user's Home Space template node
person	A node representing the current user's Person object
space	The current space template node (if you are accessing the templates through the **Space Preview** action)
document	The current document template node (If you are accessing the templates through the **Document Preview** action)
Template	The node representing the template itself
Args	A map of any URL parameters passed via the Template Content Servlet (only available if the template was executed via the servlet)
Session	Session related information (session.ticket for the authentication ticket)
classification	Read access to classifications and root categories

For example, consider the following FreeMarker template:

```
<html>
<head>
<title>Welcome!</title>
</head>
<body>
<h1>Welcome ${person.properties.userName}!</h1>
</body>
</html>
```

At run time, the value of person.properties.userName variable will be the name of the current user who is accessing the system. Hence the template generates a dynamic greeting message.

> The Alfresco Wiki website (http://wiki.alfresco.com) contains a complete reference to the FreeMarker template guide.

FreeMarker template-node model API

These objects, and any child node objects are called **template-node objects**, and they provide the following API:

Node method	Description
properties	A map of the properties of the node.
	For example, userhome, properties, name.
	Properties may return several different types of object. This depends entirely on the underlying property type in the repository. If the property is multi-valued, then the result will be a sequence, which can be indexed like any other sequence or array.
children	A sequence (list) of the child nodes. For example, a list of documents in a space.
url	The URL of the content stream for this node.
content	Returns the content of the node as a string.
size	The size in bytes of content attached to this node.
isLocked	True if the node is locked, false otherwise.
name	Shortcut access to the name property
Parent	The parent node, can be null if this is the root node
childrenByXPath	Returns a map capable of executing an XPath query to find child nodes, for example, companyhome.childrenByXPath["*[@ cm:name='Data Dictionary']/*"]
childByNamePath	Returns a map capable of returning a single child node found by name path, for example, companyhome. childByNamePath["Data Dictionary/Content Templates"]

FreeMarker directives

Like any programming language, the FreeMarker templating language also supports fundamental directives, such as the following:

```
#if, #else, #elseif
#switch, #case
#list
#assign
#function
#include
<#-- comment -->
```

For your reference, a complete guide is available at `http://FreeMarker.sourceforge.net/docs/`.

Custom template to preview web pages

Let us develop a custom template to preview the HTML documents.

Log in as admin, go to the **Company Home | Data Dictionary | Presentation Templates** space and create a new template and name it appropriately (say, `chapter11_web_template.ftl`). The template should display the web page layout, as shown in the following screenshot. The template can be applied on any text or HTML document in the Alfresco repository to generate a web page with layout, as given in the following screenshot:

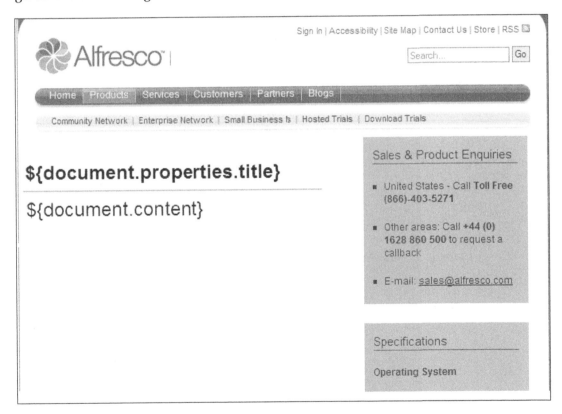

You can consider using the following code to create a custom template. The code uses the images in the Alfresco repository to display the horizontal bar on the top and the vertical bar on the right side. Note that the image URLs may change in the code based on the location of the actual images in your repository. You can use your own images or you can even create the HTML header and table structure as per your application.

The template extracts the document titles and displays them as page heading. Refer to the FreeMarker template code ${document.properties.title}. Similarly, the template extracts the document content and displays it in the center portion of the page, as shown in next screenshot. Refer to the FreeMarker template code ${document.content}.

```
<#------------------------------------------------------------------->
<#-- Extracts Title and Description from Content and          -->
<#--                      shows in web template               -->
<#------------------------------------------------------------------->
<table width="100%" border="0" cellspacing="0" cellpadding="0">
  <tr>
    <td colspan="2" valign="top">
      <img src=
"http://localhost:8080/alfresco/download/direct/workspace/SpacesStore
                            /bfcc8130-4537-11db-972a953696db55bc/
                            chapter11_template_top_image.png" />
    </td>
  </tr>
  <tr>
    <td valign="top">
      <BR>
      <H4> ${document.properties.title} </H4>
      <HR>
      ${document.content}
    </td>
    <td valign="top">
      <img src=
          "http://localhost:8080/alfresco/download/direct/workspace/
                SpacesStore/c87378c9-4537-11db-972a-953696db55bc/
                            chapter11_template_right_image.png" />
    </td>
  </tr>
</table>
```

Create a new HTML document in one of the spaces in your Alfresco Explorer. Use the **Preview in Template** action button on the document and choose the custom template (in this example, it is chapter11_web_template.ftl) to display the document content. The sample preview screen is shown in the following screenshot:

Custom template for XML content

The FreeMarker templating engine can be used for XSLT (XML transformations) to transform XML content to HTML, with an appropriate look and feel.

This is a classic solution to store the data in the Alfresco's repository in native XML format and use FreeMarker custom templates to display the XML data in an HTML format.

To test the XML transformation features, you will need to create an XML document in Alfresco. You can either create this as an XML file (say, book.xml) on your desktop and upload it to Alfresco web client or you can directly create this XML document in Alfresco. Create a document called mybook.xml in one of your **Company Home | Intranet** spaces with the following content:

```
<?xml version="1.0" standalone="yes"?>
<book title="Book Title">
  <chapter>
    <title>Chapter 1</title>
    <para>p1.1</para>
    <para>p1.2</para>
    <para>p1.3</para>
  </chapter>
  <chapter>
    <title>Chapter 2</title>
    <para>p2.1</para>
    <para>p2.2</para>
  </chapter>
</book>
```

Create a template in the **Company Home | Data Dictionary | Presentation Templates** space called xmlbook.ftl with the following code:

```
<#if document.mimetype = "text/xml">
  <#assign dom=document.xmlNodeModel>
    <h1>${dom.book.@title}</h1>
  <#list dom.book.chapter as c>
    <h2>${c.title}</2>
    <#list c.para as p>
    <p> ${p} </p>
    </#list>
  </#list>
</#if>
```

The template displays the title of the book and chapters using the HTML tags. When you apply the xmlbook.ftl template on the book.xml document, you will observe the output, as shown in the following screenshot:

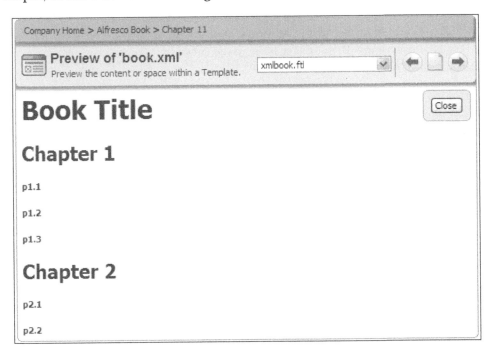

Custom templates for custom space view

Custom space view is a portal window, which shows up on the top of each space when a **Custom View** is selected. If you are implementing Alfresco for various departments and groups, you might consider having custom home pages for each department or group space.

As an example, let us build a custom view for all the department spaces. Let us say each department space contains two files: home_image.png and home_page.html. Let us apply a presentation template as a **Custom View** on the department space, which displays these two local files in that department as the department home page.

Create a template in the **Company Home | Data Dictionary | Presentation Templates** space called chapter11_dept_home_template.ftl with the following code:

```
<#------------------------------------------------------------------->
<#--        Displays Home Page for each department using    -->
<#-- (1) Home Page Image file home_image.png and                 -->
<#-- (2) Home Page HTML file home_page.html                      -->
<#-- By Snehal Shah, March 18, 2013                              -->
<#------------------------------------------------------------------->
<H4> Welcome to ${space.properties.title} </H4>
<#list space.children as child>
  <#if child.properties.name = 'home_image.png'>
    <img src="/alfresco${child.url}">
  </#if>
</#list>
  <#list space.children as child>
    <#if child.properties.name = 'home_page.html'>
      ${child.content}
    </#if>
  </#list>
```

Next, create a sample space (say **Department A**). Within that space, create two content files with names home_image.png (the department image) and home_page. html (the department description). Now select the chapter11_dept_home_ template.ftl template as a custom view for your space (the **Department A** space).

The steps to apply a presentation template as a **Custom View** are already explained in the *Applying Custom View on a space* section of this chapter. You will notice the custom view of your space is as shown in the screenshot on the next page.

This can be applied to each and every department and group within your organization. Consider having the department space as the space template, so that you could re-use the department space template to create spaces for many departments. More information about space templates is provided in *Chapter 5, Implementing Document Management*.

Department members can update the image file and the HTML file, as required, to alter the home page information dynamically. Similarly, you can think of various presentation templates to display the information in a specific space.

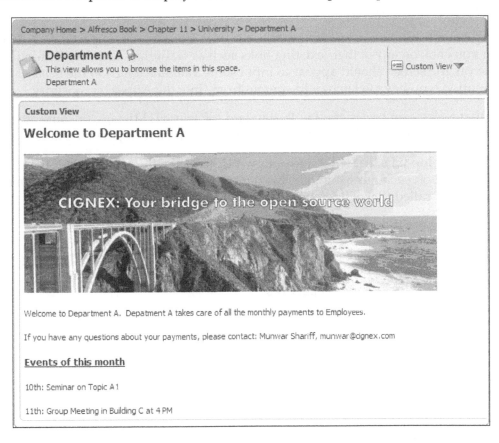

Customizing JSP Client

You can develop a custom user interface using JSPs and Alfresco Foundation APIs. The following is a list of some of the Foundation APIs:

- NodeService
- SearchService
- DictionaryService
- ContentService
- FileFolderService

Suppose there is an existing portal for a travel agency named **Fun Travels Ltd**. This portal is developed on another platform. The agency has various galleries, articles, guidelines, forms, and so on. They want to store as well as fetch all this content from the Alfresco repository.

To implement this, you have to customize the user interface of this portal such that when you click on any of their existing links such as **Galleries**, **Articles**, **Guidelines**, and so on, the screen should appear to input some valuable data. On the basis of this information, you have to fetch/add content from/into the Alfresco repository.

Note that a form can be designed with standard JSP tags, HTML tags, or some other standard UI frameworks. In this chapter, we are covering it using the JSF Framework.

For this, develop JSPs that will have our own UI to deal with Alfresco, and these JSPs will be called on each link asking for the data to be entered. On submission, Alfresco beans will be called that will fetch the content and send it to the portal.

The following are the code snippets provided:

1. Define a managed bean that contains the properties of the UI elements and properties for the Alfresco services:

```
Custom UI Properties

Public class ArticleBean implements Serializable{

    private  String contentTitle = null;
    public String getContentTitle() {

  return contentTitle;
   }
   public void setContentTitle(String contentTitle) {
  this.contentTitle = contentTitle;
     }


//Alfresco Service properties
Private SearchService searchService = null;
   /**
   *    @return the searchService
   */
   public SearchService getSearchService() {
  return searchService;
   }
   /**
   * @param searchService the searchService to set
   */
   */
```

```
      public void setSearchService(SearchService searchService) {
    this.searchService = searchService;
        }
Public void addContent(){

}
```

2. Provide the following code in `faces-config-custom.xml` (for a Tomcat installation, it is in the following folder: `<alfresco_install_folder>\tomcat\webapps\alfresco\WEB-INF`):

```xml
    <managed-bean>
   <managed-bean-name> ArticleBean</managed-bean-name>
         <managed-bean-class>com.alfresco.bean.ArticleBean</
managed-
          bean-class>
         <managed-bean-scope>session</managed-bean-scope>

         <managed-property>
           <property-name>searchService</property-name>
           <value>#{SearchService}</value>
         </managed-property>
     </managed-bean>
```

3. Provide the following code in `faces-config-navigation-custom.xml` (for a Tomcat installation, create the file in the following folder: `<alfresco_install_folder>\tomcat\webapps\alfresco\WEB-INF`):

```xml
    <navigation-rule>
      <from-view-id>/jsp/extension/displayAllTravels.jsp</from-
          view-id>
      <navigation-case>
        <from-outcome>addContent</from-outcome>
        <to-view-id>/jsp/extension/addContent.jsp</to-view-id>
      </navigation-case>
    </navigation-rule>
```

4. Write various JSP pages. These JSPs will access the bean properties for setting the elements and for displaying the content:

```
        <h:inputText ="#{articleBean.contentTitle}" />
        <h:outputText ="#{articleBean.contentTitle}" />
        <h:commandButton action="#{articleBean.getContent" value
="ADD"/>
```

5. Attach the JSP to the links provided on the portal. Click of each link, and a custom JSP page will be called, as shown in the following screenshot:

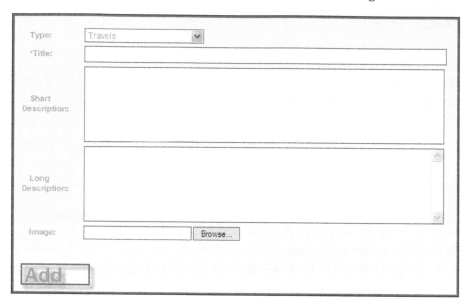

6. The Alfresco custom JSP integrated with the external application is shown in the following screenshot:

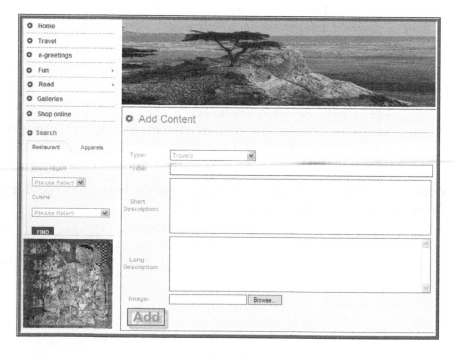

7. On clicking the **Add** button, the content is fetched from the Alfresco repository and is displayed in the portal, as shown here:

Various user interface options

Alfresco can be integrated with various other external systems. It can be integrated with Flash, Liferay, Drupal, iPhone, Facebook, iGoogle, Outlook, Adobe, Quark, FFMPEG, and ViewOnePro. For more details about configuring external systems, refer to *Chapter 9, Integrating External Applications with Alfresco*.

Summary

The Alfresco Explorer user interface can be customized to display your personal dashboard information, such as the pending tasks, checked out documents, and a list of press releases. Presentation templates can be applied to spaces, as well as to content. By using a **Custom View** on a space, you can consolidate all the important information in one place.

You can store content in the Alfresco repository in native XML format and use FreeMarker custom templates to display the XML data in various formats, such as PDF and HTML. You have an option of separating the actual content with display information so that you can leverage the ability of having multiple views of the same content.

In the next chapter, we will go through the power of Alfresco's search mechanism, which gives you a required content in fewer clicks. Also, it will cover various options for categorization and other search integration mechanisms.

12
Search in Alfresco

The success of content management systems depends on their ability to locate the required content with the least amount of clicks. The way you choose the content name, the way you categorize the content, the location where you place the content, and the meta-data property values you provide will help you to easily locate the content. You will realize the benefits of having a powerful search engine when you have a large number of files in your content management system. In this chapter, you will examine the advanced search features of Alfresco, and extend the capabilities of search.

By the end of this chapter, you will have learned how to:

- Use the advanced search form
- Extend search capabilities
- Define and save search criteria as re-usable reports
- Use Alfresco's OpenSearch features
- Configure Alfresco's search engine Lucene
- Configure and use the Solr search engine with Alfresco

Overview

Unlike many commercial content management systems, Alfresco includes free and very powerful search engines called **Lucene** and **Solr** as part of its installation. Therefore, you don't have to buy and install a third-party search engine. Moreover, you don't have to deal with integration issues and upgrades.

Using Alfresco, you will be able to search both content and properties. You can do a full-text search on any word in the content, regardless of the format. You can search for content in a particular space. You can also search for content belonging to certain categories or of a specific type. You can search for content created or modified between certain dates, created by a specific person, and so on. You can extend the search capabilities to search for custom content type and custom property values.

By default, the content in Alfresco is full-text searchable. Any content that is uploaded to Alfresco, such as the following types, will be internally converted to text, indexed, and made searchable:

- Microsoft Office documents, MS Word, Excel, PowerPoint
- Open Office documents
- XML/HTML
- PDF
- E-mails
- Content in foreign languages

Search using Alfresco Explorer

Alfresco Explorer provides a web-based user interface to search and locate the content. When you log in (to `http://<servername>:<port>/alfresco`), you will notice a search box in the upper-right hand corner.

Simple search

Performing a search on Alfresco is easy. Simply type one or more search terms (the words that best describe the information you want to find) into the search box and hit the *Enter* key or click on the search icon (), as shown here:

You can use Google-style query syntax to search the content stored in the Alfresco repository. The following table lists various search syntaxes along with their descriptions:

Search string	Description
Customer	Returns all of documents that contain the text "Customer" (as filename or file content)
-Customer	Returns all of the documents that do not contain the text "Customer"
Customer Alfresco	Returns all of the documents that contain "Customer" or "Alfresco". Equivalent to Customer +Alfresco
Customer +Alfresco	Returns all of the documents that contain "Customer" or "Alfresco"
Customer -Alfresco	Returns all of the documents that contain "Customer" and do not contain "Alfresco"
inter	Returns all of the documents that contain any portion of the word "inter", such as International, Interest. This is also known as wild card search.

Search filenames only

It is faster to search the content by filenames if you know the filename or some portion of the filename. When you click on the search options icon (📧▼), you will see a list of the options available to you, as shown in the following screenshot:

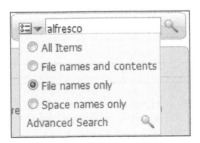

You can select an option by clicking on the corresponding radio button, as shown in the screenshot. You have the following options:

- **All items**: Search the entire content and all the properties
- **File names and contents**: Search the entire content and the filename property
- **File names only**: Search only the name property of the file's content
- **Space names only**: Search only the name property of the space's content

Advanced search

You can view the advanced search form by clicking on the **Advanced Search** link provided in search drop-down options, as shown in the preceding screenshot. By using the advanced search form (shown in the following screenshot), you can search content:

- Within a space, optionally its sub-spaces
- Matching a given category, optionally sub-categories
- Of a specific content type or a mime type
- Matching properties such as title, description, author
- Created or modified within certain date ranges
- Matching custom properties

The menu bar of the advanced search form contains a **Reset All** button (refer the following screenshot), which is useful for clearing all the options selected in the form. You can save the search options and execute the saved searches as reports. More information about saved searches is provided in the later sections of this chapter.

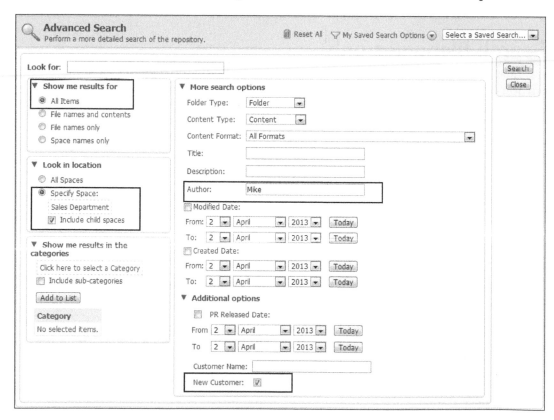

Search by content location

The options provided in the **Look in location** block of the advanced search form will allow you to search content by its location. Clicking on the **Specify Space** radio button will list the spaces for you to choose, as shown in the next screenshot. From the list of spaces, click on a space name to browse to sub-spaces. You can click on the ⊕ image to select a space and optionally choose to search in all sub-spaces by checking the **Include child spaces** option. You can choose only one space and its sub-spaces to search the content at a time.

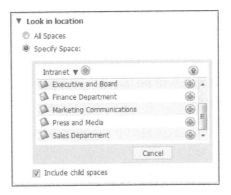

Search by content category

The options provided in the **Show me results in the categories** block of the advanced search form will allow you to search content belonging to one or more categories. Clicking on the **Select Category** link will list the categories, as shown in the screenshot on the next page. From the list of categories, click on category name to browse the sub-categories. You can click on the ⊕ image to select a category and optionally choose to search in all sub-categories by checking the **Include sub-categories** option. Click on the **Add to List** button to add the category to the list of selections. You can choose as many categories as you want to search the content.

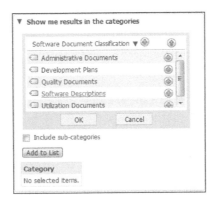

Search by content properties

The options provided in the **More search options** block of the advanced search form will allow you to search content based on the property values. You can search for content that belongs to a specific content type by selecting the **Content Type** drop-down option. You can search for the content created by a specific author by providing full or partial name of the author in the **Author** textbox, as shown in the previous advance search dialog screenshot. You can search for the content created within certain date ranges by selecting the **Created Date** checkbox and providing the **From** and **To** dates.

If you choose more than one option, then the content that satisfies all the conditions will be listed in the search result. For example, if you have provided the author's name and a **Created Date** range, then the content created within that date range and authored by that specific person will be listed. This is equivalent to a logical AND criteria to select the content. The current limitation with the advanced search form is that you cannot provide an OR criteria. For example, you cannot search the content within a date range or which was created by a specific person.

Extending the search form

In *Chapter 7, Extending Alfresco Content Model*, you have created a custom content called **Press Release** and a custom aspect called **Customer Details**. You can search content of the press release type. You can also search the content having a specific custom property value.

For the advanced search form to recognize and list the custom content types and custom aspects, you need to customize the web client.

Configuring the web client user interface

Edit the `web-client-config-custom.xml` file in the `extension` (`<alfresco_ install_folder>\tomcat\shared\classes\alfresco\extension`) folder and add the following XML code to extend the advanced search form:

```
<config evaluator="string-compare" condition="Advanced Search">
  <advanced-search>
    <content-types>
      <type name="custom:pressrelease" />
    </content-types>
    <custom-properties>
      <meta-data type="custom:pressrelease"
                                  property="custom:PRDate" />
      <meta-data aspect="custom:CustomerDetails"
```

```
                                          property="custom:CustomerName" />
            <meta-data aspect="custom:CustomerDetails"
                                          property="custom:NewCustomer" />
        </custom-properties>
      </advanced-search>
    </config>
```

This code in the `<content-types>` block will list this content type in the advanced search form. The code in the `<custom-properties>` block will list the given custom properties in advanced search form.

After making changes to the configuration file, restart Alfresco.

Searching custom content and properties

After you log in to Alfresco Explorer, open the advanced search form and click on the **Additional options** block, you will notice the custom properties, as highlighted in the next screenshot. Similarly, when you click on the **Content Type** drop-down list, you will notice the custom content type listed, as shown in the next screenshot.

You can search content by providing various values in the **Additional options** block. For example, you can list the documents belonging to new customers by selecting the **New Customer** checkbox and clicking the *Enter* button on your keyboard or by clicking on the **Search** button in the advanced search form:

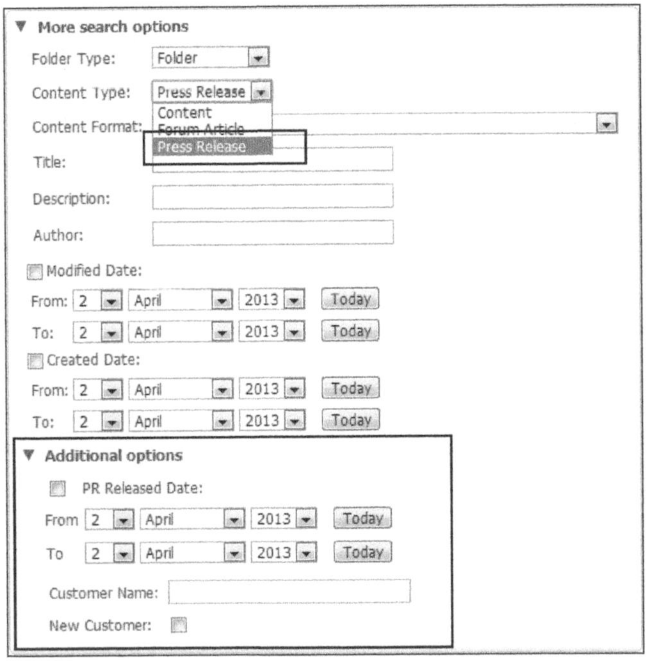

Saving search as a report

Some times, you will have to repeatedly search for some content that satisfies a specific search criterion. Instead of typing or selecting the same options in the advanced search form again and again, you can save the search criteria to reuse. This is like a personalized report for you. You can choose to share this report with others by making the saved search as **Public**. You can keep certain reports to yourself by not sharing them with others and these reports will be listed for you as private reports.

Defining complex search criteria

As an example, generate a report to list all of the sales documents authored by Mike for new customers.

In order to define these search criteria, open the **Advanced Search** form. Under the **Look in location** block, select the **Company Home | Intranet | Sales Department** space and select sub-spaces. Under the **More search options** block, type **Mike** for **Author**. Under the **Additional options** block, select the **New Customer** checkbox.

You can further complicate the search criteria by selecting a date range for **Created Date**.

Once you are done with your search criteria, click on the **Search** button to display the search results.

Saving search criteria as a public or private report

The search results page is shown in the following screenshot. You can save the search criteria by clicking on the **More Actions | Save New Search** option, as shown in the following screenshot:

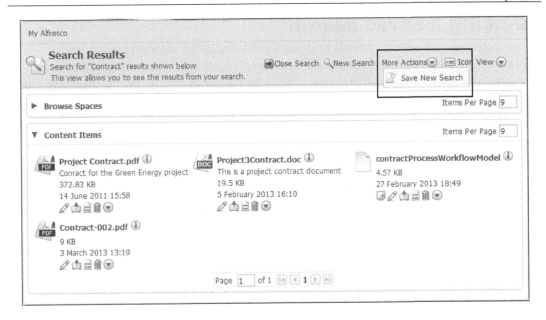

Clicking on the **Save New Search** link will open up the **Save New Search** dialog, as shown in the following screenshot:

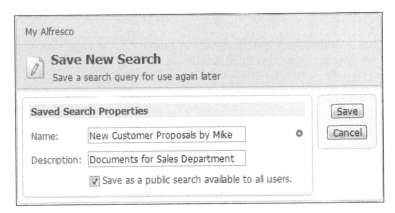

In the **Save New Search** dialog, give some meaningful **Name** and optional **Description** to your custom report (saved search).

If you select the **Save as a public search available to all users** option, then this custom report becomes a public report and is visible to all other users in the advanced search form. If you have not selected this option, then the report is visible only to you, as a private report.

All saved searches can be found at the **Company Home | Data Dictionary | Saved Searches** space.

Re-using a saved search

You can re-use the search criteria that are saved earlier by selecting them in the **Advanced Search** form. In **Advanced Search** form, click on the **My Saved Search Options** link and then on **Public Searches**. The right-hand side drop-down box will list all of the available public reports (saved searches).

Selecting a saved search will automatically create the search criteria by selecting the options in the advanced search form. Similarly, you can re-use **Your Searches**, which are types of private reports for you.

OpenSearch

OpenSearch is a standard format of sharing search results across many systems. It helps various search engines and search clients communicate, by introducing a common set of formats to perform search requests and syndicate search results.

 Refer to the OpenSearch website at `http://www.opensearch.org` for specifications and documentation.

Alfresco has adopted open standards throughout the framework, and OpenSearch is one such standard. This enables a standards-based interface to search the content in repository. For example, you can search the content in Alfresco from any application written in any other programming language running on any platform.

Alfresco exposes its search engines via OpenSearch and also provides a new aggregate open search feature in the Alfresco Explorer.

Alfresco's open search engines

You can discover the available open search engines using the following URL:
`http://<servername>:<port>/alfresco/service/api/search/engines`.

There are two open search engines available out of the box. One is a keyword (Google-like) search and the other is a person (registered member) search. Click on a specific engine to view the description and usage:

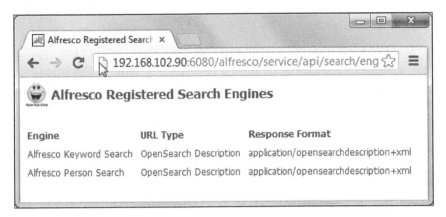

Keyword search description

This search is similar to the keyword search of the Alfresco Explorer. Documents containing the specified keywords in their name or content are returned.

The search URL format is as follows:

```
http://<servername>:<port>/alfresco/service/api/search/keyword?q={sea
rchTerms}&p={startPage?}&c={count?}&l={language?}
```

The parameters to be provided are given as follows. The optional parameters are listed with a question mark:

- searchTerms: Keyword or keywords to search on
- startPage (optional): The page number of search results desired by the client
- count (optional): The number of search results per page (default: 10)
- language (optional): The locale to search with (XML 1.0 Language Id, for example, en-GB)

The output response can be in either HTML, ATOM, or RSS. The default output format is HTML.

Sample keyword search in HTML

Consider the following keyword search sample:

```
http://localhost:8080/alfresco/service/search/keyword.
html?q=alfresco&c=3
```

In the URL, `keyword.html` indicates that the desired output is HTML. The search term is `alfresco` and the number of search results to be listed per page should be three. The following screenshot displays the search results. If the search results are more than the count specified (which is three in our example), then you will notice the links to subsequent results pages in the bottom of the screen:

Sample keyword search in RSS

You can also consider using the RSS output if you have RSS reader, or if you would like to display the search results in your custom application, such as a Portal. The URL format remains the same, except that the extension is rss:

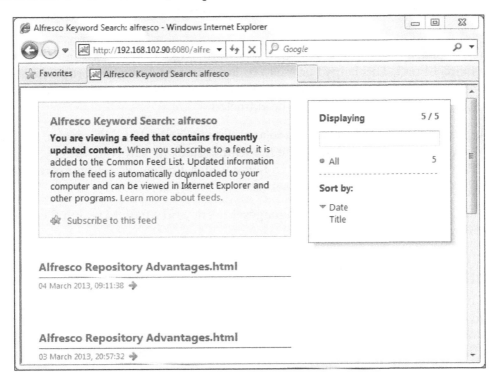

The search interface is provided using Alfresco web scripts. You can customize the search result format by customizing these web scripts. More information about web scripts is provided in *Chapter 9, Integrating External Applications with Alfresco*.

Configuring the Alfresco search engine

The Alfresco search engine is configurable and highly scalable. This section provides information about the underlying search engine and the process to configure it.

The theory behind the search engine

Alfresco supports full-text search capabilities, using Apache's powerful Lucene search engine (http://lucene.apache.org). Lucene is an open source, highly scalable, and fast search engine. Lucene powers searches in discussion groups at Fortune 100 companies, in commercial issue trackers, e-mail search from Microsoft, and the Nutch web search engine (that scales to billions of pages).

Lucene's logical architecture is such that it performs a search on a document based on the fields of text. This helps Lucene to be independent of the file format. So any kind of text (PDF, HTML, Microsoft Word documents, and so on) can be indexed as long as their textual information can be extracted.

Lucene stores the search indexes and related data in the backend filesystem, similar to Alfresco binary files. You can locate the search-index files in your <alfresco_ installation>\alf_data\lucene-indexes folder. Lucene also supports federated searches by combining various data sources.

Currently, Alfresco supports two languages: Lucene and XPath to search the content in the Alfresco repository.

Limiting the search results

By default, a search returns all the results that match the search criteria. Let us say you have millions of documents in your repository. If a particular search results into thousands of documents, the web client creates pagination to display search results in multiple pages. Quite often we never see the search results in the later pages of the search. Have you ever remembered clicking on page number 10 (or later) in search results page to locate content? It is very inefficient to get all the search results and display in pages.

You can limit the search results by customizing your web-client configuration file web-client-config-custom.xml in the extension (<alfresco_install_ folder>\tomcat\shared\classes\alfresco\extension) folder.

Edit the web-client-config-custom.xml file and add the following XML text after the first line (<alfresco-config>). If you have already created this XML block in your web-client-config-custom.xml file, then insert the following lines that are highlighted:

```
<config>
  <client>
    <!-- Override the from email address -->
      <from-email-address>mike@cignex.com</from-email-address>
        <!-- the minimum number of characters required for a valid
```

```
                                                  search string -->
      <search-minimum>3</search-minimum>
      <!-- set this value to true to enable AND text terms for
                              simple/advanced search by default -->
      <search-and-terms>false</search-and-terms>
      <!-- Limit search results. -1 for unlimited. -->
      <search-max-results>100</search-max-results>
   </client>
</config>
```

The code ensures that the search engine will return a maximum of 100 results. The minimum search string length is set to three characters. The Boolean AND search option is disabled by default to improve search performance.

Restart Alfresco to make sure the above changes are effective.

Indexing properties

In Alfresco content model, the data dictionary settings for properties determine how individual properties are indexed in search engine.

Refer to the custom aspect called **Customer Details** in *Chapter 7, Extending Alfresco Content Model*. In earlier sections of this chapter, we have configured the advanced search form to search for the **Customer Name** property of this custom aspect. It is recommended to index the values of the **Customer Name** property to improve the performance of search.

Edit the customModel.xml file in your <extension> folder, where you declared the **Customer Details** aspect. Add the following highlighted code to the aspect declaration to index the property:

```
<property name="custom:CustomerName">
    <title>Customer Name</title>
    <type>d:text</type>
    <protected>false</protected>
    <mandatory>false</mandatory>
    <multiple>false</multiple>
  <index enabled="true">
      <atomic>false</atomic>
      <stored>false</stored>
      <tokenized>true</tokenized>
  </index>
    <constraints>
        <constraint ref="custom:name_length"/>
    </constraints>
</property>
```

If the `enabled` option for the index is set to `true`, then this property will be indexed in the search engine. If this is set to `false`, there will be no entry for this property in the index.

If the `Atomic` option is set to `true`, then the property is indexed in the same transaction of the node that a repository is creating. If not, the property is indexed in the background. Lucene search engine is the only one that supports In-Transaction management of search indexes.

If the `Stored` option is set to `true`, then the property value is stored in the index and may be obtained through the Lucene low-level query API. Setting `Stored` to `true` is only useful when you need to read the Lucene indexes directly from any third-party application.

If the `Tokenized` option is set to `true`, then the string value of the property is tokenized before indexing; if it is set to `false`, then it is indexed as it is as a single string. The token is determined by the property type in the data dictionary. This is locale-sensitive as supported by the data dictionary. For example, you have `xyz.txt` content with a property set as `company_name=Fun Corporation`. Based on how you have set the tokenization of the `company_name` property, you would have different search results. Let's say you want to search for content for which `company_name` property contains the value `Corporation`. Now if you have set `tokenized` to `true`, you would be able to get `xyz.txt` in the search result. If you have set `tokenized` to `false`, you would not be able to search, in this case you need to search for complete text `Fun Corporation`. You can refer to the `http://wiki.alfresco.com/wiki/Search` link for more details on how to use and create Lucene query for search.

If you have not specified any indexing values to your custom properties, then Alfresco assumes default values to your properties. By default, the properties are indexed atomically. The property value is not stored in the index, and the property is tokenized when it is indexed.

Controlling indexing of a node

In Alfresco, there is an important `cm:indexControl` aspect, which helps us to control the indexes of a node. This aspect provides two properties with which we can control indexing of metadata and binary content of node. Both these properties are of the type Boolean, with a default value of `true`:

- `cm:isIndexed`: This property allows you to control whether a node will be indexed or not. If it is set to `false`, neither metadata nor binary content of any node would be indexed.

- `cm:isContentIndexed`: This property allows you to control the indexing of binary content of node. If this is set to false, only the metadata of a node would be indexed.

Let's consider an example where we have some documents stored in Alfresco. These documents should be searchable on the metadata of document and not on the content of document. In such kind of requirement, the `indexControl` aspect is very useful.

Configuring Lucene in Alfresco

The `repository.properties` file in your `config` folder defines a number of properties that influence how all indexes behave. You can improve the search performance by setting appropriate values in the `properties` file.

 We recommend you NOT to change the values in the `repository.properties` file. Rather, we would like you to override settings in the `alfresco-global.properties` file in the `/extension` folder in the Alfresco classpath.

Make sure the following properties are set to `lucene` in `alfresco-global.properties` file, and then only the following search-index properties will have an impact:

```
index.subsystem.name = lucene
```

The following are the default search-index properties:

- `lucene.query.maxClauses=10000`

- `lucene.indexer.batchSize=10000`

- `lucene.indexer.minMergeDocs=1000`

- `lucene.indexer.mergeFactor=10`

- `lucene.indexer.maxMergeDocs=100000`

- **Max Clauses** (Lucene standard parameter): Lucene queries limit the number of clauses in a Boolean query to this value. Some queries are expanded into a whole set of Boolean query with many clauses under the covers. For example, searching for `luc.*` will expand to a Boolean query containing an OR for every token that the index knows about that matches `luc.*`.

- **Batch size** (Alfresco indexing parameter): The indexer stores a list of what it has to do as the changes are made using the node service API. Typically, there are many events that would cause a node to be re-indexed. Keeping an event list means, the actions can be optimized. The algorithm limits re-indexes to one per batch size, and it will not index if a delete is pending. When the list of events reach this size, the whole event list is processed and the documents are added to the delta index.

- **Min Merger Docs** (Lucene standard parameter): This determines the size of the in-memory Lucene index used for each delta index. A higher value of Min Merger Docs would mean that we have more memory but less IO writing to the index delta. The in-memory information will be flushed and written to the disk at the start of the next batch of index events. As the process progresses, the event list requires reading against the delta index. This does not affect the way information is stored on disk, just how it is buffered before it gets there.

- **Merge Factor** (Lucene standard parameter): This determines the number of index segments that are created on the disk. When there are more than this value, some segments will be combined.

- **Max Merge Docs** (Lucene standard parameter): This value determines the maximum number of documents that could be stored in an index segment. When this value is reached in a segment, it will not grow any larger. As a result, there may be more segments than expected from looking at the merge factor.

You can refer to the following links to fine-tune the Lucene-based on your requirement. Values of the preceding parameters mainly depend on the usage of Alfresco system, like you have more read operation or write operation:

- `http://wiki.apache.org/lucene-java/ImproveIndexingSpeed`
- `http://wiki.apache.org/lucene-java/ImproveSearchingSpeed`

Using the Solr search engine with Alfresco

Solr is a widely used open source search server provided by apache. It uses Lucene as its search engine, but addition to that it provides full enterprise search server capabilities. Solr provides a web based application that accepts http request and returns http response.

Here are some advantages of Solr:

- Advanced full-text search capabilities
- Provides faceted search
- Performance optimized for high volume web traffic
- Single server for indexes of multiple applications
- For clustered Alfresco servers, indexes can be maintained at a single Solr server
- Solr is highly scalable, provides clustering of Solr server.
- Web-based Solr administration interface
- Solr supports Lucene-style queries, so no need to change the queries
- Path queries are significantly improved in Solr

Solr Core is a very important term in Solr. Single Solr instances can have multiple Cores. Each core contains indexes and related configuration files, schema for that index. The advantage we get with core is that all indexes are isolated. Multiple cores in a single instance of Solr also allows us to have a unified administrator for the entire index.

The main difference between the Solr and Lucene subsystems in Alfresco is in-transaction indexing. Solr doesn't support in-transaction indexing. If your application has a requirement of in-transaction indexing, then you have to opt for Lucene. Also, currently Alfresco doesn't support Solr for records management and multi-tenancy. So, if you want to use any of these features, then you need to go for Lucene.

Installing Solr on an independent server

Solr comes embedded with Alfresco. But on a production server, we should install Solr on an independent server. This will allow us to leverage the scalability feature of Solr. You have to use the Solr search engine provided by Alfresco. The following are the high-level steps to be followed to install Solr:

1. Download the Solr distribution zip bundle provided by Alfresco.
2. This zip contains a Solr WAR file, SSL keystore, certificate files, and Solr core configuration files.
3. Install the Tomcat server and deploy the WAR file in Tomcat.
4. Generate the SSL Certificates and configure with Tomcat.

5. Refer wiki for detailed installation steps: `http://wiki.alfresco.com/wiki/Alfresco_And_SOLR#Setting_up_the_Solr_web_app_from_the_distribution`.

6. Follow the upcoming configuration section to configure with Alfresco.

Configuring Solr in Alfresco

Alfresco and Solr use HTTP requests to search the content and update the index. Alfresco has done some customization on top of Solr to integrate with it. Solr downloads the entire content model deployed in Alfresco to index the content as per your custom model.

Solr has two cores:

- **Workspace**: Contains all the live content indexes and configuration files
- **Archive**: Contains all the archived content indexes and configuration files

The following diagram shows an high-level overview of how Alfresco and Solr work:

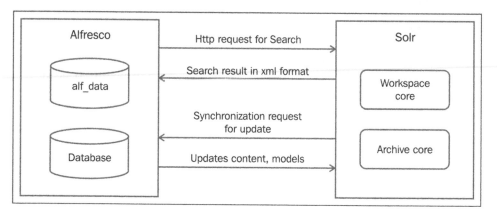

The `repository.properties` file in your `config` folder defines a number of properties to configure the Solr server with Alfresco. Make sure the following properties are configured in the `alfresco-global.properties` file.

- `index.subsystem.name=solr`: Used to specify use of the `solr` subsystem
- `dir.keystore=${dir.root}/keystore`: As Alfresco and Solr do a secure HTTPS call, all certificates are stored in this folder
- `solr.port.ssl=8443`: The SSL port of your Tomcat server

Now all the Solr cores (indexes and associated configuration file) are stored in the `<alfresco_installation>/alf_data/solr` folder. The following table shows the important files and folders for any core that you can configure to improve the search performance by setting appropriate values.

The folder hierarchy of Solr:

Name	Description
`Workspace`	All the indexes of the live content
`workspace-SpacesStore`	Configuration files for live content indexes
`Archive`	Indexes for archive contents
`archive-SpacesStore`	Configuration files for archive contents indexes
`workspace-SpacesStore/ alfrescoModels`	Stores all the models XML files of Alfresco. Each core has such a folder.

The following section lists the important files for each core.

- **The Solr property file** (`solrcore.properties`): This file contains important properties to configure the index location for a particular core and Alfresco tracking time to update indexes. The following are the important properties; you can configure this as per your needs:
  - `data.dir.root=D:/alfresco_setup/Book/tomcat/alf_data/ solr`: The Solr root directory
  - `data.dir.store=workspace/SpacesStore`: Specifies the index path for Alfresco core. Above two properties are used for index location
  - `alfresco.host=localhost`: The Alfresco server details
  - `alfresco.port=8080`: The Alfresco port number
  - `alfresco.port.ssl=8443`: The SSL port
  - `alfresco.cron=0/15 * * * ? *`: The cron expression by when the solr server should track alfresco to create/update indexes
  - `alfresco.stores=workspace://SpacesStore`: Specifies the store of Alfresco that will be indexed in this core

- **The Solr config file** (`solrconfig.xml`): This file contains all the configuration of Solr. This file can be configured to fine-tune the Solr search.

The Solr admin console

Solr provides a very cool web-based GUI for administrating and monitoring the Solr server. With this admin console, you can do the following:

- View detailed statistics of the Solr indexes
- Enable / disable different loggers, which can help in tracing any issues
- View the Solr configuration parameters for any core
- View all of the XML schema files that are used for indexes in Solr
- Test behaviors of different analyzers for any fields
- Web-based query interface to search any content
- Can take the thread dump of the Solr server from the admin console

After installation of Solr, you can access the Solr admin console using the `https://localhost:8443/solr` URL.

You need to import the `browser.p12` browser certificate located at `alf_data/keystore`. You can see a list of cores. Click **Admin alfresco** to access the workspace core, as shown in the following screenshot:

Some important direct URLs:

- **Summary Report**: `http://localhost:8080/solr/admin/cores?action=SUMMARY&wt=xml`

- **Detail Report**: `http://localhost:8080/solr/admin/cores?action=REPORT&wt=xml`

- **Transaction Specific Reports**: `http://localhost:8080/solr/admin/cores?action=TXREPORT&core=alfresco&wt=xml&txid=<TXID>`

- **Node Specific Report**: `http://localhost:8080/solr/admin/cores?action=NODEREPORT&wt=xml&nodeid=<Node DB ID>`

Rebuilding Solr indexes

As part of regular maintenance of the server, it is good practice to rebuild the indexes in specified time intervals. Rebuilding of indexes would remove any stale indexes and merge the indexes, which in turn improves search performance. Follow these steps to rebuild the Solr index:

1. Stop the Tomcat server in which Solr is deployed.
2. Take backup of indexes of the workspace core located at `<SOLR_HOME>workspace/SpacesStore`.
3. Delete indexes of the workspace core in `<SOLR_HOME>workspace/SpacesStore`.
4. Take backup of indexes of the archive core located at `<SOLR_HOME>archive/SpacesStore`.
5. Delete index of the archive core in `<SOLR_HOME>archive/SpacesStore`.
6. Delete all the models inside the `<SOLR_HOME>workspace-SpacesStore/alfrescoModels` folder.
7. Delete all the models inside the `<SOLR_HOME>archive-SpacesStore/alfrescoModels` folder.
8. Restart the Tomcat server in which Solr is deployed.

Solr also supports for re-indexing of any specific node, transaction, or acl. This is useful in cases where some index got corrupt. The following URL can be used for that:

```
http://localhost:8080/solr/admin/cores?action=REINDEX&txid=<TXID>&acl
txid=<ACL TXN ID>&nodeid=<Node DB ID>&aclid=<ACL ID>
```

Let's suppose you have a node with `node db-id` set as `3456`. If you want to re-index that node, you need to hit the following URL:

```
http://localhost:8080/solr/admin/cores?action=REINDEX&nodeid=3456
```

Integration of Solr with Alfresco has really enhanced the search in Alfresco. Biggest advantage of Solr is scalability, which allows maintaining a huge amount of indexes. Now, along with document management, we can also leverage other advantages of Solr.

Summary

In this chapter, we covered the full-text search capabilities of Alfresco using an open source based, highly scalable, and a fast search engine called Lucene. You also learned about how the content as well as content properties are indexed in search engine automatically. We also covered the usage of the **Advance Search** form to create complex search criteria to search content and save the searches as a re-usable report. We also learned about the extending the advance search form to include custom content types and properties, and also learned how to configure and use an external search engine, such as Solr, provided by Alfresco.

In next chapter, you will learn about the various imaging and form processing implementation in Alfresco. The next chapter will also provide you more detail about the various scanning and OCR technologies integration with Alfresco.

13
Implementing Imaging and Forms Processing

Alfresco is integrated with scanning and **Optical Character Recognition (OCR)** technologies. This chapter helps you to implement an end-to-end solution by collecting the paper documents and forms, transforming them into accurate, retrievable information, and delivering them into an organization's business applications. The information is full-text searchable, and goes through the various approval workflows, based on the organization's defined business process management.

By the end of this chapter, you will have learned how to:

- Connect a scanner to a network drive and map it to a space within Alfresco
- Specify a business rule to automatically extract metadata from the scanned document
- Bulk upload scanned documents into the Alfresco repository
- Integrate Alfresco with Ephesoft

Introduction

You can extend the value of your ECM investment by implementing imaging and automated forms processing solutions, as per your organizational requirements. Increasingly, electronic document images are starting to have the same legal status as a paper document.

Alfresco integrates with various image-capturing systems to provide flexible and intelligent form processing. This results in greater control and management of crucial information and documents, within and outside the firewall. These joint solutions enable you to include forms and the captured data as content types that can be version controlled, repurposed, and integrated into workflows, and managed by the ECM environment. This simplifies compliance with enhanced archiving and audit capabilities. You can also reduce the cost of printing, storing, and distributing paper forms.

You can implement various solutions by leveraging the Alfresco's content management and business process management features. Some are listed as follows, for your reference:

- Order fulfillment
- Claims processing
- Underwriting
- Loan origination
- Contracts management
- Accounts payable, managing checks and invoices

Electronic imaging and the paperless office

Managing paper documents is not easy. Distribution of paper documents is manual, and is a slow process. The high cost of filing and retrieving them makes them expensive to manage. The electronic imaging technology offers an effective solution to these problems. The concept of the **paperless office** is picking up to scan and digitize the business documents, and to process the images instead of the paper itself.

Electronic imaging gives us the following benefits:

- It reduces shortage space.
- The documents are stored as magnetic or optical images. This eliminates the possibility of their deterioration due to age, adverse temperatures, or weather conditions.
- It facilitates instant retrieval of the documents.
- It provides a document's security by providing view, edit, and delete access to the concerned people.
- It provides simultaneous access to documents for multiple users.
- It provides usage and tracking of documents.

- It provides a centralized database for documents belonging to various departments.
- It helps speed up business decisions that require an approval process.
- It provides file integrity—as the use of read-only files prevent document images from being altered.

In early years of imaging, the absence of a workflow was the main barrier to customer acceptance. The development of robust workflow systems has driven widespread adoption of electronic imaging by allowing web-based approval processes.

Forms processing

Automated forms processing is used to capture data on forms that are filled manually using handwriting, machine print, and checkboxes. These forms are then returned to a centralized location for batch processing. Imaged hand or machine print is of little value until it is converted into computer-usable (ASCII) data.

Forms automation is **Intelligent Character Recognition** (ICR) intensive, and involves a process to convert a bitmapped image data into ASCII data. Since, over 80 percent of all of the business documents are forms, manual data entry forms conversion constitutes an enormous expense, which can be significantly reduced through the use of recognition-based automated forms processing.

The following is a typical process to convert and manage forms in a content management system:

- **Scanning**: Pages of forms are scanned and converted into bitmapped (usually TIFF) images of forms, which are either compressed or stored for later batch processing, or are passed immediately in an uncompressed format to an ICR engine for recognition.
- **Image enhancement**: The document image is cleaned up and character images are enhanced, using image enhancement techniques.
- **Information extraction**: An information extraction template identifies which individual fields on the form image require recognition, and what is the nature of those fields. They can be barcodes, signatures, hand prints, machine prints, numeric, alphabetic, or alphanumeric.
- **Electronic content**: An image with the converted ASCII data is then moved to a content management system as a content item. The information extracted from the form is stored as the properties of the content item.
- **Workflow**: The content goes through various workflow approval processes and is finally stored for future access.

Alfresco for imaging and forms processing

Alfresco already has imaging solutions with Ephesoft and Kofax. You can also use the network drive features of Alfresco to automatically upload all of the scanned documents to the repository without having a tight integration between your scanner and the Alfresco repository.

The following figure shows a sample architecture diagram that Alfresco for imaging and forms processing. A remote office can be connected to your central Alfresco repository to bulk upload the scanned documents. The documents could be forms, checks, invoices, engineering diagrams, legal contracts, or any other kind of paper document.

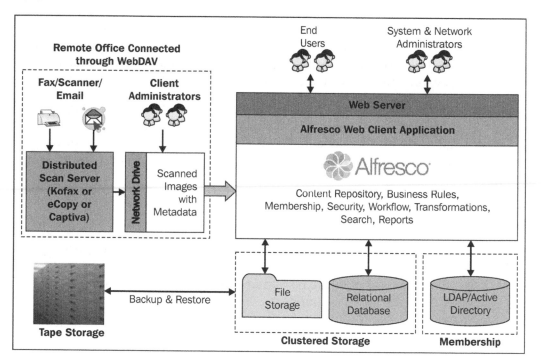

Once a document is uploaded to a space, business rules could be triggered by moving the document through a workflow process. The documents and the search indexes can be stored in a high-end file storage and the metadata can be stored in a relational database, such as Oracle or MySQL. The storage can be clustered for high performance and heavy loads. You can even consider having single sign-on with an existing **Active Directory** or **LDAP** membership system.

Alfresco is highly scalable in terms of storage and performance. Alfresco is being used by a large French bank for loading all faxes of client trades into the repository. On a low-powered machine, they were getting around 350 TIFF images loaded per minute (21,000 documents per hour), and the scalability tests showed that this could be scaled up pretty easily, with more horsepower.

Example of an imaging solution with workflow

Let's consider a sample imaging use case scenario. Let's say that you have remote client offices, which scan all of the checks, OCR them, extracts metadata, and sends them over to you for approval, payment, and storage.

The sample solution provided in this section uses all of the features you have learned so far, including business rules, transformations, security, and workflow. The solution is useful for scanning a paper document (such as a check or a claim form), OCR it, extracting important data, transforming the document to a required format (such as in a GIF format), and delivering it to your business application and database.

Refer the architecture diagram that was shown in the previous figure. A remote office can be connected to your central Alfresco repository to bulk upload scanned documents. Once a document is uploaded to a space, business rules will be triggered thereby transforming the document to a required format and moving it through a workflow process.

You are going to perform the following steps in a demo application:

1. Set up a space and security for your remote office. You can create a separate space for each remote office to get the scanned documents.

2. A remote office connects the scanner to a network folder, and maps it to an Alfresco's space via WebDAV (HTTP protocol).

3. The scanned documents (checks, claims, and forms) will enter the Alfresco repository in TIFF format.

4. The Alfresco business rule extracts metadata, and attaches it to the scanned image.

5. These documents will be automatically transformed from the TIFF format to a GIF format, and sent to the **Review** space. When a document gets into the **Review** space, the workflow kicks off.

6. The reviewer can visit this space, and review the document. He/she can approve or reject the document.

7. The approved document will then be moved to the **Approved** space and then to the **Cut Check** space.

8. The rejected checks will be stored in the **Rejected** space and an e-mail notification will be sent to the concerned people.

Setting up space and security

Log in to the Alfresco web client, and go to the **Company Home | Intranet | Finance Department** space, and create a new space called **Office Accounts** for the imaging solution demo application.

Under the **Office Accounts** space, create the following sub-spaces:

- **01_Inbox**
- **02_Under Review**
- **03_Approved**
- **04_Rejected**
- **05_Cut Checks**
- **Offices**

Under **Offices**, create two office sub-spaces called **OFFICE1** and **OFFICE2**:

- **Offices**
  - ◦ **OFFICE1**
  - ◦ **OFFICE2**

Set up the security for each office accordingly so that only the office personnel have write access to that space. Go to the **Company Home | Intranet | Finance Department | Office Accounts | Offices | OFFICE1** space, and set the security. For example, you can add a user (say user1 from your remote **OFFICE1**) and give the user the **Contributor** role so that he/she can add documents to the **OFFICE1** space. To ensure security, make sure nobody else has a write access to this space, except some of the employees of **OFFICE1**. For more information about securing spaces, refer to *Chapter 4, Implementing Membership and Security*.

Similarly, you can set security for the **OFFICE2** space.

Business rule to extract important metadata

Define a single business rule that does the following three actions on all the incoming documents in the **Offices** space and all of its the sub-spaces:

1. Add the **Customer Details** aspect.
2. Execute a script to extract important metadata, and fill the document properties.
3. Move the document to the **01_Inbox** space.

Refer to *Chapter 7, Extending Alfresco Content Model*, where you have added a custom aspect called **Customer Details** to add customer-specific properties to the documents. The properties include CustomerName, CustomerContactName, CustomerContactPhone, CustomerProjectID, and NewCustomer.

You can create your own script in the JavaScript language to automatically fill the document properties on all of the incoming scanned documents. As an example, create a file called chapter13_fill_metadata.js in your personal computer with the following code. The following JavaScript fills three properties. The CustomerName property is filled with the name of the office space, and the other two properties, CustomerContactName and CustomeContactPhone, are filled with some fixed values, as shown here:

```
if (document.hasPermission("Write"))
{
    if (document.mimetype == "image/tiff")
      {
        var l_currentSpace = document.parent;
        document.properties["custom:CustomerName"]
                                        = l_currentSpace.name;
        document.properties["custom:CustomerContactName"]
                                               = "Office Admin";
        document.properties["custom:CustomerContactPhone"]
                                             = "111-222-3333";
        document.save();
      }
}
```

Go to the **Company Home | Data Dictionary | Scripts** space, and click on the **Add Content** button and upload the chapter13_fill_metadata.js file. Now, you have your own custom script that can be used in the business rules.

Go to the **Company Home | Intranet | Finance Department | Office Accounts | Offices** space and create a new business rule.

In **Step One-Select Condition** drop-down list, select items with the specified mime type, and click on the **Set Values and Add** button. In the **Set condition values** pop-up window, select the **TIFF Image** value as the **Type** and click on the **OK** button, and then on the **Next** button.

In the **Step Two – Actions** pane, create the following three actions:

- Add the **Customer Details** aspect
- Execute script chapter13_fill_metadata.js
- Move to **O1_Inbox**

In the **Step Three – Enter Details** pane of the **Create Rule Wizard**, provide an appropriate **Title** and **Description**, and select the checkbox that says **Apply rule to sub spaces**.

Now, when a document gets into the **OFFICE1** space, additional properties will be added to the document (due to the **Customer Details** aspect), and some properties of the document will be prefilled with data (due to the chapter13_fill_metadata.js script file), and finally the document will be moved to the **01_Inbox** space for further workflow and approval.

Connecting the scanner to the network folder

The scanner in your remote office can be connected to a local network folder (refer the first figure in this chapter). The network folder can be mapped to the Alfresco repository as a space via WebDAV or CIFS. More information about mapping a drive to Alfresco using CIFS or WebDAV is provided in the *Chapter 5, Implementing Document Management*.

You can map the network folder in your remote **Office1** to a secure space in Alfresco (**Intranet | Finance Department | Office Accounts | Offices | OFFICE1**).

To map the **OFFICE1** space in Alfresco in the local Windows Explorer as a network drive, follow these steps:

1. In Windows Explorer, click on the **Tools | Map Network Drive** option. The **Map Network Drive** dialog appears.

2. Select an unused drive letter (say, O for the **OFFICE1** space).

3. In the folder textbox, type `\\<AlfrescoServer>_a\Alfresco\Intranet\ Finance Department\Office Accounts\Offices\OFFICE1`. Replace `<AlfrescoServer>` with the actual server name.

4. Check on the **Reconnect at logon** checkbox.

5. Click on the **Finish** button. As the space is secured, the system will prompt for your authentication. Only users defined on the **OFFICE1** space will be able to connect to the **OFFICE1** space.

6. Type your Alfresco username and password when prompted.

Uploading scanned documents into the repository in bulk

To test the network folder setup, drag-and-drop a few TIFF files from your personal computer to the O drive, which is mapped to the **OFFICE1** space. In a production environment, the scanner will be connected to the O drive to upload the scanned images.

You will notice that as soon as the scanned documents (TIFF files) get into the **OFFICE1** space, additional properties are added to the documents, and the documents are moved to the **01_Inbox** space.

You will also notice that the original documents (TIFF format) are in the **01_Inbox** space and the transformed copies of the documents (in GIF format) are in the **02_Under Review** space for further workflow approval process.

If you examine the transformed documents in the **02_Under Review** space, you will notice a set of properties added and prefilled due to the business rules already applied on the document. The following screenshot is the **Details View** of one of the documents in the **02_Under Review** space:

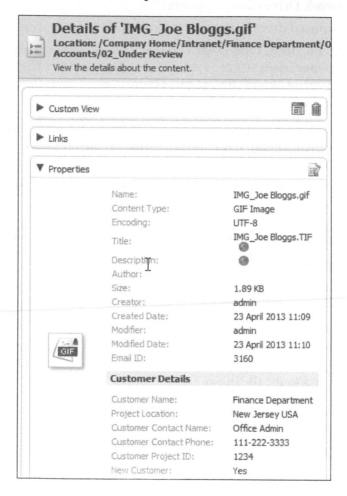

You can examine the documents in the **02_Under Review** space and either approve them or reject them. You can write a presentation template to have a custom view of all the documents in the **02_Under Review** space, as shown in the next screenshot. More information about custom views is presented in *Chapter 11, Customizing the User Interface.*

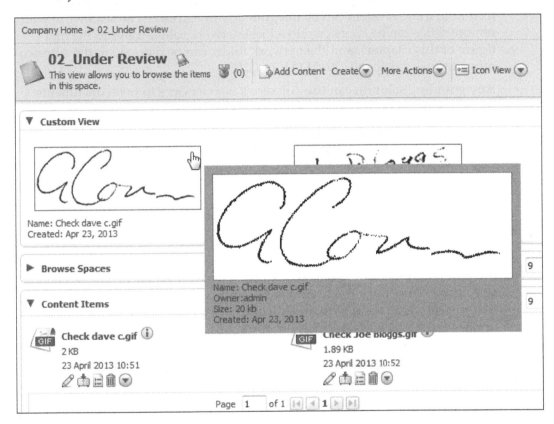

When you approve a document in the **02_Under Review** space, the document moves to the **03_Approved** space, and an e-mail notification is sent to the concerned people. When you reject a document in the **02_Under Review** space, the document moves to the **04_Rejected** space, and an e-mail notification is sent to the concerned people. Test the workflow by moving documents through various workflow spaces. Now that you have got an idea about implementing a solution, create a custom solution to solve your business problem, and test it.

Scanning solutions with Alfresco

There are many scanning solutions that you can integrate with Alfresco. Here, we will discuss with various such options:

- Any standard scanner that scans and saves the document in PDF/TIFF format to the filesystem can be integrated with Alfresco. The scanner in your remote office can be connected to a local network folder (refer to the first figure of this chapter), and the network folder can be mapped to the Alfresco repository as a space via WebDAV or CIFS.

- Any scanning solution can use Alfrseco's web services to push documents into the repository. It is a very easy integration.

- Alfresco supports integration with Kofax. Kofax is the world's leading provider of information capturing solutions. Their product, **Kofax Ascent Capture**, is integrated with Alfresco, offering customers access to a comprehensive production capture solution. This product includes automatic document classification, data extraction, and validation for both Internet-based distributed capture and centralized environments.

  Refer `http://docs.alfresco.com/4.1/topic/com.alfresco.enterprise.doc/concepts/kofax-intro.html` for more information.

- Integrating with eCopy-enabled scanners. eCopy provides products, enabling anyone in an organization to transform paper documents into information that is easily integrated with all of their existing business workflows and applications. **SIRA Systems Corporation** (`http://www.sirasystems.com`) created a connector to integrate Alfresco into the eCopy suite, which allows users to scan an image via eCopy and place it directly into Alfresco.

- Alfresco also supports integration with Ephesoft, which is open source scanning solution.

In the following section, we will discuss more about how Ephesoft can be integrated with Alfresco.

Integrating with Ephesoft

Ephesoft is an open source document capturing solution. It provides automatic classification, extraction of data, and sorting scanned documents. Most important, it is web-based which makes it easy to use. It also supports the OCR/ICR engine. Ephesoft provides a complete imaging solution. Ephesoft support CMIS, using which documents can be stored in any ECM.

Let's consider our example. You have remote client offices that scan the customer details documents, OCR them, extracts metadata, and sends them over to you for approval and storage. For this, we will need integration of Ephesoft and Alfresco. Ephesoft will take care of capturing of document and extraction of metadata. Alfresco will store the document.

You are going to perform the following steps for a demo application:

1. Install Ephesoft.
2. Create a custom type in Alfresco.
3. Create a custom document type in Ephesoft.
4. Configure the CMIS plugin in Ephesoft.
5. Process batch in Ephesoft and store documents in Alfresco.

Installing Ephesoft

Ephesoft provides an installer file, which can be downloaded and installed from `http://www.ephesoft.com/products/on-premise`.

Creating a custom type in Alfresco

Next, we need to create a custom type named `customer:document` in Alfresco. From Ephesoft, when a document is uploaded in Alfresco, this type will be applied and all the metadata would be captured. Create the custom type, as shown in following code snippet. More information on content model is provided in *Chapter 7, Extending Alfresco Content Model*:

```
<type name="customer:document">
        <title>Customer Document</title>
        <parent>cm:content</parent>
        <properties>
           <property name="customer:customername">
              <title>Customer Name</title>
              <type>d:text</type>
           </property>
           <property name="customer:projectlocation">
              <title>Customer Project Location</title>
              <type>d:text</type>
           </property>
           <property name="customer:customercontactname">
              <title>Customer Contact Name</title>
```

```
            <type>d:text</type>
        </property>
        <property name="customer:customerprojectid">
            <title>Customer Project Id</title>
            <type>d:text</type>
        </property>
    </properties>
</type>
```

Creating a custom document type in Ephesoft

Ephesoft comes with some default document types. Whenever we process any document in Ephesoft, the document type is specified, which helps you to classify the documents and extract and store the metadata information. You need to create a custom type name CustomerDocument with the same properties as we created in Alfresco. Refer to the following link to create a custom document type in Ephesoft:

```
http://www.ephesoft.com/wiki/index.php?title=Tutorial#Adding_A_New_
Document_Type
```

Once you have created the Customer document type, you need to map it with an Alfresco type. For that, add the following mapping in the DLF-Attribute-mapping. properties file at <Ephesoft_Home>/SharedFolders/BC2/cmis-plugin-mapping:

- CustomerDetails=D:customer:document <First map the custom types>

- CustomerDetails.customername=customer:customername <Now map the properties>

- CustomerDetails.projectlocation=customer:projectlocation

- CustomerDetails.customercontactname=customer:customercontactna me

- CustomerDetails.customerprojectid=customer:customerprojectid

Configuring the CMIS plugin in Ephesoft

After completely processing the document in Ephesoft, it should be uploaded in Alfresco. For this, you need to configure the CMIS plugin in Ephesoft, which will specify the repository in which the document should be stored.

You need to follow these steps to configure the CMIS plugin:

1. First, you need to get the repository ID of Alfresco. Hit the following URL to get the **repositoryId** of Alfresco. This ID is required while configuring CMIS plugin in Ephesoft:

   - ° `http://localhost:8080/alfresco/cmisbrowse?url=http://localhost:8080/alfresco/service/cmis`

2. Next, log in to Ephesoft Admin Console using the following URL. The default username is `ephesoft` and password is `demo`.

   - ° `http://localhost:8080/dcma/BatchClassManagement.html`

3. Select the batch class with ID **BC2** and name as **TesseractMailRoom** and click on **Edit**, as shown in the following screenshot:

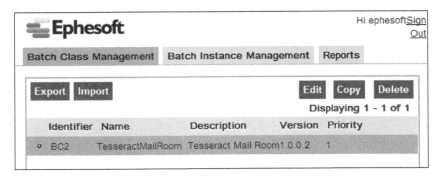

4. Select the **Export** module and click on **Edit**. Then select **CMIS_EXPORT** and click on **Edit**. Now configure the CMIS plugin, as shown in the following screenshot:

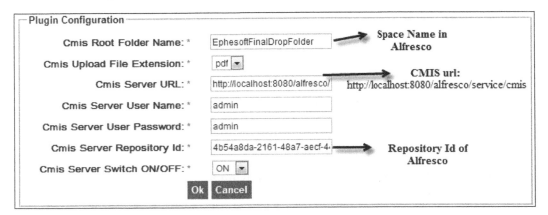

Processing batch in Ephesoft and store in Alfresco

Once all the configurations are done, you are ready to process any batch in Ephesoft. To begin this, get any sample document.

Now follow these steps to process it:

1. Log in to **BatchList** (`http://localhost:8080/dcma/BatchList.html`) using the same Ephesoft credentials.

2. Navigate to the **Upload Batch** tab and upload your scanned document. Select the default **TesseractMailRoom** batch and click on **Start Batch**, as shown in the following screenshot:

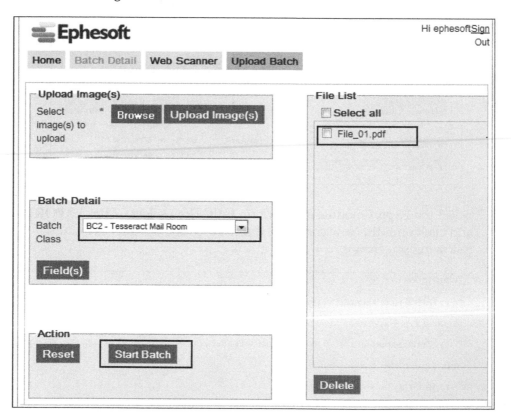

3. You can view the status of your batch using `http://localhost:8080/dcma/BatchInstanceManagement.html`.

4. The next step will be to review and validate the document. After some time, your document would appear for review, as shown in the following screenshot:

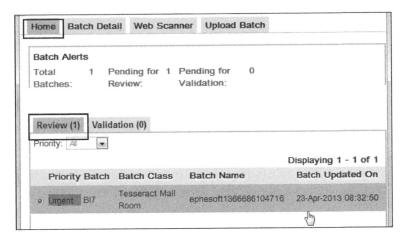

5. Click on the link to open the document for review. Once reviewed, press *Ctrl + q* to move the document to next stage of validation. After sometime, the document will appear in the **Validation** list.

6. Now navigate to **Validation** list and open the document to validate. Associate the document type and related metadata with the document, as shown in the following screenshot. Once validated, press *Ctrl + q* to complete the process.

7. The document would now be uploaded in Alfresco. Navigate to Alfresco and verify the document. A PDF file should be created along with the information entered from Ephesoft.

For more information on Ephesoft, you can refer to `http://www.ephesoft.com/wiki/`.

Summary

Alfresco integrates with various image-capturing systems. This adds to the flexibility, and provides intelligent forms processing that result in greater control and management of crucial information and documents, within and outside the firewall.

You can implement an OCR solution within Alfresco using the transformations framework. The Ephesoft integration also allows documents to be captured and stored in Alfresco, enabling customers to review and approve documents for long-term archival or records management purposes.

The next chapter will cover in detail about administrating and maintaining the Alfresco system. The chapter will also provide you with all the details on export import process in Alfresco, JMX, an the backup process. You would also learn about upgrading Alfresco.

14
Administering and Maintaining the System

Maintaining and upgrading the system is equally important as implementing it. A well-maintained system will give the highest return on investments. This chapter provides a high-level overview of administering and maintaining your Alfresco implementation. It includes information about backing up your valuable content, upgrading your system to newer versions, managing sub-systems using JConsole/JMX, and understanding utilities of the bulk import tool. You will also find general maintenance tips, such as maintaining logfiles, and periodically updating your admin password.

By the end of this chapter, you will have learned how to:

- Export and import your personal or departmental information
- Back up your data on a regular basis for storage and retrieval
- Perform general maintenance tasks, such as examining logfiles
- Set up replication for high availability
- Upgrade your Alfresco application to newer versions
- Managing sub-systems using JConsole

Exporting and importing content

Export and import functions are useful to bulk extract and load the personal, departmental, or team information from one location to another location, within the repository or to some other repository. In some situations, you can use this to integrate with third-party systems. For example, you can send the exported contents from the Alfresco repository to another content management system, or an internal system. Similarly, you can package the external content and import into it the Alfresco repository.

Alfresco Content Package (ACP)

The Alfresco Explorer has web-based utilities for exporting and importing content using an **Alfresco Content Package** (**ACP**). An Alfresco content package (otherwise known as an ACP file) is a single file (with an extension of `.acp`) that bundles together the metadata, content files, business rules, and the security settings on content.

The process for export and import is simple. Export produces one or more ACP files that hold the exported information. As with all of the files, you can place them somewhere secure, or transfer them using transports such as e-mail, FTP, and so on. Security settings only allow the export of those items that are readable by the user performing the export.

The import of an ACP file is the reverse of an export. The information held in the ACP file is placed into the repository location chosen at the import time. By default, the import process creates a copy of the ACP-held information.

An ACP file is simply a ZIP archive whose structure is as follows:

```
/<packagename>.xml
/<packagename>/
    contentNNN.pdf
    contentNNN.txt
    ...
```

The `packagename` is assigned on export. The XML conforms to the export and import view schema, which describes the transported nodes in terms of their types, aspects, properties, associations, and permissions. Content properties are handled specifically where the binary content of the property is held in a separate file under the `packagename` folder of the ZIP archive, and the XML contains a reference to the file.

While the repository provides several different ways to create an ACP file (export), it is also possible to create one manually. This is very useful for system-to-system integration.

Exporting and importing space content

Any Alfresco user may perform an export and import of folders and files that they have access to. You can choose any space (personal or departmental) to export.

The scope of information to export is configurable, but typically involves specifying the location within the repository to export. For example, if you choose to export content in one specific space (say **Company Home | Intranet | Finance Department**), then the exported data includes:

- The current space and all of the sub-spaces
- All documents (files, images, HTML/XML content, custom content, all versions) within the space and sub-spaces
- Complete meta data (aspects, audit, versions) associated with the documents
- Business rules set on spaces
- Invited users to a space or content

Export of a department space using Alfresco Explorer

The process to export a space within the Alfresco Explorer is as follows:

1. Select a specific space to export (say, **Sales Department** in your sample Intranet application)

2. Select the **More Actions | View Details** link to view the **Details** page of the space.

3. Select the **Export** action to launch the **Export** dialog, as shown in the following screenshot:

4. Fill in the export options, as follows:
    ○ **Package Name**: The name of the resulting export ACP file
    ○ **Destination**: The location within the repository to place the ACP file
    ○ **Include Children**: If selected, it will also export subfolders
    ○ **Include this Space**: If selected, exports the selected folder, otherwise only exports the children
    ○ **Run export in background**: If selected, the export will take place in the background, eventually creating the export ACP file

5. Select the **OK** button.

On success, the destination location will contain the ACP file. At this point, the ACP file can be saved to a local filesystem for safe backup or for transfer via e-mail.

Importing a department space using Alfresco Explorer

The process for importing an ACP file within the Alfresco Explorer is as follows:

1. Select a space to import the information into.

2. Select the **More Actions | View Details** link to view the **Details** page of the space.

3. Select the **Import** action to launch the **Import** dialog, as shown in the following screenshot:

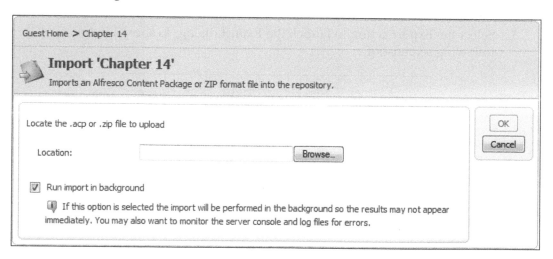

4. Fill in the import options, as follows:

   ° **Location**: Select an ACP file to import from the filesystem
   ° **Run in background**: If selected, the import will take place in the background, eventually creating all the folders and files held in the ACP file

5. Select **OK**.

On success, the information exported is held in the ACP file, and it will now reside in the destination space.

Using business rules to import data

Using Alfresco rules and actions, it is possible to set up an automated import, whereby an ACP file is automatically imported into the repository when placed into a designated space.

For example, the following rule (shown in the next screenshot) is defined against an **Import Drop Zone** space, where, if the incoming file name property matches *.acp, then it imports that ACP file's contents into the **Imported Content** space.

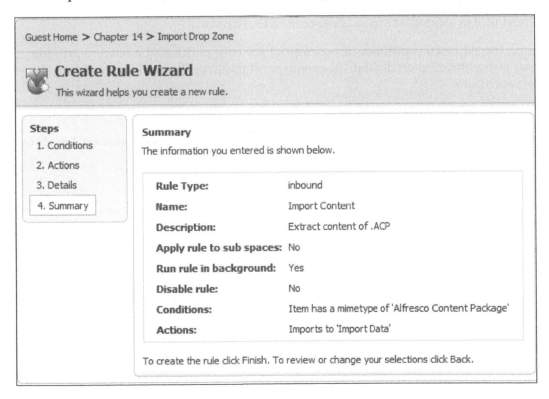

When an ACP file is placed into the **Import Drop Zone** space, it automatically kicks off the import process and places the items held in the ACP file into the **Imported Content** space.

An important point to remember is that the import will be initiated regardless of how the ACP file was placed into the folder. For example, the import will initiate if the ACP file was placed there via CIFS, FTP, WebDAV, Alfresco Explorer, or API. This is particularly powerful for system-to-system data integration.

Using command-line tools

The Alfresco export and import tools are developed directly against the Alfresco repository foundation APIs. This means that they execute standalone with an embedded repository. To perform an export and import via these tools requires configuration of the repository to ensure the appropriate storage locations (for example, database and filesystem folder) are used.

The export tool

The export tool is useful when you want to extract certain data from the Alfresco repository without using the Alfresco Explorer application. The Java class file for the export tool is located at `org.alfresco.tools.Export`.

Since, the Alfresco repository imposes strict security policies, you need to provide your authentication credentials (username and password), no matter how you access the repository.

The usage of the tool is as follows:

```
Usage: export -user <username> -pwd <password> -s[tore] <store> [options]
<packagename>
```

Where,

- `<username>` is your login user ID
- `<password>` is your password
- `<store>` is the store to extract from, which is in the form of `scheme://store_name`
- `<packagename>` is the filename to export to (with or without extension)

Other important [options] include:

- -path: The path within the store to extract from (default is "/", which is the root folder)
- -nochildren: Does not extract children
- -overwrite: Forces overwrite of existing export package if it already exists
- -quiet: Does not display any messages during export
- -verbose: Reports the export progress

For example, to export the **Intranet** space from the repository, you would use the following command:

```
export -user admin -pwd admin -s workspace://SpacesStore -path /
companyhome -verbose Intranet.acp
```

The import tool

The import tool is useful when you want to upload certain data into the Alfresco repository without using the Alfresco Explorer application. The Java class file for the import tool is located at org.alfresco.tools.Import.

The usage of the tool is as follows:

```
Usage: import -user <username> -pwd <password> -s[tore] <store> [options]
<packagename>
```

The [options] are as follows:

- -path: The path within the store to import into (default is "/", which is the root folder)
- -verbose: Reports the export progress
- -uuidBinding: You can use any of the keyword from this as per your requirement. It will instruct import process to perform import operation accordingly: CREATE_NEW, REMOVE_EXISTING, REPLACE_EXISTING, UPDATE_EXISTING, THROW_ON_COLLISION (the default is CREATE_NEW)

For example, to import the **Intranet** space into the repository, you will use the following command:

```
import -user admin -pwd admin -s workspace://SpacesStore -path /
companyhome -verbose -uuidBinding REPLACE_EXISTING Intranet.acp
```

It is possible to import from an ACP file or just an XML file. Importing just XML is useful if you want to import nodes without associated binary content, for example, **People**.

The bulk import tool

The bulk import tool helps you in importing files from the Alfresco server's filesystem to the repository. You can use this tool to migrate your legacy system's content to the Alfresco repository. There are two types of import operation you can achieve with help of this tool:

- **Streaming import**: It streams the input files to the Alfresco repository. It allows you to replace already existing content and enable/disable business rules applied on folders while the content is being imported. This feature is available in the Alfresco community version as well.

- **In-place import**: It imports file to the Alfresco repository; it assumes that files are already available in content store and that it just need to copy them in the repository database. This feature is only available in the enterprise repository.

There are certain limitations of this tool, such as it does not support import to the AVM repository. Only one import job can be run at a time and only admin can run the import tool.

You can use this tool programmatically as well as through the user interface. Let's first see how to use this tool using the user interface:

1. Write the following URL to your browser's address bar to see the next screen for the import tool. It will ask for the admin user's credential.

   ° `http://localhost:8080/alfresco/service/bulkfsimport`

2. You can provide the folder's path from where you want to import the content and target path from where you want to copy content in Alfresco. There are few more options you can use in the import utility. If you don't want to run business rules during content import, you can select the checkbox. To replace already existing content in the repository, select the checkbox shown in the following screenshot:

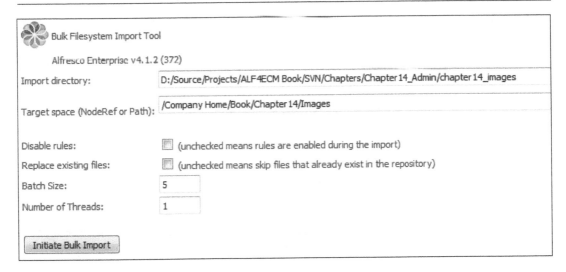

You can also use this tool through your code. Let's see how to use this tool programmatically.

You will need the `StreamingNodeImporterFactory` Spring bean to perform stream import and the `InPlaceNodeImporterFactory` bean for the in-place import operation.

 Since this import tool can be run only by the admin user, you need to authenticate it with the admin user before running this script.

Following is the code to run streaming import:

```
UserTransaction txn = transactionService.getUserTransaction();
    txn.begin();

    AuthenticationUtil.setRunAsUser("admin");

    StreamingNodeImporterFactory streamingNodeImporterFactory =
    (StreamingNodeImporterFactory)ctx.getBean("streamingNodeImporterFacto
ry");
    NodeImporter nodeImporter = streamingNodeImporterFactory.
getNodeImporter(new File("importdirectory"));
    BulkImportParameters bulkImportParameters = new
BulkImportParameters();
    bulkImportParameters.setTarget(folderNode);
    bulkImportParameters.setReplaceExisting(true);
    bulkImportParameters.setBatchSize(40);
```

```
    bulkImportParameters.setNumThreads(4);
    bulkImporter.bulkImport(bulkImportParameters, nodeImporter);


    txn.commit();
```

Here is the code snippet to run in-place import programmatically:

```
txn = transactionService.getUserTransaction();
    txn.begin();


    AuthenticationUtil.setRunAsUser("admin");


    InPlaceNodeImporterFactory inPlaceNodeImporterFactory =
(InPlaceNodeImporterFactory)ctx.getBean("inPlaceNodeImporterFactory");
    NodeImporter nodeImporter = inPlaceNodeImporterFactory.
getNodeImporter("default", "2011");
    BulkImportParameters bulkImportParameters = new
BulkImportParameters();
    bulkImportParameters.setTarget(folderNode);
    bulkImportParameters.setReplaceExisting(true);
    bulkImportParameters.setBatchSize(150);
    bulkImportParameters.setNumThreads(4);
    bulkImporter.bulkImport(bulkImportParameters, nodeImporter);


    txn.commit();
```

Data backup

This is one of the most important, yet also one of the most neglected, areas of computing. Backing up your data should be at the top of your computer maintenance list, right next to virus protection. Without data backups, you are running the risk of losing your data.

Data loss can happen in many ways. One of the most common causes is the physical failure of the media the data is stored on. In some situations, users of the system might have deleted the content due to some error. No matter what, your data is your intellectual property and you have to protect it by taking proper backups regularly.

List of items to back up

Alfresco stores content information in both the database and the filesystem. You need to back up both the filesystem and relational database. As a part of implementation, you might have customized Alfresco, and hence you also need to back up customization files. If you have used an external membership system, such as Active Directory or OpenLDAP, then you might have to back up the user and group data as well.

You can set up automated processes to back up data periodically. On Linux operating systems, you can write a cron job to run a backup script on a regular basis. Similarly, all other operating systems support backup utilities.

Most often, people tend to store the backup data on the same server. This might create issues when the server crashes. Hence, it is recommended to move the backup data on to some other external server to store.

Now, let us examine various types of data that need to be backed up.

The content stored in filesystem

Typically, the content in the filesystem is stored in your <install_folder>\alf_data folder, as shown in the next screenshot. The contentstore folder contains the binary content with all the versions. The lucene-indexes and backup-lucene-indexes folders contain search information. The audit.contentstore folder contains audit trail details.

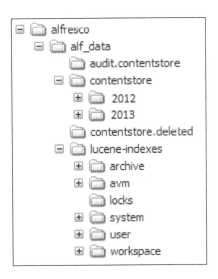

You need to back up the entire alf_data folder, as well all of its contents.

If you are Windows user, you may use the backup utility that comes with Windows XP (it is installed by default in XP Home). You will find it from the **Start** menu under **All Programs | Accessories | System Tools | Backup**. When you start it, you are presented with the backup wizard.

The metadata stored in the relational database

The relational database contains a bunch of tables defined as per the Alfresco schema. These tables hold information about users, security, audit, spaces, metadata, rules, scripts, and various business processes (jBPM).

Most database vendors (commercial or open source) provide utilities to take a database dump. Based on the database you have selected while installation (MySQL, Oracle, or MS SQL Server), you can use an appropriate utility to take a database dump.

MySQL database provides a utility called `mysqldump` to back up both the database table definitions and contents. It can be used to dump a database or a collection of databases for backup or for transferring the data to another SQL server (not necessarily a MySQL server). The dump contains SQL statements to create the table or populate it, or both.

The following is the command to take a database backup in MySQL:

```
Syntax: mysqldump [options] db_name [tables] [> output_file_name]
```

An example command is:

```
> mysqldump alfresco > alfresco_outfile.sql
```

Customization files

You might be customizing your Alfresco application over a period of time. Typically, you might have added or updated the following files:

- Logos, images and stylesheets
- JSP files (dashboard)
- Presentation templates

- Configuration files, property files
- Files in the extension folder
- Custom application code (WAR files, source Java files, and so on)

The process you follow to maintain and back up your customization files depends upon the development process you follow within your organization. It is useful to maintain your customization files in some configuration management system, such as CVS or SVN, which helps you to easily maintain and back them up.

Logfiles

The location of the logfiles depend upon the application server. For a Tomcat installation, the logfiles are located at <install_folder> itself. The Tomcat application server creates a logfile per day. The current logfile is named alfresco.log and at the end of the day, the logfile will be backed up as alfresco.log.YYYY-MM-DD (for example, alfresco.log.2013-03-08).

Based on the usage of the system, and based on the logging level, the size of these logfiles might be pretty big. Hence, it is a good practice to back up the older logfiles and remove them from the current location to save hard disk space.

Backup frequency

The frequency at which you take backups really depends upon the nature of the application, your high availability requirements, and the Alfresco deployment option you have chosen.

For example, you can consider only a single backup of customization files. You can back up the files whenever you enhance the application or upgrade the application to newer versions.

Since the content, metadata, and tasks change very frequently, the regular back up of the Alfresco filesystem and relational database is required. You have to consider the business risk and system resources availability while deciding on the backup frequency.

Backups based on the Alfresco deployment

If your application is highly accessed by thousands of users, then it is important for you to deploy Alfresco in a clustered environment. If it is a critical application, such as a finance, or insurance app, then you should consider deploying Alfresco in hot backup mode with a master-slave configuration. The data backup policy and process might be different based on the way you have deployed Alfresco.

A typical process to backup Alfresco repository is as follows:

1. Stop Alfresco to ensure that no one can make changes during the backup.
2. Export the MySQL (or other) database.
3. Back up the Alfresco `alf_data` folder.
4. Start Alfresco.

To restore the Alfresco repository:

1. Stop Alfresco.
2. Delete the `alf_data` folder and restore the `alf_data` folder that you backed up earlier.
3. Drop database, and then import the database that you have exported.
4. Start Alfresco.

Alfresco deployed as a repository application server

In this deployment (as shown in the following figure), the web application becomes the host for an embedded repository and remote access is via the application, that is, through HTTP. This is the default deployment option chosen by the Alfresco installer. This means the repository automatically benefits from any enhanced features provided by higher-end web application servers. For example, the repository can be embedded inside Apache Tomcat for the lightest weight deployment, but also embedded inside J2EE compliant-application servers from JBoss, Oracle, and IBM, to take advantage of distributed transactions, and so on.

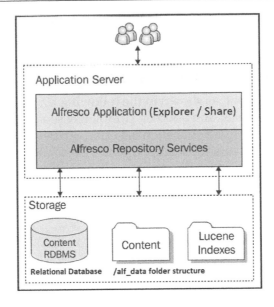

In this deployment option, you need to take the back up of the `alf_data` folder and the database. There will be one copy of customization files.

Alfresco deployed as Clustered Repository Server

A **Clustered Repository Server**, as shown in the following figure, supports large numbers of requests by employing multiple processes against a single repository store. Each embedded repository is hosted in its own Web Server and the collection as a whole (that is, the Cluster) acts as a single repository.

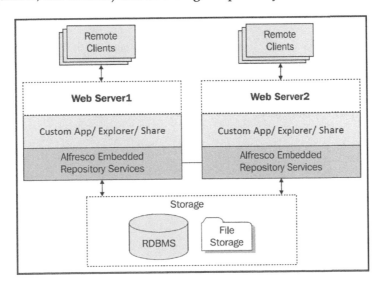

In this deployment option, you need to take the back up of the `alf_data` folder and the database. The customization files need to be provided per web server box.

Alfresco deployed as hot backup

In this method of deployment, as shown in the following figure, one repository server is designated the master and another, completely separate, repository server is designated the slave. The live application is hosted on the master and as it is used, synchronous and asynchronous replication updates are made to the slave, that is, the backup. The backup remains in read-only mode. If for some reason, the master breaks down, it is a relatively simple task to swap over to the slave to continue operation.

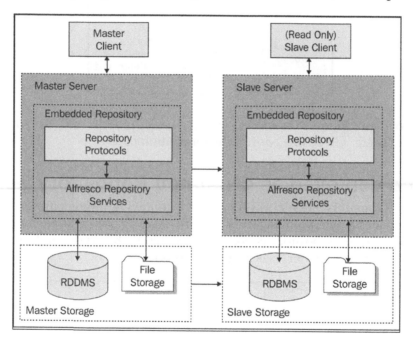

In this deployment option, you don't have to take regular backups as the data is getting backed up automatically.

Upgrading to newer versions of Alfresco

You can consider upgrading to new version of Alfresco if you are expecting one of the following benefits:

- Security patches
- Bug fixes
- New features
- Compatibility with other systems

Even if you are not getting these benefits, sometimes you might consider upgrading to a newer version as you do not want to maintain a big gap between the Alfresco version on which your application is currently running, and the latest Alfresco version. If this gap is too big, it might be very expensive for you to upgrade later on. This is the scenario with most of the enterprise software.

Alfresco has upgrade scripts that helps you to upgrade to newer versions automatically. However, it is essential to follow certain best practices while upgrading your system. Always try upgrading the test or staging server first before trying on production server. It is essential that you back up your existing data before attempting an upgrade. Follow the information and instructions given in the *Data backup* section.

Upgrading to a minor release

Alfresco minor (or dot) release, typically contains bug fixes and minor enhancements. There will not be any new features. An example is, upgrading from Alfresco 4.1 to 4.1.2 release.

Since there are no new features, typically, the database schema remains the same. In this situation, you can replace only the web application (WAR) file to upgrade.

The WAR file (`alfresco.war`) for a Tomcat installation is located at the `<install folder>\tomcat\webapps` folder.

Follow these steps for minor upgrades:

1. Download the latest `alfresco.war` file from the Alfresco website.
2. Stop Alfresco.

3. Back up all the data, including customization files (as explained in the earlier sections).

4. Delete the `<install_folder>\tomcat\webapps\alfresco` web application folder.

5. Replace the `alfresco.war` file in the `<install_folder>\tomcat\webapps` folder with the latest one.

6. Restore the customization files.

7. Start Alfresco.

Test your application after upgrading it to ensure that the upgrade is successful.

Upgrading to a major release

Alfresco major release typically contains new features, performance enhancements, and bug fixes. An example is upgrading from Alfresco 3.x to 4.0 releases.

Before planning a major release upgrade, you should always check its upgrade path from the Alfresco site. For Alfresco 3.0 to 4.0, you can find the upgrade path in at `http://docs.alfresco.com/4.0/index.jsp?topic=%2Fcom.alfresco.enterprise.doc%2Fconcepts%2Fupgrade-path.html`.

In order to upgrade Alfresco from version 3.0 to 4.0, you need to first upgrade Alfresco from version 3.0 to version 3.4, and then after from version 3.4 to version 4.0.

Once you finalize the migration path, you should also confirm software support stack for the target Alfresco version. In our case, it's Alfresco 4.0. In order to upgrade Alfresco 3.0 to 4.0, you need to update your MySQL version from 5.0 to 5.5.

You should also refer to the support stack information for other software you may like to use with Alfresco. Based on the demand of the target Alfresco version, you should change them as well.

The upgrade scripts will be executed automatically by the server when starting up against an existing database. Scripts that support the various Hibernate dialects can be found in the `<configRoot>/alfresco/dbscripts/upgrade/*` folders. This means that you don't have to do manual upgrades any more.

For example, let us assume that you are using the Tomcat bundle of Alfresco 3.0 (installed in the `C:\alfresco3.0` folder) on the Windows operating system, and you want to upgrade to a Alfresco 4.0 release.

Follow the steps for major upgrades:

1. Stop Alfresco in your current `C:\alfresco3.0` installation folder.

2. Back up all the data, including customization files (as explained in the earlier sections).

3. Download the complete Alfresco package and the Tomcat bundle for Windows operating system.

4. Perform a new installation in a different folder (say, `C:\alfresco3.4`).

5. Copy the older Alfresco file content folder to the newer installation (copy `C:\alfresco3.0\alf_data` folder to `C:\alfresco3.4\alf_data`)

6. Create a new database table and restore the relational database content from the older database. Update the Alfresco configuration file in a new installation to point to this new database (`alfresco-global.properties`).

7. Start Alfresco in a new installation. Verify that Alfresco is starting up properly without any error on the console.

8. Now, you have Alfresco 3.4 in working condition. You need to follow step 1 to 6 for upgrading Alfresco 3.4 to 4.0.

9. You need to install the license file for Alfresco 4.0 before you start it to verify installation. You can copy the license file in the `<classpathRoot >/alfresco/extension/license` folder.

10. Now, you can restore the customization files in new installation. Before you install it, you need to compile it against Alfresco 4.0 SDK.

11. Now, start Alfresco in a new installation and confirm it starts without any error in the logfile.

Although most of the upgrade happens automatically, you might have to perform some manual steps to restore your customization files in a new installation.

There are some configuration files and a properties file in Alfresco's config folder (`\tomcat\webapps\alfresco\WEB-INF\classes\alfresco\`), which you might have updated, that requires manual updates.

Test your application after upgrading it to ensure that the upgrade is successful.

General maintenance tips

If you maintain the system regularly, by cleaning up the database and by fixing the system errors, your system runs faster. Some tips for doing so are given in this section.

Regular maintenance of deleted items

When you delete an item (content or space) in Alfresco, the item will not be deleted from the server, it will be moved to a temporary store called **archive space store**. This gives you an opportunity to recover the content that you have deleted earlier.

Deleted items will be in the temporary store forever, consuming significant amount of storage space. It is best to purge them periodically. Purged items are deleted forever, and cannot be recovered. It is recommended to take regular backups of your data before purging.

Examining logfiles

Your logfiles inform you on very important issues and problems about your system. The level of details logged will be based on level of logging (INFO, ERROR, or DEBUG). Refer to *Chapter 3, Getting Started with Alfresco*, where you have set the level of logging to DEBUG.

The logfiles are named as alfresco.log (current one) or alfresco.log.YYYY-MM-DD (older ones). Examine one of the logfiles and you will notice that the log entries made in the following categories:

- ERROR: Error occurred (requires FIX)
- WARN: Warning messages (requires your attention)
- INFO: General information about the system

The sample messages are as follows:

```
14:20:42,088 WARN  [org.hibernate.cache.EhCacheProvider] Could not
find configuration [org.jbpm.graph.def.Node]; using defaults.
14:21:45,056 ERROR [org.alfresco.repo.action.ActionServiceImpl] An
error was encountered whilst executing the action 'import'.
org.alfresco.service.cmr.view.ImporterException: Failed to import
package at line 8; column 19 due to error: A complete repository
package cannot be imported here…
15:03:19,308 INFO  [org.alfresco.repo.admin.patch.PatchExecuter] No
patches were required. .
```

You have to fix the errors listed in the logfile, and make sure there are no ERROR messages in the logfiles. There are many utilities (based on the operating system) that examine the logfile for ERROR messages, and send you notifications as required. Consider using such tool or develop such tool to be notified as soon as an ERROR occurs.

Resetting the administrator password

The administrator has the highest powers in the Alfresco application. It is a good practice to periodically change the administrator password as a security process. You can change the password using the Alfresco Explorer's user profile option.

If, for some reason, you forgot the administrator password, you can reset the password as follows:

1. Configure the authentication component to accept all logins, using the `external.authentication.defaultAdministratorUserNames` property in the `<configRoot>\subsystems\Authentication\external\external-authentication.properties` file. You can set a comma-separated list of usernames in this property, which will be able to log in Alfresco as an admin user.

2. Log in as anyone who has admin rights.

3. Reset the password.

4. Revert the configuration.

Resetting the complete repository data

If you are setting up an environment to test your Alfresco application, you might want to remove or reset the data once the testing is done. There might be other circumstances, where you want to remove the existing users, spaces, rules from the repository, and start fresh. Before deleting or resetting the complete repository, you might want to back it up.

The following is the process to reset the complete repository data:

1. Stop Alfresco.
2. Remove the `alf_data` folder
3. Drop the Alfresco database and create an empty Alfresco database.
4. Start Alfresco.

When you start Alfresco, the `alf_data` folder will be created and the default database tables will be created automatically.

Migrating servers

The process of migrating an instance of Alfresco, running on one server to another server follows a similar pattern to the backup process, with additional steps for ensuring that any configuration is also copied over.

The Java Management Extension (JMX) interface

Much like other applications, you can configure Alfresco and restart it to make it effective. Alfresco offers the **Java Management Extension (JMX)** interface to access Alfresco through a standard JMX console that supports JMX Remoting (JSR-160). Using that, you can perform the following:

- Change log levels
- Set server read-only mode
- Manage Alfresco subsystems
- Enable or disable file servers (FTP/CIFS/NFS)
- Set server single-user mode
- Set server maximum user limit, including the ability to prevent further logins
- Count user sessions/tickets
- User session/ticket invalidation

You can use JConsole, MC4J, or JManage to perform the preceding activities. JConsole is supplied with Java SE 5.0 and higher versions.

Connect to Alfresco using the JMX client (JConsole):

1. Open the JMX client. In case of JConsole, it comes with JAVA SE. You can find its executable file from the `bin` folder of your Java installation directory.

2. Provide the Alfresco JMX service URL to the remote processor:
   - ° `service:jmx:rmi:///jndi/rmi://<hostname>:50500/alfresco/jmxrmi`

3. Provide default JMX username as `controlRole` and default JMX password as `change_asap`.

4. To change the default username, you can change the `<configRoot>/alfresco/alfresco-jmxrmi.access` file. For the password, make changes in the `<configRoot>/alfresco/alfresco-jmxrmi.password` file. A best practice is to copy these files to the `<classpathRoot >/alfresco/extension` folder and then make the change.

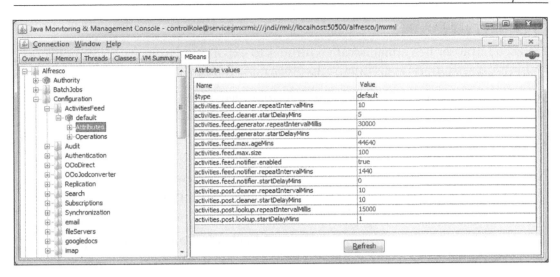

This is how you can manage Alfresco using JConsole:

1. Select the **MBeans** tab from the **JConsole** window. All Alfresco-managed beans would be displayed in JConsole.

2. Now, navigate to the **Alfresco | Configuration** option from the left-hand side tree panel. You will see Alfresco subsystems in an expandable tree structure. To check its settings, check **Attributes** and **Operations**, displayed below in tree.

3. You can select an attribute and set proper Alfresco subsystem values to it. Possible editable fields are displayed in blue text.

4. Once you change a configuration setting, the subsystem will automatically stop.

5. You can restart the Alfresco subsystem to make your change effective by clicking on the start button from operation. You can similarly stop a sub-system without making change to it.

6. To revert back previous edit values of a Alfresco subsystem, restore the default settings. Navigate to the subsystem, select the operation, and click on the **Revert** button.

Summary

Alfresco Explorer has administrative utilities to export data from Alfresco repository and import within the repository or to other repository.

You must back up data at regular intervals to protect your data from hardware failures. Consider the hot backup-deployment option of Alfresco for high availability. If you need a high-performance repository, you must consider deploying Alfresco in a clustered environment.

The upgrade scripts in Alfresco help you to upgrade to newer versions automatically. It is recommended that you try an upgrade on a test or staging server before going into production server.

Alfresco sub-systems can be managed from JMX clients. You can start, stop, or revert sub-systems without restarting the Alfresco application server.

In this book, you read about Alfresco, right from its installation to administration functionalities. Now you know to how leverage various features of Alfresco for your organizational needs. Throughout these 14 chapters, you learned the usage of Alfresco, starting from document creation to maintenance, its integration aspects with different application, user interface customizations, usage of out-of-the-box workflow, developing custom workflows for various business processes, creating or extending content model in Alfresco, different ways to manage users, roles and permissions in Alfresco.

Index

Symbols

Session Timeout property 356
FileServers subsystem configuration
about 81
CIFS, configuring 81
File System Transfer Receiver
configuring 81, 82
File Transfer Protocol. *See* FTP
Flash Player
installing 45
installing, steps 45
folder structure
installing 46
Form key 267
forms processing
Alfresco, using 428
forum space
about 151
defining, for groups 153
departmental forums and security 152, 153
discussion forums, creating 151
topics, creating 152
topics, replying to 152
FreeMarker dashlet
Alfresco objects 387
custom template, developing 389, 391
custom template, for custom space view 393, 394
custom template, for XML content 391, 393
directives 388
FreeMarker template engine 386
presentation templates 385
template-node model API 388
FTP 30, 145, 146, 294

G

gateways 264
general maintenance tips
administrator password, resetting 463
complete repository data, resetting 463
deleted items 462
logfiles, examining 462
servers, migrating 463
Google Docs
enabled property 370
integrating 369, 370
password property 370

username property 370
groups
creating 349
deleting 351
editing 351
managing 349
memberships, managing 351
subgroups 350, 351
top-level group 349, 350

H

Have Fun Corporation
people groups 86
Header 57
Heart Beat Disabled property 359
Hello World example 298-300
high availability
about 84
clustering, setting up 84, 85
components, of Alfresco 84
holder property 358
Home Folder Path property 369
Home Root Path property 369
Home Store property 369
Host Announce property 356
host property 369
HTML file
creating, in spaces 128

I

Icon View option 127
ICR 427
imaging
Alfresco, using 428, 429
imaging solution example
workflow, using 429
imaging solution example, workflow used
about 429
important metadata extraction, business rule 431, 432
scanned documents, uploading 433, 435
scanner, connecting to network folder 432
security, setting up 430
space, setting up 430
IMAP emails
enabled property 369

X

XML configuration file, for scheduled actions

Thank you for buying
Alfresco 4 Enterprise Content
Management Implementation

About Packt Publishing

Packt, pronounced 'packed', published its first book "*Mastering phpMyAdmin for Effective MySQL Management*" in April 2004 and subsequently continued to specialize in publishing highly focused books on specific technologies and solutions.

Our books and publications share the experiences of your fellow IT professionals in adapting and customizing today's systems, applications, and frameworks. Our solution based books give you the knowledge and power to customize the software and technologies you're using to get the job done. Packt books are more specific and less general than the IT books you have seen in the past. Our unique business model allows us to bring you more focused information, giving you more of what you need to know, and less of what you don't.

Packt is a modern, yet unique publishing company, which focuses on producing quality, cutting-edge books for communities of developers, administrators, and newbies alike. For more information, please visit our website: www.packtpub.com.

About Packt Open Source

In 2010, Packt launched two new brands, Packt Open Source and Packt Enterprise, in order to continue its focus on specialization. This book is part of the Packt Open Source brand, home to books published on software built around Open Source licences, and offering information to anybody from advanced developers to budding web designers. The Open Source brand also runs Packt's Open Source Royalty Scheme, by which Packt gives a royalty to each Open Source project about whose software a book is sold.

Writing for Packt

We welcome all inquiries from people who are interested in authoring. Book proposals should be sent to author@packtpub.com. If your book idea is still at an early stage and you would like to discuss it first before writing a formal book proposal, contact us; one of our commissioning editors will get in touch with you.

We're not just looking for published authors; if you have strong technical skills but no writing experience, our experienced editors can help you develop a writing career, or simply get some additional reward for your expertise.

Alfresco Share

ISBN: 978-1-84951-710-2   Paperback: 360 pages

Enterprise Collaboration and Efficient Social Content Management

1. Understand the concepts and benefits of Share

2. Leverage a single installation to manage multiple sites

3. Case Study-based approach for effective understanding

Alfresco 3 Cookbook

ISBN: 978-1-84951-108-7   Paperback: 380 pages

Over 70 recipes for implementing the most important functionalities of Alfresco

1. Easy to follow cookbook allowing you to dive in wherever you want

2. Convert ideas into action using practical based recipes

3. A comprehensive collection of Alfresco recipes covering the API, Freemarker templates, external integration, web client, and much more

Please check **www.PacktPub.com** for information on our titles

Alfresco 3 Business Solutions

ISBN: 978-1-84951-334-0   Paperback: 608 pages

Practical implementation techniques and guidance for delivering business solutions with Alfresco

1. Deep practical insights into the vast possibilities that exist with the Alfresco platform for designing business solutions

2. Each and every type of business solution is implemented through the eyes of a fictitious financial organization - giving you the right amount of practical exposure you need

3. Packed with numerous case studies which will enable you to learn in various real world scenarios

Alfresco 3 Web Content Management

ISBN: 978-1-84719-800-6   Paperback: 440 pages

Enterprise Web Content Management made easy and affordable

1. A complete guide to Web Content Creation and Distribution

2. Understand the concepts and advantages of Publishing-style Web CMS

3. Leverage a single installation to manage multiple websites

4. Integrate Alfresco web applications with external systems

Please check **www.PacktPub.com** for information on our titles

CPSIA information can be obtained at www.ICGtesting.com
Printed in the USA
LVOW02s0959290713

345111LV00008B/227/P

9 781782 160021